Cass Turnbull's Guide to Pruning

3RD EDITION

CASS TURNBULL'S

Guide

to

Pruning

3RD EDITION

WHAT, WHEN, WHERE & HOW TO PRUNE FOR A MORE BEAUTIFUL GARDEN

BY THE FOUNDER OF

PLANTAMNESTY

ILLUSTRATIONS BY KATE ALLEN

SASQUATCH BOOKS
SEATTLE

Printed in the United States of America
Published by Sasquatch Books
17 16 15 14 13 12   9 8 7 6 5 4 3 2 1

Cover design: Rijuta Trevedi
Cover photographs: Mark Sullo (author photo)
                    © Rigsby8131 | Dreamstime.com (Pruning A)
                    © Elinamanninen | Dreamstime.com (Apple Tree)
Book design and composition: Stewart A. Williams
Interior and cover illustrations: Kate Allen
Copy editor: Alice Copp Smith
Proofreader: Amy Smith Bell

Library of Congress Cataloging-in-Publication Data is available.

ISBN-13: 978-1-57061-751-5
ISBN-10: 1-57061-751-1

Sasquatch Books
1904 Third Avenue, Suite 710
Seattle, WA 98101
(206) 467-4300
www.sasquatchbooks.com
custserv@sasquatchbooks.com

SUSTAINABLE FORESTRY INITIATIVE — Label applies to the text stock

Certified Sourcing
www.sfiprogram.org
SFI-00341

Contents

Foreword

I first met Cass Turnbull many years ago at a conference for Women in Horticulture. After I spoke about my experiences as a writer, gardener, and single mom, she walked up to me and said, "I thought I wanted to be you when I grew up, but today I realized I'm already older than you." I still chuckle over that, and I think Cass has grown up to be Cass, which is an even better plan.

Cass is a remarkable person, a woman of vision and character capable of uniting people of all ages and persuasions into a cohesive action group that has created positive horticultural change. Not only is this an outstanding achievement, but she does this unifying with grace, wit, and sparkling humor. I suspect she learned long ago that you can get people to do just about anything if you can make them laugh first. It's a great lesson, one I've absorbed as well.

Cass is a passionate person with a serious commitment to plant rights, plant health, and, if such a thing exists, plant happiness. Cass cares what happens to trees—all trees, everywhere. Through her teaching, her programs, and her writing, she makes many other people realize how deeply *we* care as well.

It is a testimony to her persuasive powers that the thousands of people who have been positively influenced through her organization, PlantAmnesty, all regard her with respectful fondness approaching love. They come away from Cass's programs with a healthy respect and informed appreciation for trees that changes the way they plant, prune, feed, and water their woodies.

If you've ever been to a Cass Turnbull class, you'll never forget the lessons you learned there. If you can't make her classes, or want a deeper, fuller, more explicit understanding of how to prune plants for optimal health, this book is for you. It's a keeper, one you'll use over and over, share with friends, and pass on to your kids. In fact, if Cass has her way (which I bet she will), all kids will learn how to prune properly before they get out of high school.

So read this book, not just when you know you need it, but when you have time to ponder. This is great material, presented in a clear, unfussy manner that's a pleasure to read. Savor Cass's words and thoughts at leisure and your plants will thank you. So will your kids, and their kids, and the generations to come who will love and appreciate the trees we plant, prune, and cherish wisely today.

—Ann Lovejoy

Acknowledgments

I must thank my wonderful illustrator, Kate Allen, for the many hours and years she has spent creating a kinder, gentler world for the plants. I know that it is her pictures that will make it possible for the reader to master the mysterious art of pruning. I am equally grateful to Glen Grantham, the illustrator of my first book, *The Complete Guide to Landscape Design, Renovation, and Maintenance*, who agreed to let Kate redraw his illustrations in her hand for this book. Thank you to Ron Brightman for his editing; to Linda Chalker-Scott, Warren Copes, Ciscoe Morris, and Don Brooks, who all contributed to the second edition; and to Steve Priebe and Donna DiFrancesco, who compiled the plant lists for the "Arizona Low Desert" section of Appendix 1, Regional Pruning by Plant Habit.

Most of all, I thank my husband, John, for underwriting PlantAmnesty over these many years (without really consenting to it, I'm afraid) and for his short-deadline, free editing service and his steadfast love and support.

Introduction

Thomas Jefferson said, "Though I am an old man, I am but a young gardener." I feel much the same. I've been a professional gardener for more than twenty years and I'm still learning how to prune, observing how each species responds over the course of years. I have taken many classes on pruning and have read many books, but it is only by combining such education with field experience that I have come to know how to prune. I started out wanting to control Nature, bending her to my will with loppers, pruners, and saw. I now believe, instead, that I've been trained by Nature, in that patient, silent way that she has. I've come to understand that I must obey her laws if I hope to achieve a modicum of success in pruning and gardening. And only by giving many classes have I learned how to communicate the skill of pruning to others. I think that it is this combination of field experience, academic training, and experience teaching others that uniquely qualifies me to explain pruning to the beginner, both homeowner and professional.

When I was first learning to prune, the books I read were of little help. They showed pictures of shrubs that looked so good I wouldn't have bothered pruning them. I found a lot of information about pruning situations I rarely encountered, like how to fan-prune a peach tree, and yet there was little about *my* most common pruning problems. For example, people always wanted me to prune the giant rhododendrons that were blocking

their windows. The pruning books I read tended to say something utterly unhelpful like "requires little pruning." Also, most pruning guides told me that the purpose of pruning was to improve the bloom and health of shrubs. Although I care about these things, what I mostly needed to know was how to make plants smaller.

Nothing about pruning is obvious. In fact, most of it is downright counterintuitive. People try to prune plants the way they cut lumber. But that doesn't work if the goal is a smaller plant. Instead, the plants respond by going into a spasm of regrowth, locking the homeowner into a high-maintenance battle against water sprouts and suckers.

I suspect that soon after man emerged from his cave with the first cutting tool, he whacked a limb off a bush, and it felt good. Bad pruning (what I call *mal-pruning*) accounts for more than 80 percent of all the work done by homeowners and professionals alike. And this sad state of affairs has persisted for decades. It was as if I were a member in a small secret society of people who somehow knew how to prune. We were doomed to watch helplessly as the rest of the world crashed through the greenscape with tools of destruction in their well-intentioned mission to restore order to their yards. Needless to say, it troubled me that so many plants were being treated exactly opposite of how they should be. People wasted so much time and money, cutting in ways that would eventually make their plants unhealthy, unpretty, unmanageable, and costly to maintain. It was just crazy!

Then one day, as part of a self-actualization seminar, I brainstormed the end of mal-pruning. In my unbridled imagination the most common forms of mal-pruning—tree topping, shrub shearing, and overthinning—became the topic of newspaper articles and the evening TV news. In the future, everyone would know what a heading cut was, and everyone would know how to prune. Or if not, they would know whom to hire to prune their yards: professionals who really did know how to prune.

Why, there would have to be an organization. It would be called "PlantAmnesty," and its mission and first goal would be "to end the senseless torture and mutilation of trees and shrubs caused by mal-pruning." The name made me laugh. What started as something of a lark soon got away from me. Twenty-three years later our nonprofit group had a thousand members.

PlantAmnesty has three major goals, the first of which is *to alert the public to the crimes against Nature* being committed in their own backyards, mainly mal-pruning but other things as well. The problem is that the topic of pruning is so dull that most people don't pay much attention, or money, to see that it is done right. Our mock-militant name, the combination of humor and controversy, made the topic of pruning newsworthy, and what followed was media coverage occurring with amazing regularity. PlantAmnesty was featured on the evening news, in the local papers, and then in an Associated Press article published across the country. I was also interviewed regularly on the radio, both locally and on the CBC (Canadian Broadcasting Corporation) and even the ABC (Australian Broadcasting Corporation), thus raising the public's awareness of the problem. We made people laugh with the idea of "the Ugly Yard Contest," but at the same time we instilled a low-grade fear among individuals that they might be doing something wrong and might even wind up being featured on the evening news!

During my years as executive director, PlantAmnesty used other methods to alert people to common plant "abuses." We developed the popular slide show of pruning horrors, a "Hall of Shame" educational booth, and TV public service announcements. We employed a nasty letter writer, distributed "arrest warrants," instigated two mutilated tree protests, and lobbied various city and state governing bodies. On the lighter side, we entered local parades with the precision marching gardeners' drill team and float, or sometimes we entered as the walking forest. We had Father Weedo Sarducci attend our events with his confessional, giving absolution to all those who confessed their horticultural sins.

Actually, it was Weedo who told me that when Moses was talking to his burning bush (see Chapter 10, Mounding-Habit Shrubs), he was given an additional ten commandments for gardeners:

1. Thou shalt not shear thy bush.

2. Thou shalt not top thy tree.

3. Thou shalt not plant thy sun lover in the shade, nor thy shade lover in the sun.

Weeping willow

4. Thou shalt mulch.

5. Thou shalt not leave stubs.

6. Thou shalt not flush cut, neither shalt thou paint wounds.

7. Thou shalt not cover up the base of thy plant, or thy tree, or thy shrub. Neither with mulch, nor with soil, nor with any landscape material.

8. Thou shalt cut circling/girdling roots.

9. Thou shalt not compact the root zone of thy tree, nor trench near the trunk of thy tree.

10. Thou shalt not weed-whip the trunk of thy tree, nor bash it with thy mower, nor leave anything tied on thy tree or the branches of thy tree, as is done in the land of the philistines.

The second goal of PlantAmnesty is *to provide the solutions* to the problem of poor pruning. We released a video on pruning, and a book, created the good gardeners and arborists' referral service, staffed the pruning hot line, published pamphlets of pruning information and articles, published a list of local classes on pruning, and gave classes. We organized volunteer pruning work parties for trees and needy landscapes.

PlantAmnesty's third goal is *to engender respect for plants*, which we did through many of the activities mentioned above, as well as by inventing the Seattle Heritage Tree Program.

We raised money for our group with tours, grants, plant sales, auctions, and such. Membership dues provided the major funding for our good works. In return, members attended regular meetings of horticultural interest and free pruning classes, gained access to the "cyber library," and received an educational and amusing newsletter. The newsletter contained (along with the usual organization updates) "Tales of Hope and Tales of Horror," the adopt-a-plant column (a listing of free plants), how-to pruning articles, cartoons, and other articles of horticultural/arboricultural interest.

After starting PlantAmnesty and teaching many pruning classes, I realized that people don't want to read an entire book just to figure out what to do with their camellia bush. But most encyclopedia-type pruning books leave a lot to be desired, devoting only a sentence or two to each plant. So, in each issue of the PlantAmnesty newsletter, I explained how to prune a specific plant or group of plants. I found that I could say everything needed in two or three pages. Most of these species-specific "pruning tips" have finally been collected in one place—this book. Each piece is meant to stand by itself. You will find in-depth information on specific plants in a variety of circumstances. As it

turns out, there is more than one right way to prune a forsythia, as there is more than one wrong way. This means that you will find a fair amount of repetition within the book. But you will also be free to read it one bit at a time, as needed, though I recommend first reading the general-information Chapters 1 through 9.

I have also included information about corrective pruning for previously mal-pruned plants and tips on how to "read" the responses of plants. This will equip you to learn how to prune other plants, and indeed, will enroll you in Nature's training course. You will find that the Goddess Flora is an easy mistress to please. She readily forgives your mistakes and generously rewards those who are willing to serve her.

PART ONE

The Basics

CHAPTER ONE

Basic Cuts

If people understood plants' responses to basic cuts, they probably could figure out all the rest of pruning on their own. I wish it were taught in grade school along with how maple and oak leaves look. I suspect that people think that pruning plants must be the same as cutting hair. But it's not. If your hair worked like a plant, after a haircut your hair would grow 3 inches in a day or two (instead of a month) and the ends would be very, very bushy.

Kind pruning is not just a matter of the size of the cut, or even how the plant looks soon after pruning. The true test of success is "Are you retaining the long-term health and beauty of the plant?" Your pruning should succeed in getting you what you want, with minimal effort and without destroying the purpose of your tree or shrub (which in most cases is its natural beauty, or fruit production on fruiting trees).

Learning the kinds of cuts and how plants respond to them is the difficult part of learning to prune. It takes a little concentration, but once you understand it, you are more than halfway home. I often tell people that pruning is a skill like any other. You must pay attention and then practice. Learning to do a decent job of pruning takes more time and effort than learning to vacuum, but less than learning to play basketball. The sport of pruning takes about as much time as learning to play a decent game of ping-pong.

Pruning for beginners is often made more confusing by the fact that the experts disagree on the definitions of types of pruning cuts.

Below is the system I learned, and still prefer, for defining the types of basic pruning cuts.

PLANT TERMINOLOGY

Before learning about different pruning cuts, it helps to understand how plants grow. The theory behind a plant's mechanism for regrowth is called *apical dominance*. The end bud on any branch is called the *apical bud* (apex, the top) or *terminal bud* (terminal, the end). This bud releases a chemical called an *auxin* (like a hormone) that travels down the stem (via gravity) just below the bark and keeps all the *dormant* (sleeping) buds from growing. If the terminal bud is removed (i.e., with a heading cut) then dormant buds down below on the branch are released from apical dominance and are free to grow out (*break bud*). This is the plant's system of replacing damaged parts.

This brings me to more plant terminology. A shorthand way of saying "a bud or side branch" is to say *node*. (And, if you say "soil" instead of "dirt" and "shrubs" instead of "bushes," you are well on your way to speaking gardenese.) Knowing to cut to the node

Figure 1.1 Types of nodes. Always cut to a node. A *node* is a place where a bud was or is. **A.** Branch node **B.** Leaf node **C.** Bud **D.** Leaf scar **E.** Bud scale scar

separates the pros from the amateurs in gardening. A node can also be a place where a leaf or branch used to be and where a dormant bud remains. Such a node will look like a bulge in the stem with a line or leaf scar where the leaf once was. If you cut to the node, a dormant bud will begin to grow out and form a new branch (see Figure 1.1).

Plants are categorized by their branching pattern into *alternate, opposite,* and *whorled* (see Figure 1.2).

The vast majority of plants are alternate in branching (with branches first to the left and then to the right). Opposite plants (with branches directly opposite one another) are harder to prune because it's difficult to

squeeze the tips of your hand pruners into the "V" to cut so as not to leave a stub to die back. A *stub* is the dead section of branch that occurred when the last person didn't cut to the node and so the branch died back. If buds or twigs are opposite each other, just cut off straight and as close to the paired side branches as you can (see Figure 1.3).

There's another reason why it's harder to direct the growth of opposite plants: Often the branch you chose because it was headed in the right direction (out from the center) is mirrored by one going the opposite (wrong) way. Do the best you can.

HEADING CUTS

Heading cuts are cuts that shorten branches, trunks, or twigs. There are two types of heading cuts, *nonselective* and *selective.*

Nonselective Heading

Nonselective heading means basically whacking back a branch to no place in particular. This sort of a cut is good for making things bushy, though not particularly good

Figure 1.2 Branching patterns: **A.** Alternate **B.** Opposite **C.** Whorled

Figure 1.3 Pruning oppositely branched plants is difficult without leaving a small stub.

for general height reduction. It's the nonselective heading cut that gets most people into trouble (see Figure 1.4).

Wherever a cut is made, hidden dormant buds located directly below the cut end are stimulated into growing out into new branches. Furthermore, the shrub or tree speeds up its growth rate. The new growth on larger plants is most often skinny, unsightly, straight *water sprouts*. I call this the "Hydra effect," after the many-headed snake that Hercules battled. Every time Hercules cut off one of the snake's heads, two grew back in its place. People who cut back their tree or shrub in hopes of reducing its size are surprised to find that, by the end of the next year, the plant has grown back vigorously and thickly. Worst of all, for every one cut made, the pruner now has to make five or six new cuts. An exception is when you cut back into the older, barren wood of most conifers, such as junipers and firs. These

conifers can't force new buds or regrow from barren wood! You are left looking at ugly brown branches for eternity. Oops!

Nonselective heading is also hard on a plant's health. All pruning cuts are an injury to a plant, but nonselective cuts are the hardest for a plant to take; and the bigger the cut, the harder it is for the plant to deal with it. In some pruning literature the nonselective heading cut is simply referred to as the "heading cut."

There are four types of nonselective heading cuts, based on the size of the cuts: topping, heading, tipping, and shearing. *Topping* is a term reserved for the large, nonselective heading of tree branches. *Heading*, or *heading-back*, refers to smaller cuts on trees or shrubs; heading can be either selective or nonselective. *Tipping*, or *tipping-back*, refers to small cuts. *Shearing* refers to using hedge shears (they look like a giant scissors) to cut back a plant uniformly.

Inappropriate Shearing

Shearing shrubs planted as a formal hedge, as the lower story of a Japanese formal garden, or as real topiary (plants sculpted into geometric shapes or animals) is perfectly all right. Unfortunately, most people, both professionals and homeowners, shear shrubs because they don't know how to selectively prune (see "Selective Heading," on page 11 as well as Figure 1.5). One of the reasons I started PlantAmnesty was to stop what I call "inappropriate shearing" of shrubs. Shearing everything in sight is considered tacky by horticulturalists, but if it were simply a matter of taste, or if it were rare, I probably

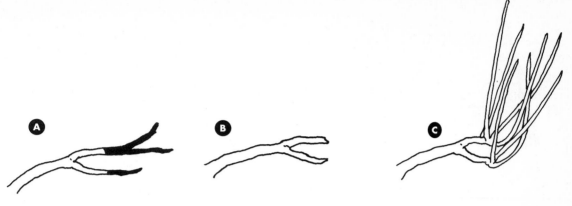

Figure 1.4 The *nonselective heading cut* creates bushiness. **A.** Removing tips **B.** stimulates dormant buds and **C.** results in rapid growth of water sprouts.

Figure 1.5 *Selective heading cut* **A.** Original branch **B.** Parent stem removed, leaving smaller side branch **C.** New growth continues through remaining existing branch.

Figure 1.6 *Thinning cut* **A.** Original branch **B.** Smaller side branch removed **C.** Next season's growth is channeled into remaining limbs.

would have just ignored it. But I estimate that more than 90 percent of the work done on shrubs is exactly "inappropriate shearing," and although many garden writers have railed against it for, believe it or not, centuries, it persists throughout the world!

Aside from considerations of taste, there are other good reasons to avoid the use and misuse of shearing as a pruning technique:

Shearing is not a way to control size
Because shearing is nonselective heading, it will stimulate bushy regrowth, creating

Figure 1.7 Shear madness: very tidy at first, but twice as messy in between prunings.

a twiggy outer shell on sheared plants. This layer of twigs shades out the interior, which then becomes leafless and full of dead leaves and deadwood. Meanwhile the outer shell becomes thicker and larger every year because, as it is sheared repeatedly, it must be cut a little farther out to retain its greenery. This dense, twiggy outer shell makes size reduction difficult because cutting back too far exposes that ugly dead zone inside the shrub. It is also physically difficult to cut through the thick twiggy mass. Although most plants will eventually green back up when they are pruned back into the dead zone, most needled evergreens, such as junipers, won't. Therefore, shearing is not a good way to control the size of a shrub. Selective pruning utilizing the selective heading cut (which I'll discuss later) ensures that there will be a green twig or branch to cut back to and can therefore be employed to reduce a shrub's size while retaining its natural look.

Only tough plants can take shearing

Shearing is also a drain on the health of plants. Selective pruners spend most of their time opening up the plant to let in more light and air and to reduce the buildup of deadwood and disease. Shearing plants creates the antithesis of a healthy environment, making shrubs more prone to insect attack, deadwood, and dieback. It adds a general stress on plants because the rapid, profuse growth promoted by repeated heading depletes their energy, and their resulting weakness and tender growth makes them more susceptible to injury from freeze or drought. This is why care must be taken to choose plants that are tough enough to take repeated shearing. Even then, the shearing must commence when the plants are young in order to avoid the sudden stress of shearing after they have reached maturity. Even with plants for which shearing is appropriate, the good gardener will take time to reach inside and clean out the buildup of deadwood and dead twigs.

Shearing is high maintenance

Another problem with shearing is that it is a high-maintenance chore. The new shoots (water sprouts) that result from heading cuts are thin and straight, and look quite wild. Heading cuts stimulate rapid regrowth, which soon destroys the tidy look that the first shearing created. Although shearing a plant may take little time, the tidy appearance vanishes very quickly, and shearing locks the practitioner into frequent reshearing (see Figure 1.7).

On the other hand, when a plant is selectively pruned, the new growth matches that which already exists and the plant ends up looking more natural (see Figure 1.8). The new growth continues at about the same rate as before, meaning that a selectively pruned plant doesn't look out of control quickly as one that has been sheared.

Figure 1.8 *Selective heading* reduces size, allows a shrub to bloom and to retain its natural habit, and produces no ugly water sprouts between maintenance sessions. **A.** Original shrub **B.** Reduced with selective heading cuts (grab and snip) **C.** 1–3 years later **D.** Reduced with selective heading **E.** 2–5 more years **F.** Grab and snip again. . . , and so on and so on. . .

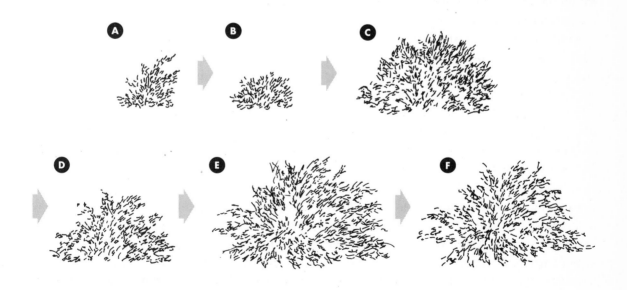

Shearing is a counterproductive form of pruning

I have even heard it compared to drug abuse—the first time through is very gratifying and very quick, but the unwary wielder of hedge shears will soon be locked into a high-maintenance habit. It will take more and more shearing to keep a plant looking its same tidy way, until one day the hapless homeowner will not be able to see out the window or open the door that's blocked by a giant ball or box. And eventually, the plant's health will begin to show signs of deterioration.

Shearing subverts a plant's natural beauty

Aside from maintenance and health considerations, the gardener must also consider the purpose of plants when deciding how to prune them. Shearing often defeats the purpose of shrubbery, usually by cutting off the flowers, but other characteristics get subverted as well. True genius in landscaping is obtained by balancing theme and contrast. One of the elements of contrast is texture (for example, the fine leaves of a boxwood, the fluffy look of bridal wreath spiraea, or the bold, deep leaf of a viburnum). Shearing will eliminate contrast of texture, and everything will begin to look the same.

Shearing also does great violence to plants that have been chosen for their secondary characteristic of fine branch patterns. Such a plant is the star magnolia tree, which is valued for its flowers but is also valued for its beautiful branch patterns and fuzzy buds. Other shrubs and trees highly valued for their fine branch patterns are the doublefile viburnum, Harry Lauder's walking stick, Japanese

maple, and eastern dogwood. Shearing ruins them. (See Chapter 12, Tree-Like Shrubs, and Chapter 14, Trees, for details on how to prune these plants.)

So, if you have a sheared hedge and you do rent a pair of power shears, restrain yourself from taking on the rest of the yard. Don't get carried away with shear madness.

A Word About Tree Topping

Tree topping is the other major reason I started PlantAmnesty; it has been variously described as "vandalism for hire," "tree butchery," and a "disgrace to the tree service industry." It is estimated that 80 percent of the work done on trees, as a national average, is tree topping. In my opinion it constitutes a form of consumer fraud.

The large, nonselective heading cuts (topping cuts) cause rot (decay) to enter the tree trunk, much as gangrene follows a war wound. But there are no antibiotics for trees, and pruning paints have been shown to be ineffective in preventing the spread of decay in trees. Why do we care? Decay in trees shortens their lives and creates dangerous, weakened trunks. Topping also causes branches to die back, which is ugly, and at the same time, it stimulates watersprout formation. These water sprouts are also ugly, but worse yet, they are weakly attached. Many years later, after they have become large, these new branches will be more prone to breakage than the original tree branches.

The perversity of tree topping is that it achieves none of the things people think it will. It makes a tree more dangerous, not safer, and it ruins the tree and the "water view" (since the topped tree rapidly reaches its original size again, except now it's ugly). Topping is not even a cheaper form of "pruning." It is paying to mutilate a tree on an ever increasing maintenance program (as water sprouts regrow exponentially in number every time they are cut off). Proper pruning of trees is actually done less and less frequently (not more and more often), though it does take more time on the original go-through than the few quick and dirty cuts of the tree topper.

The bottom line on tree pruning is that it should always maintain or improve the tree's natural beauty, health, and safety. Proper pruning will never increase maintenance by creating water sprouts or deadwood. Given that, you can prune a tree to solve a problem—such as creating access to a path, letting in more light, or decreasing limb breakage—or just to improve the looks of the tree itself.

Correct Uses of Nonselective Heading

Shearing is a correct way of pruning certain plants chosen to be topiary, formal hedges, or the lower story of Japanese gardens. In almost all cases the plants chosen for shearing have small leaves spaced closely together and are tough enough to take repeated shearing. The ubiquitous shearing of all other plants in the landscape into globes or cubes is not good pruning.

There are other correct uses of nonselective heading. A nonselective heading cut can be used to train young trees called "whips." Such young trees are sometimes cut to the ground to force regrowth of a straight new trunk. Sometimes the trunk of a sapling or whip is headed to force the branching that will become the tree's crown.

The nonselective heading cut is also used correctly on apple and pear trees to stiffen up young branches or to force production of fruit spurs. The ability of apple and pear trees to set up spurs distinguishes them from other trees, and you can prune them differently because of it.

Selective Heading

Selective heading is the "right way" to shorten the branch of a tree or shrub. It reduces the amount of regrowth, looks more natural, and is easier on the health of the plant. Because of the Hydra effect, a combination of selective heading and thinning (see Figure 1.6) is the correct method for pruning the vast majority of shrubs and trees.

A *selective heading* cut—also called the reduction cut—reduces the length of a branch by cutting off one of two forks of a branch. The pruner selects the longest fork, follows it back to where it joins a shorter side branch, and cuts it off there. The side branch should be big enough to take over as the branch's end (see Figure 1.5 again).

How big a side branch is "big enough"? Well, it depends. The International Society of Arboriculture's Western Chapter Standards define it as "large enough to assume the terminal role." This means that the remaining fork will *not* respond by producing water sprouts (straight, skinny, ugly shoots that grow out at the site of a pruning cut). As an average, the remaining side branch should be at least half the diameter of the parent stem. Other authorities say that no more than a third of the foliage of the branch should be removed. "Big enough" is, however, a sliding scale, with many exceptions, based mostly on the requirements of the species in question. The questions to ask about any potential cut are "Will it rot the branch?", "Will it cause unsightly regrowth?", and "Will it eventually starve the branch, causing it to die?" If the answer to each question is no, cut away.

Selective Heading of Trees (Dropcrotching)

In general you could say that the bigger, older, and woodier a plant is, the harder heading cuts are for its health. Heading-back a privet, a spiraea, or a Japanese holly is no big deal. But when it comes to trees, we run into trouble.

No one knows why people often decide one day that their tree is too big. People don't declare all of a sudden that their dog, their house, or their kid is too big. But this subconscious assessment often leads to mal-pruning of the worst kind. Selective heading of trees (also called *dropcrotching*, *crown reduction*, or *de-horning*) is not as bad as topping, but it poses severe risks and is not the magic solution to the "too big" tree.

Dropcrotching is unsuccessful as an overall size control measure. After a *young, healthy* tree is pruned back, it increases its rate of growth. The remaining limbs elongate rapidly and very soon the tree is the size it was before. A tree that took five years to grow five feet taller will now grow five feet in a single year. Repeated dropcrotching will make the tree limbs leggier and the entire crown broader. But ten years later the tree will be the same height as its unpruned counterpart.

Very *large* dropcrotch cuts, or crown reduction, on very *old* trees may succeed in constraining size, but at an unacceptable cost to the health, safety, and longevity of the tree. The rot invades the main limbs, the tree expends valuable energy to deal with the wounds, and it may decline and die as a result. Even if the tree recovers, it will be more dangerous as a result. The lateral branches that take over as the main branches of the tree will likely be weaker and more prone to breakage even thirty years later.

When done, dropcrotching should probably be limited to a relatively few branches of a mature tree, say 2 percent of the total leaf area (for example, the branch hanging over the chimney or blocking the window). It should not be done for the sole purpose of trying to contain the size or height of a tree. Arborists estimate that an average tree's height can be reduced 5 to 10 percent without doing significant damage to the tree's health or natural beauty (depending on the tree's age, species, and health, of course). You would be hard pressed to find a tree (outside of a Japanese garden or a commercial orchard) that has been kept small by ongoing pruning. Trees are genetically programmed to reach a certain size, and unless you want to make it your life's work, you'd better plan on them getting to that size a lot sooner than you think. In places where trees are annually pruned for size control, using many small selective heading cuts (along the streets in Japan, for example, or where beech trees or hemlocks are used as hedges), you will find that the natural, characteristic branch pattern of the trees has been eliminated.

Dropcrotch pruning will always sadden an arborist who sees no good reason to cut other than the public's ever present arborphobia (fear of large trees) and the increasing obsession with water views. There would be no size reduction of trees in the best of all possible worlds.

Many people think that dropcrotching is an acceptable "heroic measure" to save certain special trees growing under powerlines. However, directional pruning, a sort of V-shaped pruning, has taken precedence for these situations (see "Pruning Trees for Powerlines" in Chapter 14, Trees). In this case pruning is used to redirect growth rather than to restrict the overall size of the tree.

Selective Heading of Shrubs and the Grab-and-Snip Method

With shrubs it's a different story. The smaller the leaves, the finer the branches, and the smaller the plant, the more you can use selective heading to tidy up the shrub and to reduce size within moderation. In general, I would say that you can successfully make a shrub a quarter smaller than it would be without pruning. If you do more (even using the correct selective heading cuts), it sends up water sprouts, looks funny, and/or grows back so fast that pruning is not worth the effort.

There is a decision-making process involved in pruning to reduce the size of a given shrub. It is not simply a matter of selectively heading-back every branch, as you might assume. Instead, you blur your eyes and stare at the offending shrub. Look for the branch that sticks up the highest or farthest into the walkway. Grab it with your left hand (assuming you're right-handed), then follow it down with your hand pruners into the interior of the shrub. Follow it down, down to where it meets a good-sized side branch that faces outward, and cut it off there. Or sometimes, if it is a wispy branch without internal side branches, you follow it down into the shrub and cut back to no place in particular, knowing that it will force buds to grow out at that point. Sure, it may "Hydra-back," but since the cut is located deep inside the shrub, the new growth will grow several months or perhaps a year before it reaches the surface; by that time it will have assumed a natural, pretty form, instead of sticking out awkwardly, as it would have had you made the cut closer to the surface.

After making the cut, toss the cut stem to the lawn. Repeat the process, always looking for the next-longest branch, not the next-closest one. In this way, the longest branches are removed. What remains are the unpruned branches that were already the size you want the shrub to be. (Figure 10.1 should help you visualize this.) By way of analogy, the difference between a shearing cut and a selective heading cut is like the difference between a blunt haircut and a shag haircut.

When you are done, the shrub retains its natural form, it is just smaller. And because many branches were not pruned at all, they still have their flower buds at the tips and the shrub will bloom no matter what season you prune.

"Selective pruning" means that you consciously select which branches to cut and which to leave in place, and that you have a clear idea of the purpose of the pruning session. "Selective pruning" is the name of real pruning, and PlantAmnesty's motto *Secare selecte* means "Prune selectively" (in Latin, of course).

THINNING

The *thinning* cut removes a branch (or twig) completely (see Figure 1.6 on page 7). In other words, you cut a smaller, or "side," branch off of its larger, parent stem. Generally speaking, thinning cuts don't make plants smaller overall, they just reduce the bulk and clutter of the plant, making it sort of "see-through." Thinning off the lower, most interfering branches of a tree (called *skirting, limbing-up,* or *crown raising*) is more permanent and less harmful than crown reduction. Dr. Alex Shigo, the renowned research scientist known as the Isaac Newton of arboriculture, says in his lectures, "Trunk wood is different from branch wood." Trees are much better adapted to losing side branches than to having their major limbs or the *leader* (top part of the main trunk) cut in half.

Similarly, with many shrubs the correct approach is to take off the lower interfering branches that lie upon, or reach into, neighboring plants. You find the branch that stretches out most obtrusively into the pedestrian's way, follow it back to the main trunk, and cut it off there. General thinning throughout a plant, especially deadwooding, creates definition. It also increases air circulation, which is good for plant health. The plant just looks better (and, we assume, "feels" better). With those plants that resent being made smaller (being headed-back), we try to get what we want with thinning and raising.

Overthinning

As with so much in life, people get into trouble with "too much of a good thing." New pruners are apt to overthin. Once you can spot "wrong branches" (i.e., crossing, rubbing, wrong way, too straight, duplicating, etc.), you will be tempted to eradicate all the offenders. However, if you take out everything that is wrong, you are often left with an overthinned plant or tree. Overskirted plants look top heavy, and in the case of trees, can be dangerous. Similarly, when all the internal branches are "skinned out" of a large tree, all the weight is dangerously concentrated at the ends of the scaffold branches. It is preferable to distribute the weight of foliage evenly throughout the tree. Overthinning the internal branches of a tree is called *lion's tailing*, and it should be avoided.

Correct Thinning

One consideration in thinning is aesthetics: An overthinned tree or shrub can look anorexic instead of artistic. Trees and shrubs vary in the degree to which they can be successfully thinned out. Here again the determining factors are "Will it water sprout?" and "Can this branch live if I remove this much foliage?" Most pines, for example, can't water-sprout back. They can also withstand an incredible amount of thinning before the overthinned branch in question dies (usually in a drought or freeze, or from sun scald some years later).

On the other end of the scale, some trees, such as ornamental cherries, plums, and crabapples, naturally have sort of a "messy" look and many crossing branches; but if you prune them too much (and it doesn't take much), they respond by producing a host of water sprouts. If the water sprouts are repeatedly removed every year thereafter, the tree's branches will rapidly age, crack, and eventually die. This is not to mention the incredible amounts of time and money that you are apt to waste by battling the mess of your own creation.

Most people want to prune to reduce the size of their plants, and you can moderately reduce many plants in size, always thinning as you do so. But let me add that most of what I do as a professional landscape renovator is prune out internal branches so that you can see into or through the plant. I also thin to break up the exterior solid-ball appearance of both old and young plants. This gives a shrub more character and definition. In addition, I prune to create definition between shrubs, so that instead of a mass of giant greenery jammed against the house, you can see three shrubs of different types, with room between them and the house. You will be able in some cases to see the soil beneath them.

It is not immediately apparent how following the rules (as often stated in pruning books: cutting off dead, crossing, and crowded branches) will result in a nicer, less-oppressive-looking shrub. So beginning gardeners will just have to follow the recipe with faith until they see the connection. When you make your cut on a shrub, do so just above a side branch or bud, slanting the way the bud is facing. Don't cut too close, but don't cut too far away. In the beginning, don't agonize over which one is the right branch, just take your best shot and see how it goes. Then stand back and observe the effect on the plant's overall appearance.

SUMMARY
Pruning—especially heading—stimulates growth. Thinning cuts are preferred. Avoid cutting ends or tips of branches to make things smaller; this technique often backfires.

Heading Cuts
Nonselective heading is good to stimulate bushiness. Examples: sheared hedges, chrysanthemums.

Selective heading is the cutting back to a side branch or bud. The remaining branch should be at least half the size of the one being removed. This reduces the plant size and is less likely to stimulate water sprouts or create dead wood.

Thinning Cuts
Thinning cuts remove branches to the point where they began as buds, or remove entire canes by cutting them off at the ground.

Thinning reduces the bulk and sometimes the height of shrubs (when the tallest canes are removed).

Thinning cuts are better for the health and good looks of plants, especially trees, than heading cuts.

Shrubs and trees vary in degree of thinning they can withstand. A pine tree will take a lot of thinning; a cherry tree resents even moderate thinning.

CHAPTER TWO

Selective Pruning Techniques

17

Selective pruning takes into account a plant's natural shape (habit) and characteristics. The kinds of cuts (heading or thinning), the total number of cuts (how much foliage is removed), and the size of the cuts should be matched to the specific plant. I call the combination of these factors a plant's "pruning budget." A large cut is harder on the plant (taking more of the pruning budget) than a smaller-diameter cut. A heading cut is harder on the plant's health (and therefore spends more of the budget) than a thinning cut. A nonselective heading cut is even harsher than a selective heading cut. And taking more foliage off a plant spends more of the pruning budget than taking off less.

THE PRUNING BUDGET

Some plants have a large pruning budget and others are very touchy. Too bad the budget isn't posted on the plant. It should be. Like the beeper at the do-it-yourself car wash, the plant should start beeping loudly as you are about to run out of allowable time. Instead, you continue pruning till it looks good to you now, by which time you may have unknowingly overpruned it. The plant waits until the next growing season and then explodes into water sprouts.

If your pruning budget is small (because the plant is, say, a deciduous viburnum), you may choose to spend it in any number of ways. You could make one medium selective heading cut and sixteen small thinning cuts. Or you might choose to make three large thinning cuts and a few smaller thinning cuts. Alternatively, you could do thirty small thinning cuts. It's up to you how you want to spend the budget, but you may not exceed your total budget allotment.

PLANT HABITS

When I gave my first lecture on pruning, I had to decide what to say. The principles of pruning are the same for every plant, but I knew that I approached a forsythia with a different mental attitude from the one with which I approached, say, a star magnolia. I concentrated on different kinds and sizes of branches. With the forsythia I spent most of my time sawing out large canes to the base; I didn't worry about its ability to recover. The magnolia, on the other hand, required dainty, thoughtful pruning that was more a matter of art. I realized that there were many plants that I pruned pretty much like forsythias and that I could tell how to approach most plants by simply observing their "habit" or natural shape.

This is how I came to divide plants into three broad categories. This classification is convenient, not scientific, but it will help you decide how to prune your shrubs by learning to read their habits. I have labeled these groups *mounding-habit, cane-growing,* and *tree-like.* This book is divided according to these habit categories and then by individual species within each group.

MATURE SIZE VS. ULTIMATE SIZE

The *mature size* of a plant is the size it will be in about ten years (give or take a few). It is what is listed on the plant tag that came with the plant from the nursery or what you found in your plant encyclopedia. It is just the average size of a given tree or shrub. The plant doesn't stop growing when it reaches its mature size; it slows down but continues growing to what I call the plant's *ultimate size,* roughly twice what is on the plant tag. Then it stops getting taller—although, like people, it may continue to get wider. It is good to know this fact of Nature, since I often hear people say odd things such as "My plant is out of control." It is, in fact, just growing up.

Over several years, I have tried to keep almost every plant I have encountered smaller with diligent pruning. My observation is this: You will be unable to keep a plant smaller than its mature size. The plant will just redouble its efforts, eventually exhausting you. Given that fact, you may have some success in moderating a mounding-habit or cane-growing shrub's size, keeping it in the mature size range with selective pruning. You don't need to let these types of shrubs grow to their ultimate size. However, it is best to let trees and most tree-like shrubs grow to their ultimate size. For these, thinning or removal of some of the lowest limbs may make them seem less oppressive or solve a perceived size problem.

Size Reduction and Root Mass

I have found that you can successfully reduce the size of a shrub by about one-quarter of what it would be without pruning. In the most obvious cases, you simply run out of green-leafed branches to cut back to; pruning such a shrub lower would mean reducing it to a jumble of barren branches. But even if there are still green-leaved branches to cut back to, you should not reduce the plant further than one-quarter of its current size. Plants will respond to size reduction based on their root mass. If you prune back too far, they simply grow back faster.

For example, some years ago a client asked me to reduce some Japanese holly shrubs (mounding-habit plants) so that the raised sprinklers could deliver irrigation over them, out to other shrubs. I easily accommodated her request, selectively reducing the size of the plants in a relatively short time. It took several years for them to get "too big" again. But every year it gets harder to achieve size reduction, as the plants gain in root mass. They regrow faster each year, and I must prune more and more frequently. The new growth no longer matches the old, but has begun to show the characteristic watersprout look. And I know that, eventually, it will become impossible to keep the plants down.

REHABILITATIVE PRUNING

Given that most pruning is really mal-pruning, it is often necessary to restore plants to their original structure. I call such a process *rehabilitative pruning*. Whereas regular selective pruning (as an ongoing maintenance chore) goes quickly, rehabilitative pruning is quite time consuming. A plant may look better after just one long session, as in the case of, say "unshearing" a previously sheared azalea. But it may take years of patient work to return a previously topped tree to a decent form. On some occasions the plant in question will look worse, a lot worse, before it looks better.

The good news is that, given enough time, most trees and shrubs will reestablish their natural habits on their own. Our job is simply to assist them in doing so. Eventually, even water sprouts turn into thick, curved branches. Thinning and deadwooding will make mal-pruned plants look better as they recover, and simplifying tangled branch ends will move the process along.

RADICAL RENOVATION

I often tell my students that what the guy down the block did to his shrub is *plant butchery*. What I did is *radical renovation*. The two can look much the same. Sometimes a previously mal-pruned shrub can be more quickly and effectively returned to its natural habit by cutting it to the ground or to a low, uneven framework. This is called *radical renovation*. It works best on the cane-growing category of shrubs and with somewhat lesser reliability on the mounding-habit shrubs. Even many tree-like shrubs can

withstand this treatment. It does look quite terrifying, though, and is a serious stress on the plant. But this practice is horticulturally accepted and is commonly referred to in many British garden books as "cutting back hard."

Occasionally, when it becomes necessary in the course of human events to radically reduce the size of plants, radical renovation is called upon. Such a practice is not to be entered into lightly or unadvisedly, but only when all other options have been exhausted. Radical renovation is done only once in a great many years to start a shrub over, giving it a second life. It is not done to keep a shrub small. This is an important distinction. And, like surgery, radical renovation is a calculated risk. Sometimes the plant dies. Most often it grows back and looks better than ever.

Timing is important. Pick the season with the longest period of benign, warm, wet weather so that the plant has the best chance at recovery. That usually means early spring. When most people radically renovate, they err on the side of not cutting back far enough. They wind up with the barren "legs" of a mature plant topped by the thick regrowth of a new crown. It looks bad. On broadleaf evergreen plants (like camellias and rhodies) I also recommend cutting all the branches back at once—not in thirds, as is often recommended. If you whack back a single branch that is then shaded by the remaining leafy stems, it is more likely to die than to break bud and grow back. In summary, radical renovation is a "sink or swim" proposition.

As a note of interest, some plants are cut to the ground annually as a regular maintenance

Figure 2.1 Victim of radical renovation **A.** Monday, Tuesday, Wednesday, Thursday . . . **B.** . . . Friday

procedure. This is then called either *stooling* when done to shrubs or *coppicing* when done to trees. The reason it is done is to accentuate some special feature of the plant. Red twig dogwood shrubs regrow with brighter red canes to add winter interest to a garden. Smoke bushes and paulownia trees will develop enormous leaves, adding interest to a mixed border. Though it isn't technically stooling, some people also cut hydrangeas and butterfly bushes (*Buddleia*) to the ground annually to get plants with even bigger blooms. In all cases, this kind of annual pruning is extremely high maintenance and is not to be confused with a way to keep other shrubs or trees small.

CHAPTER THREE

Suckers and Water Sprouts

23

Many gardeners have picked up a bad habit of using the word "suckers" to indicate both suckers and water sprouts. Both terms refer to the rapidly growing, straight-up, skinny, unsightly shoots found on trees and shrubs.

Water sprouts, however, occur on the crown or on the natural trunk and are usually a response to injury or mal-pruning (although a few plants grow water sprouts generally as a way of life, and natural new shoot growth occurring at the ends of branches can look like water sprouts on some young plants). Examples of injury include bashing the tree trunk with the lawn mower, topping, heading, overthinning, and *flush cutting*, which means cutting into the *branch collar* (the bulge of trunk wood at the base of a tree branch). (See "How to Prune a Tree Limb," page 211.) In fact, the number of water sprouts on your tree or shrub is a pretty accurate reflection of too much or the wrong kind of pruning. This is bad news for many of you, I know. But it gets worse. Water sprouts exponentially increase in number every time you prune them off.

Other causes of water sprouts could be sudden, rapid freezing, as I have seen in the spring when side branches of budding plum trees freeze back to the scaffold limbs. And stress on an old tree, such as severe soil compaction, can cause water sprouts (properly, *epicormic shoots*) to form on the upper part of the limbs as a survival mechanism.

Suckers, true suckers, arise from the roots, rootstock, or on a trunk below a graft union. A *graft union* is the point at which one plant (for example, a rose with

desirable blooms, or a weeping cherry tree) has been spliced (or grafted) to the rootstock or trunk of another vigorous, related-species plant. "Suckers" also refers to any other young shoots arising from the base of a shrub. Many naturally "suckering" shrubs, like quince or forsythia, can have old canes or branches cut to the ground and new suckers will arise as replacements.

Another important difference between water sprouts and suckers is how you deal with them. Water sprouts are best left to regrow into branches. True suckers come from below a graft union and must be removed regularly, forever. Naturally occurring suckers from a shrub's own roots can be removed or let grow as preferred.

I used to use the terms interchangeably, especially using "sucker" as a verb, as in "The tree suckered-back like mad when he topped it with the Sawsall." But I realized that in other parts of the country, people use "sucker" to refer exclusively to new shoots coming up from the ground.

HANDLING A FEW WATER SPROUTS

If the water sprouts are the result of a small wound—say, a Weed Eater™ "Whoops!"—you can try removing them all, and it might work. Cut them off in the summer (pruning in the summertime has a somewhat dwarfing effect). Cut them clear off; don't leave stubs. Some people recommend ripping or snapping them off, sort of like pulling out your little sister's hair. But I have also heard that this doesn't work any better than cutting them off. Don't cut too close or wound the bark with your pruning tool either. Every once in a while a grounds crew member gets the idea that a whole cluster of water sprouts should be removed with one big slice. This causes major new damage to the plant (letting rot into the trunk of a tree, for example); and such cuts will only stimulate new water-sprout formation. You may care to rub off the buds as they reappear at the wound site with your thumbnail, thus catching them early and expending less effort.

Some people have reported moderate success using a product called Sucker Stopper that you spray on the cut ends. However, the product stops suckers for only about a year, and it is a chemical. The active ingredient (NAA, Ethyl 1-napthaleneacetate) damages new growth and should therefore be used only on wounds (pruning or otherwise) that are tiny, like the size of the base of a sucker. Don't spray the product on pruning cuts to prevent water sprouts as it will damage living tissue and interfere with wound closure.

HANDLING A LOT OF WATER SPROUTS

If you have many, many water sprouts on your tree or shrub, it won't work to take them all off. They will just keep returning, and always with some friends. They are, after all trying to replace that branch that was so rudely removed. They needed that branch and its leaves (solar collectors are how plants make food—you remember, photosynthesis). Since the plant can't regrow a nice big branch, it's regrowing many small ones (water sprouts) so that it won't starve. So what can you do if your tree is a mess of water sprouts? In some cases the kindest cut is the one to the ground level, then use a stump grinder. Like a car that's been in a crash, at some point many plants are considered a "total loss," aesthetically speaking.

However, I have been watching the progress of mal-pruned trees and shrubs for about twenty years, and I can tell you that not only many but most trees and shrubs can recover given enough time. This is, I realize, more bad news for people who don't want to keep looking at a forest of unsightly water sprouts. On trees, especially, you need to let water sprouts grow for several years. Usually about the time the water sprouts get to the height that the tree once was, they will stop growing straight up and will begin to curve again, fattening up, growing side branches, and becoming the new crown of the tree. The same thing applies to shrubs, except that they take less time to recover.

You can help hasten the process and make the afflicted plant look better for now by prompt removal of deadwood and by gradual reduction, over the years, of the number of water sprouts. At each cluster of sprouts, choose a few to cut off (usually the smallest and most crowded, and those headed too far down, too far up, or back toward the center). The ones you leave in place will help stop new ones from reappearing. Come back next year and get some more. Sneak up on them.

Narrow the number of water sprouts down to the few that you have chosen to become replacement branches. If you remove too many too soon, you just get a spasm of water-sprout regrowth.

Patience is the greatest gardening lesson. In the end, should you develop an affinity for gardening, the forced delays (everything is on the five-year plan in gardening) will cease to be frustrating. Haven't you noticed how fast time is beginning to race by? Well, here's the way to slow it down.

Some plants are more prone to water-sprout growth than others. Heavily water-sprouting plants include ornamental cherry trees, ornamental plums, crabapples, witch hazels, deciduous viburnums, cotoneasters, dogwood trees, and magnolias. Prune these plants very lightly indeed, and avoid the heading cut. For moderately better success, in mild climates such as Seattle's, prune in the summer. If the plant begins to grow water sprouts (at the site of the cuts, the first growing season after pruning), do less, not more, next year.

As you now know, it is advantageous to let water sprouts grow unchecked for a year or two before doing anything except deadwooding. People often feel that they should jump on a water sprout right away, before it gets out of hand. Wrong! Let it grow. Let the plant regain what it needs. I realize this is all terribly counterintuitive, but there you have it.

TRUE SUCKERS

Occasionally suckers (true suckers) will appear from the roots of a plant or at the graft union. In this case you must remove all of the offending shoots. If you don't, the undesirable part of the tree or shrub can totally overtake the good part. Unfortunately you will probably have to remove suckers year, after year, after year. In the case of rootstock suckers—say, on a grafted rose—this means digging down to where they originate on the roots and cutting them off there. What a pain! If the suckers are from the base of a nongrafted plant, such as a lilac or a forsythia, you can let them grow up into trunks or canes. Some people use them as replacements for old canes that they prune out. Suckers are more common on younger plants and will eventually cease coming up on mature shrubs as long as the base remains shaded, healthy, and relatively unpruned.

STOPPING WATER SPROUTS AND SUCKERS

The only successful way to beat suckers and water sprouts is to not create them. Don't plant your tree too deep. Don't let plants suffer from drought, or compact the soil, or wound trees, or overprune or mal-prune. (You have already taken the first step in prevention: getting and reading this book on pruning.)

SUMMARY

Water sprouts are the straight-up, unsightly, skinny shoots that occur on the limbs of a tree or shrub. They are usually the result of mal-pruning—either too much or the wrong way (flush cuts or heading cuts). The best way to get rid of them is to let them grow for several years until they turn back into branches. It won't work to cut them off. They just keep coming back with their friends.

True suckers (also straight-up, skinny, unsightly shoots) from below a graft union on a trunk, or off the base of a tree, or from the rootstock of a grafted plant, must be removed every year. What a pain.

True suckers arising from a nongrafted plant can be removed or left alone to grow up into nice-looking replacement canes.

CHAPTER FOUR

Looking For Deadwood

One of the great secrets of successful pruning, and the only overall rule, is "Prune out the deadwood" (it's also a favorite adage of politicians). Pruning out deadwood is called "deadwooding" by gardeners. Deadwood makes an amazing subconscious impact on the viewer: Before deadwooding the landscape seems messy and dirty, but after deadwooding it looks clean and healthy. I estimate that over 80 percent of my pruning work is simply pruning deadwood. You cannot hurt a plant by cutting out deadwood; there is no incorrect season for such pruning; deadwood cannot possibly grow new leaves or add any beauty. Equally important is pruning off any dead stubs you may find. These stubs also have a profound effect on the overall appearance of the plant.

Summer is a good time to prune out deadwood on deciduous plants; in the winter it is much more time consuming to sort out which branch is dead on shrubs like deciduous azaleas, viburnums, and lilacs. In the summer, you need only note which branches have no green leaves.

SIGNS OF DEADWOOD

New gardeners will have to train their eyes to see deadwood. I can't stop seeing it. I see it on houseplants; I see deadwood even when I'm driving 60 miles an hour on the freeway. You can tell if a branch is dead even in the winter, because the wood is a different color from the plant's live wood and it is brittle. Experienced gardeners are always gently bending branches to see if they are brittle and dead, and shaking them to see where they go. Sometimes merely tapping the branches with your pruners will snap them off; cotoneasters, for example, are easy to clean up this way.

Another clue is that dead branches have dead buds. Any time of year your healthy plants will have live-looking, plump buds on the tips of branches. Dead buds are smaller, browner, and, well, dead looking. Dead or dying branches will sometimes have coral spot fungi on them, sunken spots or wounds, or persistent dead leaves. Finally, you can always nick the bark with your pruners to see if the wood is alive or dead: If the layer just under the bark (called *cambium*) is green, the branch is still alive; if black or brown, it is dead. Eventually you will be able to tell how "dead" a branch is simply by looking at it.

HOW TO CUT BACK DEADWOOD

Many branches are in a state somewhere between totally alive and totally dead. When you cut back the suspected dead branch, you need to cut it back a little bit at a time until you find out where it is alive again (branches die from the tip back). Check the interior of the part of the branch you just cut off by looking at its cut end. If it's brown inside, it's dead. If it's light tan surrounded by green or all green, it's alive. When a branch becomes more dead than alive (when, say, it's died back by two-thirds), it's better to remove it entirely than to make a selective heading cut to the too-small remaining live-side branch.

It is not possible to prune deadwood at a distance—you are going to have to put on your grubbiest clothes, get on your hands and knees, and crawl into the shrub! Now sit there and stare at the branches. Spot the deadwood? Sometimes it helps to start from the bottom and work up, following one branch at a time. Don't just take the largest ones, get all the tiny twigs, too. Be patient, move slowly. If you are in a hurry, you will not see what is needed, and you will probably put your eye out, not to mention cutting off some nice live wood. Keep in mind that major cleanup needs to be done only once—the task will be only a minor job in coming years.

Soon your underwear will be full of twigs and you should be feeling about as awful as your shrubs have been. But when you have finished, after, I estimate, between half an hour and two and a half hours per old shrub, then walk or crawl outside and see what you have unveiled. I promise a miraculous improvement in any shrub, if you prune out the deadwood before you do anything else. Most people ignore this part, and yet this *is* the real pruning.

Once you are done pruning out the deadwood, employ another great secret of professional gardeners: Use a fan rake to clean everything up. Raking out the leaves and pruning mess from under trees and plants invariably makes things look enormously better.

YOUR PLANTS WILL THANK YOU

When I was a novice gardener, I wondered what the big deal was about improving air circulation and the health of shrubs, which the professionals kept saying was the point of pruning. Your plants will love you for taking out the deadwood and raking up the dead leaves. (They'd do it themselves, but they can't move.) I have brought many plants back from death's door by pruning out the deadwood. Not only do they look infinitely better, but they grow better and are able to ward off disease better as well.

SUMMARY

Take out the deadwood. Do it first; do it always. Use your fan rake to remove debris. The signs of deadwood:

1. No leaves, or dead leaves, on dead branches.

2. Dead-looking buds.

3. Wood is a different color.

4. Branch or twig is brittle.

5. Cambium layer just under the bark is not green.

CHAPTER FIVE

Timing

Timing is a very simple matter. Just remember not to prune shrubs and trees that flower on the current season's wood till the first growing season after the winter solstice. Plants that bloom on last year's wood and lateral growth can be pruned any time in months that have thirty-one days except months with the letter R. Some trees will bleed if pruned in the spring or winter, but only if they are cambial tip-bearers or are in the family Rosaceae.

Just kidding! I have always been confused by timing, and I have been paying attention for several years now. But what I can tell you with utmost certainty is that *when* you prune isn't nearly important as you have been led to believe. *How* you prune is what counts. In beginners' pruning classes you are quite apt to hear such silly questions as "When is the best time to top my tree?" The answer, of course, is "Never."

People are fairly phobic about pruning and bloom time. There is almost a cult about timing. If you ask your garden columnist how to prune a forsythia, you are more apt to be told to wait to prune it until after it blooms, without much information on correct procedure. But if you are selectively pruning (as opposed to cutting it all back with heading cuts) the plant will still bloom. It will just be missing the flowers from the buds that you cut off. The casual observer of a camellia pruned at the "wrong" time will still see a shrub packed with lovely flowers on the now-more-graceful branches.

BLOOM TIME

Bloom-time considerations are only really important when you are considering radical renovations or any other wholesale heading-back, like stooling a butterfly bush (*Buddleia*) or cutting a clematis vine to the ground (as is often done), or shearing, which you probably shouldn't be doing to your flowering shrubs anyway. I will do my best to explain when to prune blooming plants. I'm probably oversimplifying, but here goes.

There are basically two kinds of plants: the ones that bloom in the spring, such as lilacs, rhododendrons, and forsythias, and the ones that bloom in the summer/fall, such as roses and cistus. How a spring bloomer works is that it wakes up in the spring with its flower buds already formed. It blooms. Then it grows for the summer. Then it sets flower buds and goes to sleep for the winter. Summer/fall bloomers wake up in the spring and grow for a while. Then they set flower buds and bloom. Then they go to sleep in the winter *without* setting flower buds.

Now if you were to cut back all the branches on a forsythia for some perverse reason and you did it in February just before it bloomed, it wouldn't. Bloom, that is. You just cut off all the flower buds. If you wait till after it blooms, and then cut the shrub to the ground, it regrows all summer, sets flower buds, goes to sleep, and blooms next spring. So you get flowers both this year and next.

With a summer/fall bloomer, you can head all the branches back in the spring and still have it bloom that year. Take, for example, a hybrid tea rose. We traditionally shorten all the canes way, way back in February. Then it wakes up, grows, sets up flower buds, and is blooming like crazy in June. Then it goes to sleep for the winter without flower buds (just the fruits, called rose hips) on the branches. In the spring it wakes up, grows, sets up flower buds, and blooms. Some summer/fall bloomers, like hybrid tea roses and cistus, will repeat-bloom if you prune them just after they bloom too. Others, like hydrangeas, continue to confuse me the more I read about them and the more people tell me what happens when they cut theirs to the ground.

That's the best I can do. If you selectively prune by removing some of a plant's branches, but leave many intact with their flower buds on them, then it doesn't matter when you prune them. I like to selectively prune forsythias *before* they bloom so that I can bring in the cut stems to force them in a flower vase. I like to selectively prune camellias while they are in bloom, and beautyberries (*Callicarpa*) too, so that I can use them in arrangements. If you prune a plant at the wrong time, you won't shock the plant into not blooming; there are just fewer blooms left on the plant—the ones you cut off. Knowing this, however, will not stop people from pouring out of the condo units to tell you that you are pruning the forsythia or the rhody at the wrong time. When this happens just turn to them and say, "I am selectively pruning it." For people who like timing rules or those who want to preserve the most blooms, I have made up a maxim: "Prune spring bloomers in the early summer, summer bloomers in the early spring." Another maxim that works is "Prune soon after the plant is through blooming." My favorite timing maxim is "Prune when the shears are sharp."

There are many things to know about timing that will help you make wise decisions, but thinking in terms of "a best time" to prune too often turns into a rule about "the only time" to prune. If you are selectively pruning in moderation, the best time to prune is any time. The following are some generalities on timing, along with a few nice-to-know specifics.

PRUNING BY SEASON

Springtime Generalities

This is the time when plants will grow back fastest and most vigorously. Spring pruning stimulates growth the most. Shoots are elongating. It is a kind time of year, weatherwise.

Springtime Specifics

Early spring (February–March) is a good time for radical reduction of shrubs—say, for example, your camellia (it will grow out quickly, hiding the dead-looking stumps).

This is a good time for bud work (in the Northwest, we wait until spring to find plumping buds on hybrid tea roses to cut back to). Later in the spring you cut buds (called *candles*) on pines to achieve the Japanese cloud-pruned look and to control growth. You can score the bark just above plumping buds on rhododendron bark to force them to grow (see "My Rhody Is Too Big" on page 163 in Chapter 12).

Some plants "bleed" if you prune before their leaves are out. This means that the sap flows out at a terrifying rate. It doesn't hurt the plants, we are told, but it will scare you. I remember cutting off a branch on a birch and it veritably squirted sap as if I had severed an artery! Therefore, avoid pruning dogwood trees, grapes, birches, maples, and walnuts in early spring.

Spring or early summer is a traditional time to prune rhodies and many other broad-leaf evergreens.

Summertime Generalities

Summertime, especially hot, dry summertime, is very hard on the health of plants. So is heavy pruning, so go easy. Summertime pruning has a less stimulating effect on plant growth (some even say it has a dwarfing effect, but I think that overstates the case).

In August the Pacific Northwest is often in the throes of drought (referred to as "summer" by the locals). It is a terribly stressful time for plants, and if they have been hanging on to life in poor health, this is the time they will finally succumb to *permanent wilt*, which is a real technical term. If bark that has been shaded all year is suddenly exposed to direct, 80-degree sun, bad things happen. I generally ease up on the pruning in August. Deadwooding is always okay. And it does sort of depend on how hot the weather is in any given year. Was it Mark Twain who said the mildest winter he ever spent was a summer in Seattle?

Summertime Specifics

I do almost as much pruning in the summer as I do in the winter, but nothing drastic. Just after rhodies are through blooming they send up soft new vegetative shoots that are easy to snap off if you absolutely have to keep the plant from getting bigger. I do most of the rhody control work at this time. A little later in the year, about June or July, it becomes obvious to all my clients that everything is growing "out of control!" The tree branches that have dipped down under the weight of leaves are bipping dog walkers in the face. The Japanese holly has grown up over the sprinkler heads. The shrubs are too crowded. I like to wade in and restore order.

Also, summer is a great time to spot deadwood—dead branches have no leaves! On some shrubs it is especially difficult to distinguish deadwood in the winter, so I like to nip inside them in the summer and clip, clip, clip. The plants that come to mind as good summer deadwooding candidates are the deciduous azaleas, hydrangeas, a lot of the deciduous viburnums, and lilacs.

In the summer, prune those shrubs and trees that water-sprout easily (that is, if you have a choice in the matter). But don't fool yourself into thinking that this will stop them from water-sprouting if you *overprune*—and remember, it doesn't take much to overprune these plants. Briefly, they are dogwood trees, cherries, crabapples, plums, magnolias, plants related to witch hazels, and deciduous viburnums.

Summer is a good time to prune plants like cherry trees and quince that are plagued by fungal-bacterial-canker diseases spread by rain, drizzle, fog, and mist. Summer is a good time to thin your apple and pear trees so that the fewer fruits will receive more sun and energy thus making bigger and better fruits. I like to prune Japanese maples, both upright and laceleaf, in June or July. That way their lovely branch structure can be enjoyed in the green season too.

Fall

September is a continuation of the drought summer, in my mind, and I avoid heavy pruning. More and more I am reluctant to do a lot of pruning in the fall. I'm not sure why, but I have a few ideas. If you shear or otherwise head-back the more tender shrubs, you might stimulate regrowth, which may subsequently freeze. Also, fungal diseases are all sporulating and looking for ways to attack plants. I think of plants as tired and worn out from all the summer work, or maybe that's me. But moderate pruning is always okay, especially thinning and deadwooding. Pines are often pruned in the fall.

Winter Generalities

Winter is when all your deciduous plants are sound asleep and your evergreens are sort of dozing too. Winter is the traditional time to prune deciduous plants because they are safely dormant and because, now that the leaves are gone, you can see what's going on with the branches. And gardeners are finally through mowing and weeding and have the time to do major pruning. It's cold, so you can do major sawing and hauling without getting overheated. Winter pruning stimulates growth almost as much as spring. The evidence is just delayed until spring.

Winter Specifics

I am told that if temperatures drop much below freezing you might hurt brittle wood (and slowed-down cambium) on some trees and tree-like shrubs. Branch collars may suffer dieback if exposed. I'm not thoroughly convinced that these are dangers. It is true that radical reduction of tender plants may expose them to freezing.

IVY AND WISTERIA

If you are unfortunate enough to take care of a landscape with English ivy in it, and you need to minimize your maintenance time (and who doesn't?), the late summer/fall season is the most efficient time to peel off the tendrils that are climbing up the foundation, the brickwork, or the trunks of trees. Why? Because the ivy tendrils are still soft and relatively easy to scrape off with your hand pruners. If you let it go all winter, the tendrils/roots will harden off and really grab hold. Late summer is also better than spring for ivy work because if you cut ivy back in the spring it just grows back right away and you have to cut it over again.

Summer is the time that you will find yourself whacking back the new shoots (runners, whips) of wisteria vines too, just to keep them from overtaking the North American continent. You will be cutting the runners back every couple of weeks. But the most important thing to remember is to remove all the wisteria runners that have lashed themselves into nearby trees and wedged themselves under your shingles before winter. If you wait till next spring you will find that they have hardened off into unyielding tentacles. Then they can only be cut off, not pulled off—a very labor-intensive and frustrating job.

TREES

Because trees are a long-term investment in health care, good arborists may pay closer attention to specific requirements of certain trees than to the season for pruning. Generally speaking, arborists will avoid major pruning during the periods when a tree's leaves are expanding in the spring and when they are falling in the autumn. These are low energy times for the tree. Also, at some times in the spring, the bark fairly floats on sap and should not be "walked" on. Some trees have vulnerable times in their yearly cycles that make them susceptible to specific pest and disease organisms and therefore require additional timing considerations. For example, to prevent the spread of Dutch elm disease, do not prune elms in leaf.

But, hey, that branch hanging over your car that hit Aunt Martha in the head? Saw away!

SUMMARY

People make too big a deal about timing. If you are pruning the right way, and in moderation, anytime is the right time to prune.

CHAPTER SIX

Pruning Tools

Man, the tool user" is a phrase that has stuck with me since junior high school. I usually quote this phrase when I'm trying to convince my husband to use something other than his hands as a hammer. It is certainly true that whenever you become engrossed in a project you are apt to resist taking the time to go search out the necessary tool. But it is an important lesson. It saves work in the not-too-long run, and saving work is intrinsically enjoyable. Furthermore, getting the right tool will save wear and tear on your most important tool— your hands.

HAND PRUNER

Occasionally, when I'm out on a garden consultation or doing a class demonstration, I borrow the homeowner's hand pruner (a.k.a. hand-shear or, if you are British or just well read, secateurs) to demonstrate a cut. These often turn out to be cheap tools that cut so poorly that I am tempted to give them the heave-ho into the bushes, right then and there. It's no wonder that many people give up trying to learn how to prune.

I remember my first pair of professional-quality hand pruners (see Figure 6.1). They were a red-handled Felco 2 that came in a leather holster, lay heavy in the hand, and were oh-so-sharp to the touch. Getting your first good hand pruner inspires much the same exultation you felt as a kid at Christmas. Felcos are definitely the Red Rider BB gun of the gardener's world.

Felco is the brand name of the most popular hand pruner. From time to time I try one of the many imitations. They look the same, but never seem to cut as well. I figure it must be the quality of the metal in the blade. I always go back. In all fairness, I should mention that other very good gardeners swear by Corona, Sanvik, and ARS. You might care to try them and let me know what you think. Originally I was impressed with the ratchet-type hand pruners because of the large cut they could effortlessly make. But eventually the blades splay apart, and I'm back to using my Felcos once again.

Figure 6.1 Hand pruner

There are many other Felco models that are equally as good as Felco 2. You may find that you prefer a 6 or an 8. Some people like ones with smaller, straight blades—good for propagation work. Others prefer the pruners with a smaller grip because they are less damaging to their smaller hands. (This is no small matter for people in the business. Carpal tunnel syndrome, sometimes requiring surgery, is quite common.) For the same reason, Felco makes some models with a swivel handle. I never liked the looks of a moving handle. It just seems like one more thing to break, and I suspect it would get gunked up with dirt and pitch. But other gardeners have assured me that they are sturdy and of value.

In general it's hard to find one really good source for all the tools a gardener needs, and there is a lot of junk sold in hardware stores. The better nurseries usually carry a nice selection of good tools. Nationally, you can receive the A.M. Leonard wholesale catalog that has just about every landscaping tool on the market (call 800-543-8955 or visit *www. amleo.com*).

The topic of garden tools is subjective, and what works for one person may not work for another. I wouldn't want to get in an argument about which hand pruner is the best. But I can say the following: Most good pruners I know use the "bypass" type (that work like scissors; see Figure 6.2) rather than the "anvil" type (see Figure 6.3). You get a cleaner cut. Originally, I preferred the anvil type because it had more "umpf." But I now think of it as unprofessional and was slightly

Figure 6.2 Bypass-type pruner

disappointed when Felco began offering an anvil-type pruner.

Anvil pruners always leave a tiny stub, and they purportedly crush, rather than cut, the stem. As you gain experience, you become more sensitive to the need for clean cuts. Like a chef or a surgeon, you fixate on getting ever sharper and more precise tools. Rather than searching for a small tool that can do a big job, you get a complete set of tools and keep them handy. Each one is specifically matched to a certain kind and size of job. When I worked for the Seattle Parks Department, we used to say "Get a bigger hammer." The two-pound hammer is still one of my favorite tools.

All parts of the Felco pruner, including the spring, the blade, and so forth, are replaceable. I rarely bother with parts, though. I can use the original pair for years, until the plastic coating wears off the handles. They hold up really well. And, I am ashamed to admit, I don't take very good care of them. I do give the blade a few licks with a file when I notice my pruning cuts are starting to tear. Other

Figure 6.3 Anvil-type pruner

people, people of greater tool-care virtue than I, have more extensive regimes for sharpening and caring for pruning tools. Mine is pretty simple. After a rainy day of pruning and weeding I refrain from leaving them stored in the holster, or they get rusty. I take them inside and wash them off, scrubbing them in the sink. Then I spray them with WD-40 and store them open until dry.

In fact, when they are not inside my holster, my pruners are always open. This is because Felcos have a flaw. That little latch (supposed to keep the blades shut when not in use) loosens up and starts closing the pruners in between each and every cut. Very annoying! And there's no use trying to tighten it back up. I always just take the whole mechanism off and throw it away. The holster keeps the pruners shut when they're not in use, so I don't really need the latch anyway. And the spring-loaded tension of the open blades against the holster sides may even help the pruners stay inside the holster (say, for example, when I'm pruning upside-down). I think that Felco may have tried to fix the latch once, but it still fell open. Instead of fixing the problem, they just succeeded in making it so I couldn't unscrew the latch and get it off. Then I had to use a little piece of duct tape to keep it stuck open. It looked really professional, as you can imagine.

HOLSTER

Having a holster is essential. It keeps you from losing your very expensive pruners in a debris pile inside a shrub (for this reason, the hand-pruner handles are usually red). They make different kinds of holsters: One is sort of cone shaped, another is more U shaped to fit the different models of pruners. There is also one with a clip to attach to your pocket (good for women with hips), and the kind with slots that you thread your belt through. Having a holster means that you are always ready to act with quick-draw pruning whenever a stub is sighted. It's like having a pair of scissors with you at all times.

I use my pruners to stab open bags of soil, cut string-trimmer twine, and clean around sprinkler heads (more apologies to the people who take good care of their tools). On the Felco there is even a wire-cutting notch on the lower blade that you can use to cut free the odd strangled tree you might run across. And there are several uses for worn-out holsters.

Besides, having a leather holster makes you feel like a real cowgirl at the end of the day when you hang up it up (my husband, John, and I have His and Hers pegs for our belts). When you walk into a store or bank with it on, people immediately suspect that you are a person of some authority, like an electrician or a robber.

Figure 6.4 Uses for retired holsters **A.** Piercing object **B.** Chia Pet **C.** Lunch box

And, if perchance you find yourself waiting in a long line, you might even sidle up to the potted ficus to do a little absentminded deadwooding. I am so attached to my belt, holster, and pruners that I have been known to pack them up to take on vacation. Note that arborists don't have a separate holster for their hand pruners. I believe the pruner holster is built into their saw scabbard.

LOPPERS

I swear, the second most mispronounced word in gardening is "loppers" ("cotoneaster" is the first). People tend to rhyme it with "dopers." Actually it rhymes with "toppers." I prefer the Coronabrand. And as with all pruning tools, it pays to buy the more expensive ones.

Figure 6.5 A person of authority

I like the wood-handled loppers because they are not as cold in your hands in the winter as the metal-handled ones (see Figure 6.6). Also, wood handles tend to break, not bend, when pushed too far, and it is much easier to discard, or repair, a broken-handled lopper; a bent-handled one tends to stay on board to annoy its users indefinitely. I know just how far I can push my wood-handled loppers, and I haven't broken a pair in years (and years).

When cutting up brush, I do sometimes brace one handle with my foot on the ground (hook side on the bottom, slip in the branch, and then push down, slowly, with both hands on the upper handle). The power of leverage is evident. It also always helps to make the cut at a slant (as anybody who cuts bamboo poles can tell you). At the risk of contradicting the "Get a bigger hammer" adage, I sometimes brace one handle against my breast bone and pull toward me with both hands to prune a large branch. This pruning technique can make for some interesting bruises.

Be prepared to shell out a little extra money for the loppers with a rubber lopper bumper at the hinge. (Go ahead, say "rubber lopper bumpers" five times, fast.) This cushions the blow to your hands when you're making repeated cuts. When I have not pruned for a while, cutting back a laurel hedge can ruin me for a week. Thank heaven I rarely do this. Like most professional gardeners, I got out of doing hedges as soon as I could. The last time I arborized and pruned 50 feet of laurel, I borrowed my husband's compound loppers. They really paid off. But in general,

Figure 6.6 Loppers

I avoid using heavy and/or complex tools, preferring instead to get the next-sized "right" tool. When pruning, this means you trade the loppers in for a saw.

Pruning loppers, or lopping shears, are used for cuts from about ⅛ inch to 1 inch depending on the hardness of the wood. The long handles are good for extending your reach above your head or for reaching inside a thorny shrub. Loppers are also used to further reduce the size of pruned branches in order to fit them compactly into your truck. Finally, loppers are the tool of choice for cutting down a blackberry bush. You cut canes with it, you bash the bush bits down with it, and you also use it to fish out the cut brambles.

PRUNING SAW

The invention of the ARS-type blade and pruning saw practically put my loppers out of business. This revolutionary blade (also called Japanese style or tri-faceted) cuts twice as fast as a similarly sized regular pruning saw. All the gardeners I know now carry a red, plastic-handled, folding Felco 60 in their back pockets (see Figure 6.7).

I used to have an old wood-handled folding saw, and it sufficed for years. But when I got my first ARS-type saw I found that it cut so fast that I rarely turned to my loppers. I would be clear across the yard before I noticed that I didn't have the loppers with me—I even made it home one day without them. And when I discovered that I had lost my loppers, I felt a twinge of pain just because we had been together for so long. It's not good to get emotionally attached to your tools.

In the beginning, I liked the bow saw—once again, because it seemed to have more power. But they are really no good for pruning. Bow saws are designed for cutting firewood. Pruning saws are crescent shaped with a narrow, pointed end so that they can fit into tight spaces. The bow of a bow saw often prevents you from making the proper-angled cut on a tree.

The idea behind the Felco 60 blade folding into the handle is, I assume, to protect your truck upholstery and yourself from inadvertent cuts. Once, when I was pruning inside an 8-foot shrub, I tossed a cut branch out to the

Figure 6.7 Folding pruning saw

lawn by throwing it up and out. Unfortunately, I still held my pruning saw open in the other hand and managed to make a significant pruning cut on my forearm. Just before the blood started to gush and the shock set in, I remember noting with some interest that the wound looked like an anatomical illustration showing the layers of skin.

Danger is everywhere, don't you know! A good way to cut off your finger is to reach around to the back side of the shrub in front of you with your hand pruners and prune it "backwards." The ARS-type pruning saws are frequently seen with the tips broken off: When new users try to force the blade through a branch, the tips snap off. I know someone who suffered an eye injury as a result. Like all pruning saws, the ARS ones cut on the pull stroke, which may account for some of the problem. I think the ARS-type saws have more slender blades than the old saws did, too. But really it's mostly a matter of learning how to finesse the cut, and only experience can teach you that. The saws with the broken tips still cut well, and you can always relegate them for use as root pruners, or "dirt saws" as my husband calls them.

Although I never think twice about using my loppers to cut roots, and I use my hand pruners to prune roots even though I know I shouldn't, I never let my good hand saws touch the dirt. The ARS-type blades cannot be sharpened, or at least not easily. The replacement blades are sold separately and are quick to install. Still, I guard the blade like a mother hen.

READY TO WORK

When preparing yourself to do a pruning job, suit up with all your tools. The Felco is in the holster, the loppers are slung over the shoulder, and the pruning saw is tucked in the back pocket. If it is raining out, the saw may be tucked into the rubber boot, since the rain gear has made the back pocket inaccessible. Then, as the size of the cut exceeds the limits of the tool, you can readily trade up.

I have taken to keeping an arborist's saw in a scabbard hanging from my tool belt. It looks pretty pretentious, I must admit, but comes in real handy for the larger cuts, if there aren't too many. Unlike the chain saw, it always starts on the first pull. You don't need to spend fifteen minutes filling it up with fuel and bar oil, or straightening out the new chain and putting it on. And it doesn't annoy the neighbors. The arborists' saw I use has the same tri-faceted blade as my little saw. It's called the "Turbo Cut." I guess that's sort of an arborist's joke. Which reminds me, how do you get a one-armed arborist out of a tree? Answer: Wave.

In conclusion, remember what Mr. Natural says: "Use the right tool for the job." You'll be glad you did.

SUMMARY

The starter kit for pruners includes Felco 2 hand pruners, a holster, a Felco 60 pruning saw, and a pair of good, wood-handled loppers with rubber lopper bumper. Buy only high-quality (expensive) pruning tools.

CHAPTER SEVEN

How to Prune Hedges

Hedges can be grown in two styles, the formal and the informal. Formal means that you shear them; informal means that they look more natural, and you selectively prune them to control size and maintain their good looks.

A big difference between formal and informal hedges (see Figure 7.1) is the amount of time it takes to maintain them. Formal hedges have to be sheared all over to keep them looking tidy—which may be fast, but must be done frequently. To control size, you cannot miss a year. Informal hedges can be selectively pruned, and therefore they generally need only touch-ups of unruly branches. They are easier to reduce in size and look better when reduced this way. Both styles of hedge have the purpose of providing a natural screen or wall. A formal hedge (in addition to performing this function) is a style that makes a good contrast to other plants, and contrast is one of the major elements of an aesthetically pleasing yard. So, whereas an entirely sheared yard may look dumb and dull, a perfectly straight sheared hedge behind your perennial flowerbed constitutes valuable contrast in your yard and is very tasteful.

AVOID LEGGY HEDGES

A hedge with legs looks pretty uncouth. You want a hedge that is dressed to the ground, as in totally formal. Hedges get leggy when sun cannot reach down low, so that the lower leaves get shaded out and die. The way to prevent this is to shear your hedge in a slightly pyramidal fashion so that the top does not shade the bottom. By fall, the top

Figure 7.1 Hedge styles

Formal   Semiformal   Informal

| Formal | Semiformal | Informal |

hedge template and move it along. Some choose a part of their body to cut to. Once Norman the Foreman at the Parks Department where I worked told the crew to cut at knee level—which, of course, varied according to whose knees you were talking about. We sang it to the tune of "She's Got Bette Davis Knees."

For very tall and very long hedges, rent scaffolding to help you cut the hedge perfectly level. The best method I've found for general hedge cutting is the haircut method: Take a little off at a time, and constantly, frequently, stand back and walk around, looking at your hedge from different angles. Get it right the first time, using loppers; then you can follow your old cuts the next year, using shears or your hand pruner.

will have grown back more vigorously than the bottom, and the hedge will look more nearly square. If it snows, the pyramidal form also helps prevent damage to the top.

CREATING A NICE HEDGE

The major criteria for nice formal hedges are levelness and straightness. This is a lot harder to achieve than one might suppose. As people who have sided a house or laid bathroom tile know, the work may look even close up, but when you stand back, *oops*!

Mistakes to avoid are (1) following the ground level, (2) lowering the hedge top as your arms get tired, (3) following last year's mistakes, cutting just above the old cuts, (4) having two people do it, and (5) following a sagging string tied between two posts or tied along the adjacent chain link fence.

Some people try using a carpenter's level on a board, or they rig up a two-dimensional

Hedge Width

A hedge needn't, shouldn't, be wider than one person can reach across on a ladder. If your hedge has gotten very broad, consider serious reduction. When you drastically reduce the height (or, more likely, the width) of your hedge, do it in spring, when the new growth will most quickly and vigorously hide those ugly bare branches. Be sure your hedge is the type that will green back up if pruned hard; many needled evergreens won't. If you are a lazy gardener and want to shear only once a year, try a tidy cut in June or July, when shearing is least likely to promote new shaggy growth. If you have a truly giant laurel or boxwood hedge with only one side facing the public, you may want to turn it into a false front (see Figure 7.2) by taking out the unseen inside, the same as making it into a horseshoe by chainsawing out the inside. This will make it possible for you to set up your ladder inside and shear the top.

Have you ever wondered about those giant sheared things on English estates? How do they do that? That giant holly gumdrop? That two-story yew that looks like an elf hat? Well, first off, these plants have been sheared from the time they were little, every year, so that they are incredibly bushy and dense right through to the very inside, and the gardener actually stands or ties the ladder onto the shrub itself. The plants chosen are slow growing, so they usually need to be done only once a year, and generally their leaves are small.

Hedge Size

Which brings us to the point of your laurel or photinia hedge. You (or someone else) planted laurel or photinia because you wanted a wall *fast*. Since these bushes really want to be trees, they oblige you by growing fast. But they don't stop when they get to the size you want, they keep growing—fast. They are prone to developing legs, and their big leaves don't look as nice sheared as do those of fine-leaved plants. That's what you get for being so impatient.

Figure 7.2 Making a false front hedge

You will probably want to shear laurel and photinia more than once a year to keep them looking nice. After you shear them, go back and go over everything with your hand pruner and selectively prune out the ugly stubs and exposed branches. If you've let either of these tasks go, so that now you have to place a twelve-year-old on a plywood board on top of the hedge to shear its 8-foot-wide expanse, you may rest easier knowing that these incredibly tough plants can be pruned back hard, which is gardenese for cut way, way back, to a couple of feet off the ground if you like.

Do not, however, try this radical reduction with your needled evergreen. It won't work. Most conifers and needled evergreens, except yews, develop a dead zone of bare wood on the inside of a sheared plant. The dead zone gets bigger every year. If you shear deeply into it, it will not green up again. So, generally speaking, every year your needled evergreen hedge must get incrementally larger. Hemlock, Atlas cedar, and, recently, Leyland cypress (*Cupressocyparis* x *leylandii*) are used to make elegant sheared hedges. These conifers can break bud only at the very tips, not deeper inside. They also want to be big trees. The Leyland cypress, especially, wants to be 125 feet tall (it grows to 20 feet in five years). But it doesn't stop there, and shearing it can become an expensive annual chore. You can never miss a year. Of the conifers, "pyramidalis" (*Thuja occidentalis* 'Pyramidalis') is not recommended as a sheared hedge. No matter how slightly you cut into the dead zone, it will not break bud and green back up. (It is also unnecessary to prune them. The pyramidalis is bred to be the perfect evergreen hedge—never wider than 4 feet, nor taller than 20.)

The qualities that make good shear material are small leaves, spaced closely together; slow growth; the toughness to take hard shearing; and the ability to break bud on barren wood.

DECIDUOUS HEDGES

Some people plant deciduous shrubs for hedges—privet, hornbeams, and the like. They often need more severe early training than conifers in order to build a dense bushy framework, especially around the base. It's even possible to use blooming things like forsythia, escallonia, quince, and camellia. (I wouldn't, but I'm prejudiced.) Pyracantha is often used as hedge material and is also valued for its decorative berries. You might time your pruning so as to retain as much "show" on all of these berried and flowering plants as you can. Unlike a conifer hedge, which should not be headed until it reaches the height you want it to be, deciduous material should be sheared all over repeatedly as it grows to its desired height.

POWER TRIMMING

If you have inherited a home with a veritable fortress of hedging around the perimeter and you want to keep it (I'd take it out and plant a perimeter of tasteful groupings of shrubs), you may choose to invest in a pair of electric or gas-powered hedge trimmers. The two most hated pieces of power equipment in the Parks Department were chainsaws and power hedge shears. That's because they rarely made it through a group project alive. I always loaded up as many as I could lay my hands on, so that when one died I could switch to a new one. It reminded me of a Pony Express rider changing to a fresh horse. I also brought two extra chains for the chainsaw and some WD-40 for the blades of the power hedge shears, to use when they got sticky and wouldn't move.

It's a wise idea to sharpen both of these pieces of equipment before, during, and after a big job. This is because the amount of physical effort required increases exponentially with the dullness of the blade. Also, you can get into serious accidents with both these power tools, the chances of which increase as you get tired from forcing dull blades through your shrubbery. People are very reluctant to stop to rest once they start this equipment, especially when it's taken thirty-five pulls to get it started, thus ensuring operator exhaustion from the beginning. Tired people with dull chainsaws cut their foreheads open (tip kickback); tired hedgers tend to saw into their thighs. These tools are, on the other hand, useful timesaving and labor-saving devices, if you use the best and the sharpest and take the

Shrubs Good for Formal Hedges

Box honeysuckle (*Lonicera nitida*)

Boxwood (*Buxus*)

Japanese holly (*Ilex crenata*)

Privet (*Ligustrum*)

Pyracantha

Yew (*Taxus*)

Shrubs Okay as Formal Hedges (Some people would argue)

Cotoneaster

English laurel (*Prunus laurocerasus*)

Hemlock (*Tsuga*)

Holly (*Ilex*)

Osmanthus

Photinia

---

time to rest and resharpen. I use my local saw sharpener a lot, and I keep extra chains on hand. I sharpen things after I'm done, so that my chainsaw or trimmer is ready when I go to use it six months later. Electric saws and shears tend to start more easily than gas-powered ones and are much lighter in weight, so you don't get as tired. Also, you don't get gassed to death by the exhaust fumes. Be careful with your cord in the rain, however: Don't cut it and get a nasty shock.

People just don't realize the danger, drama, and high excitement that waits for them in their own back yards. Now that you know all about hedges, you are ready for the assault. Let's be careful out there!

SUMMARY

• Good plants for shearing have small leaves spaced closely together. They are slow growing and tough. They will not become diseased or die back as a result of repeated shearing.

• A formal sheared hedge should be level, and narrow enough for one person to reach across.

• Needled evergreens (hemlock, pyramidalis, etc.) cannot be radically reduced in width. They will not readily break bud and green back up, as will most broadleaf plants.

CHAPTER EIGHT

Principles of Landscape Renovation

53

Most people want to learn to prune to restore order to overplanted or overgrown yards. But pruning is only one of the tools that should be used to achieve a satisfactory look. Pruning itself comes in several forms. You can prune for size restriction or to thin out a shrub so that it seems less oppressive. You can prune to raise up a tree or shrub by taking off lower limbs—perhaps to accommodate foot traffic, or to get a tree off the shrub beneath it. Then there is "radical renovation"—cutting a shrub drastically to the ground, or nearly so, in order to give it a new lease on life. Which pruning technique will work best depends entirely on the type of shrub or tree and on the situation. All techniques are described more fully in future chapters.

PRUNE, MOVE, KILL

Pruning, especially pruning for size control, is really only a temporary fix for a given situation. After several years of pruning, I yearned for longer-lasting solutions for overgrown gardens. Here are a few: enlarging beds; eliminating some plants altogether; rearranging plants (transplanting); adding lower-story plants (those under 5 feet, and ideally more like 3 feet); and separating the layers (that is, getting the ground covers out of the shrubs and the shrubs out of the trees). These solutions might sound like more work than just pruning things back, but trust me, they are not.

POPPA BEAR, MOMMA BEAR, BABY BEAR

I have decided that what makes a landscape look right is the correct quantity and placement of different-sized plants. I call it the "poppa bear, momma bear, baby bear" theory of landscape design. The big trees, over 80 feet, are the poppa bears. Momma bears are those plants that max out in, say, the 10- to 20-foot range. In the Pacific Northwest, momma bears dominate our landscapes. In some other parts of the country, they may be missing altogether. The momma bear category includes all of what we call the "small" or "ornamental" trees, such as Japanese maples, flowering cherries and plums, dogwoods, and magnolias. Also, most of our shrubs max out around this size: rhodies, lilacs, camellias, pieris, mock orange, forsythias, etc. etc. etc. As a percentage of plantings, the baby bears are much less common here than in other parts of the country. They are shrubs that max out at less than 5 feet, plus most perennials and ground covers. Examples are skimmia, evergreen azalea, sarcococca, sword ferns, and heather. I suggest that the optimal ratio is one poppa bear to three momma bears to twenty or so baby bears.

Now go look at your yard from afar, squint your eyes, and ask, "Do I have the right proportions?" Would it look better if half the momma bears went away? You can't add poppa bears (because they take 40 years to get up to size), but you can add lower-story plants, or baby bears. Maybe you just need to add a lot more baby bears.

You can add baby bears by limbing up some old mature shrubs and underplanting them with such things as hellebores, sarcococca, and sword ferns. But beware, only the toughest shade lovers can do well under established shrubs and trees, and supplemental irrigation might be required. Optionally, you could enlarge your beds by removing sod, and then plant lower-story shrubs *in front of* existing large shrubs. Try to get the small shrubs from other places in your yard. Perhaps there are some azaleas or sword ferns buried somewhere under the rhododendrons. Same-aged plants look right together, whereas bringing in new, young stock from the nursery can seem, somehow, wrong. It's because they are mismatched. Adding new perennials can work, though. And some of the soft-wooded lower-story shrubs, like rosemary and lavender, can grow fast and look "right" rather soon. (See Figure 8.1.)

You can make the bed so big that the 15-foot camellia in the back of the bed is dwarfed. Then add a sea of perennials and baby bear shrubs that will become the focal point, bringing your eyes down to a more comfortable, human scale. Enlarging beds or adding new lower-story plants sounds like a lot of work. But it can give you fifteen years of not having to prune everything back. In fact, a well-designed or well-rearranged landscape looks great with practically no pruning.

Sod as Gold

When you enlarge the shrub beds, don't throw the sod away. It is extremely valuable stuff! To enlarge the beds, cut the lawn out in strips, following the existing bed line, sort of like railroad tracks. Cut sod into 8-inch by 8-inch squares that are about 1 to 2 inches thick. The best tool to use is called a half-moon edger, though a square spade will do. Pry up the brownie squares of sod with a spading fork and set them gently in the wheelbarrow. Don't overload it and tucker yourself out. Slow and steady, slow and steady. Drive the half-filled wheelbarrow to an unseen part of your yard. Dump it. Then, on your knees, stack the squares carefully and slowly like a bricklayer, piece by piece, upside down (not a speck of green showing). Make a sod wall 2 to 3 feet wide, 2 feet high, and as long as you like. Water it and then cover it over in black plastic, or simply ignore it, for a year. Come back, scrape off the top, and find the best soil on God's green earth. Better than you can buy. It's a miracle! Use this soil to create or enlarge the next bed.

Musical Plants

Aside from enlarging beds, you are most apt to find me fixing people's yards by moving shrubs around. Good gardeners are always rearranging the shrubbery. It's a lot like rearranging the furniture, except heavier and

Figure 8.1 Typical overgrown landscape (left to right): Cane-grower (sheared forsythia); mounding-habit shrub (spreading yew); tree-like (rhody); conifer (Alberta spruce); mounding-habit shrub (evergreen azalea); tree-like (pieris); and tree (maple).

Solutions (left to right): Radically renovate forsythia; grab-and-snip the yew; move rhody; remove Alberta spruce; leave evergreen azalea; thin out pieris; and remove low-limb maple.

One year later (left to right): Renovated landscape includes enlarged beds and additional low-story plants.

dirtier. And, unlike furniture, plants continue to grow, so it doesn't stay done forever. People always think that they should be able to "finish" their gardens the way a carpenter finishes building a house. But gardening is more akin to riding a horse than to making something. It is a process, not a task.

Depending on the exact nature of your soil and the species of shrub you are dealing with, you can move things around to suit yourself. In the Arizona desert they move big cactuses (with mattresses); in California they transplant 400-year-old oaks; in Seattle we move 15-foot rhododendrons using backhoes. With certain exceptions, whether or not something can be transplanted is mostly a matter of your back and your budget. There are some species that resist transplanting (for example, daphne, magnolia, juniper, camellia, madrona, heather), although my husband swears that if you take a big enough rootball you can move anything. Some things that transplant well are rhododendrons, azaleas, sword ferns, and plants that haven't been in the ground for longer than two years. (For more on how to transplant rhododendrons, see "My Rhody Is Too Big" on page 163 of Chapter 12, Tree-Like Shrubs.)

It's good to know that clay soil is good for something. If your plants are in clay soil, you have a much greater chance of transplant success because the rootball will nicely hold together. On the other hand, the perfect, wonderful, soft, fluffy sandy loam that everybody wishes they had falls off roots when the plant is dug up. And once the roots are exposed to air, they are in big, big trouble.

Wherever you live, there will be a list of plants that are good transplant candidates. Unfortunately, this list probably resides in the brain of your local experienced landscaper. Seek that person out, and hire him or her to help you decide what to prune, move, or kill in your landscape.

JUSTIFIABLE ARBORICIDE

People sometimes hire me to help them make these decisions. I carry the "red tape of death" (you know, flagging tape) to tie onto shrubs and trees that I decide must come out. I know that what I am doing is really giving the homeowner permission. They probably already knew that shrub was in the wrong place. PlantAmnesty isn't against death of plants, we're against torture! Lots of folks believe that they must keep every crummy plant that came with the house. You wouldn't keep all the furniture that someone left, so why suffer some ill-sited, sick, unpleasant plant, when there are many wonderful ones looking for a new home? Some may even be elsewhere in your own yard! In fact, the removal of one wrongly placed tree or shrub can easily transform a yard, and fast, into something more agreeable. And, I gotta say, it feels good. Some days I wake up and instruct the crew to load the chainsaw, announcing (like the Indian chief in the movie *Little Big Man*), "It's a good day to die." But be careful, chainsaw fever is apt to set in and before you know it you could remove half your yard. It will take thirty years to replace one nice, fully mature plant. So go slowly.

If you do cut something down, make sure that it won't grow back. Do this by digging out the root, by having it ground out by a tree service (they have a tool called a stump-grinder), or by using a nasty chemical painted on the cut stump (as described in "How to Kill Your Wisteria" on page 203 in Chapter 13, Vines).

PEELING THE ONION

The process of renovating an entire landscape is a lot like pruning. When I begin either of these chores, I often haven't got a clear picture of how it will turn out. I can't foresee all that I will wind up doing. In fact I'm likely to be a bit confused, a bit anxious, and sometimes overwhelmed by the task at hand. A lot of people get paralyzed by this inability to see the final product in their mind's eye. Just know that it's natural to feel this way and that you can train yourself to push through it. As with pruning, you should start with "the worst first." Another way to say this is: Start with what you know needs to be done, then step back, reassess, and then make your next move. It's like peeling an onion, one layer at a time. Only after you've completed several moves will more ideas on what needs to be done occur to you. With the pruning of a shrub, these first steps might mean taking out the deadwood and a few of the branches that touch the ground. In renovating a yard, the first steps might mean killing the birch under the powerlines, and transplanting the rhody that obscures the living room window (to a temporary holding pen, which is just a big pile of mulch).

I've been doing this work a long time. For me a typical renovation starts with the murder of a few undesirables. Then my crew and I enlarge some beds and even make some brand-new ones, irrespective of what could, or should, go into them. Then we dig up all the crowded shrubs and drag them to the middle of the yard. Then, with arms waving and sweeping hand gestures, I direct the crew to drag the plants around seeing how they look in this place or that. The crew loves this part. "Move it forward a foot, no, back, now spin it, spin it the other way, tilt toward me, okay, sink it." You will find that, in the end, some shrub that took half an hour to dig up will wind up back in exactly the same spot. And know that it is not uncommon for a particular shrub to be moved two or three times in the course of a year, at great effort, before it finds its final perfect place. The end result, I assure you, is worth it.

SUMMARY

• In renovating an overgrown or overplanted yard, pruning is only one tool. The other tools to use are enlarging beds; adding lower-story plantings; removing some plants altogether; and rearranging existing shrubs for a better overall picture.

• Pruning can be used to shorten some shrubs, limb some plants up, or thin out plants to make them seem less imposing. Pruning is often done to create definition between the layers of the landscape and between crowded plants.

CHAPTER NINE

The Most Common Design Errors

People often want pruning to fix things that pruning won't fix. More often than not, pruning is used to mitigate the ill effects of *bad planning*. As I've mentioned previously, a well-planned yard needs little pruning on an annual basis (except the vines, espaliers, hedges, raspberries, and roses), and one large-scale reworking every fifteen to thirty years or so.

OVERPLANTING

New yard owners usually buy and plant enough trees and shrubs to make their gardens look good *now*. This leads to the most common error: overplanting. But plants are only a fraction of their adult size when they are purchased, and they will inevitably grow from one to one hundred and thirty sizes larger before they stop. For the first five years, plant owners long for larger trees and shrubs; then the next twenty years are filled with angst that it's all gotten "too big" and is "out of control."

Unfortunately, homeowners are not the only people who overplant. Landscape designers and architects commonly overplant "to satisfy the customer" and because they, too, fail to understand the laws of nature. This technique usually backfires ten years later, giving the green industry a well-deserved bad reputation.

A couple of myths commonly accompany these overplantings. One is that the customer can selectively remove half the plants later. This works rarely in practice. I read a great placard recently: "In theory, theory and practice are the same. In practice, they are not." It seems like such a waste to cut out plants just coming into their prime that

most people won't do it. No one remembers the initial plan, and selective removal rarely even occurs to a landscape owner. Instead, they hire a gardener "to prune."

The second myth is that "If the pruner is good (and if they get on top of it early), they can keep plants small and even shrink them in size." Although some pruning does entail size reduction, the vast majority of pruning cannot and will not succeed in stopping plant growth to the degree that the average homeowner expects. Total size control, as achieved in some Japanese gardens and topiary gardens, takes incredible diligence and enormous budgetary outlays. It is seldom

---

Figure 9.1 Trees and tree-likes under windows and next to doors achieved elsewhere. I compare such pruning to lion taming: an interesting exercise for the devoted professional, but not suitable for the average person. The level of commitment is high, and there is a large downside risk factor involved. Perhaps a house cat is a better option for the animal lover, and a good long-term (and low-maintenance) design for the landscape owner.

According to my pruning system, plants are divided into categories according to their malleability. Cane-growers and mounding-habit shrubs are the easiest to keep down or return to their *mature heights*. Tree-like plants are those best let to grow to their *ultimate* size (twice their mature height).

MIS-SITING TREE-LIKE SHRUBS

Another common design error is siting tree-like shrubs under windows and next to walkways (see Figure 9.1). The most mis-sited plant in the Northwest is the rhododendron, difficult to reduce in size or keep small. Most conifers and other needled evergreens (except for yews) are also impossible to reduce dramatically in size. If one cuts a laurel hedge clear back into a mass of dead-looking stumps, it will surely grow back and be fine in a year's time. Not so for a dwarf Alberta spruce or a row of junipers. If cut heavily into the barren wood, they will rarely grow back. Unfortunately, there are always a few exceptions around (the amazing juniper comeback, the made-short rhody) to spawn homeowner hope and instill self-doubt in the minds of professional gardeners.

In some parts of the country, landscapers and landscape architects advise homeowners to shear conifers all over, every year, to keep the size controlled. What an incredible waste of time and natural beauty. All such plants eventually become unwieldy giants. Instead, needled evergreens can be carefully situated to allow for their ultimate size, requiring little maintenance and assuring maximum beauty for decades to come.

MISMATCHED PLANTINGS

Another common design error is placing large-growing shrubs under relatively small trees. (For example, the rhododendrons that are growing under my cherry tree.) One of my favorite "deadly dull" landscapes consists of five purple-leaf plum trees surrounded by masses of photinia. Both species will max out at about the same size. The futility is built in.

Similarly, planting a small shrub in a coarse-textured ground cover is unsightly and doomed to failure (see Figure 9.2). The commonest of these combinations is ever-green azaleas and young Japanese laceleaf maples surrounded by coarse-leaved and vigorous English ivy or vinca. Creeping thyme, fine-textured sedums, or other diminutive ground covers are preferable.

A landscape can be planned so that trees and shrubs retain their size relationships (tall, medium, low) throughout most of its life. A huge bank of Pfitzer junipers at the local warehouse installation will look over-bearing after fifteen years if it has been planted with small cherry trees. But the same mass planting will look "right" if the designer has chosen tree species that will stay "in scale"—plane trees, for example. The term

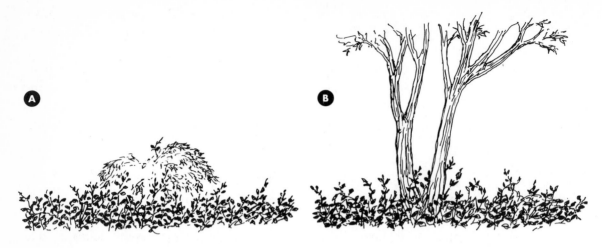

Figure 9.2 **A.** Japanese maple and coarse ground cover **B.** Mid-size tree and coarse ground cover is a better design.

"not in scale" is too often incorrectly used to mean "too big." (See Figure 9.3.)

TOO MANY FOCAL POINTS

Some people develop a taste for the rare or unusual. They begin a collection of plants with weeping or curlicued branches, or striped or peeling bark, or dwarfs, spikes, or other specialty items. The most common error for such a plant lover is to fill a yard with these oddities. What happens is that the specialty plants steal the show from each other. The eye jumps from one to another. In order to properly show off a specialty plant, you need to surround it with relatively unobtrusive mass plantings. I call them "the chorus line." Close neighbors should be nice-looking, but fairly uniform and relatively non-eye-catching.

TOO MANY AND MIS-SITED SMALL TREES

The final myth leading to design error is the commonly repeated sentiment that "city lots are too small for big trees." There is a grain of truth to this statement, but in some ways a tall tree can fit a small space better. At eye level, the vast majority of "headroom" is taken up by a 2-foot-diameter trunk. The really large part of the tree, the crown, is way above even a two-story house, interfering with nothing but air, and sun, I suppose. On the other hand, a small tree can take up a great deal of the yard where it is least wanted—in front of windows, or next to walkways, paths, or streets—thus dooming the tree to a life of bashing, snipping, and skirting. A saucer magnolia, for example, *needs* to be broad and low. Instead of deeding one quarter of the yard to it and mulching the bed beneath, people forever limb it up and up, just to get the mower under it. But the tree never seems to look quite right.

Figure 9.3 Keeping plants in scale over time

Newly planted plane tree and pfitzer junipers.

Plane tree and pfitzers in 15 to 30 years are still in scale.

Newly planted cherry tree and pfitzer junipers.

Cherry tree and pfitzers in 15 to 30 years are mismatched.

Good planning is by far the cheapest and best way to ensure a low-maintenance landscape. Unfortunately, that's in direct opposition to the "instant" landscape upon which everyone seems so intent. The clever designer will compromise by "overplanting" mounds and cane-growers that can be more easily pruned, renovated, or removed as the landscape matures. He or she will carefully locate the trees and tree-like shrubs, however, in the middle of beds, far from roofs, walks, and wires, so that they will be allowed to reach their ultimate height without molestation.

No doubt, one of the laws of the universe is "It costs less to build and take care of a good one than it does to replace it." Better to do it right the first time than to do it over. One might equally assume that in sheer numbers the instances of "doing it over" will always exceed those of "doing it right," be the arena politics, ecology, infrastructure, business, home, or yard.

SUMMARY

Common design errors are:
• Overplanting
• Siting conifers and tree-like shrubs near windows and walkways
• Planting shrubs that will grow large beneath small trees, or planting aggressive ground covers around smaller shrubs
• Using plants that all max out at the same size
• Siting small trees near paths
• Too many focal points

Clever design includes:
• Planting low-growing plants near walkways and under windows
• Siting tree-like shrubs in the middle of beds or bordered by lawn, which can later be removed
• Surrounding tree-like shrubs with mass plantings of cane-growers, mounding-habit shrubs, or low-growing plants that will be shaded out or removed as the others mature
• Spacing shrubs correctly for mature size and filling in with perennials and annuals

PART TWO

The Plants

CHAPTER TEN

Mounding-Habit Shrubs

Mounding-habit shrubs are basically the blobs of the plant world. They tend to be wider than tall, and most have small leaves or supple (soft, more herbaceous) branches. Examples are spiraea, evergreen azalea, choisya (Mexican orange), and escallonia. They are often used in mass plantings as opposed to being the featured plant (the specimen plant) of a garden area.

PRUNING MOUNDING-HABIT SHRUBS

Mounding-habit shrubs are the easiest shrubs to keep at a certain size, which means that (aside from the conifer shrubs of this type) they are better suited for placement under windows and next to walkways than other categories of shrubs. Mounding-habit shrubs have a generous pruning budget. You can generally remove a third of the shrub's leaf area without getting into trouble

(see Chapter 2 for a discussion of "the pruning budget"). They are most often pruned to keep them tidy and relatively smaller using the grab-and-snip method (see Figure 10.1).

ABELIA *(Abelia)*

Abelias are nice mounding-habit plants with graceful arching stems and small leaves. They have profuse, small pink blooms late in the summer and fall, adding interest to the garden when most shrubs are just

Mounding-Habit Shrubs

Abelia	*Abelia*
Aucuba	*Aucuba*
Barberry	*Berberis* (except *B. julianae;* see Chapter 11, Cane-Growing Shrubs)
Boxwood	*Buxus*
Box honeysuckle	*Lonicera nitida*
Broom	*Cytisus*
Burning bush	*Euonymus alata*
Ceanothus	*Ceanothus* (some species)
Cinquefoil	*Potentilla*
Escallonia	*Escallonia*
Evergreen azalea	*Rhododendron*

Evergreen euonymus	*Euonymus japonica*
Heath	*Erica*
Heather	*Calluna vulgaris*
Juniper	*Juniperus*
Japanese holly	*Ilex crenata*
Laurustinus	*Viburnum tinus*
Lavender	*Lavandula*
Mexican orange	*Choisya ternata*
Pernettya	*Pernettya mucronata*
Rockrose	*Cistus*
Snowberry	*Symphoricarpos*
Spiraea	*Spiraea*

Also see the list "Not One or the Other: In Between Mounding-Habit, Cane-Growing, and Tree-Like Shrubs" on page 180 of Chapter 12.

Figure 10.1 For mounding-habit shrubs, use the grab-and-snip method, hiding cuts inside the plant. **A.** Before **B.** After: shorter and tidier but still natural looking.

plain green. After blooming, the leaves and sepals remain with bronzy tints. If the winter weather is not too cold—more than 20°F—an abelia will keep its leaves.

When I was first learning to prune as one of the grounds maintenance crew of the Seattle Parks Department, I remember going through one of the city parks with a senior horticulturist. When we got to the abelias I said, "I suppose these are okay to shear?" "No!" was his adamant reply.

The Most Common Mistake

Abelias fit the criteria for plants that can take shearing: small leaves, evergreen, and tough. But shearing should be avoided on abelias, or on anything that is not planted as a formal hedge or topiary. It's not healthy and it's not in good taste.

The main reason I hate sheared shrubbery, though, is because of what happens next. Every place a cut is made, three shoots, wild and straight, leap up from the cut end. This is especially true for abelias. I call the long, arching branches "moon shots."

My husband, John, calls such regrowth "the fright." Although shearing is fast and a real no-brainer, it is self-defeating. The newly stimulated regrowth quickly destroys the neat and tidy sheared look. Therefore, in the not-so-long run, it is more expensive than selective pruning. The more you shear, the more moon shots you get, which need to be re-sheared, leading to a greater number of shoots, and on, and on. One is locked into a constant battle, and the plants look like heck half the time because of it.

General Maintenance Pruning

As with all shrubs, one can improve the looks of abelias by pruning out the deadwood and by cutting off a few of the lowest branches, especially ones touching the ground. Moderate height reduction can be achieved using the grab-and-snip method. Locating the longest branch first, you follow it down to a side branch and selectively head (snip) it off there. Repeat the process, always looking for the longest, most offending branch to prune next. In this way the shrub will be shorter, but natural looking.

Because abelias have small leaves, many people assume that the mature height of their shrub should be lower than it actually is. They think the shrub will be about 2 or 3 feet tall. Your average abelia (*A. grandiflora*) is 8 feet at maturity (as tall as the ceiling) and often more. The so-called smaller abelias (like *A. grandiflora* 'Edward Goucher') are 5 feet tall, which is not waist high, it is shoulder high. To prune in an attempt to keep a shrub, even a mounding-habit shrub, and especially a touchy abelia, smaller than its mature size is to ask for water-sprout trouble. So if you want an abelia that is smaller, pay close attention to the plant tag. 'Sherwoodii' and *A. grandiflora* 'Prostrata' are two cultivars that mature at less than 5 feet.

Avoiding Moon Shots

Abelias make water sprouts not only in response to shearing, but even when subjected to overly ambitious selective heading. This is especially true of young plants, which seem to naturally increase in size with those straight, ugly moon shots.

A common scenario is for the homeowner to purchase an abelia with a nice curved and arching branch structure. The plant looks great when it's first put into the ground. But the next spring it sends up these wild, stretched-out overachievers that ruin its good looks. The unsuspecting homeowner cuts off the offending shoots, which only results in a greater upsurge of them. Help!

So, how do you get rid of those long shoots? Well, you wait—maybe a couple of years. Eventually the plant sorts itself out. The only abelias I know that don't have any of those long upshots are ones that nobody has been trying to keep small. One in particular that I have finally tamed is currently 7 feet tall. It looks great all the time and now needs very little pruning. You could never convince me to try to shorten it. I'm not looking for trouble.

Rehabilitative Pruning: How to Deal with the Mess

For those whose abelias have a really bad case of the fright, I have developed the following technique. It is utterly counterintuitive. Every fiber in your body will tell you that the solution is to cut off the moon shots and leave the prettier, curvaceous inner branches. But that won't work!

The goal of this rehabilitative pruning is not to make the plant prettier but to make it more uniform in appearance by modifying both the top (which is all straight branches) and the bottom (which has all pretty, curving branches). Then it will be less annoying to the viewer.

Step 1: *Thin up a portion of the skirt that touches the ground.* **Step 2:** *Take out some of the nicest curving branches from the lower portion.* (I know this is hard to do since these are often the prettiest.) **Step 3:** *Modify the top portion of mostly straight branches.* Remove a few of the longest, most upsetting branches, but leave the vast majority in place. You may head-back some branches to a promising bud, cut some off

Figure 10.2 How to deal with a messy abelia **A.** Lift up the skirt. **B.** Cut out a few of the most arching (prettiest) branches, including interior, not just outward-facing, growth. **C.** Looking better! **D.** Deal with moon shots: Head some, remove some, leave many. **E.** Plant is more uniform, top and bottom.

inside the shrub where they join a stem, and remove some stems at ground level (see Figure 10.2).

In this fashion, the shrub becomes more uniform in appearance, and over time, as the shoots and branches age, they arch out and assume the characteristic pleasing habit of the plant. You cannot force branches to become more arching and beautiful. Only the aging process does that.

Radical Renovation

Cutting down a shrub, clear to the ground, to start it over is a radical step, but it is recommended for any abelia that has been sheared for numerous years. The plant will grow back remarkably fast, since it has the root system of a full-size plant. But the new growth will be unpleasantly straight for a year or more. When the shrub reaches its previous height, or even higher, the branches will begin to arch out, thicken up, and set more flower buds. If you choose this method, do it in the spring to lessen the chances of killing your shrub, and be sure you (and your neighbors) can stand the shock of seeing the initial results.

Summary

Abelias can be a bit difficult pruning-wise because when pruned for size control (either by shearing or even by selective heading) they respond with water sprouts. Even the normal new growth can be in the form of straight shoots. Therefore, avoid size control, and patiently wait for the plant to grow into graceful form. Be certain that the variety purchased has the desired mature size for the site. Other than that, abelias can be thinned, taking unwanted branches out at the base or to a parent stem. Deadwooding and removal of a few of the lower branches makes these shrubs look better. Abelias can be cut to the ground and regrown if necessary.

BOXWOOD *(Buxus)*

My husband, John, is the charter member of the S.O.B.s of America. That's an acronym for Stamp Out Boxwoods. John is a *complete* landscape maintenance gardener. That means he does lawns and hedges as well as the sort of bed maintenance that I do in my own separate but equal landscape business. Yes, he does do hedges, lots of them, including many boxwood hedges. And he hates them. I have done just enough to know why I don't do hedges anymore. It's tedious and frustrating, unless you like to shear. And we know that many people must *love* to shear, given what we see done to shrubs in yards everywhere. In such cases, a formal hedge or a sacrificial boxwood ball is just the thing to keep the industrious out of trouble.

Box Hedges

Boxwoods are good plants for hedges and topiaries because they have small leaves, grow slowly, and break bud if you have to cut into barren wood and want the plant to green back up. Even so, box hedges are higher maintenance than selectively pruned plants and need to be sheared annually to keep them in shape. Really anal-retentive hedgers (isn't that a redundancy?) must also go through their hedges every few years, thinning the crowded branch ends and cleaning out the extensive collection of dead leaves that has accumulated within. This helps offset disease potential created by tight shearing. Another problem with a boxwood hedge is that if a piece flops out, it's hard to get it back in place.

Which leads me to another reason the S.O.B.s hate box hedges. By their very design these hedges make it impossible to rake leaves and other debris out of beds that are hemmed by the hedge itself. And if it is a rose bed, well, there you are—bending over in a cramped corner, trying to hand-rake leaves. It's uncomfortable and occasionally painful, as you can imagine. John also hates the commonly quoted admonition to clip hedges narrower at the top than the bottom. He says it is unnecessary, and he's probably right with regards to box hedges. But what can I say? People like how box hedges look. And gardens are there for looks, and gardeners are there for the sake of gardens.

I personally am not a member of the S.O.B. society; my philosophy is "No Bad Plants," just poorly situated or poorly used plants. Yet I know that someone will still accuse me of hating boxwoods and topiary. It's not true. In fact, at PlantAmnesty we once got a call from a representative of a local elementary school. As with most Seattle schools, the school grounds were utterly dull and empty as a result of years and years of budget cuts. What it did have was a boxwood hedge—a full 100 feet of 5-foot-tall, lumpy box hedge. PlantAmnesty volunteers sculpted it into a bookworm, with an open book to celebrate reading week. There's nothing wrong with topiary, if you do it right.

An Alternative to Boxwood

In the Northwest, boxwoods are slowly being replaced by Japanese holly (*Ilex crenata* 'Convexa'), which looks just like boxwood except that it stays a nice, glossy, dark green. Boxwood tends to turn various shades of icky yellow or gray for a variety of reasons: too much sun, too cold, not enough water, sheared at the wrong time of year, mites, scale, a nitrogen deficiency, dog damage, and so on.

Not only is Japanese holly the superior plant in color, but it is also easier to shear because its branches are stiff. Boxwood stems and leaves are very soft: They jam in hedge shears and drive gardeners crazy. And the tiny shorn leaves are equally frustrating, resisting cleanup like so much confetti on a wet wood floor.

Tools

John works on many box hedges of the 3-foot-and-under variety, including a real knot garden. A knot garden is a set of low, interwoven sheared hedges (often of different colors such as gray, green, and gold) used in a design that is reminiscent of macramé. It is a particularly interesting formal garden feature that is best viewed from an upper-story window.

For precision hedging, John uses a special long-handled power hedge shear (the Maruyama brand). He claims it cuts his time by two-thirds *and* that his lines are infinitely straighter since he stands back as he cuts. John recommends doing the top of the hedge first, and then the sides, because it's easier to get the sides perfectly square this way. However, listening to thirty-five minutes of power shearing, followed by a good blow down, is no treat, I can tell you. In Europe during the Age of Aristocracy, gardeners had to work at night so they wouldn't be seen—laborers look so uncouth, spoils the whole ambience of the garden, don't you know. But times have changed. Modern garden maintenance has all the auditory charm of *Saving Private Ryan*. Well, I guess that's what people deserve if they insist on formal box hedges and yards with no leaf out of place.

Timing

Correct timing is very important if you shear a box hedge. If it's too cold when you shear, or shortly thereafter, all the leaves turn gray. If it's too hot when you shear, or shortly thereafter, all the leaves turn gray. So the most opportune time is about a three-week window in April—which is, unfortunately, the busiest time of the year for gardeners.

The Natural Look

I think boxwoods are underutilized as a non-hedge plant. Their natural habit is billowing and fine leafed, making them the perfect counterpoint to the overabundance of really broad broadleaf evergreens (such as rhododendrons, camellias, and the like) in the

Northwest. I especially like to see boxwoods planted in a little shade—the variegated form of *B. sempervirens*, 'Aureo-variegata', or the silver-edged form of true dwarf boxwood, *B. s.* 'Suffruticosa', will really brighten up a dark corner.

When keeping a plant in its natural form, it is imperative to accommodate its mature size. The mature size of an English or common boxwood (*B. sempervirens*) is 15 to 20 feet; the mature size of the true dwarf boxwood (*B. s.* 'Suffruticosa') is 4 to 5 feet, although it can be kept to about 2 feet with annual pruning. For even smaller places there are some incredibly cute super dwarfs, such as *B. s.* 'Rotundifolia' and *B. microphylla japonica* 'Compacta.' Consult your local nursery for more details.

Size Reduction

Given enough room to grow, boxwoods, like most plants, don't need pruning to look their best. Taking out dead twigs and branches is always in order. Any time is the right time. If and when boxwoods reach beyond the size of their allotted space, they are easy to reduce using the grab-and-snip method. First locate the branch that sticks out the most, that most interferes with the next shrub over, or the one that grows into the walkway. Grab the tip with one hand, and with your other hand (in which you hold a pair of Felco hand pruners) follow the branch to a place deep inside (say 6 inches or more on a 3-foot shrub). Cut it there. Most novice pruners don't go deep enough. If your pruners actually run up against a major side branch (clunk), this is an even better place to cut.

Figure 10.3 You can prune boxwoods for a more natural look.

Repeat the process. Between pruning cuts, scan the entire plant for the *worst* longest branch of all. Otherwise, you simply shear your plant one twig at a time. After a while you will find that your boxwood is miraculously shorter and tidier, but still loose and natural looking.

Thinning for Definition

Alternatively, a big old boxwood can be thinned out to make it open and airy, accentuating its branch structure (see Figure 10.3). You really can't get into too much trouble. If you thin "too much" it will easily break bud (growing numerous leaves on internal branches); the new growth looks just like the old growth and is not a mess of water sprouts. The natural features of the plant will not be compromised, since boxwood is a dense, small-leaved plant to begin with. "Overthinning" the shrub may simply become an annual maintenance chore. And, if abandoned, the shrub will easily revert to its natural full form, none the worse.

To thin a shrub, you must physically open it up and look inside. Push branches gently aside and search for lateral branches (side branches) to cut. Work from the bottom up and the inside out, taking and leaving some branches, cutting both some large-ish and smaller branches.

Summary

Boxwoods can be sheared, thinned, selectively reduced in size, or renovated. If you shear, do it in April or all the leaves turn gray. Japanese holly makes a better hedge plant.

BURNING BUSH (*Euonymus alata*)

You may have a *Euonymus alata*, or you may have a lotta euonymuses, or both. In any case the burning bush is not to be confused with the smoke bush or smoke tree (*Cotinus coggygria*). The burning bush is a deciduous shrub that is generally a big green globe. It grows easily 9 feet tall and 12 feet wide.

The *E. a.* 'Compacta' version, sold more commonly to homeowners, still gets pretty dang big, around 5 feet by 6 feet. It used to be pretty rare but lately it has been turning up in freeway plantings. You probably don't notice it until banks of them turn brilliant garnet red in the fall. I approve. (There is a spectacular planting of *E. alata* and Virginia creeper that turn color at the same time at the bridge entrance to the I-90 tunnel on the east side of Seattle, no doubt brightening the miserable commute of thousands.)

Because *E. alata* is now common on freeways, it is no longer considered good enough for many landscape owners. I think this is a mistake. Aside from its good fall color, *E. alata* has other attributes that make it a good choice for the garden. In my opinion, Northwest gardens are overwhelmingly composed of broadleaf evergreens (pieris, rhody, camellia), and the addition of deciduous shrubs helps create foliar contrast even in the

Figure 10.4 Burning bush with corky ridges

Figure 10.5 Corky Ridges and the Burnin' Bush Boys

summer. *E. alata* has a stiffish branch structure, with leaves that are arranged *opposite*, giving it a nice double-ranked textural quality. Subtle, I know, but there. New gardeners tend to pack their yards with all *choice* plants, forgetting that, in order for the star performer to show off, she needs a good chorus line. *E. alata* is one of those good chorus-line plants—tough as nails, always tidy, globe shaped, with its own moment in the spotlight during the fall. Sometimes the burning bush is called the winged euonymus because the twigs of the plant have corky ridges, interesting to note (Figures 10.4 and 10.5). The shrub will color up better if planted in the sun.

Size Reduction

As you probably know from reading other sections of this book, shearing a burning bush, or any other plant not used as a formal hedge, is a no-no. Also, it doesn't pay to try to reduce a shrub by more than a quarter. It's just too much work. The harder you prune, the faster it grows.

That said, you can somewhat shorten and tidy your *E. alata* with selective pruning. Locate one of the branches that sticks out the farthest. Follow it inside the plant and prune it off, cutting to an internal side branch or sometimes just to a pair of leaves. Now scan the shrub to find the next worst branch that sticks out the farthest and repeat the process. Slowly work your way over the entire shrub—for example, pruning it to get it away from a walkway. Be sure to keep it sort of globe shaped, feathering it back from the walkway, instead of making

one side a veritable straight wall of foliage. If it is up against a house or crammed next to another shrub, prune a bit where they interface. I usually start at the bottom of a plant and prune it and the back side first. It just seems to work out better that way. I call it the "round-down" when fitting a shrub to a wall. I think of it as creating tunnels or shadows by pruning between plants that are too crowded.

The burning bush, unlike most of the mounding-habit plants, can also have all the remaining branches headed-back too. This is true because *E. alata* is not notable for flowers (which would be cut off with every branch headed). And, too, the regrowth is not an unpleasant looking hydra. The new growth, if the heading cut is moderate in size, will pretty well match the shrub's natural growth. The main point is to stagger your cuts at different heights.

Selective pruning, as opposed to shearing, also maintains the texture and natural character of the plant. And unlike shearing, selective pruning keeps some internal foliage green so that the size can be reduced (with shearing you can't cut into the outer twiggy shell without running into barren branches).

Thinning

You can also thin *E. alata* to make them more open and thereby show off their nice branch structure. If your shrub seems oppressively big, sometimes thinning will make it less imposing and more interesting. Spend most of your time at the base. Taking off a few of the lowermost limbs almost always lends some definition to a shrub. Then selectively thin off other branches—some small, some large—evenly throughout the shrub. I don't think of the burning bush as particularly sensitive or prone to the water-sprout response, so prune as much as you like. If you prune too much, it will regrow, but not with a billion ugly shoots that take years to turn into anything decent looking, as will happen with many other shrubs.

Radical Renovation

One of our PlantAmnesty members complained bitterly about the hack job done to the rows of *E. alata* in the median strip by a local mall. A similar hack job was done to scores of these shrubs along a main city arterial, cutting the plants to about a foot off the ground. Actually, both these instances were the correct use of the radical renovation technique, where oversized shrubs are started over by cutting them nearly to the ground. In one growing season the plants in these two places put on an average of a foot of new growth. One planting grew much faster than the other. I think it had to do with the time of year. I wish I had been taking notes.

The mistake most people make when they decide to do hard pruning is that they don't go down far enough. They cut the plant to the size they want it to be, trying to be nice. Unfortunately, with the heading cut, growth starts at the cut and goes up. And when a plant is pruned hard, it grows up very fast, much faster than its previous growth rate. So the very next year the shrub is too big

again. By cutting very, very low, you allow room for the new growth to shoot up. And it gives the plant some time to reestablish its natural shape. If the new shoots grow rapidly and long, you may want to whack (shear, cut) it all again at the 2- or 3-foot level to create more internal bushiness. Be aware that radical renovation is not a maintenance procedure to keep a shrub smaller than it is programmed to be. It can be done once every fifteen years or so if there is a good reason. Usually this reason is that the plant has been horribly pruned for many, many years.

If you don't have automatic irrigation, do radical renovation in the early spring. It is also advisable to give the plant extra water in the summer. Hard pruning is tough on a plant, and so is summer drought. The two together can kill a shrub, even one as tough as *E. alata*.

Design Solutions

I know of another mass planting of *E. alata* in a median strip between four lanes of traffic that recently got a quasi-renovation. The crews just whacked them back to fit the bed. Wrong! Whenever possible, it is better to adjust the site to the growing plants, not the other way around. It turns out to be too much work to stop plants from growing by pruning. In fact, it is a study in the law of diminishing returns. Here was the perfect opportunity to just remove the narrow strip of lawn. Really, who wants to mow a 4-foot strip of lawn between the bed and the street, dragging mowers across two lanes of angry, smelly traffic every week? Similarly, at the mall described above, they could have just removed the bordering planting of low-growing holly (*Ilex crenata* 'Mariesii'). Many of the low shrubs had died because of car exhaust or a broken sprinkler system. Instead, the crew chose to renovate the burning bushes and replant the hollies. That was okay, but they could have taken the other tack.

A clever landscape designer does not depend on pruning to keep a yard looking good. He or she uses several design tricks so that the young yard looks good, and later as the yard matures, lower-story plants can be removed or beds enlarged so that it ages gracefully and with minimal maintenance.

Summary

A burning bush may be pruned to make it somewhat shorter using the selective heading technique. Stagger the cuts to retain the plant's interesting texture. Or the shrub can be thinned for definition. It is a good candidate for radical renovation. Placed in the correct location it—like most plants—requires no pruning.

EVERGREEN AZALEA *(Rhododendron)*

What is the difference between azaleas and rhododendrons? Well, any horticulture student can tell you that all azaleas are a subset of rhododendrons. We tend to think of azaleas as smaller shrubs, but in truth, many true rhodies are quite small (*R. impeditum*, for example), and azaleas can be big, especially the deciduous ones (like the royal azalea, *R. schlippenbachii*). But evergreen azaleas (as opposed to deciduous azaleas) are the small-leaved, mounding-habit, low-growing shrubs most people think of when you say "azalea."

A Useful Plant

Many horticulturists dismiss the evergreen azalea as being too common and uninteresting to be a "choice" plant. I think they are common because they are very, very useful plants. Unlike the vast majority of shrubs, evergreen azaleas remain "small," providing the much needed lower story in our gardens. I find that most shrubs mature in the 7- to 10-foot range, overwhelming the average yard. I recommend that people plant 50 percent of their gardens in shrubs, perennials, and groundcovers that are less than 5 feet tall. Azaleas fit the bill.

Furthermore, they are evergreen, naturally tidy looking, have nice flowers, and many even have reddish tints to their foliage in the fall and winter. Azaleas take sun and part shade. If watered correctly they live in loam or clay. Best of all, they transplant like a dream. When renovating old yards I often enlarge the beds and transplant all the sword ferns and azaleas to make the new lower story. It's sort of like rearranging the furniture. And lastly, evergreen azaleas are agreeable to all sorts of pruning.

No Pruning

As with all shrubs, if it's not broken don't fix it. If your azaleas look good and are doing their job, just leave them alone. Plants don't need to be pruned.

The Most Common Mistake

People usually err by shearing shrubs into balls. Evergreen azaleas are no exception. On the one hand, evergreen azaleas fit the criteria of good plants to use in formal settings, such as true formal Japanese gardens, where they can be sheared as individual plants or in masses. They have small, closely spaced evergreen leaves, they break bud everywhere down each stem, and they can put up with constant shearing. This is high maintenance, however, requiring frequent shearings to keep the plant looking tidy. And with shearing, timing is important. To preserve flowers, shearing must be timed soon after the plants are through blooming. If you shear at the wrong time, evergreen azaleas won't bloom, and if you shear at the right time, you increase the number of flowers. I almost lost it when I heard that for the first time. (That's one reason I like selective pruning. No matter what time of year you prune, there will be plenty of flowers left. Don't let anyone tell you differently.)

Although evergreen azaleas can take it, shearing them in most gardens is the hallmark of bad taste. It just shows the world that you don't know how to selectively prune, to "enhance the natural shape," as gardening books say. I remember consulting in a yard where all the azaleas had been sheared into separate balls. When they bloomed, all in different colors—white, pink, orange, carmine, and deep purple—it looked like a giant gumball machine had spilled. Luckily, evergreen azaleas are the easiest of all the shrubs to convert back into their natural form. My friend Tina calls it "ball busting." In print we call it rehabilitative pruning.

Deadwood

Deadwood is pretty obvious in evergreen azaleas—there are no live leaves at the tips. The dead twigs inside azaleas are so brittle that you can brush, or "crunch," them out with your hands (your *gloved* hands, that is). Such a course makes the biggest difference in the shortest amount of time (see Figure 10.6).

Figure 10.6 Deadwooding azaleas **A.** Collected dead leaves and dead twigs **B.** After deadwooding

You are supposed to go back and carefully cut the dead stubs cleanly from where you "crunched" off the deadwood. But sometimes you can save that for when there is more time. Whenever I see stubs left from a unknown previous gardener's hectic deadwood job, I feel a kinship that transcends time and space.

A grade-A deadwood job leaves no stubs. You should be able to run your bare hands down the stems and feel bumps (nodes), but no sharp edges. I sometimes tell new gardeners that they should be able to pass through their shrubbery with a knitted sweater on, and not have it catch.

Puppy-Dog Tails

Evergreen azaleas often have a few branches that stick out strangely beyond the rest. Northwest garden columnist Marianne Binetti calls them puppy-dog tails; I call them stick-ups. We both allow that people may want to remove them. To do so, use the grab-and-snip method: Follow the offending branch down to a place inside the shrub and

cut it off where it meets a side branch or a parent stem (see Figure 10.7).

The most common mistake is to just cut a branch off at the shrub's perimeter. This is nonselective heading, or mal-pruning, and it will just stimulate the dormant buds situated directly below the cut. Those buds will spring into action, growing out rapidly into a whorl of unattractive straight shoots, or water sprouts. On the other hand, cutting back to a side branch (selective heading) reduces or eliminates the water-sprout rebound effect.

There are other plants that are prone to growing stick-ups (or puppy-dog tails). They are enkianthus, evergreen huckleberry, deciduous azaleas, and Pacific wax myrtle (see Chapter 12). The stick-ups are these plants' natural way of increasing in size. This is true for evergreen azaleas too. You are ill advised to eliminate all of them in an effort to tidy the mounding outline of the shrub. This tends to stimulate even more stick-ups over time, even if you are pruning selectively, as the plant struggles to increase its size. So, as a general rule, I prune only a few of the most offending branches (look for the worst first). The goal of pruning is not absolute control. Pruning can only make a plant better, not perfect.

Size Reduction

If your azalea has gotten too large, use the same grab-and-snip technique described for puppy-dog tails above to make it smaller. Always locate the branch that sticks out too far and follow it back inside the plant. Cut where it meets up with a side branch, the larger the side branch the better (see Figure

---

Figure 10.7 Cut puppy-dog tails off at a point deep inside the shrub.

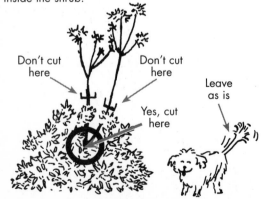

Don't cut here

Don't cut here

Leave as is

Yes, cut here

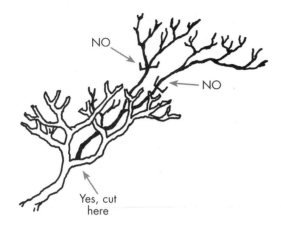

Figure 10.8 To make evergreen azaleas smaller, selectively cut out the tallest branches.

10.8). Then look for the next *worst* branch of the entire shrub that sticks out too far. Don't go for the next *closest* branch that sticks out.

Be aware that most novices err by concentrating on the top portion of the plant. The part of the azalea that actually prevents people from walking past it or that crowds nearby shrubs is often the *lower* part. Check out those branches. In fact, I think taking off a few of the lowest branches almost always makes azaleas look better. Remove any aggressive groundcovers trying to swallow them up. Only the most diminutive plants can be used around azaleas, say the smaller sedums/sempervivums. Tear out ivy and periwinkle. They shouldn't be anywhere near these shrubs.

Thinning

Evergreen azaleas have a very nice branch structure, which can be better featured by thinning. Thinning out means pruning off smaller side branches throughout the shrub.

Generally you should do more thinning where a number of branches meet up, thus simplifying the cluster. Also prune out some of the worst branches that cross and rub others, drag on the ground, wander too far, or clog up the interior. It doesn't matter much which ones you choose. Just follow a side branch back to its parent stem and prune it there. Generally speaking, you prune to "open up the center," leaving branches that head up and out, while removing some (not all) of the ones that cross, rub, wander, and head back through the center. (See Figure 10.9.) Simplifying crowded branching inside the plant will allow dead leaves to drop through to the ground rather than collecting like a bird's nest.

Although this sort of pruning does improve the health of plants, it's mainly done to improve the looks of them. It makes evergreen azaleas look airy and delicate. Don't worry about pruning too much (except during

Figure 10.9 Simplify branches by cutting out the crowded center.

a drought). It's okay if you get a little over-zealous on these particular plants. Azaleas readily break bud (grow back from barren or headed branches) just about everywhere. And the new growth is attractive, not a billion water sprouts.

Rehabilitative Pruning

To turn a sheared evergreen azalea back into its natural form, you prune the same as you would thin (described earlier), only there will be a great deal more of it to do. Be patient. You could easily spend twenty minutes dead-wooding and thinning the first time through. You need to crawl around, behind, and inside the plant, gently pulling branches apart or reaching in from the bottom up to get to the multitude of black, dead, brittle twigs that clog the interior. While you're in there, drag out the huge piles of dead, composting leaves that have been collecting on limbs and at the base. Use your hands. After that, a tidy-up prune will only be needed every two to four years and it will only take a minute or two.

When a shrub has been sheared into a box or globe, it pays to spend more time at the base of the plant, pruning off the lower branches to break up the geometric look (see Figure 10.10). By cutting off as much as the lower third you will return the azalea to its more characteristic chevron form. Up top, where thickly branched hydras interlock, look for the worst parts and prune them out, fearlessly cutting them off with selective heading or thinning cuts. Evergreen azaleas are very resilient and are among the easiest and fastest shrubs to return to a natural form.

Radical Renovation

I see part of my job as pushing the limits of pruning. Although reluctant to do it, I have used the radical renovation technique on evergreen azaleas. It works well. They survive and regrow in good form. (Although I must warn you that they grow back to their previous size quite quickly, in a year or so.) Since radical renovation is a serious stress on most shrubs, it shouldn't be done but once every ten or fifteen years. Which brings up the question, Why do it? I usually renovate as a quick way to return a shrub to its natural form if it has been mal-pruned.

Figure 10.10 Rehabilitating a "boxed" azalea **A.** Before: Concentrate on lower branches, looking for a more natural chevron shape. **B.** After: Remaining growth has been directed to renew natural form.

Rooted plantlet

Potted plantlet

Radical renovation is the cutting back (way, way back) of a shrub to a low, uneven framework, leaving 2 to 7 inches of horribly headed branches to regrow. Timing is important. Pick the season with the longest period of benign, warm, wet weather so the plant has the best chance at recovery. That usually means early spring.

Summary

Azaleas are easy to prune and can be pruned many ways. They can be selectively pruned to reduce size, they can be thinned, and they can be radically renovated. They are also quite easy to transplant. Always take out the deadwood and some lower branches to make these shrubs look better.

HEATH/HEATHER, LAVENDER, ROCKROSE, AND BROOM

(Erica/Calluna, Lavandula, Cistus, and Cytisus)

The most common pruning transgression is not tree topping. Though topping may be the worst of the horticultural sins, the most *common* one is the inappropriate shearing of shrubs. People, nationwide, seem to share a deep-seated, unconscious drive to make their bushes into green boxes, balls, buns, and corn dogs. None of this is good pruning and, aside from being tacky, it also gets people into horticultural hot water.

PlantAmnesty's general advice is: *If it isn't planted as a formal hedge, don't shear it!* That's a pretty simple rule. Unfortunately, exceptions do exist. All the plants listed here can benefit from regular shearing.

Horticulturists use shearing to keep certain rangy plants *more compact and tidy*. These plants are the brooms (*Cytisus* spp.), lavender (*Lavandula* spp.) and other silver plants, heaths (*Erica* spp.), heathers (*Calluna vulgaris*), and rockrose (*Cistus* spp.). When using hedge shears to keep these plants compact, timing is important. If you shear right before they bloom, you will cut off all the buds, and so the plants won't bloom. That's just common sense. One of the main reasons I like selective pruning is because it can be done anytime without eliminating the flower show.

Heaths and Heathers

The problem with heaths and heathers is that their old flowers fall off, leaving barren stems. If the plants are not sheared they may eventually develop ugly barren centers. Spring bloomers are sheared shortly after blooming (in the spring). Summer/fall bloomers are also sheared in the early spring (just as new growth starts), so that the attractive seed heads are left in view all winter. An annual light shearing is all that is needed. Don't wait. Do it now before the plants get too old and woody. When cut too far into old brown, barren branches, a plant may not break bud and green back up. If you have inherited a mature yard, it may be necessary to severely prune an old neglected heather. It will either regenerate, or die. Probably the latter. An exception is the tree heath *Erica arborea*, which purportedly responds well to radical renovation (and I have witnessed it).

Shearing is done to prevent "bald spots," but selective pruning can also be used to

Figure 10.11 Pruning as refereeing **A.** Two heathers compete. **B.** Two heathers relax.

alleviate overcrowding and sprawling. In this situation, "undercut" the heathers that are running into each other or out into the walkway. To do this, simply lift up the top and cut off handfuls of the lower branches as far back as is practicable. Then drop the top back down. I rarely think of my job as making plants smaller with pruning, but rather as refereeing between them (see Figures 10.11 and 10.12).

Lavender and Other Silver Plants

Gray- or silver-leaved plants such as lavender, senecio, and artemisia have always intimidated me because some books warn that hard pruning can kill them. Lavenders quite commonly get leggy, ragged looking, and sprawl apart. They do so more often and sooner than we all would hope. Because cutting back into thicker, older wood can kill lavender, preventive pruning (a light shearing, taking off the seed head and about an inch of stem) is what is usually done in hopes of keeping the plant a tidy dome, longer (see Figure 10.13).

In mild season climates a very light shearing can be done soon after the plant is through blooming. In colder areas, wait until spring to shear. And note that even dutiful annual shearing will sometimes fail to keep a plant compact. If, in the spring, you see new growth breaking at the base of young stems, you can also prune down to it, encouraging replacement foliage.

Kate Allen, Seattle gardener and this book's illustrator, says that there is an art to timing when cutting back *Artemisia* 'Powis Castle' (see Figure 10.14). You should cut it back early enough and far enough, in the spring, so that it stays compact. Otherwise it sprawls and develops that telltale deadish spot in the middle. But don't prune too much, or too soon, or it suffers a total setback, becoming a gray smudge the rest of the year. Ah, the trials and tribulations of the perennial gardener! Just as with fertilizing, when pruning one is admonished not to do too much,

Figure 10.12 "Heather Tending," from a tea service ca. 18th century, origin unknown. Note how the heather is being lifted up and clipped from beneath. The movement of the branches is reminiscent of waves breaking on rocky shores. The tarp is, of course, from the plastique period.

Figure 10.13 Lavender should be sheared lightly soon after it is done blooming.

too little, or the wrong kind, or to do it too soon or too late!

I suspect that a lot of these plants that become old, woody, and scraggly are meant to just be replaced every ten years or so. Open any pruning book to the section on lavenders and it will mention replacement. See, it's not you or your pruning skills. It's the plant. Lavenders are just like that.

Rockrose

I am increasingly fond of the rockrose, since it blooms in the summer and it actually likes living on hot, dry banks, making it a logical alternative to junipers. In most years it's evergreen. I was heartbroken to hear that, like many others in this pruning category, it may not reliably return if cut back hard (meaning that it's cut to a few inches from the ground or cut deep into older, thicker branches). If rockrose would regenerate easily, it would be the perfect choice for play areas and traffic circles. So if you have information to the contrary, be sure to write. Like other drought-tolerant sun lovers, rockrose is apt to freeze to death in a hard winter in

the Northwest. Its main drawback, however, seems to be its somewhat rangy habit.

New gardeners of course, want all things from all plants—not just a tidy habit, but attractive blooms, fast growth to full size yet easily made smaller, and evergreen. As you become more sophisticated horticulturally, you begin to appreciate the diversification and specialization in the plant world. Then the game becomes one of "mix and match," a game that is infinitely more fun.

The rockrose's rangy habit can be modified somewhat by heavy shearing early on in its life (in the nursery they shear hard in the spring, delaying bloom) and by annual lighter shearing later in its life, timed after bloom. This is not to say that cistus cannot be selectively pruned using the grab-and-snip method as an alternative. As I said, I like selective pruning because you can do it any time of the year and still have plenty of flowers.

As with heathers, I find most of my time is spent undercutting rockrose where it has flopped onto some nearby desirable plant. By the way, Seattle gardening expert Ciscoe

Figure 10.14 Left unpruned, *Artemisia 'Powis Castle'* quite happily flops out and roots, assuming the position of a doughnut or an octopus with silver pom-poms.

Morris says that he has used mass plantings of rockrose to effectively smother horsetail. Please make a note of it.

It pays to know the limits of each plant. At a recent slide show, an audience member confessed that she had given up selectively pruning her rockrose and had resorted to heavy-handed hedge shearing. Eventually, I explained, such methods would also fail her. The reason was that she had overplanted the shrubs along her driveway to begin with. I have noticed people have an almost universal habit of mentally downsizing plants. Although the plant tag clearly states that the shrub will get *4 to 5 feet high and as wide,* the purchaser crowds them into a *3-foot strip.* Five years later, the holler is heard, "They're out of control!" What did they think was going to happen? The shrubs won't stop when they have reached the size you wanted. And neither wishing nor pruning can make it so.

Broom

Another family of plants that are correctly sheared as a maintenance procedure (or so I read) are the brooms. Christopher Brickell, in his famous book *Pruning: Roses, Deciduous Shrubs, Evergreens, Hedges, Wall Shrubs, Fruit Bushes and Trees and Deciduous Trees,* actually shows someone taking scissors to a broom's outer perimeter. As with lavender, this removes the untidy spent blooms and encourages a more compact form. But like most pruning, it will not stop a plant from reaching its mature height, though it may take it longer to get there. Avoid heavy pruning of brooms, as with the similar plants I have mentioned. If the plants are young, they may readily resprout, although I fear older plants will simply die if all the green is removed.

Brooms, like many of these plants, like the sun but lack the architectural structure for people to regard them as "choice." But hey, they are evergreen and tough, and they can be used effectively in mass plantings. I have often admired our city's freeway plantings. At 65 miles an hour and over (or more likely under, these days), the plants that are too large or too coarse for the average back yard find their highest and best uses. I especially like the contrast of the mass planting of deodar cedars against fields of 'Moonlight' broom (apologies to hay-fever victims). I think the broom is especially well suited for slowing the cars that are involved in freeway accidents without stopping them cold.

A Final Word of Caution

Just because the above plants can be sheared does not mean that they must be sheared. I find that this assumption is commonly made by students of pruning. "Can" becomes "should." "Might be harmful" becomes "always is harmful." A well-planned landscape needs very little pruning. I believe that the natural habit of plants is their best habit. One person's "rangy" could be another person's "freestyle texture." If plants could talk, I'm sure that their only request would be for deadwooding and removal of the occasional crossing/rubbing branch. With the exception of heathers mentioned earlier, these plants don't *need* to be pruned. If the shrubs in your yard look good, then let them be and enjoy the time off. Maybe you could use the time to do some weeding—which, unfortunately, *always*, should be done.

Summary

Heaths, heathers, lavender, rockrose, and broom can be sheared to keep them tidy and compact. Shear lightly soon after blooming, or in the spring. Take care not to cut deeply into old, barren wood, as these plants in particular might not grow back. Undercutting, by removing the lowest, sprawling branches, may solve a crowding problem. Hard pruning is a kill-or-cure method (more likely kill) that can be used to renovate an old, leggy plant.

JUNIPER *(Juniperus)*

I think junipers are an overly maligned group of plants and I'm not afraid to say so. If the truth be known, I'm even fond of Pfitzers (*Juniperis chinensis* 'Pfitzeriana'). They remind me of the way waves are shown in Japanese paintings.

Every once in a while you run across a phrase or passage that changes the way you think forever. In a 1988 article printed in the *Ornamentals Northwest* newsletter ("Some Practical Tips on Pruning Shrubs"), Tom Cook eloquently wrote about the problems of inappropriate shearing of shrubs. Here is what he said about junipers: "Junipers by nature are irregular in growth and come in a multitude of colors and forms. Pruned naturally, they retain this delightful variation. Sheared, they all look like boxes or pompons. Advocates of natural pruning have been known to get physically ill while walking in a neighborhood where junipers have been sheared."

It wasn't until reading that passage that I realized that junipers could be "delightful." Many people's dislike of certain plants is based on the fact that the ones they have known were ill suited to the site, or mistreated and sick. Why hate junipers just because they are overplanted and mal-pruned? In truth, they are wonderfully tough, sun-loving, drought-resistant (and even shade-tolerant) plants. Junipers come in shapes, sizes, and textures to match any taste or place, from the tidy, flat *J. horizontalis* 'Blue Rug' to the wild and crazy 'Hollywood'. They have it all.

Prune, Don't Shear

I'm not sure that junipers should put in the mounding-habit category. Many are pruned using the grab-and-snip method, yet they are still relatively to difficult to reduce in size. The low-growing ones are used in mass plantings, and they are the ones I address here.

The first thing to know is what *not* to do. And that means don't shear them. You'll just trade in a "too-big" mass of textured junipers for "a too-big but now smooth" mass of junipers. Once junipers have been sheared, all hope of any size reduction whatsoever is eliminated. The green internal branches (ones that you could have cut back to) get shaded out and die. You are left with a thin green outer shell on a plant that gets a bit bigger every year.

Figure 10.15 Wrong way: Don't bluntly cut juniper, even next to a walkway. Such cuts reveal barren stems—the dead zone. **A.** Before **B**. After blunt cut. Barren stems will not regrow.

The Dead Zone

Like many conifers (things that remind you of Christmas trees), junipers, are difficult to adjust with pruning. A common mistake is to bluntly cut back the row of juniper tams (*J. sabina* 'Tamariscifolia') that extends too far over the sidewalk (see Figure 10.15). The uninformed pruner will saw the plants off straight to the sidewalk's edge, cutting deeply into the barren branches. These branches, now devoid of any green needles, are unable to break bud and regrow within. You will be left staring at an ugly brown stripe for a long, long time, maybe forever. (Dr. Ray Maleike of Washington State University calls it the *dead zone.*) If one radically cuts back a laurel hedge, it will assuredly resprout everywhere and be just fine come spring. But this doesn't work on most conifers.

The Lowest Limbs

When the juniper (e.g., *J. horizontalis* or *J. sabina* 'Tamariscifolia') extends over the sidewalk, the best strategy is to lift up the top (holding it back awkwardly with your ankle or leg) and cut off the lowest limbs (see Figure 10.16). Then drop the top back down. *Voilà!* The juniper no longer extends so far over the walkway, but miraculously it still looks natural. This process is sort of the opposite of sweeping things under the rug.

The same technique is used to help ameliorate the generally oppressed and invaded feeling you get as the junipers begin to crowd the other plants and trees in the landscape. By incorporating a little empty space between the juniper masses and other objects—tree trunks, lamp posts, the building—you can make the landscape seem more under control. You do this by removing the lowest juniper limbs as described above. On the other end, you can help by limbing up trees and shrubs a bit farther above the masses of low-growing junipers. Often this is not a perfectly satisfactory solution, but remember your options are limited by the plants' inability to take heavy pruning. "Better" may be all that you can do, aside from replanting the entire area with shrubs that will be "too small" for quite a while.

As for oceans of Pfitzers, use the same lower limb removal technique to get them away from walkways and such. In addition, a good pruner can effectively remove some

Figure 10.16 Right way: Do lift up top branches, cut off lowest ones, then drop the top back down.

of the most interfering branches up above. Here again, use selective pruning (hiding the cuts down inside the plant), rather than just whacking back the branches. Strive to retain the characteristic pointy "waves" instead of turning the shrub into an uninteresting ball. Before cutting, grab the intended victim and move it aside. Ask yourself, "By cutting this branch off, will I expose barren-looking branches?" If not, cut away. This works best for eliminating the branch that prevents you from walking out to the garage. I rarely try to keep an entire mass planting lower by doing this. It's just too much work. Besides, the best-looking junipers are the ones that are left alone but kept weeded (yes, you need to put the loppers down, crawl inside the plant, and weed out that grass).

Rehabilitative Pruning

A previously sheared or headed mass of Pfitzers can be made to look better by selectively eliminating branches and encouraging more of the natural chevron shape. In this case, pruning is used to accentuate texture. It creates shadows. In a sense it is the opposite of shearing. The mass of junipers might

still be too big, but now it will at least be more interesting looking.

Grab-and-Snip Method

What about the juniper tams or other low-growing junipers that are encroaching on both sides of the entryway? If you don't do something they will soon close off access completely. Use the time-honored grab-and-snip method to keep on top of the problem. Every year locate the branchlets that extend the farthest out and snip them off, hopefully hiding the cuts beneath other greenery. If such a cut is not possible, try to cut back to a bit of green that faces forward. Be sure to selectively prune the shrub all the way back at a slant so that the entire plant stays looking natural.

Deadwood Torture

What hope is there for people who have unwittingly exposed the dead zone or for those whose artistic pom-pom or Kmart bonsai didn't quite come out looking right? (See Figure 10.17.) Well, as in so many cases, the best solution to the pruning "oops" is thorough, meticulous deadwooding. And with a

Figure 10.17 Avoid shearing junipers: no Kmart bonsais.

juniper this can be a lengthy and very painful experience. Every tiny, yucky, dead twig must be individually cut off at the parent stem. A good, sharp pair of high-quality hand pruners is essential. I have spent a lot of time helping mal-pruned junipers look better, and I always dream of inventing the "Lady Juniper"—a limb shaver for just this purpose. The tiny needles on junipers always prick your skin and sneak into your underwear. You develop a juniper rash that stings, and it will sting again when the shower water hits it later. To make matters worse, why do you always seems to be pruning junipers in either 80-degree weather or pouring rain?

But try to remember that after an hour or two of patient deadwood removal, you will be gratified to see that those horrible plants look "almost human" again. And note: You will not have to do it again next year. Unlike "bad" pruning, "good" pruning stays done a long time.

Removal

Occasionally, previously mal-pruned junipers are so ugly that a more attractive solution is to remove them entirely. Junipers are relatively easy to dig out with a mattock, loppers, and a shovel. Old (or I guess I should say experienced) gardeners keep a chain in their truck for the specific purpose of murdering junipers. You attach one end of the chain to the truck bumper and use the other end as a "choker" around the plant. Then drive off slowly. It works amazingly well.

Oh dear, there I go again, telling people how to kill plants. Not only should we prune selectively (*Secare selecte*), we should also kill selectively (*Necare selecte*). The Plant-Amnesty creed reads: "We promise that when we take what we want from nature, we will do so selectively and with respect. Always we will preserve the health and integrity of the whole, be it a plant, a rain forest, or our planet." Good advice for a troubled yard and a troubled world.

Summary

Junipers, like most conifers, are difficult to prune. This is because the barren portions of the branches can't produce new greenery (break bud) once the exterior green has been removed (headed-back). Never expose those ugly, barren internal branches. If you do, your next step is to deadwood like crazy. Or take the whole plant out. What little can be done to help an overgrown planting involves removal of the lowest limbs, and/or selective heading (grab and snip) or thinning off the worst, most interfering branches.

Always hide the cut beneath some natural-looking greenery.

SPIRAEA *(Spiraea)*

My first gardening mentor, a woman named Andrea, once said to me, "If you don't know what a shrub is, it's probably a spiraea or a viburnum." This is sort of a horticulturist's joke, and one of some truth too. She said it because both genera have a huge number of plants in them.

The spiraeas all have a mounding habit and are tough, deciduous flowering shrubs. They take sun or part shade, survive in a wide range of soils, and take all sorts of abuse and neglect. Some bloom in the spring, others in the summer or fall. Their sizes range from 2 feet to 8 feet tall and as wide. One of my favorites is *S. trilobata* 'Swan Lake', which the *Sunset Western Garden Book* says "is like a smaller bridal wreath spiraea [and] gives a massive show of tiny white flowers in May and June." It is dainty and feathery and looks like sweet spring to me. The other spiraea I particularly like is a summer/fall bloomer and is a variety of *S. japonica* named 'Anthony Waterer'. It, too, is a fluffy little bun. *Sunset* describes it as having "flat-topped, bright carmine flower clusters and maroon-tinged foliage." Now there are some with golden foliage. I planted a group of them around some taller purple barberries (*Berberis thunbergii* 'Atropurpurea') and a purple smoke bush (*Cotinus coggygria* 'Purpureus') and together they look stupendous! If I do say so myself.

I think the spireas are best used in groups or as a ring at the border of a more distant bed, since their winter branches aren't particularly pleasant looking.

General Pruning

As with most of the plants in the mounding-habit category, the grab-and-snip method works well to tidy spiraeas and reduce size within moderation. There are limits to size reduction that don't result in a wild upsurge of new growth. In general, you should be able to successfully reduce a spiraea's height by about a quarter. And know that, no matter how dutifully or determinedly you prune, eventually you will be unable to keep the spiraea smaller than the size listed for it on the plant tag. "Eventually" means after it has been in the ground about ten years.

But, as stated above, moderate pruning is fine. As you follow the offending branch with your hand pruners, reaching down deep inside the shrub, you may find that there are no likely lateral (side) branches to which you can cut back. Take heart! You can just cut to no place in particular—snip. The branches on most spireas are so slender that cutting to a bud will do, and there are dormant buds hidden all along the stems. Yes, it might hydra back, but since you cut low, it will take a while for it to get "too tall" again. And, by the time the new growth reaches the surface of the shrub, it will have branched gracefully and put on flowers, instead of being an ugly straight shoot. Or maybe it will just die back and become deadwood for some future pruning session. In any case, by making a low cut, you will have bought some time before it gets "too big" again. You will have retained the shrub's natural texture and flowers no matter when you prune.

While you are inside, look for chunky, too-stiff-looking, older branches. Prune them out to the ground level. And, as always, remove deadwood, weeds, and litter.

Bloom Time

Spiraeas and most flowering shrubs don't really need to be pruned in order to flower, as many have been led to believe. But you may have a very tired old bush and the flowers may be getting puny and few. If the reason for this isn't too much shade or not enough water, you might want (and be able) to force some new growth. New shoots will come up from the base of the plant if you cut some of the branches down to the ground, pruning it more like a cane-grower (see Chapter 11). The new growth may start out thin and straight, but by the end of this year or the next, it should become graceful, arching, flowering branches.

If you are selectively pruning, you can do so any time of the year. If the shrub is blooming, you can use the cut flowers in a vase. The shrub that remains will still be full of flowers. Really, timing matters only if you are shearing (which you shouldn't do anyway) or if you cut the entire shrub to the ground.

If you are still compelled by the notion of right-time pruning, know that you will get *maximum* flowers by pruning the spring bloomers soon after they are done flowering, and the summer/fall bloomers soon after they are through flowering or even in the early spring.

Rehabilitative Pruning

A spiraea looks horrible when sheared, developing dead bits and losing its flowers, and, in the winter, you can see what looks like rats' nests of leaves and debris collecting inside. The sheared branch-ends soon begin to look like the snarled hair of a feral child. Rehabilitative pruning for previously sheared

Figure 10.18 Radical renovation of a spiraea **A.** Freshly cut to the ground **B.** 1 year later **C.** 2 years later spiraeas may require that the pruner remove a third of the "split ends" for three years in a row, always hiding the cuts inside the plant. If possible, cut back to a side branch and choose branches that grow outward from the center of the shrub.

Radical Renovation

If you have a nasty mal-pruned spiraea, and you are bold, you can just cut the entire shrub to the ground or an inch above, all at once. If you do so, do it in the spring. In a year or two the shrub will regrow and be just fine (see Figure 10.18).

Radical renovation of this sort is a serious stress on a shrub's health, so be sure it is well cared for otherwise. By this I mean it should have enough sun, and enough water, both the year before and the year after renovation. And please refrain from pruning this way as a regular maintenance procedure. Plants don't need to be pruned to look and do their best. Spiraeas are no exception.

Summary

Spiraeas are easy to prune, though they don't need to be pruned to bloom and look their best. You can lower and tidy your shrub using the grab-and-snip method. Remove deadwood. Prune off the branches hanging onto the ground. If it has been mal-pruned (sheared), restore the natural habit by thinning out crowded branches over three years (rehabilitative pruning), or cut the entire shrub to the ground (radical renovation). If you are selective pruning, it doesn't matter when you prune. If you like timing rules: Prune spring bloomers in the early summer.

Prune summer bloomers in the early spring (February–March). If you are going to cut your shrub to the ground, do that in the spring.

THREE MORE MOUNDERS

Is Your Frozen Shrub Dead?

After an extraordinarily cold winter in Western Washington, many garden owners wanted to know what to do about the damage to many of our not-completely-hardy shrubs. Two of these are escallonia (*Escallonia* spp.) and Mexican orange (*Choisya ternata*). As with many of our broadleaf evergreens, it is common after a hard winter for their leaves to turn brown or black and eventually fall off. The plants themselves will probably still be alive. To check, use a hand pruner blade to peel back a little bit of the "skin" to see if the cambium layer just beneath is alive (green) and not dead (brown). If it is alive, the plant will likely flush out with a new set of leaves. So don't panic if your shrub looks dead. Wait and see. How long should you wait? By June you will have an answer. By then, those that will put on a new set of leaves will have done so. If you can't stand the sight of the stricken brown shrub until June, try running your hands along the branches to knock off the brown leaves. Then the plant might appear to be deciduous rather than dead.

And by the end of August, the final report will be in. Freezing weather sometimes does internal damage that doesn't show up until after the stress of the summer "drought." A choisya might look okay through June and July, but then, as it is pumping water like crazy trying to keep up with the heat demand in August, some portions can just collapse and you will see dieback. (This nonscientific explanation is my own and may be a little, well, anthropomorphic.)

PRUNING ESCALLONIA AND MEXICAN ORANGE

Repairing Winter Damage

If your shrub has really suffered freeze damage, it will most likely die from the tip back. Both escallonia and choisya respond well to radical size reduction (with big, horrid-looking heading cuts to the point of green wood). The plants will break bud just below your cuts (not farther down), and many new green-leafed shoots will rather quickly grow out. They will hide the cuts and provide you with a new-looking plant by the end of the growing season.

Frequently, choisya also suffers mechanical damage from snow loading: Branches split, break, or splay flat to the ground. What a ragged mess! No problem. Get your loppers out and whack everything back to 4 to 6 inches off the ground. Yes, it's really okay. I promise. I have done this thing many times. As soon as the growing season begins, the majority of cut plants will spring into action. (The ones that don't are, well, dead. But then, that's no great loss.) As the renovated choisyas grow up that spring and summer, it is advisable to pinch them back every so often. That will force them into more branching and thicken them up. "Pinching" conventionally means a very light heading done by just nipping out the end bud of each

Figure 10.19 Pinch for fullness

branch with your fingernail tips. But to me, pinching can also mean using your hand pruner to nibble back the branch ends, forcing them to become bushier.

Cutting a plant back to a few inches from the ground or to a low—say, 2- to 3-foot—uneven framework is called radical renovation. It can be done to many shrubs if one knows what one is doing, and why.

The Wrong Reasons for Radical Renovation

Radical renovation is *not* a regular maintenance procedure (done every year) but one that can work in certain circumstances to "start a plant over" (done once every twelve or twenty years). It is also *not* a way to control size. Plant size is determined by species genetics and the age of the plant. A radically renovated choisya or escallonia will quickly grow (in one to three years) to the same size it was before. This is the reason radical renovation is preferable to replacement when a shrub has been damaged. You will get a full-sized shrub much faster than if you plant a new one, and it's free!

The Right Reasons for a "Rad Reno"

Two acceptable reasons for radical renovation are *to repair weather damage* (as above) or *to correct mal-pruning* (usually when the plant has been inappropriately sheared for many years). I can remember an occasion where I used the one as an excuse to fix the other. In a client's yard was a *Ternstroemia* that had been sheared by previous gardeners into a whisky barrel. It did not look good. But to return it to its natural shape with a radical renovation (whacking off every leaf to a stubby framework) would have been too scary for my homeowner. Then the freeze hit. Every leaf turned yucky brown/black. The shrub looked horrid. The homeowner wanted me to do something, so I whacked away. By the end of the year I had a nice, natural-looking shrub again.

Plant Criteria for a Rad Reno

As a general rule, a good species candidate for radical renovation has several of the following qualities: It is a broadleaf evergreen; it breaks bud readily; it is tough enough to take rad reno (that is, it won't die back from heading cuts); it has closely spaced, small leaves; the new growth will match the old; and it will be no great loss if the shrub does

die (which occasionally happens). Some other plants are not particularly good candidates for radical renovation. Juniper won't green back up. On rhododendrons, the new growth is squiggly. With witch hazel, you can see the ugly heading cuts in the winter, and then the plant explodes into water sprouts, which are not pretty. In addition, the new growth does not match the old, and the plant will take a long time to redevelop its characteristic beautiful branch pattern.

In summary, the three questions to ask when considering whether or not a certain plant is a good candidate for radical renovation are (1) Can the plant take it? (2) Will it look good again fairly soon? and (3) How bad will it be if this plant dies?

No Pruning

Given the proper location and cultural conditions, plants don't need to be pruned to look their best. A little deadwooding can't hurt. But in general, if it's not broken (literally and figuratively), don't fix it.

ESCALLONIA *(Escallonia spp.)*

Escallonia grows to a mature size of about 6 feet In time it will get even bigger, reaching an ultimate size of about 12 feet. It likes sun, so it makes a nice evergreen border for a sunny site. It can also be used in a grouping with other sun-loving, drought-tolerant plants like the lower-growing rockrose (*Cistus*), and a few other interesting perennials like maybe some sedums, some coneflowers, and something spiky.

The smaller leaves of escallonia provide some textural relief from all our really *broad*

Figure 10.20 Escallonia branch

eventually grow to its mature size. Trying to keep escallonia smaller won't hurt it or look bad; it will just exhaust the pruner, and over the course of years it will fail at meaningful size restriction. Trust me, I know. Another way of saying this is, trying to keep an escallonia to 3 or 4 feet tall (at about hip height) and as wide is plain crazy. Trying to keep an escallonia to 5 or 6 feet will work for quite a while, given annual pruning (more frequent as the years progress). But for the least work and the best results, site it where you can let it grow 8 to 10 feet high and as wide, which is its real, actual, and true size.

To generally tidy and shorten your escallonia, use the PlantAmnesty–approved grab-and-snip method. Let your eyes go slightly out of focus and scan the perimeter, locating the worst, stick-up offender. Grab it with your left hand (assuming you're right-handed), follow it down to a place hidden inside the plant, ideally (but not always) to a side branch, and cut it off there. This is a selective heading cut. Toss the cut stem out onto the lawn or walkway. Locate the next-*worst* (not the next-*closest*) too-long branch. Position yourself next to it. Cut, using the same technique. After ten minutes of grab-and-snip pruning, you will have removed the longest branches from all over the plant, leaving the perimeter of the shrub made up of the remaining, already shorter—unheaded—branches. These will still have all their flower buds on them, and therefore the shrub will bloom no matter what time of year you prune it. *Voilà!*

For people who really want a small, bun-shaped escallonia, the news is good. Those

broadleaf evergreens like camellias and rhodies. And it has a nice flower show a little later in the year. In June, when most everything else is done, escallonias hit the scene. They remind me of a fireworks show—their stems are streams of tiny pink (or white or red) flowers that shoot up and then flow down gracefully (see Figure 10.20). That's nice.

However, it is those small leaves, spaced closely together, that fool people into thinking that the shrub is going to be much smaller than it is. Good selective pruning can reduce the height of the shrub to about one-quarter less than it would be otherwise. But even with dutiful annual pruning, the plant will crazy industrious hybridizers have created a dwarf one. It's called *Escallonia* 'Compakta', and it stays a very manageable 3 feet high and wide. Ask for it or a similarly sized plant at your local nursery.

Old Escallonias

If necessary, I suppose one could limb up an old escallonia and even thin it out a bit to make it seem less massive. I've never had the need to do that. I have taken care of an informal hedge along a pathway that looked better when I pruned up the skirt where it flowed out onto the path. A little bit, just an inch or so, can make the plant seem a little tamer to whoever might be bothered by it. Doesn't mean you have to do this. You might prefer the trailing long-gown effect. In that case, no pruning will be needed. With pruning advice, too often "a possible thing to do" is misinterpreted as "something that must be done."

Mal-pruning Escallonia

The most common form of mal-pruning is, as always, inappropriate shearing (that is, shearing a plant not used as a formal hedge or topiary). Shearing an individual escallonia shrub is a senseless act, destroying the flower show and the texture. It is a poor way to control size, wasting both time and money.

Escallonia Hedges

Using escallonia as a formal (sheared) hedge is more justifiable. It seems to work, for the first several years anyway, and the species meets the criteria for shrubs that are good for formal hedges (evergreen, small leaves, breaks bud easily, takes frequent heading). But, after a while, it doesn't bloom so well. And a twiggy, dense shell develops at the exterior. It collects a rat's nest of old twigs and leaves, and it gets a little denser every year. The inside leaves of the shrub get shaded and die, leaving barren ugly branches inside. Then size reduction becomes very problematic—there's nothing green to cut back to. On the other hand, selective heading allows some light into the interior of the plant, and that ensures true size reduction, as there is always some green branch to cut back to. In contrast, the sheared hedge can go only one way, and that way is bigger—though incrementally so. Thus selectively pruning escallonia as an informal hedge works better in the long run.

Selective pruning *seems* to take more time than shearing a hedge or shrub, but that's an illusion. Add up the minutes over a year and you'll see that *selective pruning is cheaper*. Here's why: Although a session of selective pruning on a particular grouping of shrubs will take the pruner more time (and more thought), it will need to be done only once a year. (Prune slowly: 30 minutes, once a year = 30 minutes per year.) That's because the new growth will match the texture of the remaining shrubs. In contrast, hedge-sheared shrubs must be pruned more frequently to keep them looking good. The new growth from sheared shrubs sticks out all wild and straight, in sharp contrast to the ultra-tidy "shape" of the shrub. Thus it is necessary to shear three to ten times a year to keep things looking good. But each shear-session goes relatively fast, requiring little skill or thought. (Shear quickly: 10 minutes, 5 times a year = 50 minutes per year.) So you see, over the course of a year, selective pruning takes less time. And it's quiet.

Selective pruning won't work for plants sited in places that are too small for them, or in other tight quarters—for example, where there's a concrete walkway on both sides. Then shearing (dare I put it in print?) may be inevitable, and in the case of an escallonia hedge, not too horrid a thing to do. If you can, try a "shear-and-shag" (let it grow out a little in between heavier shearings, done just after bloom time). Then you may preserve some flower show.

Rehabilitative Pruning

If you own or care for a sheared escallonia and want to return it to its natural form, you can slowly rehabilitate it over the course of a few years (Option One). Do so by selectively cutting out portions of it, usually the densest parts, using selective heading or thinning cuts. Be brave. It doesn't really matter which parts you prune out. Even if you think you've made a mistake, leaving a hole or something, don't fret; you won't have done any real harm. With any plant conversion, things often look worse during the "in-between" phase. As they say, it will get worse before it gets better. Or it may not. In any case, three years (or fewer) later will return the shrub to its normal shape and texture.

Or, Option Two: You can radically renovate a sheared escallonia as described in the section on repairing damage, above. Be sure to cut it a lot lower than you want the final plant to wind up. It needs several feet of room to grow out, look right, and bloom.

Option Three is: Do nothing. It works surprisingly well. If you leave any mal-pruned plant alone long enough, it will grow out of whatever was done to it and resume its natural shape and size on its own.

MEXICAN ORANGE
(Choisya ternata)

Choisya is another evergreen, sun-loving shrub. I list it as a mounding-habit plant even though it has larger leaves than most of the shrubs I put in the mounding-habit category. Its soft (more herbaceous), nondividing branches make it most appropriately pruned with the grab-and-snip method described earlier for escallonia and other mounding-habit plants. One can even gently head back almost all the tips as long as it continues to look good. And it will be none the worse.

Choisya is not a "choice" shrub (see Figure 10.21). It is not really suitable as a specimen plant. I've never seen a choisya thinned out or skirted up. I don't think these methods work for them; their internal branch structure is too flimsy. Nor is it a good formal hedge plant. It's used more for billowing, mass plantings of something a little different. Choisya's best qualities are hidden from view. The inconspicuous flowers put out a sweet scent in April, hence its common name, Mexican orange. Second, the foliage gives off its own, somewhat pungent smell when it is brushed or pruned. Some people don't like it. I do. For me it's just another sensory gift from the garden.

Figure 10.21 Choisya

A certain husband of my acquaintance, who will remain nameless, takes care of a property where the choisya is situated too close to the walkway. Unable to keep it restrained with selective pruning, he shears it. Not PlantAmnesty PC. But, I must admit, it doesn't look half bad, except just after it is sheared. So, one (but certainly not this one) could contend that under true (and not imagined) size constraints, the shear-and-shag technique might be appropriate. I wouldn't do it. I'd see if the choisya just sort of crept out to the path by layering itself on the ground. If so, I'd rip out the roots and plants closest to the walkway. Then I'd rad-reno the flopping mess behind. And, if it grew back and looked good at a decent distance from the path, I'd let it live. If not, out it would go. (*Necare selecte*, or "kill selectively.") Then I'd

be off to the nursery to get what should have been planted there in the first place.

Summary

• After a hard freeze, many shrubs may still be alive, even though their leaves are brown or black and fall off. Wait till June to see if a seemingly dead plant recovers.

• Escallonia and choisya are both mounding-habit shrubs that can be reduced in size (by about one-quarter of what they would be otherwise), or tidied up by using the grab-and-snip method.

• Neither of these plants can be kept significantly smaller than their mature size, 8 to 10 feet for most escallonias and about 5 feet for choisya.

• Both plants respond well to radical renovation and other hard pruning to restore them after they've suffered freeze-damage or malpruning.

• The "shear and shag" technique can be applied in special circumstances.

FLOWERING QUINCE (*Chaenomeles*)

Good Quince

There are two plants called quince. One is *Chaenomeles*. The other is *Cydonia*, the fruiting quince, a tree or tree-like shrub that bears those big lumpy rock-hard pearlike fruits that, I'm told, make great jam once you've managed to cut them up. As a pruner, I am familiar only with the most common one, the flowering quince, which is *Chaenomeles*. I like to show off by saying its botanical name, which is pronounced "ky-NAHM-uh-lees." The quince's main claim to fame is its early spring flowers, which have a translucent quality rarely seen in the garden. You can choose a plant whose flowers are pink, coral, red, or white. I prefer the darker colors because on a sunny spring day they veritably glow. The coral flowers, in particular, seem backlit like an alabaster lamp. During their moment on stage, they are hard to beat.

Another good thing about the quince is that its branches have a naturally angular branch structure that seems spring-loaded (see Figure 10.22). When cut branches are put in a vase they arrange themselves in a very artistic way, making you look very talented.

Figure 10.22 Quince has a naturally angular branch pattern.

Those of you who appreciate unusual identifying characteristics (as I do) will enjoy looking closely at the leaves and their arrangement. There are the regular-shaped leaves that make up most of the foliage. But upon closer inspection, you will also see smaller disc-shaped leaves wrapped around the stems. They're kinda cool. And occasionally you can spot the little odd, lumpy quince "fruit." A less-pleasant identifying characteristic is the barb found on each branch tip.

Bad Quince

The same branch structure that makes for good flower arrangements makes for seriously aggravated gardeners who endeavor to do any major pruning. The pruned branches fight back, slapping you in the face and refusing to be pulled out of the bush. Be sure to wear wraparound safety glasses when pruning. Cut quince branches defy stacking and prick you as you try to maneuver them into the truck. Patient deconstruction of the branches using a loppers is the answer.

And the bush itself is fairly inelegant. It just looks like a giant thicket, and I guess it is. Aside for the brief show-stopping moment in the spring, many gardeners find it hard to justify the space it takes up in the garden.

Spreading Quince

The mature size of the quince (which is the average size of the plant in 10 years) is 6 feet by 6 feet for most. This is the minimum space the shrub needs to do its job and look good. Trying to keep it significantly smaller with pruning is unlikely to succeed. It simply exhausts the gardener and potentially ruins the flower show and branch pattern of the shrub.

After the quince bush reaches its mature size, it doesn't stop. It just slows down. It will continue to grow in height to its ultimate size, which is probably 10 or 12 feet, but it will especially grow much broader—very thicket-like indeed. It can become a problem as the root system moves outward, sending up new colonizing suckers in an ever-increasing circle. Some people dutifully rip up the straying suckers every year. But most watch helplessly as their nice shrub becomes a dauntingly huge clump. I am often asked in classes what to do about the spreading-root-system problem. I have no good answer. Some people have suggested corralling the shrub by surrounding it with "bamboo-barrier." I'd be interested to know if that works. If you decide to wage a battle against the spreading root system, using a mattock to grub out the perimeter roots, I doubt that you will hurt the remaining plant. Most gardeners decline this option, though, because of the thorny nature of the bush.

The problem of the "too-big" quince is not really a problem if you have a lot of room. Size is then more a matter of psychological adjustment of the owner, or perhaps a design challenge. I vividly recall a fundraising tour that Ann Lovejoy gave for PlantAmnesty. She had moved into a farmhouse on Bainbridge Island and had transformed a typically ordinary landscape into the typically wonderful garden for which she is famous. I was particularly impressed by the center-island bed. It had originally contained only one shrub—one single, enormous quince.

Instead of eliminating the overbearing beast, Ann had surrounded it with a bed five times the size of the shrub and filled the bed with an array of lower-story beauties—herbaceous perennials, ground covers, and self-seeding annuals. Genius! The quince became the foundation, the solid backdrop, if you will, for the rest of the show. Most of the year it did its job unnoticed, except for that moment in the spring when it became the main attraction.

Maintenance Pruning

If your quince has enough room, and it looks good, don't bother pruning it. The best pruning is no pruning—one more benefit that comes from correct placement. It will bloom, it will look good, and you'll get all the credit.

However, if your shrub is encroaching on a sidewalk or other structure, pruning can help. You usually prune a quince like a mounding-habit shrub, using selective heading cuts to remove the worst, most interfering branches. In this, the selective pruning process, the cuts are always hidden inside the shrub. And please note that when the shrub is located next to a walkway or house, you prune so that it rounds-down, mimicking its natural shape. Don't just cut it evenly back to the walkway, making it into a vertical wall of foliage. Also, if it's necessary, you can remove whole trunks or canes to ground level, as you would in pruning a forsythia or some other cane-grower. And too, the shrub can be moderately thinned out, like a tree-like shrub, to improve the view of the internal branches. However, most people also forgo this effort because of the struggle with thorny branches that is likely to ensue.

The Pruning Budget

As we discussed in Chapter 2, each plant has a pruning budget. The budget can be large or small, and it is made up of a combination of three factors: the kind of cuts (heading, selective heading, or thinning); the size of the cuts (big or small); and the amount of foliage removed (a lot or a little). For quince I would say that the budget is a little smaller than average. I recommend mostly small selective heading cuts (under ¼ inch in diameter), a few larger selective heading cuts (up to ½ inch), maybe a few cane removals (2 to 3 inches in diameter), and only about a maximum of one-quarter of the foliage removed. Pruning out deadwood is always in order and does not count against the pruning budget. If you exceed the budget you will stimulate water-sprout production, and that's very bad. New shoots zoom up from the site of your overzealous cuts. These shoots (suckers or water sprouts) are unattractive, impossible to get rid of by repruning (it just causes more to come back), and thornfully painful. So go easy, especially at first.

Despite the resprouting problem, quince can be successfully used as an espalier, pruned somewhat like an espaliered apple tree. Annett Normann, a Mercer Island gardener, sent me a fine photo of her 45-year-old espaliered quinces. She has tended them for 36 years, pruning them about three times a year, and states that the effort is well worth it. I wouldn't have thought it could be done.

Disease and Timing

Although I personally don't think a lot of disease is spread by pruning, I will say that the only plant I notice showing a disease response to pruning is quince. When I prune, I start seeing more and more dieback of limbs. The bark peels in places. My friend Tina Cohen, who is a professional diagnostician, tells me that it is not, as I assumed, fire blight. She tells me it's either brown rot or cytospora canker. That makes sense, as it looks just like what afflicts our cherry trees.

She tells me that I am not spreading it on my tools, but knocking around spores at the same time I am opening wounds (pruning cuts) on the plant. Therefore, when I prune a quince I try to do it in dry weather. Brown rot on quince is probably a local problem, due to our nearly perpetual drizzle and relatively warm winters. People in other parts of the country can probably prune at will. In these other climates, selective pruning just before or while the shrub is in bloom is a good idea; then you can use the cut branches in a vase. Remember, if you are selectively pruning in moderation, any time is the right time to prune. Here in the Northwest, because of the disease problem, I avoid pruning if I can. And if I have to prune, I do it in the summer. (For more information on pruning and diseases, see Appendix 2, "Three Views on Sterilizing Your Tools," on page 291.)

Radical Renovation

Radical renovation is the name for the process of cutting an entire shrub to a low framework or to the ground. It is certainly not selective pruning, and it is pretty hard on

"And for Madame —
Chaenomeles Nest Soup!"

Figure 10.23 When gardeners dine out

the health of the shrub. But it is sometimes a useful, onetime procedure for a large variety of shrubs that can withstand it. Quince is one of these shrubs. The radical renovation technique is usually used to fix a shrub that has suffered from years of mal-pruning, specifically when it has been repeatedly sheared. Instead of rehabilitating the plant slowly over many years, you can cut the whole thing to the ground with your loppers, saw, and/or chainsaw, and it will regrow and look great in as little as twelve months. One can minimize the possibility of death by keeping the shrub well-watered and healthy, and by doing the rad reno in a kind season weatherwise, meaning not during the drought or the freeze in most parts of the country. And again, because of the disease problem here in Seattle, the dry summer is our preferred season for rad reno as well as for selective pruning of quince.

I recently cut an entire quince to the ground because it had suffered greatly from brown rot and/or cytospora canker. Over the course of years, more and more canes and branches had died off, and the remaining canes flopped out and looked horrid. Cutting them back to shorten them would likely have resulted in more dieback. And the shrub was stricken everywhere with lesions and deadwood. However, behind it there was another quince that looked great. So I cut the entire stricken shrub to the ground—partially hoping to permanently finish it off. Instead it has come back nicely, is shorter, and looks quite healthy. Dang!

This event reminded me that one of the best looking masses of low (4-foot) quince bushes I have ever seen was in a spot where the homeowners had tried to eliminate them the previous year by cutting them to the ground. Several other folks have confirmed that they do, as a regular maintenance procedure, cut their quinces to the ground. I guess that would make it "coppicing" or "stooling" (done annually or even once every three years) rather than radical renovation (done once every fifteen or thirty years to start the shrub over).

It's an awful lot of work, though. Which is why I prefer one of two other options. Option One: Find an abandoned quince bush somewhere and steal branches from it in the spring. Option Two: Plant a dwarf variety such as 'Jet Trail', 'Minerva', or 'Pink Lady'. I remember seeing that the new Graham Visitor Center at Seattle's Washington Park Arboretum had masses of quince installed in the island between the rows of parking spaces. I thought, "What numbskull did this?" But it turned out to be a dwarf variety, 'Cameo', that stays nicely under 3 feet without pruning. And, unlike the disappointing flowers on other "dwarf" flowering shrubs, these plants had full-sized waxy blooms in the spring. You gotta love those hybridizers.

Summary

Quince is usually pruned like a mounding-habit shrub, using the grab-and-snip method. It can also be pruned somewhat like a cane-grower (cutting entire canes to the ground) or a tree-like shrub (thinning many smaller branches to accentuate its internal beauty). Because quinces are thorny and spread outward like a thicket, they can be unpleasant to prune and difficult to control widthwise. Some people cut the entire shrub to the ground every few years as a maintenance procedure.

CHAPTER ELEVEN

Cane-Growing Shrubs

hrubs with the habit I call cane-growing are made up of branches that arise from the ground (canes). Canes do not divide many times as do tree branches, nor do they taper. These shrubs tend to be taller than they are wide, with a vertical or vase-shaped habit. They are planted for the show of flowers (like forsythia or hybrid roses) or to add a foliage effect (Oregon grape, bamboo). The deciduous stems of some cane-growers are an interesting color, brightening the dull days of winter. Examples are the red twig dogwood (*Cornus stolonifera*) and *Kerria japonica*, which features bright green stems as well as cheery yellow flowers in the spring.

PRUNING CANE-GROWERS

These plants are very tough indeed, having a huge pruning budget, up to 100 percent! This is because they readily renew themselves by sending up new replacement canes from ground level. Often these plants are pruned by cutting out entire canes at the ground level or 1 to 3 inches above (see Figure 11.1).

Figure 11.1 Prune cane-growers by removing selected canes at the ground.

But they can be pruned other ways too. Some can be limbed up so that they look like a little tree. Others can be made less oppressive by thinning out crossing/rubbing and wrong-way branches. Deadwooding is always in order. New pruners are encouraged to practice on cane-growers because if you overprune you will be quickly forgiven as the plant reestablishes a nice form in only one year.

BAMBOO, HEAVENLY BAMBOO, KERRIA, OREGON GRAPE, AND JULIAN'S BARBERRY

(Family Poaceae/Gramineae, *Nandina domestica*, *Mahonia aquifolium*, and *Berberis julianae*)

What all these plants have in common is a very vertical habit, even more so than others in the cane-grower category. This makes them useful to put in places requiring tall, skinny plants (along fences and walkways), and they add valuable contrast in *form* for

Cane-Growing Shrubs

Bamboo	Family Poaceae (Gramineae)
Butterfly bush	Buddleia
Fatsia	Fatsia japonica
Forsythia	Forsythia
Heavenly bamboo	Nandina domestica
Hydrangea	Hydrangea

Julian's barberry	Berberis julianae
Kerria	Kerria japonica
Red twig dogwood	Cornus stolonifera
Rose	Rosa
Oregon grape	Mahonia aquifolium

Also see the list "Not One or the Other: In Between Mounding-Habit, Cane-Growing, and Tree-Like Shrubs" on page 180 of Chapter 12.

your landscape. *Contrast*, not flowers, is the stuff of great gardens. I think we tend to overplant shrubs with the rounded form, like rhododendrons, Japanese laceleaf maples, and evergreen azaleas. Some examples of contrasting forms would be horizontal (witch hazel), spiked (yucca), and vertical (bamboo). Other ways to add contrast are to vary plantings in terms of height, foliage, and color.

Bamboo

I think the bamboos (of which there are more species than you can shake a shoot at) are among the most beautiful plants in the world. Add to that that they are practically indestructible and virtually care free. And each cane grows to its ultimate height in one year. The different species grow to different heights, ranging from 2-foot ground covers to 60-foot so-called "timber bamboo."

Bamboo would be a perfect urban plant, especially the perfect screen or hedge, except for that little problem of invasiveness. Professional gardeners all have their favorite bamboo horror stories. I've heard "It's coming through the fireplace!", "It's coming through the refrigerator!", and "It's coming from the other side of the street, under the road!" The bamboos are divided into "running" and

"clumping" forms, with the clumping ones preferred for obvious reasons. I have heard that sometimes the runners don't run, and the clumpers will occasionally decide to run for some unknown reason. I have seen old stands of bamboo successfully contained in plastic pots set in the ground or with bamboo barrier or concrete borders. In other places I have seen all these methods fail. Bamboo is also extremely hard to cut, dig up, and prevent from regrowing from little bits left behind in the soil.

This isn't to say don't plant it.

Heavenly Bamboo

Nandina domestica is called heavenly bamboo, but it's not a real bamboo. I have seen some nandinas spread moderately, but it has never ruined anybody's garden or life, or their neighbor's garden or life. It is the perfect plant for the most difficult spot in the yard, which is that tight place by the front door bordered by the house, the stairs, and the walkway. And it's not likely to grow up to block the window.

People want a plant for this high-profile spot to be evergreen, tidy, and interesting. Enter *N. domestica* 'Compacta'. It looks like a bamboo. It has lacy leaves that are pinkish when they emerge and pick up purple and bronze tints in the fall. Each cane is topped with a nice white burble flower thing, followed by nifty little red berries. In most years the plant stays green all winter. It takes sun and part shade. And it has a cute story that goes as follows: In Japan the man of the household comes home and tells his troubles to the nandina instead of taking them out on his wife, before he goes inside. Hence the species name, *domestica*, as in domestic harmony. This is the other reason they are often seen planted at the front door of the gardener's home.

Kerria

Kerria japonica, like the tall bamboos, will fan out at the top, looking quite graceful. It is made up of many thin canes and spreads underground, becoming a shrub about 8 feet tall and 6 feet wide. It blooms with many small yellow or orange flowers in early spring, and adds interest to the winter garden with its bright green stems. One of my favorite spring plantings is a "yellow garden," with many different kinds of daffodils, forsythia, kerria, some gold-leafed aucuba, and spurge (*Euphorbia cyparissias*).

Oregon Grape

Mahonia aquifolium is a good foliage plant, adding textural contrast as well as the benefit of its vertical habit. The leaves are reminiscent of holly with their spines. They are rather large leaves, shiny or leathery, that appear all up and down the 1- to 2-inch-diameter stems. The multistemmed shrub is spreading, and grows 5 to 10 feet tall but can be kept to 5 feet with pruning. Oregon grape is good for a tough evergreen screen or an informal hedge, for contrast, and the foliage is nice to clip and use in vase arrangements. It grows in sun or part shade and is a tough plant, although serious drought or total shade will bring on a bad case of powdery mildew.

Julian's Barberry

Julian's barberry (*Berberis julianae*) is even thornier than Oregon grape, so it is often planted as a barrier. But it is also as tough as all the other barberries, which is very tough—taking poor soil, compacted soil, sun, part shade, and various kinds of abuse and neglect. The plants are not unpretty, having the vertical canes for variety in form; they grow to 6 feet unpruned, and have leathery, dark green leaves that turn reddish in the fall.

Pruning Mistakes

The only mistake I see people make on these plants is to crop off the tops evenly. This destroys their natural beauty. Kerria and bamboos that grow more than 6 feet tall look their best as tall, fountain-shaped plants. *Nandina*, Julian's barberry, and Oregon grape are even more vertical and should be evenly foliated all up and down the stem, not left showing bare legs. Shearing or tipping-back will cause this unwanted legginess to occur over time. *Nandina*, however, just tends to get that way, with ugly, dead "pegs" (the bit that once held a leaflet) persisting on the barren, lower stems and the foliage gathered at the top.

Believe it or not, bamboo is used as a hedge in formal Japanese gardens (and in those cases can be sheared), and Oregon grape takes well to being used as a sheared formal screen (though some would argue). However, the indiscriminate shearing of these plants is a form of mal-pruning. Deb Stenoin, an early PlantActivist and creator of the "screaming tree" logo, joined up when she witnessed a gardener shear her favorite stand of bamboo "into a refrigerator." My local bank just sheared its newly planted nandinas into a series of tidy little balls, reminiscent of a broken rack of billiard balls. When sheared, all these plants lose their nice foliar effect and develop an outer shell of green that keeps getting larger with no chance for size reduction.

General Pruning

Generally you thin out cane-growers by pruning some of the canes out, cutting them off at the ground. Assume the classic pruning position, which is on your knees, end up.

Use loppers, a crescent-shaped pruning saw, or a hand pruner. Cut the canes to the ground and them pull them down and out. This is not a delicate operation, though the closer you cut to the ground, the nicer it will look (especially with the bamboo).

How much should you take out? A bamboo expert of my acquaintance says that you can't really overthin bamboo. In fact, she recommends removing up to 50 percent of the canes. To that I would add that I clip off some of the side leaflets (to further accentuate the lines), removing somewhat more of them from the base than from farther up.

Figure 11.2 Assume the pruning position.

With the other plants in this category, I follow the same technique, although to a somewhat lesser degree. It always pays to stand back periodically and ask yourself if things are still looking better, or whether it's time to quit while you're ahead.

And remember—plants don't necessarily need to be pruned. If your plant looks good and isn't bothering anybody or anything, just leave it alone and take the credit for being a great gardener.

Counter Creeping Plants

Bamboo, kerria, and Oregon grape can all start creeping out if they aren't corralled periodically (see Figure 11.3). New homeowners sometimes find kerria canes everywhere, entwining in numerous other plants. Don't be timid. If the plant is not where you want it, just dig it up and throw it away! Use a spade and loppers (with a mattock if

Figure 11.3 Bamboo can creep along at an alarming rate!

necessary), and dig up all of it or just parts, if it's simply gotten too wide. If you are an experienced, clever gardener, you pot it up and donate it to a friend or to the plant sale. Don't worry, you will not damage the remaining plant. Some people are tempted to use the herbicide Roundup on the spreading roots, but it is not recommended since it is a translocated poison and can potentially kill off the parent plant. It has been used with success on the emerging shoots of unwanted bamboo to prevent its spread. Because of the aggressive nature of the beast, the owners of bamboo are often willing to take the risk.

Stop the Flopping

Bamboo is a very useful plant for tight quarters or narrow places, but it is known to flop into the path of foot traffic after a rain, after thinning, or all on its own. It can be easily tied into place or back to the wall with clear fishing line. You don't need to worry about girdling it. Unlike a tree trunk or other shrub stem, which gets fatter every year, a bamboo cane never increases in girth. (It's really a grass, you know.) It comes out of the ground the same size as it will always be, and reaches its ultimate height in one year.

Nandina gets floppy when it gets leggy and top-heavy. Cut out the canes that fall over, reach up too tall, or brush against the house. Saw them off at ground level. Pretty simple stuff. Use the same technique for the others.

Cover Up Their Knees

Nandina and previously sheared Oregon grape can become leggy. This is easily remedied with the "shotgun" method of pruning (see Figure 11.4). Cut some canes to the ground, but head others back to force new growth inside. Follow the cane down with your eyes, looking inside the plant, to locate a likely node to cut back to. (A node is a place where a leaf was or is, and where a dormant bud remains. It will usually look like a bulge with a line in the stem.) Cut just above the line (see Figure 11.5). New growth will commence exactly at that place and grow up from there (see Figure 11.6).

Leave several canes (the best-looking ones, or the shorter ones under the window) unpruned. In this manner you are planning for the future. You cycle out old, mottled, floppy, too tall, or otherwise unwanted canes. You cycle in new canes that grow up from the base, or that flush out with fresh, healthy new growth from the heading cuts you made.

Radical Renovation

What if you or a previous owner made the mistake of shearing these plants into boxes or balls? No problem. These plants respond

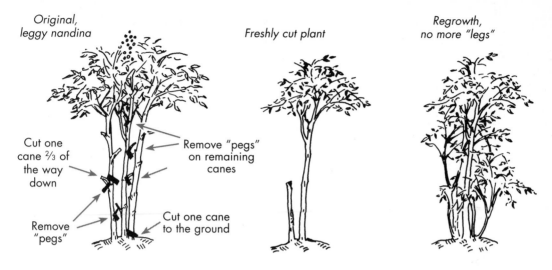

Figure 11.4 The shotgun method

well to radical renovation. That means, you cut the entire plant down to the ground (bamboo, kerria) or at least to a low, uneven framework (barberry, Oregon grape). If the plant was under stress already, and you renovate it during a drought or a freeze, I suppose you could conceivably kill it. But especially here in the Pacific Northwest, where the difference between the summer and the winter is the temperature of the drizzle, casualties are rare.

A few years ago, a television film crew was coming to my house to shoot a little footage. I noticed with some concern how crummy my nandinas looked since the freeze had hit them. I panicked and cut them to the ground lest the crew think me a less-than-perfect gardener. By the end of the growing season, the plants were 3 feet tall again and looking great! My advice to new gardeners with regard to radical renovation is: It is only for healthy plants; do it in the early spring; water well for a year; do not use fertilizer during the recovery period.

Summary
The plants in this group are easy to prune and can take a lot of pruning. Cut unwanted canes (too tall, too floppy, or too many) to the ground and remove them. Also thin some side branches or leaflets. Julian's barberry and Oregon grape can be kept short, hiding many cuts deep inside the plant and heading the rest to the desired height. Kerria and bamboo should be left unheaded (not shortened) or they won't look right. All can be pruned hard, renovated by cutting to the ground or a low framework. If these plants spread, dig up unwanted canes and throw them away.

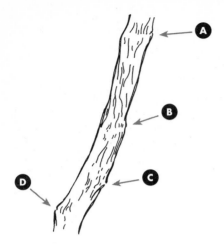

Figure
11.5 Make cuts at points **A**, **B**, **C**, or **D**—just above nodes.

FORSYTHIA *(Forsythia)*

I guess we all cut our pruner's teeth on forsythias. Like many plants in the cane-grower category, these shrubs are planted mostly for their flowers. Their yellow blooms come out in March, before their leaves emerge. After the long, drab, gray winter, the sight of these bright yellow explosions lifts our spirits. In addition, they have a reasonably nice fall coloring, which many people tend to forget.

The Most Common Mistakes

A thing people never seem to grasp is that all plants, including forsythias, have a height and width that is genetically programmed into them, and pruning really can't keep them under a certain size (for any reasonable time). For most forsythias, that size is 7 to 10 feet tall and about as wide (see Figure 11.7).

When you buy a plant at the nursery, it's just a fraction of its adult size. You imagine the shrub will grow to about 5 feet tall and 4 feet wide, so you put it in a place that such a shrub would fit. Eventually, quite soon in fact, it doesn't. Fit, that is. Then I'm apt to hear, "It's too big, it's out of control, it's gone crazy," when actually it's just grown up.

The initial reaction is to cut back the so-called overgrown shrub (and make it into a tidy globe too). Next year this results in an upsurge of straight, skinny, even-wilder shoots arising from the end of each cut tip (the common result of nonselective heading). If you know something about pruning, you might selectively head-back branches to nice laterals (side branches) or remove a quarter to a third of the canes (cutting them to the ground) each year. You will maintain the natural fan, fountain, or vase shape of a forsythia and stop it from continuing up to 12 to 15 feet tall and 18 feet wide. But you will not, trust me, be able to keep a mature plant under 8 feet tall. It's just too much work. The harder you prune, the faster it grows. In the end, you will do what you should have done in the first place: Transplant it to a location where it has room to live as a grown-up.

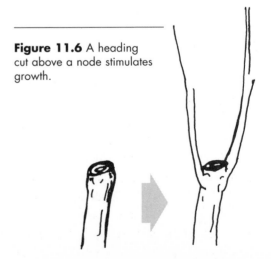

Figure 11.6 A heading cut above a node stimulates growth.

Figure 11.7 Forsythias: They get big.

The Trouble with Forsythias

Forsythias, almost as much so as quinces, have a disturbing branch pattern. It's a mess. This untidy appearance leads to mal-pruning done in an effort to smooth out the perimeter into a globe. The winter aspect is then a jumble of crossing twigs shaped into a ball, followed the next season with a ton of water sprouts, as described above. Not much of an improvement, I'd say, and certainly too much work.

Not all shrubs have a great winter structure like a witch hazel, or a tidy perimeter like a rhody. Forsythias are sort of the Isadora Duncans of the plant world. They want to be wild and free. Judicious thinning will relieve some of the crossing, crowded branches, but not all. A forsythia is just one of those plants it doesn't pay to look at too closely. At its best, a forsythia's form looks like a vase of large, arching feathers.

The other problem is that, like blackberries, forsythias tip-root. When the canes dip over from their own weight and the tips touch the ground, they will sprout roots and begin a new shrub. In this manner a single shrub can eventually colonize a whole hillside, or run through many neighboring shrubs (see Figure 11.8).

When you prune, it is advisable to cut out, or cut back, these canes and rip up the wandering rooted shrublets. You corral the plant back to the original shrub. Don't worry about using shovels, loppers, or a mattock to get them out. You won't hurt what's left.

Traditional Pruning

The traditional method of pruning a forsythia is to cut canes (with loppers or saw) out at the base. The limit is generally set at a third of the total shrub, although you can, in fact, cut an entire multicaned shrub down (as in stooling or radical renovation) and usually it will all be back in twelve months. Alternatively, when you cut out just some of the biggest, tallest canes (as fat as 2 or more inches) you are left with a smaller plant. You are also renewing growth, as new shoots will arise from the ground or the low stubs where you cut. These new shoots are very

Figure 11.8 Forsythias tip-root. **A.** Unconnect the dots (before). **B.** Unconnect the dots (after).

thin, very straight, and very rapidly growing, with few flowers and long spaces between the nodes. Eventually they arch over, put on side branches, and add flowers, becoming the new replacement canes. Sometimes a cut cane just dies, becoming deadwood for some future gardener to remove. As in a volleyball game, you are rotating the players. You remove old canes, which usually stimulates some new growth that will become new canes.

Not only does removing tall canes result in a somewhat smaller plant, it also thins the shrub out, making it seem less cluttered to the observer. (Most pruning, you know, is done to keep the plant owner calm, not to help the plants themselves.) To begin pruning your forsythia, you first stare into your shrub (most easily done in the winter when the leaves are off). Follow several canes from the tip down to the base. Your job is to locate a few of the very worst crossing/rubbing, and wrong-way (meaning they start on the outside and head back though the center and out the other side) canes and cut them off at or near the ground (for example, at 3 inches). Sometimes the selected victim is so wrapped around other canes that you must cut it in several places and take it out in pieces. Pull the canes down slowly, using the weight of your body to tug them out. Or sometimes you can toss them up and out of a very overgrown shrub. Mind your eyes!

"The Position"

Approach the overgrown forsythia on hands and knees, cutting out perimeter canes lying on the ground, and thus forcing the shrub to flow upward like a fountain. Cut out old, dead, stubbed-off canes at the base (see Figure 11.9). You'll know they are dead because they won't have any side branches growing off of them. Mostly they are so old as to be punky and you can just yank them out with your hand. Sometimes I simply step on an old dead stub and lean into it. It just snaps out. (In the tree-care business, the removal of dead limbs is sometimes referred to as "Oregon boot pruning.") Continue pruning by working your way up and out, moving in a roughly spiral fashion. Take out deadwood and some crossing/rubbing branches. Take out a few canes that crowd up the center, sometimes sawing with just the tip of your blade.

Spend a lot of time moving around getting into position for the best cut. Crawl outside

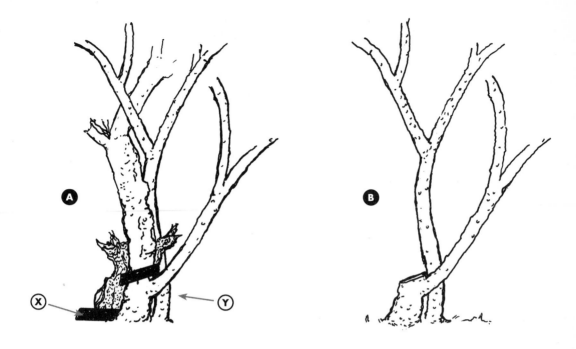

Figure 11.9 A. Before: Remove dead, spongelike wood (x). Cut back heavy growth to a fresh renewal branch near the base (y). **B.** After: Air, light, and space encourage fresh growth.

the shrub and walk around it every so often to judge your progress and plan your next avenue of attack. Why? One, you may see how much things are improving already and be encouraged to continue, or two, you may see that things are getting very thin on one side and decide to move to the other before you overthin the entire shrub. Remember, you never can get it to look perfect from all sides, so *quit while you're ahead.*

In point of fact, almost all branches in a forsythia are rubbing and crossing. This generally discourages the new pruner. Often he or she just gives up, cuts off the top, and goes back inside the house to fix a nice hot cup of cocoa. But remember, the job is not to *eliminate* wrong branches, but to *reduce the number* of them. It doesn't even really matter which ones you choose. You could blindfold yourself, throw six darts into the forsythia, cut out the darted branches, and it would miraculously look a lot better. So don't worry about which cane is the right one, just make yourself cut, and keep moving around. There is nothing that you can do to a mature forsythia (heading or overthinning) that you can't get back. So be brave. As an old client of mine says, "Prune with vigor." Forsythias are really, really tough, and can always renew themselves with new canes.

Cass's Pruning Technique

I have no trouble accepting the size of plants. When customers say they want a plant made *smaller*, I hear that they want it made *better looking*. I remove the branches lying on the ground. I thin out crossing/rubbing branches by cutting to a lateral branch, to a main stem, or to the ground. I look for stubs, stubs, stubs, and crowded branch ends where the poor shrub has been previously headed. I use the thinning cut to "simplify" these crowded, mal-pruned areas (see Figure 11.10).

I don't really spend a lot of time cutting canes to the ground. I'm just as likely to limb a plant up a bit to make it look more perky, and to cut off the worst rambling canes that head into nearby shrubs, touch the house, or look like they might poke someone in the eye. I spend a lot of time creating definition (or empty spaces between plants), so that plants seem to fit together better.

And know that selective pruning is just a series of choices—there are several correct ways to thin a forsythia (see Figure 11.11).

I very much recall working on the yard of a certain great old gal. Among other chores, she asked that I make the forsythia smaller. It was a fright of regrowth from the previous "cutting back" job. I tried to avoid the task, doing other needed work in the garden. But she pointed me back at it. So I screwed up my courage, went in, and mucked about, not trying to make it smaller, just better. Later she said, "Now, see how much better it looks?"

Stooling and Radical Renovation

An entire system of managing forsythias and other deciduous flowering shrubs is found in several pruning guides and in old British garden books. These sources recommend that the entire plant be cut down or to a low framework called a "stool." This is to be done every year after the shrubs are through blooming, which allows these tough plants

Figure 11.10 To simplify crowded branch ends, **A.** remove two outer stems, or **B.** remove the center stem. Either choice is correct.

A

Stub

B

C

D

E

Figure 11.11 There are several correct ways to prune (about one-quarter of) a forsythia.

A. Unpruned forsythia.

B. Correct forsythia pruning choice number 1.

C. Correct forsythia pruning choice number 2.

D. Correct forsythia pruning choice number 3.

E. Correct forsythia pruning choice number 4: Cut cane to the ground!

time to regrow, set buds, and bloom for the next year. I figure it worked well in olden days because labor was cheap, and it was too difficult to explain real selective pruning. I don't think it's such a good idea in very hot climates, or when done before the plant is thoroughly established (three years?). Besides, it looks mean.

I sometimes cut a shrub to the ground, or to a low, uneven framework, as a radical renovation procedure. It is a short cut (ha, ha) to rehabilitative pruning for a previously mal-pruned plant, but is *not* done as a yearly maintenance chore. The other common way to renovate a mal-pruned forsythia or other cane-grower is to cut one-quarter of the canes to the ground for four years in a row, at which point new growth will have completely replaced the old.

I recall a lady who had had all of her deciduous flowering shrubs "boxed" for years. They got too big again and she couldn't figure out what to do. They were far too dense for the one-third method. Instead, I renovated every other shrub to a low (less than 2 feet), uneven framework of headed-off canes. This was done to encourage regrowth at uneven heights, which is more natural looking. The next spring the forsythia was up and blooming and almost as tall as it was before. However, the canes were very stiff and straight and less than ¼ inch in diameter. Over the following years, the canes fattened up, arched over, and put on side branches and more blooms, thus regaining the characteristic vase or fountain shape. Then I cut down the other half of the shrubs and repeated the procedure. I could have cut them all down at once, but this is usually too great a leap of faith for the average homeowner.

Timing

When people ask *how* to prune a forsythia, they are usually treated to a lecture on *when* to prune it. The pruner is admonished to prune only when the plant is through blooming. This really is only necessary if the stooling method is used, and it's just common sense. If you cut the entire shrub to the ground just before bloom time, it doesn't bloom because it's not there. But if you wait until it's through blooming, it has all spring and summer to regrow, set up buds, and bloom the next spring. When I renovate a shrub, I often do so *before* bloom time. So the homeowner misses their flowers for a year, big deal. Heck, they're already in shock because I cut the whole thing to the ground! I prune early because it gives me a larger window of opportunity and it gives the shrub a few more weeks of warm (warm to a shrub) growing weather in which to recuperate from surgery.

But for general thinning and pruning done as regular maintenance, any time is good in my opinion. Winter is a nice time to prune because all the leaves are off and you can see what's going on in there. Spring or summer is a nice time to prune because it's nicer weather for the gardener. Thinning out just before bloom time allows you to force some branches indoors in a vase of water. The great thing about selective pruning is that it doesn't really matter when you do it, there will still be plenty of flowers left on the remaining canes.

Pronunciation

I had an interesting conversation with a British arborist over a mug of Guinness. He said he was tired of getting the "you poor, ignorant laborer" look every time he pronounced forsythia "fors-EYE-thia." He insisted that this was the correct pronunciation as the plant was named after a man called Forsythe from his country, as in "the Forsythe Saga." He's probably right, but I doubt that gardeners around here will take up that pronunciation anytime soon. After all, it took us so long to master Latin as we know it. Consider the fact that the correct pronunciation for *Pinus* (the genus of pine trees) is "PEE-noos." Our reputations would be shot.

Anyway, good luck with your forsythia and remember, "Prune with vigor!"

Summary

Forsythias are extremely tough. They can withstand any amount or kind of pruning. But don't shear them or just whack them back. It won't work.

Stare at your shrub.

Prune out the deadwood.

If you want to reduce size, cut out some big old canes, sawing them off at the ground or an inch or two above. Take out some of the tallest ones every year. Let some suckers grow back into replacement canes.

If you just want it to look better, limb it up by cutting off the branches lying on the ground, and remove a few of the worst crossing/rubbing branches. Prune to open the center a bit. Prune out the few of the worst canes that start at the outside of the shrub and then grow back into the center and out the other side (Mr. Wrong Way). Thin and selectively head-back some of the most troubling

---

Figure 11.12 Country Western forsythia: ♪ *That achey, breaky, rooty weepy* ♪... **A.** "I ache and need a break!" **B.** High as an elephant's eye **C.** Find the $52 saw in the prunings "hay stack."

branches up top. Simplify crowded branch ends that have been previously headed.

If need be, an established, multicaned forsythia can be radically renovated in the spring.

HYDRANGEA *(Hydrangea)*

A year or two after I caught the gardening bug, I entered a phase akin to being a teenager. I spoke with the authority of a garden expert and expressed strong opinions on just about everything, including the worthiness of any given plant. Hydrangeas, as well as many of the deciduous flowering shrubs, I quickly dismissed as "little-old-lady plants." Now, some eighteen years later, they are among my favorites. I wonder what all this means?

I like hydrangeas because they bloom at a time other than spring, because they bloom in part shade, because they're tough, because of their old-fashioned colors and old-fashioned lace flowers, and because the blooms change color as they fade. And because of these things I now own all but one of the shrubs described below. Like many plant lovers, my yard is becoming a collection of desirables—what I used to call a "little-old-lady" garden.

Garden and Lace-Cap Hydrangeas

The garden hydrangea (*H. macrophylla*) is the one most people think of when you say "hydrangea." It is also called the mophead or bigleaf hydrangea and is the one with big balls for flowers. I have never been particularly impressed with it, but when I met its lace-cap cousin—all understated and fabulously blue—I fell in love. Although it is the same species (*H. macrophylla*), the lace-cap form is almost like a different plant. It looks more natural to me, so much so that I will use it in a woodland border. Like other hydrangeas, it blooms later in the summer and hangs on to its fading blooms into the fall, which is nice.

Prune the lace-cap like the regular garden hydrangea, which is to say—not much (see Figure 11.13). Many of the best looking hydrangeas aren't pruned at all. So once again, if it's not broken, don't fix it. Generally speaking, garden hydrangeas and lace-caps can be made to look "better" by following the rules of selective pruning: First, take out the deadwood. (Be careful. With hydrangeas, the canes often look hollow and dead when they are not—check the cambium to see if it's tan, not live green, before eliminating.) Take out a few of the worst crossing/rubbing canes, especially those that are too crowded in the center. Cut off canes lying on the ground, growing out too far, or touching the house. This will make the shrub more attractive.

Figure 11.13 Pruning garden and lace-cap hydrangeas

Where to Cut

When pruning, canes can be cut to the ground or to a promising side branch, node, or bud down inside the shrub.

Size Reduction

I have never successfully made a hydrangea shorter using the grab-and-snip method (as used for mounding-habit shrubs), or by cutting out a few of the tallest canes every year (the method used for cane-growers). And believe me, I've tried. The next growing season the shrub zooms up to its previous size, except now all the branches are weak and floppy.

For years, however, I have read and heard that hydrangeas can be managed by annually cutting them down to a low framework. That would be 3 inches to a foot above the ground. Whenever this sort of hard pruning is done, you will also get much larger blooms and larger leaves. The shrub grows back into a 2- or 3-foot (somewhat floppy) globe. Many people have told me that shrubs cut to the ground in April are blooming by the end of summer. Other people say that their shrubs didn't bloom the first year after hard pruning. I am at a loss to explain these conflicting reports. But I do know that in two years, three at the most, the hydrangea shrub pruned in this manner will be the same size as before, except it will be floppy. I therefore don't use this method; besides, it's too frightening looking and too much work. You are welcome to try cutting to 8 inches from the ground if you like, because hydrangeas are tough and you won't hurt them in doing so.

And if you know the answer to the puzzle, be sure to let me know.

Transplanting

The good news is that hydrangeas are easy to transplant and rarely die as a result. If the plant is too large for its current location, transplanting is a much wiser choice than pruning for size control. It is best done in the dormant season, but a hydrangea will survive when moved in other seasons, too. If you move your hydrangea in the summer, the leaves will wilt and look horrible, but if it is watered well, it has a very good chance of recovering. Because hydrangeas are so tough, you can even cut a shrub to a low framework and then move it, if that makes things easier for you. Remember to water it immediately and a lot next year. In fact, you should know that hydrangeas really want a lot of water. Is that the reason for their name?

Deadheading

Should you deadhead hydrangeas? In the late fall, people are tempted to cut off the fading flower heads to make the shrubs look cleaner. Some gardeners claim that removing the faded blooms will prevent snow from collecting on them and causing limb breakage. In parts of the country with colder climates, it is recommended that you leave the flowers on to protect the buds beneath from frost damage. Then in the early spring (when the danger of frost is past, but new growth hasn't started, perhaps February), these cold-climate gardeners will cut off the old flowers. When doing so, look for the four or five pairs of plump buds just beneath the old flower (see Figure 11.14).

If you cut back to the lowest, or second-lowest, set of these plump buds, the shrub will have flowers this year, and they may even be larger flowers. This is not a necessary thing to do, but a tip for those people who desire the most from their shrubbery. I deadhead in early spring just before new growth commences.

Oakleaf Hydrangea

When I encounter a landscape that has had all the mature shrubs tied back, I take it as a sign that the previous gardener didn't know how to prune. And I suppose I'm thankful that they used tying, as opposed to whacking, in trying to restore order. The damage is less severe with tying—except, of course, where the ties have been left on too long and the shrubs have become girdled.

The only plant I am known to tie up is the oakleaf hydrangea (*H. quercifolia*), because it is a particularly floppy shrub. I don't want to cut it to the ground as some books advise. I love this plant. The new leaves on the tips emerge in the spring like two tiny pressed shirts, crisp and white. The fully emerged leaves, which

Figure 11.14 Hydrangea pruning: In early spring, cut back to any of the four topmost pairs of buds.

look like large oak leaves, turn lovely scarlet in the fall. (The oakleaf should be planted in more sun than the other hydrangeas to encourage this fall color.) The late-summer flowers are like an old lace flounce on a blouse. They're a creamy white that fades to pink.

In the winter, the shrub looks like heck, as do all the hydrangeas after the first frost. Then all the leaves hang down—limp, slimy, and brown. But I'm not spending much time in the backyard in the winter, which is why it is a wise idea to locate hydrangeas there. I do try to nip out once a year and retie the oakleaf, so it doesn't get girdled. It is also okay to thin off or head-back a few unwanted branches at any time of the year.

Climbing Hydrangea

The only really well-behaved vine I know is the hydrangea vine (*H. anomala petiolaris*). And I like to say the words out loud too—hydrangea vine. The hydrangea vine has little suction-cup dealies on its "aerial roots," which means it can climb up structures like walls or tree trunks without a trellis. In fact it needs a solid surface, as opposed to a wire or wooden trellis, to climb on. The vine has white, lace-cap–type blooms, and the winter branches are presentable, unlike those of some other deciduous vines I could mention.

What's to know about the hydrangea vine is that it can be a bit slow to get established on the wall or tree trunk, failing to get a good grab for the first few years. And the young leaves and those closest to the ground always seem to look a little moth eaten. I don't know what's getting them, but I ignore it.

If you have to prune an old vine (say it's all piled up on itself growing on top of a wall for twenty years and is getting dangerously over-extended), take heart. It, like all the hydrangeas, can take a lot of pruning, including heading. You will just lose the blooms on the parts you cut off, and only for a year. So it's best to stagger your work over a few years.

Peegee Hydrangea

In the late summer both my husband and I are apt to call out "peegee alert" when driving together in the same car. The peegees (*H. paniculata* 'Grandiflora'), grown as either a small tree (25 feet) or an enormous shrub (15 by 15 feet), burst on the scene with their giant white to pink, cone-shaped flowers covering the entire bush. I have never taken care of a peegee myself, but the books say that it can be pruned hard (to a few inches from the ground) every year. If done in the late winter or early spring, it will bloom that summer/fall. Personally, I wouldn't bother doing that as a regular maintenance chore. But I might consider it if my blooms became too small over the course of many years.

Summary

Hydrangeas don't need to be pruned to bloom and look good. But hydrangeas resprout easily from the base and from heading cuts and therefore *take* a lot of pruning, including cutting them to the ground or a foot above. Unfortunately, *moderate* size reduction on garden hydrangeas and lace-caps is doomed to failure (they grow right back, except floppy). All hydrangeas are extremely easy to transplant. Some thinning, deadwooding, and removal of unwanted canes can help many plants look better. Deadheading (taking off dead flower heads) is not necessary, but it makes the shrub look a lot nicer in the dormant season and in the spring.

HYBRID TEA ROSES (*Rosa*)

"They've butchered our roses!" exclaimed the woman on the phone. She was calling to report this crime to PlantAmnesty. "There was nothing wrong with them. The grounds crew just came through and hacked them down to a foot off the ground. My God, there's not a leaf left on them!" At the time I was the official answer person for the Plant-Amnesty hotline and referral service. I did my best to calm her, saying, "Correct rose pruning can look very severe." And I followed up with some illustrated literature.

It's true. To the novice, the annual pruning of hybrid tea–type roses (the kind most people have) can look quite frightening. Half of the canes are removed at the base and then those that are left get reduced in height to 2 feet or so. One rosarian I know teaches his students a chant: "You can't kill a rose by pruning it, you can't kill a rose by pruning it." Novice pruners repeat it to give themselves courage.

The Most Common Mistakes

Underpruning

This is not to say that a rose can't be mal-pruned. But the most common mistake, I believe, is not pruning "teas" sufficiently. Often a homeowner moves into a house with a yard wherein lives a towering 8-foot rose bush. Its canes are as thick around as your aunt's ankles. The new owner, not knowing what else to do, props a trellis under it and maintains it at that height. Which brings me to the reason we prune hybrid teas so heavily. I have concluded that it is to keep them down where we can pick and enjoy the flowers. If left unpruned, who knows at what great height a tea could top out? To restore an overgrown tea, cut half of those giant canes to the bottom, in hopes of stimulating new cane growth from buds on the graft union (looks like a bulge at ground level just above the roots). Lightly tip-back the remainder.

The heavy, annual thinning and pruning commonly done to teas results in fewer but larger roses, too. Let's face it, cut flowers for the vase is the reason to have teas. They have little to offer in the way of form for the landscape. And in the winter they are just a jumble of straight sticks. Therefore I think they look best segregated into their own bed with an edging of lavender or something else to give it a feeling of tidy formality. Some expert gardeners I know have incorporated tea roses into mixed borders with excellent results. I have not had such luck. Whenever I try to plant them closely with perennials, they succumb to black spot and die a horrible and prolonged death. Often I find solitary rose bushes scattered about in the gardens I visit. They look as out of place as a pink chiffon prom dress at the pizza parlor.

Overpruning
On the other hand, people who have been pruning roses for a few years are often tempted to prune too hard. A famous treatise on the topic surmises that people do this just because they can get away with it. Until, of course they finally starve the poor plant to death. Or so claims the author, a rosarian from Portland, Oregon (the "Rose City"). By "too hard" I mean that canes are cut down to three or four buds from the ground. That's about 2 to 3 inches tall. Yikes! Such pruning, I am told, produces long stems and enormous flowers. Thus it is justified for growing show roses (in conjunction with *disbudding*, which is the removal of young buds to force more growth into the remaining flowers). For the rest of us mere mortals it is best to prune back the average rose bush to 2 or 3 feet tall. I am sorry to report that some variation exists in the preferred height even among hybrid teas.

It's Not a Tea Rose
Sometimes people move into a yard with a neglected landscape. The original tea rose suffered dieback in a drought or freeze. The rootstock survived and now grows out wildly, with long arching canes that defy tea-type pruning. These canes are often put on a fan-shaped trellis as well. Although rootstock roses, which are usually red-flowered, are not unpretty, the homeowner should feel no guilt over tearing out the usurper and replacing it with something better suited to the site.

Other times people fail to realize that what they have are actually climbers or shrub roses. These are pruned differently from teas. Some are labor intensive, others can be practically ignored.

I have a great little book on rose varieties. It has wonderful drawings and descriptions. It includes pruning and other cultural information and the occasional historical tidbit. It's out of print, but you might still be able to find a copy at the library or a used bookstore Its title is *Roses*, by Kenneth A. Beckett, published in 1984 by the Garden Library, Ballantine.

The Unfinished Job

The only other mistake I see is when people don't take the time to finish their pruning job. They leave dead canes, and bits of dead canes and twigs. Some cut to the correct height but not to an out-facing bud, or they leave too many canes in the bush. Not that you need to be overly concerned. A recent field test showed that pruning a rose hedge with power hedge shears produced as good an effect as careful hand pruning. Of course, I couldn't recommend hedge shearing roses (around here they would become black-spot magnets), so don't quote me.

Other Roses

For those who like to incorporate roses into a larger bed design, know that there are many wonderful kinds (wonderfully confusing in number and variety). These include hedge roses, bush roses, shrub roses, climbers, and ramblers. Oh, and let us not forget pillars, species, antiques, and miniatures. And pom-poms. And standard roses (roses trained to look like lollipops in a pot). The topic of the ancestry and breeding of roses can itself fill several volumes. I like the older shrub-type

roses because of their history. And many have better scent, rose hips, and other desirable traits. I am not alone in finding shrub-type roses interesting. They are presently enjoying renewed popularity nationwide. Breeders have created many "new" old roses that combine the best of all worlds, meaning scent, repeat bloom, smaller size, and disease resistance.

February, by the way, is the traditional time to buy roses, *bare root* (sold in a baggie with no dirt on the roots), either in the store or through the catalogs. Roses are harder to find in the summer, though nowadays some nurseries carry them potted up. But then the plants are more expensive.

Old shrub roses are tough, and some can be care free—your basic glorified blackberry bushes, to my way of thinking. But many are very large, and space must be provided. The largest rose in the world is in China and goes on for several acres. Climbers and ramblers and pillars can be low maintenance if run through a tree, as the Brits have taught us to do. I thought my neighbor had a blackberry vine growing out of the top of his 20-foot Port Orford cedar until it turned into a waterfall of red roses in midsummer. Delightful!

But climbers can be high maintenance too, since most are forced to grow on a wall, fence, arbor, or trellis. Still, nothing is quite so evocative as the sight of a rose spilling over a wall or an archway. Certainly it is worth the constant tying and snipping required to keep them from becoming a menace to foot traffic. What other plant blooms after spring, and blooms and blooms and blooms? And smells so sweet? I suspect that it is the wedding of classic beauty with the danger of thorns that makes pruning roses so enjoyable. *Regarde la femme fatale!*

Tools

Be prepared. Wear tight-fitting leather gloves (hard to find, I know). Also wear a long-sleeved shirt, not a sweater. Have a sharp pair of bypass pruners, loppers, and a pruning saw. Gardeners tend to use the new ARS-type of folding saws. They are easily carried in the back pocket, and fit into tight spaces between canes.

Deadwood

Deadwood removal is first. This means mostly sawing out dead canes and stubs (see Figure 11.15).

The stubs, which are many and rather large, can be found close to the graft union.

Figure 11.15 Hybrid tea pruning: Saw out dead stubs and canes.

Take your time and saw each and every dead cane or stub off carefully and completely.

Old Canes

Remove sick canes and big old canes. How can you tell if canes are sick? Usually they are the older, thicker canes, but not always. The bark on "unhealthy" canes is mottled and blackish. The perfect, healthy cane (rarely seen in real life) is about as thick as your thumb and the outer bark is a clear, unblemished green.

Unthrifty Canes

Canes die from the tip down, as a result of freeze or drought. If the cane you are looking at fills an otherwise empty spot, you may want to keep it but shorten it to healthy, or at least healthier, tissue. To find out where that point is, cut a bit off the top and look at the cut end. The pith of an unhealthy cane is black, or partially black and brown. As you continue cutting back the cane, the wood usually becomes a more clear, tan color. Then you finish off by cutting to the nearest side branch or bud facing outward.

Completely remove canes that are *too skinny*, cutting them off where they meet the graft union. One recommendation is to prune out canes that are smaller than a pencil.

Remove Rootstock Suckers

Cut or tear off all suckers. Many roses are sort of spliced (grafted) to the roots of a tougher plant. Suckers are canes that arise from any portion *below* the graft union. These suspicious canes have different-colored bark, have different leaves, and grow in a different form. If the cane originates from the graft union itself, it is probably okay. If the cane originates from the roots, dig down to where it meets the parent root. Twist and pull (yank, actually) it off. If you simply cut a sucker off at ground level, you will get twice as many growing at the same place next year.

Crossers/Rubbers

Remove canes that cross or rub others and some that fill up the center. The perfect rose bush, should such a thing exist, would have five or six clear, green canes, each as thick as a thumb, radiating evenly from the center (see Figure 11.16).

In reality, you do the best with what is available. Sometimes all the canes are weak and spindly. Sometimes the only decent-sized cane that exists goes horribly the wrong way. Sometimes all you have are crusty, mottled, and huge canes. Just do the best you can. Keep in mind, it's no big deal. For all the disease, dieback, and death found in roses, they are tough, tough plants. A rose's strategy for survival is to constantly renew itself by sending up replacement canes every year.

Cut Everything Back

Shorten the canes that remain. How much? One rule of thumb is to cut no shorter than half a cane's original height. I like to prune most teas to about 1 to 2 feet. Some people like them shorter, some like them taller. The thinner the cane, the shorter it is pruned. The fatter the cane, the higher you cut (see Figure 11.17).

Figure 11.16 The perfect rose bush would have five or six clear, green canes as thick as a thumb and radiating evenly from the center.

Where to Cut

Cut to an out-facing bud, generally speaking. In the late winter/early spring these are easier to spot as they begin to plump up. They are about the size of pencil tips (see Figure 11.18). Some books call them eyes, since they look like eyes. Teeny-weeny eyes.

In February, one is apt to find gardeners out in the rose beds on their knees with one hand down, practically standing on their heads, peering at the canes, their faces perilously close to thorns. They are trying to locate the optimum buds. Invariably, the bud at the right height is in the wrong place—that is, it faces into the center. As you prune, the height of some canes will be

Figure 11.17 Hybrid tea pruning **A**. Graft union **B.** Sucker

Why Prune?

All this thinning opens up the rose bush, allowing for increased light and air circulation. This is more important on roses than on many other plants because roses are perpetually plagued by a host of fungal and bacterial diseases. Open pruning helps, but rarely cures. Roses, like cherry trees, are sort of the sick kids of the plant world. The homeowner is well advised to put up with a certain number of cruddy leaves. And the first criterion for buying a new rose is whether or not it shows good disease resistance.

What Next?

If you find evidence of a nasty bug called a cane borer (little holes) you may want to *seal the cuts*. There are commercial products for this, though a dab of clear nail polish or Elmer's glue works well, I am told. Most Rosarians don't bother things. By the end of summer your rose bush will be an astounding 5 feet tall and full again.

Deadheading

Once the rose starts blooming, it is common to deadhead throughout the rest of the summer season. This means that every few

a little too high or too low. It's a balancing act. Sometimes the buds are a bit to one side or another. It's even okay to have a few that fill the inside.

When you cut, the bud just below will be stimulated into growing out. It grows out the same way the bud is facing. You can anticipate how your rose bush will look by imagining the shoots growing out. Later, if two little shoots grow out from the bud, snap out one with your fingers.

Make the cut at a slant, channeling the growth energy the same way the bud is headed. Don't cut too close, or the bud will die. Don't cut too far away, or the cane will die back to the bud and leave an ugly stub. Actually (should I put it in print?) I find that I tend to cut a bit high on roses. Don't ask me why, except that I know other rose pruners who do so as well. One arborist took me to task for "leaving stubs." "But it's a rose!" I pleaded my case. (See Figure 11.19.)

Figure 11.18 Bud on a rose cane and 39-cent felt pen

Figure 11.19 Cut canes back to either **A.** a bud or **B.** a leaflet, which will **C.** result in a new shoot and bloom.

weeks, you prune off the dead (spent) flowers before they turn into seeds (rose hips). This causes the shrub to continue to produce. (Really, you are preventing the bush from having babies. And so she has to keep putting on that fancy red dress to go out and try again. Poor girl!)

The general rule is to cut to a lower set of leaves with a bud in the *axil* (the place where the stem of a leaf joins the cane) facing out. We are always told to cut to a set of five leaves rather than to the other three-leaf kind (see Figures 11.20 and 11.21). The "fiver" produces flowers, not so the other kind. My husband tested this by pruning one rose bed to "fivers" and the other to "three-ers." The five-leaf bed bloomed more, although the other did still produce flowers.

Fall

Around August or September many folks let the rose finish up by ceasing to deadhead. The rose sets up hips. The theory is that, by finishing its life cycle, the rose bush will slow down and toughen up (*harden off*) for winter. This means that the rose will be less likely to freeze.

Winter

Around December or January, if and when the rose bushes go dormant, I often shorten the shrubs some. The excuse I give is to prevent "wind rock," which actually occurs in some parts of the country. But really, I do it because the roses are too tall and untidy, flapping around with dead leaves impaled on their thorns.

Spring

The major pruning is done in the late winter or early spring (gardeners in other parts of the country prune in fall or winter). In Seattle's February, most gardeners are in a state of chronic angst, wondering whether or not they should prune the roses. Especially in a warm winter the roses have already started to bud out and grow. I should market Sleep-Eze for roses.

The general rule is to wait until *George Washington's birthday* to prune. Famous media horticulturist Ciscoe Morris insists on waiting until March. If you prune too soon, the plants are stimulated into growing right then. If we have a late freeze, that tender new growth is apt to (shall I say it?) get nipped in the bud. Worse yet, the plant might freeze to the ground. The temperatures need to get down into the teens and twenties before I worry. And if a plant dies, I see it as a wonderful opportunity to go buy a new disease-resistant variety.

Now you too can start worrying and watching your roses. You can wait to prune

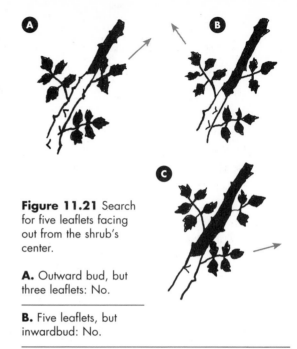

Figure 11.21 Search for five leaflets facing out from the shrub's center.

A. Outward bud, but three leaflets: No.

B. Five leaflets, but inwardbud: No.

C. Outward bud and five leaflets: Yes! Cut here.

till later, but once the new shoots are expanding, it is difficult to prune without knocking them off. And too, you'll feel guilty cutting off all that nice new growth. I doubt that it hurts the roses much. After all, you will recall, you can't kill a rose by pruning it.

Summary

Prune your roses in late February. Cut out some of the too-big old canes, some of the too-little or sick canes, and ones in the center. And deadwood, of course. Then shorten the three to six canes that are left to about a foot or so above the ground. A different rule of thumb is to reduce the rose to one-half its original height. Cut canes to an out-facing

Figure 11.20 A. Three-leaf Peace Rose **B.** Five-leaf Peace Rose bud. It's a little pink thing about the size of a pencil tip.

THREE MORE CANE-GROWERS

Here's a great trio of workhorse shrubs—tough, adaptable, easy to maintain. The first gives you big sprays of blossoms in summer, after most of your garden's bloom has faded. The second will stop you in your tracks with its intoxicating fragrance in late spring, then happily take a background role the rest of the year. The third loves wet soil and struts its stuff in the dead of winter, when not much else is happening in the garden.

BUTTERFLY BUSH *(Buddleia davidii)*

The common butterfly bush has a number of qualities that make it a useful plant to know. It is tough, fast growing, and drought tolerant, and it thrives in poor soils.

It can also be pruned heavily—and in an amazing number of ways.

This was brought home to me last summer when I was hired to make improvements to an existing landscape. The client's back yard consisted of a lawn bordering a down-slope planted with a large variety of perennial flowers. At the bottom of the slope was an unattractive chain link fence, and behind that the neighbors' *Thuja occidentalis* 'Pyramidalis' hedge and their house. But beyond that was a lovely view to the glistening waters of Lake Washington and the snow-capped Cascade Mountains. The water and mountains were visible from my client's house in all seasons, whereas the perennial bed (and the fence below) would be seen only in nicer weather,

when one stood outside at the top of the slope, looking down.

The perennials made a nice collection of flowers in the summer months but, design-wise, something was lacking. After much thought, I concluded that the perennial bed needed both a focal point (such as a sculpture or some other *objet d'art*) and, at the bottom of the hill, a taller backdrop of woody plants. This would hide the fence and add needed height and structure. Because most of the perennial flowers formed mounds and drifts, the shrubs would need to be architecturally strong and contrasting (not more round blobs).

To make matters difficult, there was no irrigation system at the bottom of the slope, and the soil was poor. And the customer didn't like purple foliage or pink or white flowers. She liked blue and yellow. Furthermore, in her seventh decade of life, she naturally wanted something that would grow fast, yet never interfere with the water view.

Enter the butterfly bush—fast-growing (8 to 10 feet), drought-tolerant, with an arching, vase-shaped habit, contrasting gray foliage, and summer-blooming blue (or violet or pink or white) flowers. Best of all, when this row of shrubs dared to grow over the allotted height, stealing from the precious water/mountain view, they could be pruned incredibly hard and be none the worse for it!

I took care to select a named variety, with less potential to spread by seed. People should know that in some parts of the world buddleia has escaped into the wild, naturalizing to the point of becoming a pest. In Western Washington, some people are getting very nervous about it too. There is talk of its potential to wreak ecological havoc. I am not yet convinced that it is a demon. I do see it naturalizing in cracks of sidewalks and freeway walls, but it has never been a pest in any of the gardens I care for. I like to think that it will naturalize peacefully, sort of like foxgloves. Then it would just add to the party. Perhaps it will divide up the territory of the Pacific Northwest, a land so recently scraped clean by glaciers that it lacks diversity, rather than shoving anybody out. But if I'm wrong, by the time I realize it, it could be too late.

In any case, hard pruning (described below under "Stooling"), if done in early winter as soon as the shrub is through blooming, should reduce the incidence of escape. This may perhaps allay the concerns of people who are unwilling to remove their buddleias quite yet (see Figure 11.22).

Stooling

The common butterfly bush can be, and often is, cut down annually to a low framework. By "low," I mean between 4 and 18 inches above the ground. Even older shrubs, never-before-pruned buddleias with stems 1, 2, or even 3 inches in diameter, can be renovated this way. Because *B. davidii* blooms on the current year's wood, pruning is done in early spring after all danger of frost is past but before new growth commences. Around the Seattle area that means late February or early March. Through that spring and summer, the new shoots (which will become canes) rapidly grow to a height that is roughly two-thirds the size of the original

Figure 11.22 Common butterfly bush "stooled" annually will grow back 8 to 10 feet in one year and bloom the same year.

shrub, and, amazingly, the shrub blooms that same year in the late summer.

This sort of hard, annual pruning of shrubs to a low framework is called "stooling." When done to trees, it is called "coppicing." (Current usage is to apply the term coppicing to both trees and shrubs.) But it should be noted that this harsh treatment works only on some plants (others could be ruined or even die as a result) and is done only for very specific reasons. For example, on red twig dogwoods stooling works to constantly renew the shrub, producing the bright red new branches that are, as the name implies, the main feature of the plant. For other plants, the object of stooling is to create ultra-large blossoms or giant leaves on relatively shorter (but much broader) shrubs.

The Results

Unpruned, the butterfly bush makes a tall, arching, fountain-shaped shrub or small tree with numerous fragrant, cone-shaped flower clusters that are attractive to bees and butterflies. In many ways it is reminiscent of a lilac, except that it blooms in summer instead spring. When a bush is stooled, it is likely to regrow with numerous, relatively thinner canes that fan out lower and more broadly than those on the unpruned plant. As a result, the blooms will be lower down, which may be the intent of such pruning. If the butterfly bush has become old and tired, its blooms, though still numerous, may have become smaller too. Then hard pruning, such as stooling, can force it to produce fewer but larger flowers, if desired.

Please be aware that in two years, or perhaps three, a stooled shrub will have reattained its previous size. Therefore, if size reduction is the object, stooling will need to be done annually or every two years. The actual size of the plant, pruned or unpruned, is mainly determined by genetics and the root mass (age) of the shrub. Put another way, you may be able to keep a butterfly bush to 8 feet tall with pruning (instead of 12 or 15 feet), but you will not, trust me, be able to keep it down to 4 or 5 feet—not for long, anyway.

Stooling has some negative effects. In my experience, the new growth is weaker, and more apt to break in winds. The new canes are also straighter and thinner and therefore less attractive than older, thicker, pleasantly arching ones. Or, in other words, one trades a taller shrub for a lower, broader one. And that could be problematic if the low canes crowd into desirable perennials or poke into the pathway.

And then there is all the labor involved in cutting an 8-foot shrub to the ground every year, not to mention disposing of the cut branches. Which leads me to suggest an alternative pruning strategy, one favored by lazy horticulturists everywhere.

Tall and Thin

I have found that, with pruning advice (and a lot of other horticultural advice as well), something that "*can* be done" erroneously turns into something that "*must* be done." In the case of buddleia pruning, the fact that it *can* be stooled does not mean it *should* be stooled. Instead, one can gently thin, dead-wood, and perhaps lightly skirt up a shrub to good effect. It will still bloom like crazy and look just fine. If flowers are wanted for a vase, one simply uses a pole pruner instead of loppers. Altogether, this technique is a lot less work as well, needing to be done only once every five years or, perhaps, even never.

The Compromise

As an apparent compromise, many pruners allow the older, thicker, taller canes to remain, constituting the main portion or framework of the shrub. They then head back these canes higher on the shrub (anywhere from 2 to 5 feet from the ground). (See Figure 11.23.) Numerous shoots arise from those points, then grow out and bloom. The next year they, too, are nonselectively headed back hard, to two or three buds (1 to 3 inches) from the original framework. In a sense, the stooling procedure is now being performed higher on the plant. Hey, it's an option.

Other Buddleias

B. davidii is the most common buddleia found in gardens, but not the only one. Occasionally, we run across *B. globosa* and *B. alternifolia*. Like their kin, both can withstand huge amounts of pruning and

Figure 11.23 *B. davidii* optional pruning using non-selective heading cuts

hard heading if it is wanted. But, unlike *B. davidii*, they cannot be stooled in spring with the expectation of blooms in summer because they bloom on old wood (that is, on the previous year's wood).

Therefore, as a general rule, these two are pruned differently from *B. davidii*. They can, like most shrubs, be left relatively unpruned. Some improvement might be had by deadwooding, doing a little light thinning, or cutting out a few annoying canes at ground level. For those who want to prune more (and my observation is that once pruning has begun, many people do), the longest part of any given cane (with the largest spent blossom) can be cut off. In contrast to pruning *B. davidii*, the longest cane is *selectively headed* back to an out-facing lateral beneath it, or perhaps to an even lower one below that (see Figure 11.24). And the tips of *those*

side branches are left un-headed (see Figure 11.25).

If you don't know which type of butterfly bush you have, just examine its branching pattern. The side branches of *B. davidii* are arranged in pairs that are opposite each other, located all along the stems. As the species name suggests, *B. alternifolia* has alternating side branches, as does *B. globosa*.

No one has ever asserted that a butterfly bush is a "choice" plant, but it is nevertheless gaining in popularity. It's easy to see why. Buddleia is tough as nails, easy to grow, and, as you can tell, incredibly tolerant of pruning.

Summary
• Butterfly bushes can be pruned like cane-growers, removing large canes to the base as needed.
• They can be left relatively unpruned, to form large vase-shaped shrubs or small trees.

Figure 11.24 Selective heading cuts are used for *B. alternifolia*.

Figure 11.25 Nonselective heading cuts are used for *B. davidii*.

• The common butterfly bush is often cut to the ground annually, or every few years, in late winter or early spring. Such a "stooled" shrub will grow back to 6 feet in one season and bloom that same year.

• An alternative method of pruning the common butterfly bush is to leave a permanent 3- to 5-foot framework. Prune back the top branches by annually heading all of them back to a few inches.

MOCK ORANGE

(Philadelphus coronarius)

Mock orange should not be confused with Mexican orange (*Choisya*), which is a completely different shrub. *Philadelphus* is one of the many giant deciduous flowering shrubs, growing easily 10 feet tall and 8 feet wide, sometimes larger. I imagine it growing at Grandma's house, in the back yard along the fence, next to the forsythia, the spiraea, and the quince. I was stunned when I found out that it's a Northwest native, one that you might run across in the woods. I guess that all plants have to be native to somewhere. I just thought philadelphus would be native to Sherwood Forest. It has shaggy bark and grows in a many-trunked form. This means that in winter it looks like all those other DFS's (deciduous flowering shrubs), by which I mean you might mistake it for a weigela, deutzia, kolkwitzia, or forsythia. I don't confuse it with forsythia because that shrub has distinctive bumps and lines (lenticels) on its canes and smaller twigs.

Philadelphus is planted mainly for its very sweet-smelling, white, roselike blooms, which appear in late spring. When I first landscaped my yard I planted it, along with two specimens of ceanothus, near my bedroom window. The idea was that when the window was cracked open at night, the sweet scents would waft in. Instead, what happened was that bees got trapped in my bedroom and I had to keep the window shut all the time. (Nobody in Seattle has screens on their windows.) Just another great garden idea gone awry.

Pruning for Size Control

I got a phone call a while ago from a lady who wanted to know when to prune her philadelphus. I immediately knew that what she really wanted to know was *how* to prune it. Furthermore, she probably wanted to know how to prune it to make it *smaller*. So after I quizzed the truth out of her, I gave her the bad news—you can't really prune philadelphus, or most other plants for that matter, to keep them significantly smaller than they are genetically programmed to be. I know because I've tried. When I was first learning to prune, my mentor at the Parks Department, Andrea, came to talk to me about a row of crowded philadelphus in one of my parks. She looked at them, scrunched up her face, and said that they were planted too close together. She informed me that "these are plants that like to be 8 feet tall." I thought to myself, "When I get through with them, they're going to like to be 5 feet tall." When Andrea left, I selectively headed them back to a size I felt was more reasonable, and I felt quite good about it. What I didn't know then was that, seemingly overnight, they would reattain their natural height. And no matter how often I pruned them, they were on automatic, fast-forward, regrow.

Mock oranges are tough and you won't hurt them with hard pruning, but you won't keep them small either. This information I imparted to my caller. The good news is that the only thing plants are usually too big for is our idea of how big they should get. A change in attitude is all that may be called for. Most people think that the size of any shrub should be about 5 feet tall and 6 feet wide and that they should be sort of globe-shaped. I am convinced that the true size and shape of the vast majority of mature shrubs is 10 to 15 feet and vase-shaped. If your shrub really, really is too big, consider transplanting it, putting it up for adoption, or outright murder.

Pruning to Make Them Look Better

In my system of pruning, plants are categorized as tree-likes, cane-growers, or mounding-habit shrubs. Unfortunately, philadelphus is sort of a cross between a tree-like and a cane-grower. It is a tree-like in that it has a branch structure that divides many times. If you feel the need to prune to make your shrub look better (Andrea was the first to tell me that a shrub should look as good in winter as it does in summer), you do so by thinning.

But don't get me wrong. Plants don't *need* to be pruned. It is just something that we do to solve a problem. Plants sited in the right place will look great and bloom just fine without any help from us. So if you like how your mock orange looks, you can, and should, just leave it alone.

But if you *want* to prune, go ahead. First and always, you take out the deadwood—old dead canes that were previously headed-back and died; dead stubs; and dead twigs that got shaded out when the plant grew. And you can thin out some of the worst crossing/rubbing branches, and the one or two that head the wrong way (that start from the outside of the shrub and head back into the center). If you find an entire cane or trunk that bugs you (maybe it leans horribly, or it blocks the path, or it clogs up the center of the shrub) go ahead and saw it off at or near ground level. In this respect mock orange is like a cane-grower. If you don't take out too many canes/trunks, you won't get sucker regrowth, and your shrub stays tidier and more cleaned-out looking.

If It's a Real Mess

I often run across old, neglected, previously mal-pruned, fallen-over wrecks of shrubs. It can be a real challenge to make these better. Follow the rules. Crawl inside on your hands and knees. Work from the bottom up. Take out deadwood, and all the junk and other plants that are growing inside the shrub.

Wow, that looks a lot better already! I remember one particularly messy philadelphus that was leaning on a fence into my client's yard. Aside from snapping out deadwood with a pole pruner, I found that thinning off a few of the *bottom-most* branches that were lying on the fence helped a lot. I don't know why this works but it almost always does. It's the same deal if the shrub is leaning and lying on the ground: Prune off some of the lowest branches (see Figure 11.26).

Another characteristic problem with a fallen and leaning philadelphus is that its branches tend to double back, making many awkward right angles. Not very attractive. Not very attractive at all. What to do? Visually, all you can do is help it a tiny bit. You do this by finding the branch that travels the farthest from its point of origin, crossing the most other branches, and pruning it off. At this point you will be tempted to continue the process. But don't do too much more. The reason is that the more you take out, the more you reveal the remaining awkward right-angled branches. So, as with much remedial pruning, your goal is to make it a little better, not to completely fix it. This might allow you to ignore the plant most of the time in the winter, and enjoy it while it is in leaf and bloom in the spring and summer. You look closely and critically while you prune. Then stand back, blur your eyes, and ask yourself if the general impression of the shrub is sufficiently better that you can now leave it alone.

The other thing that can make a mock orange look pretty bad is malpruning, which probably happened when you (or someone else) tried heading it back to make it smaller or tidier. Now it has a tangled and unpleasant branch structure. To fix this, do a combination of cane removal, thinning, and simplifying the tangled branch ends. (See Figure 11.8 in the "Forsythia" section, page 114). You may have to work on it for a

Figure 11.26 Pruning for a leaning mock orange: **A.** Cut out the cane that travels the farthest **B.** and the lowest branches.

couple of years to get it back into a good, natural shape.

Radical Renovation

But if the shrub has been sheared into a ball over and over again for the last ten or fifteen years, you may not be able to rehabilitate it as just described. Maybe you can't even beat your way inside with a loppers. Then you may have to radically renovate the entire shrub by cutting it to the ground (with a saw or a chainsaw) or a foot above, thereby starting it over. It will take three or more years to regrow into a real shrub. For a few of those years it will look like a mess of weak, wild suckers. And when it does regrow, know that it will be about the same size as it was before. But by then it will finally look right, it will bloom, and you won't have to prune it at all. Sometime during the regrowth period you may want to go inside and clean things up, but, by and large, it will "sort itself out" if left alone long enough. In this way the mock orange is like a cane-grower. It is possible to cut some, or even all, of the trunks (canes) to a low framework and it will readily renew itself.

There are other reasons you may need to renovate the shrub. I once cut to the ground a mock orange that had grown 20 feet up into a volunteer fir tree, which was by that time shading it out. The homeowner was restoring the yard to a sun yard by removing the fir. The renovated mock orange could then grow back, full and bushy. Had we not removed the tree, the mock orange would have just regrown long and lanky again as it stretched for the light. If you had to fix a chain link fence that had 30 feet of overgrown mock orange growing through it, you could, in good conscience, cut it all down to about a foot high, repair the fence, and let it regrow. But please avoid cutting down an entire shrub simply because pruning it seems too daunting. I have often felt people should need a permit to perform a rad reno: In order to get the permit, you would have to prove that you know how to prune. Like the good doctor, the good pruner employs the least invasive procedures first before doing anything too . . . uh . . . radical.

The Big Picture

And, finally, the problem you are facing may not be a pruning problem at all. If you have a mature yard (say, fifteen to thirty years old) that is one of those "grandma" yards, you probably have a design problem. It's not that the shrub is too big, it's that *all* the shrubs are *the same size* (and that size is *big*). Do a sketch of your yard from an overhead perspective. Use circles for the trees and shrubs. Now use four colors. The first color is for grass. The second is for plants that are between 1 and 5 feet tall (perennial beds, ferns, short shrubs such as azaleas). Use the third color for big shrubs and short trees, in the 10- to 20-foot range. Now use the fourth color for the tallest story: big trees, say 30 to 80 feet tall, like the Doug fir, the bigleaf maple, or the beech. Ideally, no more than half of your yard should be lawn. The rest should go 50 percent low stuff, 20 percent medium (the philadelphus and its friends), and 10 percent big trees. I have found that our mature yards are overwhelmingly made

up of medium plants: a full-grown philadelphus next to the magnolia tree, next to the
big old rhody, next to the big old lilac, and
so on.

As discussed in Chapter 8, Principles of
Landscape Renovation, the cure is to add
more lower-story plants. You might want to
delete some midsize plants too.

Be careful that you don't go overboard.
Sometimes people hire a consultant to "tag"
the plants that need to go. Bringing in a third
party can prevent a serious marital confla-
gration from igniting.

Summary

• Philadelphus is a cross between a cane-
grower and a tree-like. Generally one thins
it out a bit, and takes off a few of the lowest
branches. Deadwooding always helps. Be
sure it has room to grow 8 to 10 feet tall, or
pruning it will never work.
• Mock orange is exceedingly tough and can
be renovated by cutting to a low framework
in the early spring.

RED TWIG DOGWOOD

(Cornus stolonifera)
On a train trip I took last winter, I was
amazed to see the incredible number and
variety of things people stack and toss out
near the railroad tracks. You couldn't make
it up. I tried to list them in my journal as
we clacked along the tracks through town
and countryside. There were pretty, natural
sights to see as well—fern-covered banks,
eagles' nests in tall trees, glittering ponds,
and waterways. But most impressive were
the fields of our native red twig dogwood.

The masses of red-tipped shrubs looked like
an enormous ghost fire spreading from the
riverbeds into the forests.

In people's back yards and in public
gardens, it's standard procedure to cut red
twig dogwood to the ground (or more like
an inch or two above) every year or three.
Sounds scary, looks scary. But once the
plant is established, it works well. The reason people do this is to maintain more of
the bright red twig color, which is the main
reason these shrubs are planted: for winter
interest. (Also, they are tough as nails and
like wet soil.) As they mature, these shrubs
(which will reach 5 to 6 feet tall and as wide)
have branches that get more brownish than
reddish; the only red part will be in the new
growth at the tips. If you cut red twigs to the
ground (called stooling), they grow back to
half their original size in a year (and back
to full size in another), except that the new
canes are skinnier, straighter, and redder all
the way to the ground. One teacher I know
says a coppiced red twig dogwood looks like
a campfire.

Because they are planted to show off
their barren winter branches (best in mass
plantings), one cuts them down in early
spring. Seems cruel, doesn't it? But this
gives them all growing season to get back.
I vividly remember panicking at the sight of
a yellow twig dogwood (*Cornus stolonifera*
'Flaviramea') that I had coppiced in March.
By June it was still only a jumble of twigs
about a foot high (it had started out at 5 or 6
feet high). By November it was a reputable 4
feet tall, and a year later it was miraculously
about its original size.

Now that the new, improved variegated (two-tone leaf) varieties add a lot of visual interest in spring and summer, you may choose to forgo coppicing. A red twig can be pruned in any of the ways described in this book. You could treat it like a cane-grower, cutting out some of the oldest canes to the ground every year and leaving the rest untouched. Or you could grab and snip it like a mounding-habit shrub, to make it a bit shorter and tidier. (Be sure to hide your cuts.) Or you could thin it out, to give it more definition, like a tree-like shrub. These last three ways of pruning can be done any time of the year. Or, if you like how it looks, don't do anything.

Summary

Traditionally, red twig dogwoods are stooled, cutting the entire plant to an inch or two above the ground in the spring.

CHAPTER TWELVE

Tree-Like Shrubs

Tree-like shrubs are the Cadillacs of the shrub world. I call them "tree-like" not because they are huge or because they have a single trunk. They aren't, and they don't. I call them tree-like because they have a complex branch structure that divides many times, like a tree's branch. Examples are rhododendrons, camellias, witch hazels, and pieris. The branches of tree-like shrubs are stiffer (woodier) than those of plants such as, say, choisya (Mexican orange), which has softer (more herbaceous) wood. The complex, woodier branch structure is sort of the high cheekbones of shrubs. It makes these plants seem more elegant and tidier to the viewer than, say, a forsythia or a spiraea. And if the shrubs are deciduous, the fine branch pattern is an attractive feature in the winter. Examples are the barren curlicue branches of Harry Lauder's walking stick (*Corylus avellana* 'Contorta'), hung with catkins like dangling earrings, and witch hazel (*Hamamelis* spp.), with its horizontal and artistically angled branches.

Because the tree-like shrubs are the best looking of the three shrub categories in this book, they are often prominently featured in landscapes. They make good "specimen plants"—the ones chosen to stand alone and be admired. I feel that they are currently being overused in the new, suburban "McMansion" developments springing up everywhere. If all the plants are "special" they detract from each other. Tree-likes can be used in groupings, but great care must be given to spacing requirements. They are best allowed to grow as high and as wide as

they want (size restriction ruins their good looks). An all–tree-like landscape does not age gracefully. Therefore I believe tree-like shrubs should be combined with other shrub types (cane-growers and mounding-habit shrubs) that can be more readily moderated in size and which provide valuable contrast.

PRUNING TREE-LIKE SHRUBS

It is their articulate branch structure that makes these plants more difficult to prune than mounding-habit shrubs or cane-growers. Their pruning budget tends to be

Tree-Like Shrubs

TREE-LIKES THAT TAKE MODERATE THINNING

Deciduous azalea	*Rhododendron*
Enkianthus	*Enkianthus*
Fothergilla	*Fothergilla*
Huckleberry	*Vaccinium*
Lilac	*Syringa* (or can be pruned like a cane-grower; see Chapter 11)
Mountain laurel	*Kalmia latifolia*
Pacific wax myrtle	*Myrica californica*

TREE-LIKES THAT WATER-SPROUT READILY, SO THIN LIGHTLY

Beautyberry	*Callicarpa*
Cotoneaster	*Cotoneaster*
Doublefile viburnum	*Viburnum plicatum tomentosum*
Filbert	*Corylus*
Persian parrotia	*Parrotia persica*
Star magnolia	*Magnolia stellata*
Mountain laurel	*Kalmia latifolia*
Viburnum bodnantense	*Viburnum bodnantense*
Winter hazel	*Corylopsis*
Wintersweet	*Chimonanthus praecox*
Witch hazel	*Hamamelis*

TREE-LIKES THAT TAKE MORE THINNING

Andromeda	*Pieris*
Camellia	*Camellia*
English laurel	*Prunus laurocerasus*
Photinia	*Photinia fraseri*
Pine	*Pinus*
Portuguese laurel	*Prunus lusitanica*
Rhododendron	*Rhododendron*
Strawberry tree	*Arbutus unedo*
Thread cypress	*Chamaecyparis pisifera* 'Filifera'

TREE-LIKES TOUGH ENOUGH FOR SHEARING

English holly	*Ilex aquifolium*
English laurel	*Prunus laurocerasus*
Firethorn	*Pyracantha*
Photinia	*Photinia x fraseri*
Portuguese laurel	*Prunus lusitanica*
Privet (evergreen and deciduous)	*Ligustrum*
Sweet bay	*Laurus nobilis*
Yew	*Taxus*

Also see the list "Not One or the Other: In Between Mounding-Habit, Cane-Growing, and Tree-Like Shrubs" on page 180.

small, and size reduction is discouraged, and one should use mostly thinning cuts. Over-pruning or heading is apt to stimulate water-sprout production or otherwise undermine branch structures and diminish the good looks of these plants. Pruning these plants is often done to create definition or to show off the inner beauty of deciduous shrubs in the winter. Most of the work is simply dead-wooding. The pruner looks for crossing/rubbing branches, duplicating branches, and diseased wood. At the end of the job every space is filled, but with fewer branches. This is the art of thinning (see Figure 12.1).

Generally the pruner works from the bottom up, and the inside out, frequently getting out of the plant to judge the progress. There are no "right" branches to prune, only a series of choices. It is normal to keep a running conversation in your head: "Should I prune this branch or will it leave a big hole?

Figure 12.1 Prune tree-like shrubs for definition. You can moderately shorten some species but, in general, avoid size reduction. **A.** Too far up **B.** Too far down **C.** Parallel branches **D.** Suckers **E.** Wrong way **F.** On ground **G.** Crossing **H.** Moderate size reduction

Have I pruned too much? Should I take out this rubbing branch or the other one?" And be assured that the state of low-grade terror you feel when pruning never really goes away. You will just learn to push through it.

TYPES OF TREE-LIKE SHRUBS

I have further divided the tree-like shrubs according to their prune-ability. The *tree-likes that water-sprout readily* are very touchy and will explode into ugly, straight shoots (water sprouts) if you prune too much or attempt even moderate size restriction. They are therefore pruned only very lightly, using mostly small thinning cuts. The next group, *tree-likes that take thinning*, don't break bud easily and therefore can be thinned more extensively. Size restriction is still not

advised, since these shrubs will lose their nice branch structure or form. Some can be limbed up and made into nice-looking small trees (called *arborizing*). Exceptions to the rules always exist, and this is true for the tree-like category of shrubs. The third category is *tree-likes tough enough for shearing*. Some of the tree-like shrubs can be used for hedges, such as English laurel, English holly, and photinia, and complete information is included in this chapter. These plants can also be pruned selectively or let go *au naturel*.

CAMELLIA *(Camellia)*

When I spoke at the botanical garden in St. Louis, Missouri, one of the curators told me that her favorite task was tending the beautiful camellia collection in the greenhouse. She recounted her experience of patiently deadheading one day as she looked up past the green boughs laden in pink and red blossoms to see a wild, white snowstorm descending outside the glass windows. That image is as vivid in my memory now as if it had happened to me. There are some horticultural experiences that border on the sublime. I didn't have the heart to tell her that in Seattle camellias are generally treated as personas non grata, horticulturally speaking, that is.

I suppose, as always, it's because people plant camellias (usually *C. japonica*) too close to the house and then shear them into goofy big balls. Then, too, camellias have the unpleasant habit of hanging on to their blooms until they turn the color of aged apple cores. Finally, they drop the blossoms intact, all gawdawful orange and brown, onto the ground below. Magnolia blooms—which turn just about as yucky in color—at least have the decency to shatter and fall to the ground in pieces. Winter camellias (*C. sasanqua*) are much more appreciated since they have a looser habit, their blossoms shatter, and they bloom and smell sweet in winter months. People in gloomy climes need a lot of cheering up from November through February. The winter camellia is well placed where you park the car, so that you can see and smell the flowers as you dodge the raindrops on the way inside. They make nice espaliers too. But then I think *C. japonica* makes an even nicer wall plant. Which brings us to a major plus of both these camellias—their incredible pruning malleability.

Camellias are, in my opinion, almost as tough as English laurel. I know of an 8-foot-high, sheared camellia hedge that looks greener, tidier, and healthier than the laurel hedge next to it. And once a year it blooms! However, the average homeowner is well advised to refrain from shearing camellias (or any other plants for that matter) if they are not planted as a formal hedge or topiary.

Size Reduction

Camellias, unlike many other broadleaf evergreens, take kindly to the selective heading cut. The new growth tends to match the old growth, meaning it doesn't emerge as a fright of water sprouts. Nor do the branches tend to die when pruned hard. Always search for a nice big side branch facing out—and cut back to it, rather than to no place in particular (nonselective heading). Then look for the next branch which is too tall. Follow it

inside the shrub to a side branch and cut it off there. The uncut, shorter branches then become the perimeter of the shrub. The key to selective pruning is to hide the cuts inside, like a shag haircut, rather than cutting back each and every branch at the perimeter, nip, nip, nip.

That said, I should warn people that the average adult size of a camellia is about 6 to 8 feet tall and 5 feet wide. And they eventually get twice that size (and sooner than you think). It's best for everybody if your plant has that much room to live. Otherwise you wind up fighting against nature, which is usually too much work, even when it works well. People just have the mistaken notion that shrubs are, or should be, about 5 feet tall and 4 feet wide.

Thinning

If a camellia seems oppressive, the best way to prune it (and other plants in the tree-like category) is to thin it out (see Figure 12.2). This is the art of selective pruning. As a good pruner, start by crawling into the bottom of the shrub. Using loppers, a hand saw, and good hand pruners, work up and out. Foremost is the removal of all the dead leaves, twigs, and stubs. Then look for crossing/rubbing branches, wrong-way branches, and ones that head too far up or too far down. Don't try to eliminate all wrong branches, just take out some of the worst. Every space should be filled, but with fewer branches. Don't strip out the branches, leaving only foliage on the ends. Selective pruning means that you take some, and leave some, fairly evenly throughout.

Figure 12.2 Thinning a camellia **A.** Take out deadwood first (dotted lines). **B.** Take out a few of the worst crossing/rubbing branches. **C.** How it looks at this point. **D.** Remove smaller crossing branches evenly throughout. **E.** Finished camellia branch.

John Hushagen from Seattle Tree Preservation told me, "You know when you're done pruning a camellia when you can stand up inside it." That sounds about right. I like to finish up with a little judicious thinning from the outside, too. When you finally break up the solid wall of green, you get a lattice of foliage revealing the finely pruned internal branch structure of the camellia.

Camellias can take fairly heavy thinning and shortening because they don't tend to grow water sprouts. However, there is still a certain amount of good-sense aesthetics involved. Once I consulted at a house where I noticed, but tried not to comment on, an overthinned camellia. The husband said, "I went to a pruning class, and the guy said to prune a camellia so that a bird could fly through it. When my wife saw what I did she said, 'He meant a sparrow, not a goose!'"

Arborizing

Sometimes an ill-sited camellia that seems "oppressive" to the homeowner can be turned into a nice little tree by removing the lower limbs and thinning out what remains above. Before embarking on this path, take a moment to study the branch structure within. Imagine what it will look like without certain branches. The main trunk should be old and very thick. Otherwise you might get a "lollipop," not a "tree." But you often can't tell how it will really look until you're done. High excitement in the garden! Some people are so impressed with the effect that they proceed to strip up everything else in the yard. Good for some is not good for all.

Rehabilitation

Can a previously sheared camellia be returned to a natural, looser shape? I think so. In fact, I have succeeded in doing so. But it took all the bravery I could muster. The first spring or two I selectively thinned out the clumps of branches. Once light reached the inside, I radically (which is to say nonselectively) headed-back some branches inside the plant to try to force some new, interior green growth. It worked. As the homeowner requested, it is now several feet shorter and more natural looking. On similar plants in the future, I think I'll be more radical sooner, to get rid of the "ball" outline by staggering cuts throughout. I guess that's how you learn the limits of plants, by pushing them.

Radical Renovation

Whereas I worry about every cut, as do most of the pruners I know, the world is full of people who don't give it a second thought. Such is my neighbor who, soon after moving in, cut that too-big "green bush" in front of his window down to a 3-foot clump of stubs. He felt bad when he found out it was a camellia. It looked like heck for a couple of years. Now, about five years later, it's about 4 feet, green, healthy, and blooming again.

Cutting a shrub back to stumps (or in the case of cane-growers, back to the ground) and starting them over is what I call radical renovation. Camellias in particular are excellent candidates for radical renovation; the survival rate is high. But camellias, unlike rhododendrons, are not particularly good transplant candidates. I have successfully transplanted some large ones (6 feet tall), but many others have died. So if a very old camellia is really, really too large for its location, it is wiser to radically renovate it than to try moving it. If you decide to risk it, do your cutting in the spring, keep your plant well watered for the next year, and visit it occasionally with kind words.

Summary

Don't shear your camellia into a ball. If your shrub seems oppressive, thin it out. You can thin it a lot. And you can take off lower limbs, making it look like a little tree. Camellias can withstand heavy heading, although it isn't a nice thing to do and doesn't look very good. Mal-pruned camellias can be renovated by cutting to a very low framework (a foot or two) in the early spring.

COTONEASTER *(Cotoneaster)*

New gardeners are apt to make their first and most embarrassing phonetic faux pas when they mispronounce cotoneasters as "cotoneasters" (see Figure 12.3). "Ka-TONE-ee-assters" is correct.

Figure 12.3 Cotton-Easters

Like most plant species, cotoneasters come in a variety of sizes, from the impressive *C.* x *watereri* 'Cornubia', almost a tree at 20 feet, to the tiny-leafed *C. microphyllus*, bred for people who like cute buns. I'm partial to the ubiquitous but highly underrated *C. horizontalis*, commonly called fish-bone, herringbone, or rock cotoneaster. I think it has great architectural qualities. Planted against a fence or chimney, it espaliers itself in a tower of fans (see Figure 12.4). It reminds me of the ice feathers that form on your windshield in the winter, too.

Figure 12.4 *Cotoneaster horizontalis* espalier
A. Front view **B.** Side view

It's been so long since I took plant ID that I get my midsized cotoneasters mixed up. I think it's the *C. parneyi* (now *C. lacteus*) that I prefer to *C. salicifolius*. Latin names—I lose more of them every year. I'm surprised I can't actually see them falling out of my ears. And curse that secret society of heartless taxonomical dictators who change plant names. Did you know that common garden mums (chrysanthemums) are now really *Dendranthema* (will they be called common garden ma's?). There ought to be a law.

What cotoneasters share in common is their nice display of red or orange berries and their arching branch pattern. They like dry soils and sun, but are generally tolerant of all kinds of abuse and neglect. They get around well on their own, spread by hungry birds who eat the berries in late winter when the finer fare is gone. You are apt to find a lone cotoneaster growing in the cracks of a sidewalk or sprouting out of the middle of a field of junipers.

Although I like cotoneasters, I admit that (on the great unspoken horticultural plant-status scale) they rate rather low. I know this because of what I found myself saying when I went on a consultation with another professional gardener. We went over her client's yard together, where many plants had been mal-pruned, mostly sheared into balls. The client asked what to do about the sheared cotoneaster and the sheared evergreen azalea. I told her that it wasn't worth the effort to rehab the cotoneaster (a lengthy process). "Just dig it out." I moved on to show her how to unshear the azalea (with relatively rapid, good results).

No Pruning

Like all shrubs and trees, cotoneasters do a pretty good job on their own. My favorite *C. horizontalis* isn't pruned at all. I saw one last year, smothered in berries like a giant red bow. Next to it sat Sugar, the snow-white cat. It was as pretty as a Christmas card.

The Most Common Mistake

The most common pruning mistake people make is to shear cotoneasters (and everything else, for that matter). Actually, cotoneasters fit the criteria for plants that are good as formal hedges (small-leafed, evergreen, and tough) and can be used as such, which is to say topiaried or sheared into continuous hedges. But most selective pruners express a more than average disgust when they see cotoneaster balls because such pruning subverts the best feature of these plants—their arching branch pattern. And also because once cotoneasters are sheared, the future results are startlingly horrid. I know of no other plant that grows back from heading cuts with as many straight shoots.

Near my home, I have examples of three pruning techniques. One apartment complex sports a silly "row of soldiers"—all cotoneasters sheared into separated, tight globes. Nearer my house is a condo with a steep rockery that a hard-working, yet wholly ignorant, grounds crew swarms over once a month to shear cotoneasters into rather pleasant-looking smooth masses. It's reminiscent of some formal Japanese gardens I've seen. Between shearings, the shrubs resprout and don't look so tidy. In point of fact, the condo association is paying a lot of money to have these plants look ultra tidy half the time, and twice as unkempt the other half of the time (see Figure 12.5).

Next to the condo is a shorter rockery belonging to the church parking lot. It has unpruned cotoneasters spilling and arching gracefully, like a waterfall, down the rocks. Nobody ever prunes them and they look great *all* the time. Unfortunately, grass and

Figure 12.5 The most common mistake with cotoneasters: using nonselective heading cuts to make the plant smaller. **A.** Original plant **B.** Heading cuts make it look tidier for now, but . . . **C.** they cause ugly regrowth, making it twice as unkempt later.

weeds are starting to invade, and when that happens, can the motorheads be far behind?

Shearing also invites disease problems in plants. Cotoneasters under stress get cotoneaster webworm, ick! Thinning reduces the occurrence of this ugly bug, shearing invites it.

Size Reduction

As with most tree-like shrubs, avoid trying to shorten or otherwise restrict the size of cotoneasters. If a branch actually interferes with people walking down a pathway, rubs on the house, or sticks out too far into a neighboring plant, see if it can be removed with a thinning cut, taking it off where it joins a larger stem, or altogether, by cutting it to the ground. If this is not possible, use a selective heading cut. This is not necessarily the *smallest* cut possible along the branch. Follow the branch back from the tip trying to locate a *largish* side branch to cut back

to (see Figure 12.6). It's a difficult thing to grasp, but this is the essential part of selective pruning that retains the natural grace of the branches and reduces the amount of water-sprout regrowth.

Avoid overall size restraint, though. Even if all the cuts are selective heading, you will get an upsurge of water sprouts, impossible to eliminate and ugly to behold.

If you research the mature size of your plant in a plant encyclopedia, and your plant doesn't have enough room, by all means *take it out.* (I rarely try transplanting cotoneasters. It's just not worth the effort, since they die easily, are easy to replace, and are not considered particularly choice.) Correcting mistakes as soon as they are spotted is good garden policy.

Deadwood

In pruning any plant, 80 percent of all the cuts made should be to remove deadwood—

Figure 12.6 Selective heading is the right way to shorten a branch, but **A.** this smaller cut may not be as good as **B.** a larger cut to a larger lateral branch.

OK

Better

Figure 12.7 Deadwooding **A.** Deadwood makes plants look dirty. **B.** After deadwood removal.

dead twigs, dead limbs, and stubs (see Figure 12.7). Cotoneasters, in particular, clean up well with deadwooding. The dead twigs are often so brittle that they can be simply brushed (crunched) out with a gloved hand. Take care to remove any stubs that might remain after the quick brush-through. What a difference! You will quickly discover that most deadwood occurs on the lower parts and inside of the shrub, where growth has been shaded out. Two other plants that particularly look better after deadwooding are pines and pieris.

Bottom Up and Inside Out

God bless garden writer George Schenk for his description in *The Complete Shade Gardener* of the pruning process. He writes, "Prune from the bottom up and the inside out."

I remember when I started my business many years ago, my partner would disappear inside shrubs, sometimes crawling into the base of them on hands and knees. I felt like asking her to stop fooling around and

get to work. But as the minutes passed, and cut limbs and twigs were shoved outside the plant, the shrubs would start looking cleaner, better, and—well, more beautiful. This is the art of pruning.

Most books say to remove crossing/rubbing branches and to open up the center to improve plant health, which it does. But the real reason it's done is to make your yard look better—that's the point of gardening anyway, unless you are gardening to provide wildlife habitat. In that case some tangles, brambles, and deadwood are a good thing. So before you do any size reduction, thin a bit, doing more at the base of the plant than elsewhere, to see if that will solve the real or perceived problem.

Rehabilitative Pruning

I can't actually recall spending the time and effort to restore a previously headed or sheared cotoneaster. It's too daunting. On the other hand, it makes perfect sense to try radical renovation on a mal-pruned cotoneaster. Cut it to the ground. After three or

Figure 12.8 When pruning a shrub, work from the inside out and the bottom up. **A.** Deadwood first. **B.** Remember, sawing out a large branch also removes the small stuff attached! **C.** Testing, observing. **D.** Hmm, could lighten this up a bit . . . no, maybe wait . . .

four years you may be surprised to find it has regrown into a graceful shrub. Or maybe not. Then return to plan B, removal. If and when it does recover and regrow into a nice, natural, arching shrub, sneak hubby's hedge shears out in a Goodwill donation bag for pickup the next day.

Summary

Stay away from shearing or overall size reduction on cotoneasters, as they will explode into a million wild water sprouts. Deadwooding and removal of some lower or inside branches often makes them look amazingly better. Selectively head or thin back the few branches interfering with walkways or nearby shrubs.

DECIDUOUS AZALEA

(Rhododendron)

Deciduous azaleas, like evergreen azaleas, are a subset of rhododendrons, but they look and prune quite differently. They are larger than evergreen azaleas, seeming less formal—tall, upright, open, and finely branched. Many have spicy, scented flowers in the spring, and nice fall color, too. For this reason I think they go particularly well in Pacific Northwest woodsy areas, and they add seasonal interest to overwhelmingly broadleaf evergreen yards. They are among a very small list of plants that are suitable for "skinny" places, like next to the walkway that goes along the side of the house.

Pruning for Definition

Deciduous azaleas are best pruned for definition, which makes them more beautiful, not smaller. By following the guidelines below, you will be able to clearly "read" the shrub's branch structure in the winter. The branch structure on deciduous azaleas is intrinsically pleasing to the eye, but it will be even more so with good pruning, looking cleaner and crisper. One of those maxims that opened my eyes as a novice gardener was "A shrub should look as beautiful in the winter as it does in the summer." Before I heard that, deciduous plants just disappeared for me when the leaves fell.

Deadwood

Deadwood is hard to spot on deciduous azaleas in the winter. I often set aside some time in the summer to deadwood them (as well as deciduous viburnums and lilacs) because it takes a lot less time to sort out what is alive (see Figure 12.8.)

Size Reduction

Overall size reduction on deciduous azaleas, unlike their evergreen counterparts, is not recommended. It doesn't hurt, but it does compromise the beauty of the branches as seen in the winter. One of the things that makes the branches of tree-like shrubs beautiful is the uninterrupted tapering of the stem and the even division of branches (called ramification) to ever smaller and finer branches. It is the *taper and even division that is the source of a branch's beauty*. When a large heading cut is made, the resulting regrowth is a cluster of skinny, straight shoots heading up from a large, blunt end. This is not the smooth transition of a normally grown branch. Therefore, I avoid heavy heading (selective or nonselective) on deciduous azaleas whenever possible. But the news is good if your deciduous azalea is too big for its location. Like rhodies and evergreen azaleas, they have compact, fibrous root systems, making them among the best candidates for transplanting.

Thinning

As with most plants in the tree-like category, thinning accentuates the nice branch pattern of deciduous azaleas. Using mostly thinning cuts and a few selective heading cuts, prune evenly throughout the plant. Look for branches that actually rub others or wander too far from their point of origin (i.e., that start on the outside and grow the wrong way, through the center and out the other side). Look for laterals that dip down into the layer of branches below. Look for duplicating branches, previously headed branches, or kinked ones. Look for crowded spaces where branches meet the main stem (called crotches or branch attachments). Look for branches hanging on the ground. Prune off some of the worst of all those that are found, though never all.

Azaleas, unlike many of the shrubs in the tree-like category, can take a fair bit of pruning, both thinning and selective heading. I would say up to a quarter of the foliage can be removed. If you prune too much, the plant will not die back, but will easily break bud and send up new, straight shoots. An argument against heavy pruning, though, is that the branches will look less pleasing in the winter. The straight new shoots from *overthinning* are not as pretty as the older curved stems. The good news is that the straight new shoots of an azalea are stiffer than most water sprouts, and they rather quickly (in a year perhaps) develop a nicer, curved form.

Stimulating Replacement Stems

In several landscapes I know, old deciduous azaleas suffer from the sudden death of large old limbs. In such cases, I have had luck cutting the stems out almost to the ground (leaving, say, a 4-inch stubby cane).

The new stems of the replacement shrub will grow from it. Check to make sure it is getting enough water in the summer before you make the cut, though. It's almost like pruning a forsythia.

Pruning for Health

Certain species of plants are reliably prone to certain diseases. Good pruning can't cure them, but it can help. And bad pruning (shearing, topping, overthinning) certainly makes disease problems worse. Deciduous azaleas tend to get *powdery mildew* that turns their leaves powdery gray and crinkly. It ruins their good looks in the summer. Although the mildews are often associated in people's minds with too much moisture and a lack of air circulation, I suspect the cause may be plant stress due to *insufficient summer watering*. So if you have an automatic irrigation system, increase the time on the clock. Improving air circulation may help, but only a little bit. Thinning out deadwood and crowded branches is okay, but more effective is transplanting too closely spaced shrubs or those that are in poor locations. Also note that many experienced gardeners have learned to simply overlook a certain amount of imperfection.

Old deciduous azaleas are also known to grow a lot of gray lichen on the bark, and sometimes green or gray balls of moss may also appear in the twigs and branches. This is not usually a serious threat to the health of the plants, but it is a sign of old age. I think of lichen as the gray hair of plants. It doesn't cause old age, it is just a sign of it. The look of lichen bothers some people.

Others, including myself, think it adds interest. If you have a very, very bad case of lichen, meaning thick and covering *all* the bark, you probably should rub some of it off so the bark can "breathe." Increase irrigation if the soil is dry, and thin the shrub if that hasn't been done in a long time.

Summary

Deciduous azaleas are tough and can withstand a lot of pruning, but they look best gently and lightly thinned out for definition. Prune out deadwood in the summer when it is easier to spot. If the shrub is too big, transplanting is easy and a better solution than pruning for size control.

ENGLISH LAUREL, ENGLISH HOLLY, AND PHOTINIA

(Prunus laurocerasus, Ilex aquifolium, and Photinia x fraseri)
What do English laurel, English holly, and photinia have in common? They all have large evergreen leaves; they break bud easily if pruned back to barren wood; and they eventually grow into either very large shrubs or relatively small trees (30 to 40 feet for laurel and holly and 10 to 15 feet for photinia).

No Pruning

If your photinia, laurel, or holly looks good and isn't in the way of anything, just leave it alone. If you want to help make it look better, taking out the deadwood almost always improves the appearance of any plant.

Pruning as an Informal Hedge (Selective Heading)

Photinia, laurel, and holly make good mass plantings for background and informal hedges in the 8- to 12-foot range. If let go entirely, they can easily grow to twice that size. Don't try to keep them much smaller than 8 to 12 feet, because it won't work. Above that, they can be selectively pruned to shorten or tidy them up. Even though these shrubs can take frequent and hard pruning, it's usually the gardener who gives up because it really is too much work.

To prune selectively, locate the tallest or widest offending branch, follow it down *inside* the plant to where it meets up with a side branch or parent stem, and then cut it off there. Use a hand pruner or loppers of good quality. Then locate and shorten the next worst branch. It is very important to hide those cuts down inside the plant. It's the difference between selective pruning and shearing your shrub a twig at a time. After pruning for a while your shrub should look natural but shorter and tidier.

Pruning as a Formal Hedge (Shearing)

These big-leafed, evergreen bud-breakers are often planted as a formal hedge. However, they are really second-best as plants for sheared hedges. The truly best hedges are slower growing or have finer leaves (yew, privet, boxwood, Japanese holly). Finer leaves look more elegant. Slower growing means less work. The nicest hedge I know is a blue Atlas cedar hedge. It's 15 feet high. But only the very wealthy and devoted can afford such hedges. If you miss pruning one year and it gets away from you, you're sunk. Unlike photinia, laurel, and holly, conifer hedges can't be made small again. They can't break bud and green back up if cut back hard.

If you have (or want) a formal hedge consisting of any one of these big-leafed evergreens, go ahead and shear them. Use either hedge shears (they look like a giant scissors) or power shears (buy or rent them for the day). Rent a three-legged ladder if you don't have one. They are more stable on uneven ground than the four-legged house-painter variety. Also, the third leg can be threaded through or into the hedge, making it easier for you to get "up-close and personal" with your plants.

English laurel often looks tattered and stubby after a shearing. This can be improved by going back over it with loppers or a hand pruner to cut out the worst of the sliced leaves or barren branches. Some people have been known to selectively prune as much as 30 feet of laurel hedge, though this becomes quite tedious after a few years. Such pruning is too labor intensive for such a common and unremarkable plant. Reserve that kind of determined effort for your wisteria vine.

Photinia is just a dressed-up laurel, in my opinion. Its claim to fame is that its new growth is reddish or coppery colored. I guess I can still remember when I was mightily impressed and longed to possess some; actually, any plant is valuable when given a situation requiring its highest and best use. Every time photinia is sheared, it flushes out more interesting red leaves. Laurel and photinia are somewhat tender in regions like the Northwest, so be careful not to stimulate a late flush of growth by shearing it in the fall. It might not have time to harden off for the winter and will suffer freeze damage.

Using as Individual Shrubs

Both English laurel and photinia serve useful functions as fast-growing screens, either as formal or informal hedges. And they make nice small trees. But they are too large, in my opinion, to be used as individual shrubs in the garden. Even more difficult to accept is their use as *sheared* individual shrubs in general landscaping. You see them everywhere in commercial landscapes, repeatedly clipped into empty and meaningless boxes and balls. Each year they get a little bigger and more unwieldy. A lot of maintenance money is being spent for limited value. They don't look good sheared and they won't stay small for long. Why not use something that grows to the right size and looks good with practically no pruning?

However, I must confess a slight fondness for the giant holly gumdrops seen here and there. Other gardeners find them objectionable. If such holly bushes are sheared every year from the time they are young, they develop a useful, incredibly thick and twiggy interior. Because of it, topiarians can then strap their 20-foot ladders directly onto the bush and not fall through when they go up for the annual trimming. Even so, it's a painful and expensive proposition. Hug a holly? Not me!

Occasionally someone cuts the top off of one of these holly gumdrops, because, well, because it's gotten "too big." This won't hurt

Figure 12.9 The pruning cycle of a sheared laurel or photinia hedge: **1.** First shear **2.** Regrowth **3.** 2nd-year shear **4.** 5th-year shear **5.** 12th-year shear **6.** Radical renovation **7.** It begins again.

the holly, but it can be a visual disaster when the chainsaw reveals a trunk surrounded by a saggy donut of dead-looking branches.

Radical Renovation

The good news is that these three plants can stand to be radically renovated. I once saw a full-sized holly chainsawed into the utterly leafless shape of a lava lamp. Next year it flushed out and looked great. Radical renovations of laurel hedges are common. In the spring, saw the overgrown hedge into the desired shape, except perhaps a foot or two smaller than the final desired size (see Figure 12.9). That's because it will need that room to resprout and be sheared into a thick green coat again. Be sure to cut your

hedge narrow as well as short. It should be narrow enough for one gardener to reach across with a hedge shear. I have only seen one laurel hedge that didn't recover from this radical treatment. It has remained a perfectly square bundle of dead-looking sticks for years. I always want to stop the truck and ask the person inside the house what he or she did to kill it. But I guess that wouldn't be polite.

Please avoid heavy pruning on a hot July or August day, as you might burn up some internal leaves or scald the bark. If you renovate in the winter, you must stare at the ugly barren branches till spring. In the Northwest, spring provides the longest period of benign wet weather, which will help the plant to regrow.

Arborizing

I don't much care for laurels, hollies, and photinias as hedges or bushes, but I think they make great small trees. Arborizing, which means turning a shrub into a tree, is best done on very mature plants. Before doing anything rash, take a look inside and visualize how it will look stripped up. Are the trunks nice and thick, or will it look like an ostrich once it's limbed up? A little general thinning and cutting out of deadwood will make the crown look its best too. And don't try arborizing every plant in sight. Moderation in all things is the watchword.

When some friends moved into their new home, they inquired about what to do with the 20-foot laurel bush totally obscuring the living room window. "Limb it up and be done with it!" I replied. It turned out to have a lovely thick and sinuous trunk. Now it's a tree under which to store the firewood. There is just enough screening from the street, and just enough light is let in the window. And the birds love it for the berries. (I suspect that the delight of bird-watching is one of those pleasures that develops later in life. I don't recall being so impressed by them in my college days. But then it wasn't birds I was watching.)

The Perfect Plants for Views and Screens

Although I put laurels, photinia, and holly in the tree-like category, they are not among the Cadillacs of the plant world. They're more the utility vans of the plant world. They are quite useful for doing a specific job, though not particularly glamorous. This job is being the fast-growing screen that can be kept at a given height. For example, these plants would work for a person whose desire for water views is running smack dab into his downhill neighbor's need for privacy. He wants the tree cut down to see the water—but that would mean a sight line from his neighbor's window to the water is the same as the one from his bedroom window to his balcony. Another common problem occurs when the new neighbors suddenly add a second story to their house; the windows of their addition seem to stare out into your once private backyard.

If you are not willing to wait for a 'Pyramidalis' hedge (*Thuja occidentalis* 'Pyramidalis') to grow up (my first choice because it's no maintenance and guaranteed never to get too wide), then a planting of laurels, photinias, or hollies may be just the ticket. They will grow up quickly, providing privacy, but you can stop them from blotting out all sun and light by pruning at the exact height you want. People foolishly plant fast-growing trees for this screening purpose, and live to

Figure 12.10 Resting under his laurels

rue the day. Trees, real trees, can't be kept down successfully, and I would include in this the latest monster in the field, Leyland cypress (x *Cupressocyparis leylandii*).

Summary
Laurel, holly, and photinia are extremely tough and can take any amount or kind of pruning. They are often sheared as formal hedges. For least maintenance, use them as small trees.

LILAC *(Syringa)*
Next to roses, the most wonderfully evocative plant is the lilac (see Figures 12.11 and 12.12). In the spring the scent of its flowers is likely to transport you to a childhood time in granny's garden, even if you didn't have a granny. I think that just about everyone should have a lilac, even though they are not particularly gardenworthy the rest of the year. They get a host of pests and diseases that, though not life-threatening, will mar them. The leaves might get powdery mildew, or pucker, or get scorched tips, or they might get scored by miners. Rather than engage in a distasteful chemical battle, I suggest siting the shrub where it can be enjoyed in bloom and then ignored the rest of the year. That is to say close, but not too close, to the front entry.

Size
The adult size of a typical lilac is 8 to 10 feet tall and, left unpruned, they can get much taller. Don't bother pruning

Figure 12.11 Lilac

your shrub for the first five or ten years. Once they have reached their mature height (in seven to ten years), you may prune them if you so desire. But remember—like most all plants—they don't need to be pruned to look good, bloom, and do their job in the garden.

Tall and Open or Short and Bushy?
In the Pacific Northwest, we tend to prune an old lilac like a little tree, taking out deadwood and a few minor crossing/rubbing branches (see Figure 12.13). I'm told that back in the Midwest they prune a lilac more like a forsythia, cutting a few large canes out to about 6 inches to a foot above ground level every year or so. This creates

Figure 12.12 To ID a lilac in winter, look for double buds at the branch ends. **A.** Peace, man. **B.** Lilac, man.

a shorter but thicker shrub, as new canes (suckers, actually) arise from the base to grow into replacement canes in future years.

It's just one of those natural laws: You can prune to have a tall, open, delicately branched plant *or* a lower, broader, denser shrub. You will not succeed in pruning to create a low, delicate, open shrub. If it can't grow up, it *will* grow out—the growth energy must go somewhere. For people who desire a lower lilac without all the pruning, there are some dwarfish varieties that grow to about 5 feet tall and as wide. Examples are *S. pubescens patula* 'Miss Kim' and *S. meyeri* 'Palibin'.

Those Troublesome Suckers

Pruning books I read are always admonishing people to remove the suckers (straight, skinny shoots arising from ground level) "as soon as they are seen." I doubt that these people spend much time in the garden. After suckers are cut to the ground, they quickly regrow, except in greater numbers. This will happen year after year after year. Having fought the sucker battle on lilacs for many years myself, I have finally devised a new philosophy of sucker management. I let lilac suckers grow. Sometimes I reduce the number, cutting out the lesser ones, never expecting to eliminate them all. I call it the "country-thicket" look, which I make nicer by mulching and making sure that no weeds grow at the base of the shrub.

People often want their multitrunked young lilac to be a single-trunked, tree-like plant. I suspect that those shrubs are born, not pruned to be more tree-like. Also,

Cut

Figure 12.13 Remove crossing/rubbing branches.

older lilacs may have shaded out their own competing understory of thicket, resulting in fewer trunks. In any case, pruning the competing canes will probably just increase their number.

The lilacs of long ago were grafted onto the roots of the common lilac (*S. vulgaris*) or privet. Presumably, if you let suckers grow from below the graft union (the union will look like a bulge) the new growth will overtake and ruin your nice lilac bush. But how can you tell, unless you bought it yourself and know all about your lilac variety and whether or not it's grafted? So I tend to proceed under the assumption that the shrub is not grafted, or if it was, that it is already too late to do anything about it.

Deadheading

Books tell us to prune out spent lilac blooms (taking care not to damage side shoots just below the blooms) so that the plant's energy is not wasted by putting up seeds. Personally, I feel my own energy is wasted teetering about on tall ladders taking off spent blooms—not to mention that it puts me in danger of falling. I say, "Leave them alone." If, after many years, your blossoms get small and puny, then you may choose to deadhead to see whether it will improve them.

My Old Lilac Is Leaning

Very, very old lilacs get a hollow core and then start to fall over. As that leaning trunk dips down, dormant buds located down the trunk will break free (free from apical dominance) and begin to grow up as straight, skinny water sprouts. This is just the lilac's natural way of rejuvenating itself. If those shoots are left alone they will grow into replacement canes or trunks. That's their job. People tend to prefer the gnarly, twisted old trunk to the replacement canes, and therefore evasive action is sometimes taken. If there is something to cable the leaning trunk to, we sometimes do that. I do worry that the trunk will get half girdled by the wire-in-a-rubber-hose tie. Like the arborists, I prefer a small eyebolt actually screwed into the wood and then cabled back to the wall or other some object. An alternative is to use a "crutch" under the leaning trunk. You could use a piece of pipe or lumber for this job, but it looks more artistic to use a forked branch from some other plant. Throughout the year I keep an eye out for a few good forked sticks and gather them for just such purposes.

Radical Renovation

People are always telling me that their lilac is too tall and they can't get to the blooms. They never say that about their magnolia tree. There's nothing wrong with a tall lilac, and just about every shrub gets to be 8 to 10 feet tall. Usually the only thing trees and shrubs are too tall for is the person's idea of how big they should get. If you need some blooms for your vase, get out the loppers or the pole pruner.

That said, I must confess that I pruned my own lilac because it was too much the same size as everything around it (sounds a lot like "too tall"). Even though I know better, I first cut about half of the 10-foot canes down to about 6 feet. Sure enough, they resprouted at the cut ends and regrew to 10 feet in just one year. *Oops.* So the next year I cut those same canes way, way down to about 1 to 2 feet from ground level. Generally speaking, one cuts higher up on a lilac than on other commonly renovated shrubs. They sent out new shoots that rapidly grew to just the right height (5 to 6 feet), then they arched over and put on (bigger, better) blooms. This year I cut the other half down (see Figure 12.14).

I could have cut the entire shrub down at once, but like everybody else, I'm too scared. Such heavy-duty pruning is called radical renovation, and it is done in the winter or early spring. Do it only to well-established plants. Know that they will rapidly grow to two-thirds of their original height. Sometimes it takes a few years for the plant to bloom again. Don't do this more than once every fifteen years. It is a serious stress to cut a plant down, so be certain that it is reasonably healthy, is well watered, and has sufficient light for it to recover. There is always a chance that the shrub might die, but it's unlikely.

It Doesn't Bloom

I've heard that lilacs sometimes stop bloom-ing. Be sure that your shrub is still in the sun (did a Doug fir grow up seemingly over-night?), and also remember that they prefer an alkaline soil. You might need to spread a little lime around. Garden lime or dolomite lime is calcium carbonate and is sold in bags at your local nursery or garden center. I've also read that root pruning them can force a bloom again. I've never experienced this, but a person who called me said that she had such an experience. She said that she had used a spade to root prune, but that it hadn't helped. So then she decided to dig up the lilac bush and throw it away. She got tired of digging before the job was done, and gave up trying for the year. Lo and behold, it bloomed in the spring.

Heart Transplant

I had a nice chat with a homeowner who told me that she had coveted her neighbor's lilac for more than thirty years. When that neigh-bor died and the house was sold to someone wanting to redevelop it, this homeowner talked a backhoe operator into digging up the lilac and putting it into her own yard. It lived, and bloomed and fulfilled a dream.

Summary

Lilacs can take a fair amount of pruning. Always deadwood first. You can prune a lilac like a cane-grower by removing a few of the oldest and tallest canes to 6 inches to a foot above the ground and letting new suckers grow up into replacement canes. This gives you a lower but much broader

Figure 12.14 Renovated lilac: old cut, new growth

and bushier shrub. Or you can prune it like a tree-like shrub, keeping it as a tall, open, finely branched plant. In that case, take out a few of the crossing/rubbing and wrong-way branches. If need be, selectively shortening (heading) a few branches by cutting back to an out-facing lateral (side) branch is okay. You don't have to deadhead unless the blooms are getting puny. I have never been able to stop suckers from coming up from the base of young shrubs. You can let them grow into canes, and/or perhaps they will be shaded out later.

RHODODENDRON (*Rhododendron*)

The problem with pruning rhododendrons is, well, they're unpredictable. Sometimes you head-back a branch to a node, and when you look next month you find that, instead of sending out new shoots, the branch sim-ply gave up and died. On other occasions people reduce their rhodies to the height or width they want, only to discover that by the time the plants have developed decent, full,

Figure 12.15 Maintenance pruning: Remove deadwood, a few crossing branches, and some lower limbs. **A.** Before **B.** After **C.** Tidy up the top as needed. **D.** Finished rhody.

leafy crowns, they're back up to about the size they were before. Or the new growth is weird, all skinny and floppy. Or sometimes they do grow back shorter and look great. How are you to know? And another problem with rhodies is that all the leaves are at the outside edges of the plant. There's nothing green to cut back to.

My Rhody Is Too Big

A commonly seen situation is that of a large-growing, open-habit rhododendron (like the Loderi types) that someone is trying to keep shorter and more compact. An old gardener's saying is "Inside every rhody is a 15-foot tree trying to get out." The hapless pruner tries in vain. Even when following the "rules" by selectively heading-back branches to shorter laterals, the result is a "funny-looking" plant, which is to say it starts to grow in a roughly V-shaped pattern. With the above caveats in place, let's review seven solutions to the too-big rhododendron.

Figure 12.16 Transplanting a rhody: Turn shovel upside down to chisel out the rootball.

Prune It

A lot of people think their rhody is too big, but really it's just too oppressive and/or crowded. Real pruning for health and good looks often solves the problem (see Figure 12.15). The horticulturally correct pruner takes out all the deadwood. Do this first and always. Prune out a few of the worst crossing/rubbing branches. It often helps to take off some of the lowest branches, slowly working up and out from the inside. Also concentrate on thinning out the worst, most interfering branches that crowd into nearby shrubs, the house, the window, the gutter, or the walkway, and tidy up the top as needed. See if that just doesn't do the trick.

Increase Bed Size or Move the Rhody

Because of difficulties with pruning, it is often a better and longer lasting solution to increase the shrub's bed size to accommodate the plant. This is a creative but unpopular solution due to the removal of sod involved.

Rhodies have broad, flat, fibrous root systems and are a relative dream to move (see Figure 12.16).

Landscapers often move plants that are larger than people. Another old saying is "Your rhody will appreciate a trip around the house." It may require up to four strong backs and a tarp to slide the offending rhody out of its present home and to its new one. Don't be afraid to cut off 50 percent or more of the roots, both large and small, fishing around under the rootball with your loppers, trying to locate the roots that are keeping it tied down and foiling your shovel during the dig. After transplanting, immediate soaking is crucial. And give it lots of water throughout the first year. Moving is the only logical solution for situations where shrubs were originally planted too close together or next to the walkway, as commonly seen in new landscapes everywhere.

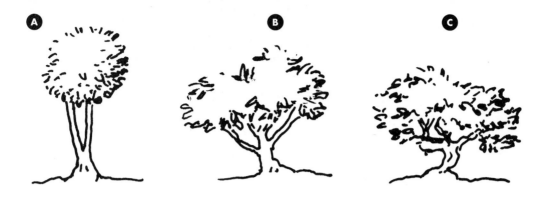

Figure 12.17 Arborizing a rhody: Turn a large shrub into a small tree. **A.** No lollipops. **B.** Limb up the lower trunk. **C.** Thin the crown to make it look less top-heavy.

Selective Reduction

Is it under the window? You can try to "work back" your rhody. You selectively head it a little every year. Locate the tallest branch and follow it down to a place inside the shrub where it meets a lower and shorter lateral. Cut it off there. Repeat with the next tallest branch. Continue until you sense you've gone too far. Quit; then come back next year. Selective reduction works better on upward-facing branches (the top of the plant). The same pruning on the more horizontal branches (sides of the plant) tends to develop new shoots that look like spaghetti.

Stop It in Its Tracks

If the plant in question borders a high-traffic area such as stairs or a path, you might try snapping off the new growth. After the plant has finished blooming, you can either pinch out the new end-bud, or let the new supple shoot extend and snap it off with your fingers or prune it off with your hand pruner soon thereafter, around May or June.

Landscapers attest that on most rhodies this will not prevent blooming next year, though it is hard to understand why not. It is also exceedingly time consuming and must be done every year to restrict growth.

Arborize It

In special cases a "too-big" rhody can be thinned-up and turned into a nice small tree (see Figure 12.17). The plant in question should be very big and old. It should have a thick, curvaceous trunk. Be sure to meticulously deadwood it as well, and perhaps generally thin the upper canopy to prevent the "lollipop" look.

Radical Renovation

In especially desperate and hopeless situations, it is sometimes appropriate to cut the entire plant nearly to the ground and start it over. Like surgery, this is a serious move, and you should exhaust other possible solutions first. Sometimes the plant dies. Most often it does not. I have been told that certain rhodies, the so-called smooth-barked rhodo-dendrons (ones with *R. thomsonii* genes in them), cannot break bud and therefore will die under hard pruning. You will not likely spot a *thomsonii* hybrid by looking at it. I can't either. Their blooms are red, I know. But you can get a good idea by looking for the plumping buds on the lower portions of the trunks. (See Figure 12.21 on page 170.) No buds? Then the shrub is not a good candidate. Renovation works best on old and/or previously mal-pruned shrubs. Don't try to be nicer to a shrub by cutting less severely. Remember, after a plant is pruned the new growth starts just below the cut and grows *up* from there. It will be too big again very soon (see Figure 12.18).

And if your reduction cuts leave too much of the framework, you wind up with a mismatched plant. The new, smaller, leafy crown is stuck on top of thick old, thick "legs." It just doesn't look right. Plus you are more likely to produce the wild regrowth common on hard-pruned rhodies. But if it is cut lower to the ground, making a framework of 1 foot or less, the new shoots have no place to go but up (see Figure 12.19).

I also think it is wiser to cut the plant down (to a foot or so from the ground) all at once, instead of in stages as some recommend. If you cut one-third of the trunks to the ground, as you would prune a cane-grower, the remaining evergreen canopy is likely to shade out the returning new-shoot growth. Others advise cutting the entire plant back by a third, and then a third again the next year, and then again lower, to achieve a smaller shrub in stages. I have come to believe that

this causes the plant more stress than a single, severe pruning to a low framework. The plant must deal with the injury three times instead of just once. But that's just my opinion.

When radically renovating a rhody, do it in the early spring, February or March. Don't fertilize. Water well throughout the next year. A radically renovated rhody will still need almost as much room to live and look good in the long run. And remember that a the rhody will take several years to recover and look like anything.

Adjust Your Attitude

Most often the only thing a rhododendron is too big for is somebody's idea of how big it should get to be. In this case, the cheapest and best solution is to learn to appreciate mature plants. A mature rhododendron can grow to be 10 to 20 feet—that's two stories high. And some get up to 40 feet. Get used to it.

My Rhody Is Too Leggy

About fourteen years ago, I saw a rhody that a brave but unskilled gardener had over-thinned. Instead of looking like a nice little tree, the plant had internal branches that were so skinny and awkward they looked like a collection of broken arms and legs. And the plant continued to look that way for most of the following fourteen years. This year I noticed for the first time that the canopy had finally grown back together, hiding the internal branch work. It looks okay. But no buds ever broke inside the shrub; all the new growth was at the ends.

Many people have skinny, leggy rhodies that are the result of bad culture, not bad

Figure 12.18 Radical renovation: The most common mistake is not cutting low enough. When the rhody on the right grows back, it will obscure the window again.

pruning. By this I mean the rhody was planted in too much sun, too much shade (for example between two buildings), or that there has been insufficient water or too much competition from weeds. These are all cultural conditions that have caused a problem as opposed to pest or disease problems.

Like the rhody described above, there's not much help for these plants. It's a good idea to try to eliminate the cause of legginess, but it will still take a long time, and the plant may perhaps never look better. The best thing you can do is deadwood like crazy. Get inside and remove each and every bit. And take out the old yellow leaves, too. On many branches you will find a tiny ½-inch pointy peg of deadwood. It is the last bit of stem from an old bloom, still hanging on. Take those off. Remove any branches hanging on the ground. Then the shrub will look cleaner and maybe sort of artistic, or at least not so annoyingly awful. And I recommend that you plant some lower-story plants to bring

the eyes down. Use sword ferns, epimedium, or Lenten rose (*Helleborus orientalis*). Or you could half-bury some interesting, low-maintenance rocks that will help shift the focus away from the rhody.

If the cause of the problem is eliminated (like cutting down the Doug fir nearby, or adding irrigation), you can try radical renovation. If the cause is not remedied, radical renovation will simply kill the plant or it will grow back leggy again. And take a moment to determine whether your rhody is one of the species that is naturally open (leggy). Most of these rhodies have large, long leaves. If so, think of yours as a tree (see Figure 12.20).

Nicking the Buds

An old landscaper's trick to renew a big or leggy rhody is to nick the buds. You can trick a rhododendron into thinking that its top is gone by doing so. In the very early spring, say February, locate the plumping buds down near the base of the plant. A bud will be about the size of a pencil-tip point. Use

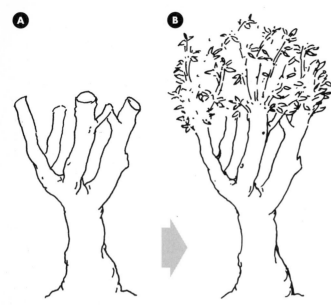

Once the flow of auxin is interrupted, the dormant bud will think the top is gone and begin to grow out.

You can select five or ten buds to nick. Be careful not to girdle your shrub by nicking the branch all the way around like a ring. The vast majority of the cambium layer must be kept or the shrub will die. The cut should be about the size of a lady's fingernail clipping (not a gardener's, because we don't have nails long enough to clip). Just a little sliver of a moon, ¼ inch long, ⅛ inch or less deep (see Figure 12.21).

That year the bud will grow into a stupid looking whorl of leaves. But next year it will branch out into several leafy stems. The year after, you will have sort of a second shrub developing at the base of your old, leggy rhody. Then you can saw the top out. Again, this process won't work if the cultural problem has not been corrected or if it is a smooth-barked type of rhody.

People love this gardening tip, so much so that it worries me. In reality most of these people have perfectly good plants that aren't too big for anything. People just think their rhody is too big. I would much prefer that they transplant or simply accept their shrubs for what they are.

Figure 12.19 When renovating a rhody, cut very low—6 inches to 1½ feet above the ground. **A.** Rhody is cut too high. **B.** Regrowth is mismatched and "spaghetti" is likely. **C.** Cut low **D.** and growth has nowhere to go but up.

a razor blade to take a tiny wedge out just above the bud. You are removing the bark and the first layer of green (the cambium) just below it. This will stop an auxin (a chemical like a hormone) from reaching the bud. This auxin comes from the apical bud (the one at the top end of the branch) and it tells the dormant buds below to stay asleep.

Layering
Another landscaper's trick is to layer mature rhodies, letting new ones grow up while

selectively cutting out some of the large parent plants. If you stake or pin down a piece of green branch to the dirt, perhaps spreading a little soil over the point of contact, it will grow roots and become a new shrub. It's called layering, and it's how some people propagate rhodies.

My Rhody Is Ugly

The hardest plants to prune are old rhododendrons previously chainsawed in half. The new growth looks horrible. Although many can be brought back to a semblance of beauty with years of rehabilitative pruning, these casualties are often so indisputably ugly that removal is a more realistic solution.

Spaghetti

Some rhodies are not just leggy, their branches are ugly in the extreme. You look inside and all you find are long, skinny, rollercoaster branches that have only one pathetic whorl of leaves on the ends. The cause

is usually mal-pruning. When a branch is headed back, the new shoot emerges, growing rapidly with soft wood. When the bud at the end blooms, the weight of the flower truss pulls the soft young shoot down. As the season progresses the shoot hardens off in that position. Next spring, off it goes again, headed up from the tip, then dipping down. I've heard these rhodies called spaghetti, and they are the most difficult plants I prune (see Figure 12.22).

Taking off deadwood as noted above may be the best you can do. If you go after the ugly branches, you are likely to open the canopy, giving an even better view of the remaining ugly branches. Remember that each of those pathetic whorls of leaves provides some valuable cover for the rest of the ungainly interior. In my experience, the internal branches never fatten up and look right. Your best bet is to encourage the canopy to cover and hide.

That said, I sometimes do try to improve the spaghetti rhody just a bit, restoring it

---

Figure 12.20 A. A leggy rhody caused by bad culture **B.** A naturally open, tree-like rhody

Figure 12.21 Nicking a bud

over many years to a better-looking plant. Here are the rules: Leave any branches that face upward and outward, no matter how horrible they seem. Cut off the lowest "hooks" of what I call "serial goosenecks." As always, I remove any branches that actually touch the ground. Aside from detracting from the appearance of the shrub, these ground-touching branches act as root-weevil freeways, making it easy for the little guys to crawl up and munch on the leaves at night.

Needless to say, spaghetti rhodies are good candidates for renovation, assuming that they have their cultural requirements met.

Powdery Mildew

Some ugly growth is caused not by bad pruning or bad culture but by a newly introduced disease that is ravaging the rhododendrons of the Pacific Northwest, especially the hybrids 'Unique' and 'Virginia Richards'. It is a powdery mildew, but not the same powdery mildew that gets deciduous azaleas and Oregon grape. This is much worse. The symptoms don't resemble the gray powder

of the other diseases either. Instead many of the leaves turn blotchy, yellow or sometimes brown, and fall off in the summer. (Some yellow, internal leaf drop is normal in the late summer.) Live buds will remain and the shrub will grow new green leaves in the spring. But then it happens again.

Rather than fight it with constant spraying of either chemical or organic compounds, I suggest removing the shrubs that continually look horrible. Some rhodies are more susceptible and others are more resistant. The disease also favors close quarters, shade, and high humidity. Some people hope that thinning will create enough air circulation to cure this and other fungal/bacterial diseases. It won't. Moving the shrub to a more open location might help. Just thought you should know.

Rootstock

And a final word about rhodies. The very first hybrids were grafted (spliced) onto the roots of a vigorous species, *R. ponticum.* When the hybrid is put under stress, the rootstock grows out and new shoots from the base eventually grow up and take over the plant. If you have a rhody with two colors of blooms, this is why. *R. ponticum* has a purple bloom (some people call it fuchsia-colored). The leaves are skinny and their edges are wavy.

Figure 12.22 How a spaghetti rhody is made: **A.** Large heading cut is made. **B.** New shoot heads upward. **C.** Flower truss weighs shoot down. **D.** Shoot hardens off in this position. **E.** New shoot emerges and heads upward in the spring. **F.** Blooms pull new shoots down. **G.** And so on. **H.** For a partial fix, remove lowest "hook."

A

B

C

D

E

F

G

H

Cut
Here

And the plants get very, very large. In parts of England they have naturalized and become quite a nuisance. I tell you this because you may have one that you want to get rid of, and now you will know that it's nothing special. And it's not even what the original gardener had in mind when it was planted. On the other hand, if you like it, by all means keep it. After all, there's nothing wrong with a big rhody.

Summary

Rhododendrons are difficult to prune, especially for size control. But they are a relative dream to move. If your rhody is too big, dig it up and drag it to a better place.

VIBURNUM × *BODNANTENSE* AND BEAUTYBERRY *(Callicarpa)*

Both these plants do one thing well: They provide us with a winter treat. Beautyberries have clusters of brilliant purple berries that persist throughout the fall and into winter (see Figure 12.23). (Beautyberry, *Callicarpa*, is not the same thing as beauty bush, which is *Kolkwitzia amabilis*.) V. *bodnantense* has extremely fragrant clusters of small pink flowers in the late winter and early spring. This makes them plants for people who like plants, and for people who like something interesting going on in their gardens all year long. These deciduous shrubs are both tall and skinny. Beautyberry is 6 feet high or more. *V. bodnantense* grows to 10 feet or more. And you should pay attention. They really will get that big, sooner than you think; and you can't stop them with pruning.

Figure 12.23 Beautyberry

The other common feature of these two plants is that they are both, well, gawky. They grow straight up with many skinny trunks or canes. From these, equally graceless laterals will shoot out in all directions in a most unpleasing and angular way. There's nothing to be done about it. It's just their natural habit, as the saying goes. People who have these shrubs are always wanting me to fix them with pruning either because (1) the shrubs are getting much bigger than they thought they would or (2) the plants just don't look right. Unfortunately, neither complaint can be fixed with pruning. The more you prune for size control, the faster the shrubs will grow (with even more and uglier upright branches). On the other hand, if you don't prune, and you just let them grow unmolested for twenty years, they eventually develop what could be termed an arching branch structure. Patience, not pruning, is the key to creating graceful, arching branches.

Horticulturists who are familiar with these shrubs don't find their habit disturbing. They know it's just how these plants look. Neophytes sort of expect all shrubs to look pretty much the same—which is to say fatter than they are tall, globe shaped, and about 4 or 5 feet tall. (That's the shrubs, not the neophytes.) It's how we drew the shrubs with crayons as kids and nobody corrected us.

It's as if we expected all animals to look like either horses or dogs. Where does that put elephants, ostriches, and eels? Beautyberry and *V. bodnantense* are sort of like the giraffes of the plant world. I'm sure they look quite natural to each other (see Figure 12.24). And when you get used to them, they will look right to you too.

Replacement Pruning

Many pruning books recommend pruning the deciduous viburnums and beautyberries like they do forsythias—by cutting some of the canes to the ground every year. This will stimulate new shoots, called suckers, to grow up from the cut and become replacement canes over the course of the next few years. With *V. bodnantense*, if you don't cut out too many canes or too large canes, you might not even stimulate new shoot growth. That would be nice because then your shrub will stay thinned out, and, if the cane (or trunk) you removed happened to be the tallest one, you will have successfully made your shrub moderately shorter. I don't know if this system works for beautyberry, but I assume it would.

Thinning

For general-maintenance pruning I suggest using a light hand with these shrubs. If you prune too much (and it doesn't take much with the viburnums) you just stimulate a lot of water sprouts to grow next season. Don't judge your pruning job just on how it looks right after you are through. If you

Figure 12.24 Hey guys, there's no sign of that escaped giraffe. . . .

prune out everything that is wrong, you will have a nightmare of regrowth the next year. Trying to restrain these really twiggy plants is especially hard on them. Just for starters, don't take out more than an eighth of these shrubs in a year. If you find that you get heavy regrowth the next season, then *do less*, not more. The plant is telling you that it must have a certain amount of leaves to stay healthy.

It is always okay to take out deadwood, dead stubs, and such. It doesn't count in the pruning budget, and it always makes things look better. It is the first thing good pruners do. Then go on to general thinning for good looks. Concentrate on taking out a few of the worst lateral branches that hit the house or that threaten to poke passersby in the eye. Then look for Mr. Wrong Way. He's the branch that starts on one side of the shrub and crosses back through the center and out the other side. And look for ones that actually touch each other. Remove one of the crossers/rubbers, if to do so will not leave a big hole or exceed your pruning budget (see Figure 12.25). Keep moving. When in doubt, just leave the crossing branches in question and move on to another side of the plant. Get out before you do too much. Young plants probably should take only sixty seconds of pruning; old shrubs, maybe fifteen minutes to half an hour.

Radical Renovation and Rehabilitation

I don't like most renewal pruning systems. However, I occasionally do a rad reno on previously mal-pruned plants (e.g., if someone tried to prune their old viburnum or callicarpa into a big ball and now have a huge mess on their hands). I cut these unfortunate shrubs to the ground, or a foot or so above, and then let them regrow for three to five years.

Radical renovation is the fast way to reestablish the natural habit of plants, although it will be a scary sight for a few years until they sort themselves out. The renovated shrubs will rapidly grow to almost their original size, and therefore the technique is not used for size control. It is also hard on plants' health. A little additional water in the summer is a good idea while the shrub is still in recovery.

There are other ways to rehabilitate these shrubs if they are mal-pruned plants. You can cut out one-third of the canes (to the ground) for three years in a row, letting new canes (suckers) replace the old. Or you can let the entire plant grow out for a few years

after such cutting. The new growth will look horribly different from the old and will start to drive you nuts. It's a lot like growing your bangs out. After a year, go inside and thin out the worst clusters of overcrowded branches and simplify the hydra branch ends, as shown in the forsythia illustrations in Chapter 11, Cane-Growing Shrubs.

Timing

I don't care what the other pruning guides say, it doesn't matter when you prune these shrubs, if you are selectively pruning them. (Note that radical renovation and shearing are not selective pruning.) You will just lose the blooms on the branches you cut out. There will be plenty of blooms or berries left on the branches that are left unpruned. I don't know how timing got to be such a big

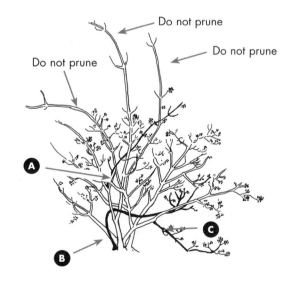

Figure 12.25 General pruning for *V. x bodnantense* and beautyberry **A.** Rubbing branch **B.** Mr. Wrong Way **C.** Branch on the ground

deal. On these plants I prefer to prune them while they are in bloom or in berry so I can bring in the cut branches for table arrangements. It's not as though you will shock the rest of the plant into not blooming next year.

The Best Siting

The ideal pruning for these plants would be practically no pruning because they had been correctly sited. In other words, they should be placed where they have all the room they need to grow as high and as wide as they want. Put them in a bed that can be enlarged to accommodate their widening skirts, or put them in the back of a border. Place them where they can be easily seen in the fall or winter (or early spring for *V. bodnantense*), near an entryway or easily viewed from a window. But neither of these shrubs should stand alone as a focal point, nor be put too close to the main entry or window. They should be tucked in among more universally acceptable shrubs (or, alternatively, segregated in a mass planting in the winter garden). In other words, put these plants where they can be admired when they are doing their thing, but where their flaws can be easily overlooked the rest of the year.

Summary

Both these shrubs are naturally tall, skinny, and gawky looking. Pruning cannot turn them into tidier round shrubs. They also water-sprout like crazy if you head-back or thin too much, and it doesn't take much. The best you can do is a little light thinning and deadwooding.

WITCH HAZEL, DOUBLEFILE VIBURNUM, AND WINTER HAZEL
(Hamamelis, Viburnum plicatum tomentosum, and Corylopsis)

These three species all possess a very desirable horizontal branch structure. The "bones" of these plants when revealed in the winter are artistic, architectural, and elegant. Many cultivars also provide fall color for the garden. And the flowers are attractive and yet tastefully understated. None of these plants are prone to any particularly awful pest or disease problem. This means that horticulturists give these shrubs ten points out of a possible ten in garden-worthiness. Unfortunately, these shrubs also share another trait. They resent pruning and especially size control. If you prune too much or the wrong way, they will respond by growing back numerous straight, skinny shoots called water sprouts (see Figures 12.26, 12.27, and 12.28).

The key to success is to site these plants in a place where they can grow as tall and wide as they like, without ever needing to be pruned. That space is usually much larger than most people suppose. The mature size of these shrubs is 15 to 20 feet tall and often as wide, which is the size of a small tree in the mind of the average homeowner. Please don't kid yourself. They will get to be this size sooner than you imagine. You or some other poor soul will have to deal with them if you put them in the wrong place. And that means they will probably have to be cut down just when they are reaching maximum glory. Because these shrubs/trees are so good looking, many people are tempted to plant them close to the walkway, close to the street, or next to the front door. Don't do it! Plant them in the middle of a bed bordered by other shrubs of lesser importance, or by lawn that can be removed to accommodate their increasing size. They can, however, be planted flat against a fence.

General Pruning Guidelines

Limit yourself to pruning only a few of the small, most annoying crossing/rubbing branches; or the one branch that heads straight up, ruining the good looks of the horizontal pattern; or some limb that hangs on the ground (see Figures 12.29 and 12.30).

Of course, pruning off deadwood is always in order and is guaranteed to make things look better. Prune the shrub while it is in bloom to bring the cut branches indoors to put in a vase, or prune it anytime the spirit moves you. For beginners, limit yourself to removing less than one-tenth the foliage in a year. This goes for witch hazels, doublefile viburnums and winter hazels.

Witch Hazel

Witch hazels rule! They have the best of everything. Witch hazel blooms are always some variation of the color yellow, running to sulfur (I'm not allowed to use the color *orange* in print), with one type even having a raspberry hue. The bloom itself is sort of odd and spidery—looking quite fascinating, actually (see Figure 12.31 on page 180).

The shrub blooms in the winter on barren, angular stems. And many varieties smell good, especially if a branch or two are pruned off and put in a vase, where they will

Figure 12.26 Don't: **A.** Making heading cuts to clear a path won't work because **B.** it causes ugly water sprouts to grow.

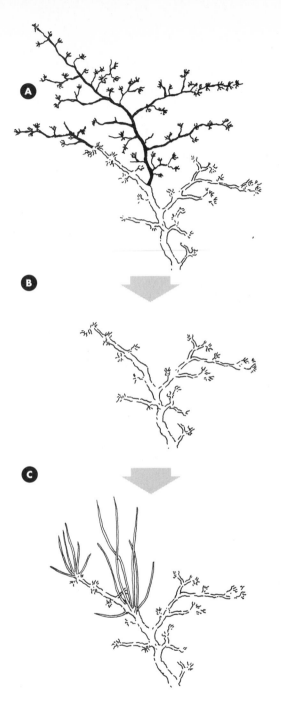

Figure 12.27 Don't: **A.** Trying to selectively reduce shrub size will look fine **B.** just after cuts, but **C.** water-sprout rebound won't be far behind.

automatically look as if they were arranged by a Zen master.

Suckers and Dead Leaves

Hamamelis mollis is one of the most commonly planted witch hazels. (I'm always tempted to say Hammammammalus mmmmolis.) It is also one of the parents of *H.* x *intermedia*, a witch hazel with great fall color. Either may be grafted to the roots of *H. virginiana*. The reason I mention this is that the graft union might fail if the shrub suffers from some serious stress. Then suckers from the rootstock will begin to grow out. If you see these suckers, you must remove them. And once suckers have begun to grow, you may need to remove them in increasing numbers every year. If you don't remove them, they will take over the shrub.

I had a client with a shrub that bloomed one color, then another, and half the plant refused to drop its ugly brown leaves. That was the rootstock that grew into half the shrub. I just killed the whole thing and started over. This unpleasant habit (of holding on to brown leaves just at the time when you should be enjoying the blooms) belongs to several of the species and cultivars, not just *H. virginiana*. If yours fails to drop, know that it's not your fault and there is no cure for it, except perhaps to carefully cut or pick the leaves off. It may vary from year to year.

As for general pruning, go easy. Use all thinning cuts, and relatively small and few ones at that. If you prune too much (and it doesn't take much) next year will bring you clusters of water sprouts at the site of each cut. Take those off and more return. Actually, more and more return. So you can see the importance of not stimulating rootstock suckers or water sprouts to begin with.

Doublefile Viburnum

Doublefile viburnums are called that because both the leaves and the flowers are arranged in two matched columns along the stems. The flowers are creamy white and quite nice. They bloom in the spring. The leaves turn a splendid fall color in the maroon segment of the color wheel. (Forgive my lack of colorful color descriptions. I flunked the "names of colors" class—just one of several "girl" subjects I missed.) But take it from me, doublefiles are really pretty in the fall. A very old doublefile can be made into a sort of small tree by removing some lower branches. You may need to do this in order to continue using the path or something. Otherwise leaving the shrub dressed to the ground is fine.

Pruning Doublefiles: True Confessions

You prune doublefiles just like witch hazels (and winter hazels). Doublefiles are on their own roots, so if you see a ton of shoots springing up from the base, you can, and should, just ignore them long enough for them to turn into regular-looking parts of the plant. If someone has been overpruning or mal-pruning the plant (and I'm not accusing anyone), just leave it alone long enough and the evidence will disappear (in one to three years).

I have been the unwilling participant in an attempt to keep a doublefile to about 2 feet

Figure 12.28 Don't: **A.** Making the right kind of cuts but too many is overthinning; **B.** it looks great just after cutting, but watch out—**C.** it stimulates water sprouts next year. Now you're stuck!

Figure 12.29 Do: **A.** Thin off one large, interfering limb, but nothing else, **B.** clearing a path for pedestrians **C.** without causing water sprouts next year.

tall. It worked pretty well for several years. But remember, if it doesn't go up, it will go out. And this doublefile spread out a lot, which is to say it's easily 8 feet wide.

Doublefiles are utterly impossible to control in width, as are all of these species. It ruins their horizontal habit. Twenty years ago I planted two doublefiles next to my house in a narrow space. With all the hubris of a new selective pruner, I felt certain that I could control them. After all, I knew the secret of the selective heading cut. But it just made the branches look funny. This is how PlantAmnesty's adopt-a-plant program began—someone with more suitable space adopted my doublefiles. I feel better knowing that the plants have probably reached their full garden potential unmolested. The scars of my early training attempts are probably no longer visible. I hope so anyway.

Figure 12.30 Do: **A.** Thin lightly if desired, using many small thinning cuts. **B.** This makes the shrub look better now and **C.** causes no water-sprout response.

Not One or the Other: In Between Mounding-Habit, Cane-Growing, and Tree-Like Shrubs

Beauty bush (*Kolkwitzia*). A big shrub that needs room to be 10 to 12 feet tall and as wide as a small outbuilding. Prune as a tree-like shrub, or renovate as a cane-grower.

Ceanothus (*Ceanothus*). There are many species and varieties of this plant; some are a low-trailing ground cover, some are mounding-habit shrubs, others will grow into open trees. All have small leaves, but many become large plants. They are drought tolerant and short lived. Pruning literature is contradictory on subjects of shearing, heading, and renovation. I suggest light thinning only.

European cranberry (*Viburnum opulus*). Preferably pruned as a tree-like or mounding-habit shrub, but can be renewed by cutting trunks/canes to the base. Wants to be 10 to 20 feet tall, the size of the garage. Cute

dwarf buns (2 by 2 feet) are available in the nursery trade.

Pearl bush (*Exochorda racemosa*). Prune as a tree-like shrub; renovate like a cane-grower. Grows to 10 to 15 feet tall. Hybrid *E. macrantha* 'The Bride' is smaller at 4 by 4 feet.

Snowball bush (*Viburnum spp.*). Several species are called "snowball." Prune as a tree-like or mounding-habit shrub. Can renovate like a cane-grower, cutting canes to the ground. All grow about 10 feet tall and wide, which is taller than you.

Spindle tree (*Euonymus europaeus*). Prune as a tree-like shrub, but canes can be removed to ground level. New canes (suckers) can be allowed to grow into replacement trunks. Mature height is 10 to 15 feet.

Even though I still long to possess a double-file, I know adoption was the best thing to do, for all those concerned.

But back to the 2-foot-tall doublefile in my customer's yard. Because of its ever-increasing width, I moved it to a new location, and I did so with an eye to the future. I looked up too. Even with diligent, knowledgeable, annual pruning, I knew that eventually the plant would be impossible to keep down. Finally, a year or two ago, I released it. Boy, it shot up! It grew to 6 feet in a year! Then I skirted-up some of the very lowest of the old growth and it looks just fine now. (Promise me, you won't turn me in to the tree police.)

Winter Hazel

Winter hazel is a lot like witch hazel, but with skinnier branches and even less spectacular flowers. I mean, we're talking so understated you might not even notice them. Actually

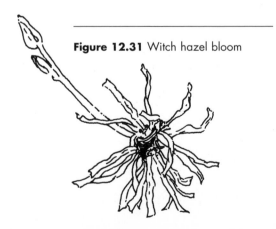

Figure 12.31 Witch hazel bloom

they're really quite nice, pale candle-yellow danglees (another Cass Turnbull technical term) that hang on barren branches in the early, early spring. I guess that makes the winter hazel the aristocrat's forsythia. And it smells nice too.

I've seen it used to wonderful effect in an early spring garden, with a yellow theme. The garden had winter hazel, daffodils of various types, and golden variegated grasses. Foliar contrast was provided by several of the always impressive *Euphorbia characias wulfenii* and groupings of the Corsican hellebore (*Helleborus argutifolius*). Their chartreuse-colored blooms added just the right pizzazz to all that understated elegance. I know that chartreuse is a horrid color for a dress or a refrigerator, but trust me, it is fabulous in a garden.

Pruning for the winter hazel is the same as the other plants in this section, which is to say, prune as little as possible and let them do all the work, making your garden a four-season delight.

Summary

These plants water-sprout like crazy, so prune them very lightly if at all. Forget size control. You may thin them out a bit to accentuate their great horizontal branch structure. Take off less than one-tenth of the foliage when you do prune, using true thinning cuts, and smallish ones at that.

MORE TREE-LIKES

Chances are that somewhere in your yard there's a shrub inside of which is a lovely small tree, just waiting for a skillful pruner to reveal it.

PIERIS AND GOLDEN THREAD CYPRESS (*Pieris japonica* and *Chamaecyparis pisifera* 'Filifera Aurea')

I prune pieris and golden thread cypress pretty much the same. Each will take a goodly amount of thinning and will look better for it. I would say that you can, if you so desire, take up to a quarter of the live foliage off without putting a healthy plant in danger. Neither water-sprouts badly.

Deadwood

These are two shrubs that really respond well to deadwooding. I can remember an awfully sick-looking thread cypress at Parsons Garden, on Seattle's Queen Anne Hill, that I deadwooded back in my early Parks Department days. It took an hour or two to carefully snip out every tiny dead twig. But when it was over, what a transformation! It looked great, and I later became convinced that I had saved its life, returning it to good health. But perhaps it just looked that way. The big ratty mop had become a lovely, rather open little tree. The threads hung like a golden veil, with glimpses of the interesting branch structure inside.

Thinning

While working inside the shrub, you can thin out branches that are too straight, that are too skinny, or that wander too far. You may care to thin off other branches, both large and small, evenly throughout the shrub so that it becomes less crowded. The art of thinning: Every space is filled, but with fewer branches.

Mock Deadwood

In every pieris shrub you will find what look like dead branches. They go on a ways, and their side branches all look dead and gray. But after you've cut, you find that there actually was a cluster of green leaves at the end. *Oops!* Don't panic, this will just give you some more general thinning. Even the most experienced gardeners have "oopses."

Figure 12.32 A. Pieris or cypress before general thinning; prune branches shown in black. **B.** Thread cypress after general thinning. **C.** Thin out more (the branches in black) **D.** Is it pruning art—or poodle-balling?

But it is something to note. Gardeners pruning inside shrubs frequently shake and bend branches to see where they go and what's on the other end.

Treat It Like a Tree

Both these plants fit the tree-like category. And they readily grow to 10, 15, and 20 feet tall. I see many three-story thread cypresses, and I've seen at least one equally large pieris. Count on them getting to be 8 to 10 feet tall anyway. When and if they become too much, try thinning. Also, you can remove lower limbs, turning the shrub into the much-sought-after small tree.

Size Reduction

As with all the tree-like shrubs, avoid size reduction. That said, these two do withstand serious cutting back. That doesn't mean it should be done. I recently taught in a landscape where someone had tried to keep the pieris down. As a result of so much heading, the top featured many upright water sprout–like shoots, spoiling the looks of it. I admonished the homeowner to let it have its head, and thinned out a few of the worst shoots just to make it look better for now.

Overthinning or Art?

Either of these shrubs can be more extensively pruned to the degree where it becomes a focal point (see Figure 12.32), reminiscent of cloud-pruned pines in Japanese gardens (see the sidebar "Pruning Art" on page 229). Or it can be thinned and poodle-balled with the use of hedge shears. (The latter option unnerves the selective pruners in the neighborhood and is to be avoided.) The difference between a well-thinned and an overthinned shrub is a matter of degree, and a certain amount of art.

Why I Like Them

I like both these shrubs. They're tidy, evergreen, and trouble free. The pieris has nice, sweet-smelling blooms, followed by copper-colored new growth. Some that have been especially bred have red new growth. The name, I believe, is 'Mountain Fire." The golden thread cypress has an interesting color—golden, without ever looking sickly yellow—and provides good textural contrast for all the broadleafs. And it is a small conifer, relatively speaking, that you can have in a small yard.

I like their names, too. Pieris is also known as andromeda, which sounds pretty, reminding me of the stars in the sky and Greek mythology at the same time. But I really enjoy the golden thread's botanical name. It reads like a poem in iambic pentameter, or perhaps a sewing machine. It (along with its common name) was an eight-pointer on the plant ID quiz when I was studying horticulture. It is *Chamaecyparis pisifera* 'Filifera Aurea'. Go ahead, try it: cam-ee-SIP-paris / pis-SIF-er-ah / fil-IF-er-ah / AWR-ee-ah. Once when I was interviewing for a job, the homeowner, unsure of my skill level, told me that her landscape architect had told her that her little tree was a rare juniper. I said, "Oh no, it's fairly common. But it is a pretty big *Chamaecyparis pisifera* 'Filifera Aurea'." That seemed to convince her that I knew my stuff.

Summary

Both these plants can be thinned extensively, and limbed up, if doing so will solve a problem. Start with deadwooding, which will be 80 percent of the job. Then thin out many small branches throughout the canopy. You can remove up to one quarter of the foliage, though less is better.

SMOKE BUSH *(Cotinus coggygria)*

One of my very favorite plants is the smoke bush (a.k.a. smoke tree). In summer, masses of flower-plume-thingies appear that look like, well, like puffs of smoke. That's pretty neat. Both the green and the purple smoke bushes have good foliage too. If allowed to have only one, I would, like most people, go for the purple-leafed one. I realized a while back how odd it was that I loved the purple of the purple smoke tree but don't care for the purple-leaf plum tree foliage that is, as far as I can tell, the exact same purple. It must be something about the leaf shape, the wonderful purple orbiculate smoke tree leaf (see Figure 12.33), that makes it such a cool foliage plant. It sort of glistens on the edges when backlit. Both the green and the purple varieties fire up in the fall—yellow, red, and orange. And the smoke tree is a tough plant. It is drought tolerant, doing best in rocky, sandy soil, but, in my experience, it can tolerate heavy clay soil too.

Unfortunately, the winter branch structure of the smoke tree/bush is not so impressive. These shrubs also get a lot bigger than people plan for. "What doesn't?" you might well ask. But they *really* get big. My *Sunset Western Garden Book* says 25 feet tall, and

Figure 12.33 Wonderful orbicular smoke bush leaf

as wide when not grown on a single trunk as a tree. That is over two stories tall and wide. Most of the mature ones I see are about 10 to 15 feet. Think about it.

Pruning Smoke Bushes

The more I prune, the less I prune for size reduction. That's because, although it seems to work for the first few years, a shrub or tree continues to gain in root mass. Pretty soon the plant is growing back so fast—faster and faster every year—that the futility of trying to keep it to a given size becomes obvious. And heavy pruning stimulates the growth of many straight-up, skinny shoots (water sprouts) that are not only ugly but impossible to get rid of by repruning. So I recommend that you don't try to keep your smoke bush smaller, even with good, selective pruning.

Smoke bushes are also hard to prune because they increase in size by sending up straight, skinny, unbranched new shoots that just sort of end in a cluster of branching and leaves. "Stick-ups," I call them. They look a lot like water sprouts (the common result of mal-pruning or overpruning), but they're not. It's just how these plants get bigger. Unfortunately, the stick-ups look awkward in contrast to the lower, internal, more arching, prettier branches. People are tempted to prune them all off—which doesn't prevent the plant from getting bigger but just stimulates more stick-ups. Whatever you do, don't go down that road.

So, when I'm asked to prune a smoke bush, I first tell the owner to forget size reduction and that I can't get rid of the stick-ups. If it is going to be too big for the spot, we move it. But things can be pruned to *look better* by following the same counterintuitive rules used in rehabilitative pruning for previously mal-pruned plants. To wit: Prune off some of the most curvaceous branches that are lying on the ground, especially if they seem floppy or extend farthest out in the bed (see Figure 12.34). Oh, and, as always, deadwood, deadwood, deadwood. A little judicious thinning of the prettier, denser areas will create less of a contrast with the straighter new growth. Don't cut off the stick-ups. Okay, maybe just one or two that bug you the most, but then you have to stop before you get into trouble

Figure 12.34 Pruning of smoke bush: Dotted lines indicate dead wood; solid black indicates branches to be removed; the "stick-up" branches remain.

Do not prune

Do not prune

Do not prune

Do not prune

(that is, stimulate the formation of more and more stick-ups). All in all, don't remove more than, say, a fifth of the foliage, and probably a lot less. Quit while you're ahead.

What I Don't Know

I read other people's pruning books and visit botanical gardens, and I was surprised to find that some books list the smoke tree as a good plant for "stooling" (sometimes called "coppicing"), which means cutting it to the ground annually or to a low framework (one or two feet high). I have even seen a young smoke bush stooled at Filoli in the San Francisco Bay area. We are told that this will make for even larger, wonderful purple leaves, and I have no doubt that that's true. And it should make for a lower—albeit very broad and uniformly straight-branched—shrub. But I have never seen a smoke bush that has been stooled for five, ten, or twenty years, and I'm not yet convinced that stooling will be successful over a long period of time.

And I suspect that an annually coppiced smoke bush will still get quite tall and wide, eventually resulting in a massive shrub probably two-thirds the size of its same-aged, unpruned counterpart. That's pretty big. But I don't know. If you know of a smoke bush that has been successfully (or unsuccessfully) coppiced for over twelve years, be sure to contact me. I am loath to make any recommendations for pruning that I have not experienced myself. What I *do* know (from experience) is that a lot of bad pruning advice is dished out in a lot of pruning books.

Furthermore, I don't really know how smoke "bushes" become smoke "trees." Is it because the plant was grown in a crowded area? Can they be pruned to a single trunk? Is it a variety? Or, like many other shrubs, do old ones just naturally turn into little trees, shading out their own lower branches? I just don't know. I almost didn't write about smoke trees because of my lack of knowledge, but then I thought maybe some reader who does know could clue me in, and until then, new gardeners will at least know more than they did before.

OTHER STICK-UP PLANTS

Several other shrubs and trees share the smoke bush's unfortunate habit of increasing in height with straight new shoots: Pacific wax myrtle, stranvaesia, enkianthus, huckleberries (especially the evergreen huckleberry, *Vaccinium ovatum*), and azaleas, especially deciduous azaleas. In general, the same pruning guidelines apply.

PACIFIC WAX MYRTLE
(*Myrica californica*)

This is a great drought-tolerant, informal hedge plant or small tree. But be aware that its mature size is 30 feet. Even if it's pruned as an informal hedge, you need to expect at least 10 to 25 feet. That is a lot of feet. Some books say it can be used as a formal (sheared) hedge.

ENKIANTHUS
(*Enkianthus campanulatus*)

A highly regarded specimen plant, *E. campanulatus* grows slowly from a shrub into a 20-foot tree. Some other species stay a bit smaller. It needs more water than most people want to give it. The trunk and branches are classy, and it arranges itself into horizontal tiers. It has good fall color and small, white-pink bell-shaped flowers. My unimpressed husband called enkianthus "a glorified blueberry." I thought that was pretty funny. Enkianthus does have the stick-up branches problem. Leave as many as you can bear. Most pruning is deadwooding and some cleaning out of branch unions (branch crotches). Although I fear to put it in print, I have seen one that was sort of "cloud-pruned." It looked great and none the worse for wear. But such pruning is too labor intensive, and it's definitely *not PC* according to PlantAmnesty.

EVERGREEN HUCKLEBERRY
(Vaccinium ovatum)
In my opinion, evergreen huckleberry is an underused shrub. It has glossy green leaves with bronzy new growth in the spring. It grows shorter in the sun, say 3 feet, and taller in the shade, up to 8 feet. It can be very useful for narrow places. As for pruning, it almost always develops the gray stems of dead wood. Prune them out. If some stick-up branches are ruining the good looks of your fine shrub, *don't* prune them off. *No, no!* Instead, thin out the remaining, thicker parts and it will look better.

STRANVAESIA
(Stranvaesia davidiana)
Stranvaesia is a fairly uncommon evergreen shrub that shares the stick-up growth habit. It is drought tolerant, grows to about 8 to 15 feet high, has reddish new growth in the spring, coppery tinted foliage in the fall, and nice clusters of reddish berries. Its main feature, for me anyway, is its usefulness in stumping young horticulture students. They can't tell what it is and wonder if it might be a cotoneaster or pyracantha. I also like to pronounce it's name like Bela Lugosi in a vampire movie, so that it rhymes with Transylvania, complete with rolling 'r', chin up and wide eyes.

I like stranvaesia. There is even a short version, low stranvaesia (*S.d. undulata*). It's more like 4 to 5 feet tall. I especially enjoy finding both planted together in the same yard. Stranvaesias are prone to fire blight, therefore avoid pruning them if possible, and especially avoid shearing.

Prune both kinds as described earlier for other stick-up plants. I recently converted a sheared stranvaesia hedge into an informal hedge using the principles of rehabilitative pruning. It took about three years to complete the conversion and it is now about 3 feet taller and 2 feet wider than it was (I took out some lawn to accommodate it). Unlike the formal hedge (which had to be pruned three or four times a year to remove the massive amounts of straight shoots), I now tidy it up about once a year removing far less foliage, and taking far less time.

Summary
• Smoke bush and other stick-up plants are difficult to prune. The new growth on these shrubs sticks up awkwardly—straight, skinny, and unbranched. Do not attempt to

tidy or shorten these plants by pruning off this new growth—it just stimulates more of the same.

• You can make these plants look better by deadwooding and thinning, and by taking off some of the lowest branches.

CHAPTER THIRTEEN

Vines

Vines are those plants that can't stand up on their own. No backbones, as it were. They need outside support to get up to the sunlight, where they will flower and/or fruit. In nature, the support system is usually a nearby tree or some other plant. Another word for "tree" is "arbor," as in Arbor Day. Was the first grape arbor a tree? Nowadays, vines have trained people to provide support for them—you know, like trellises, walls, arbors, and pergolas as well as ornamental trees and shrubs.

KINDS OF VINES

There are all kinds of ornamental and fruiting vines, and all kinds of ways to categorize them. I like to divide them into three groups, according to their support needs. Some, like clematis and grapes, *twine or lash* themselves onto an *open support system* (wire or lattice). Think of Indiana Jones using his bullwhip to lash onto a tree limb so he can swing across the open pit. Then there are those such as ivy, trumpet vine, and Virginia creeper that *cling or grab* onto *flat surfaces*. These vines have hairy, aerial roots or suction cups. Think of the suction cups on an octopus arm. Finally there are those that use the *grappling hook* method of getting up in the world, like bougainvillea and climbing roses. The pirate throws a rope with a grappling hook onto your ship and swings over with a knife between his teeth.

Why should you know these differences? So that you will use the proper support system. A *twiner* can't get up a concrete wall, but a *clinger* prefers one. Your hooker, er, I mean *hooking vine*, would like to get to the top of a pergola (or your shed roof) and

spread out. Note that most climbing roses need some canes to travel horizontally in order to bloom. If you want to train the rose on a vertical trellis, you will need to tie it on, bend new lateral canes to the horizontal, and tie them in. And be sure to periodically remove the old ties before they girdle canes.

WHY VINES?

I like vines. I study gardens trying to figure out what makes them look good, and I have concluded that the easiest way to turn an ordinary landscape into a glamorous garden is to add a vine or two. They figure prominently in garden magazine photos and coffee table books. They can double your blooms or add a second season of color to a shrub or tree. My *Clematis montana* climbed into the lilac bush one year, blooming pink at the same time the lilac bloomed lavender. Suddenly catching sight of it, framed by the lace curtains of my living-room window, almost made me swoon. Another year it ran up a rhody that appeared to bloom soft pink (the clematis) and later, dark pink (the rhody).

A clever gardener of my acquaintance planted a clematis with dainty white flowers to grow through, and contrast with, the leaves of her purple-leaf plum tree. Fabulous! She plans her garden triumphs. For most of us, they are just lucky happenstance. Vines maximize garden space by growing up, and not out. This is great for people with small urban yards. Vines are also useful for hiding unwanted views—for example, filling an empty, blank wall or covering the top of a chain link fence or the face of an ugly brown board fence.

MINDING VINES

Unfortunately, vines are not, generally speaking, a low-maintenance proposition. Along with hybrid roses and fruit trees, vines are for the industrious and forgiving gardener. I think of vines as the problem children of the plant world. If you don't constantly mind them they get into trouble. They are known to run away from home, fall off walls, and go where they have been forbidden, and some can damage your house. Periodically, they get really scruffy looking. Many don't play nice with others. Some are rightly considered juvenile delinquents—English ivy (*Hedera helix*) and silver lace vine (*F. aubertii*). Still others have been tried and convicted as adults: kudzu in the South, morning glory here, and of late, the escaped clematis that is naturalizing and taking over greenbelts. But, don't get me wrong. I like vines; really I do. I own several. And my friends tell me there are even some well-behaved ones. Give me a minute and I'll try to think of them.

PRUNING VINES

Now that you know that your vine's mission in life is to climb up your tree and smother it, you can start to think of pruning as a way of keeping it controlled. A common scenario is that of the new gardener bringing home a vine from the nursery, say a clematis, and planting it next to the house. They tie it to that cute little fan-shaped trellis on the wall. The first two years it grows to the right size, blooms, and looks great. But a few years later, all the flowers are at the ends of the vine that has grown over the roof, into the neighbor's yard, and up his tree. The bottom of the vine (the part still on the cute fan-shaped trellis) has turned into fat, barren, ugly stems. And in the winter, the vine looks pretty bad. In fact, it looks like what the plumber pulled out of the P-trap under the clogged sink.

Pruning is done to keep a vine, especially the flowering or fruiting part of a vine, where it is wanted, which is to say, nearby. And pruning a foliage vine—say Boston ivy that has reached the top of the house—is done to keep it from heading into the gutters and onto the roof. And from covering up the windows. Pruning can also minimize the ugly periods in the life cycle of many vines, and that includes the evergreen *Clematis armandii* and the semievergreen *Akebia quinata*.

Such pruning can be quite radical looking. Some clematis vines are cut to a foot off the ground annually. Sometimes you take the power hedge shears to the tangled clematis or honeysuckle mess gathered on top of the fence. Sometimes you chisel, rip, and cut the clinging vine halfway back down the wall, or maybe even back down to the bottom. Don't worry. It will grow back as much as 10 feet or more in two years. Other vines have 90 percent of all *new* growth cut off annually, like the climbing roses, grapes, and wisterias. The practice of this large-scale pruning seems so radical that it is often incomprehensible to the new gardener.

WHAT CAN GO WRONG?

I suspect that not much can go wrong with pruning on vines, at least not the common ones listed here. If you prune your clematis at the "wrong" time it will just delay, not prevent, blooming. This is only a big deal if, say, you chose the variety of clematis to bloom simultaneously with the climbing rose it is threaded through. If you are pruning just to get it off of the woodpile, timing is not very important. And, I suppose if you pruned a vine too often, say every other week, it wouldn't have enough time to set up flower buds and bloom.

You must *allow time and space* for the plant to grow and set up flower buds. This is why it doesn't work to cut the vine back to the *top* of the fan-shaped trellis. After pruning, it resumes growth from the cut ends. It grows new shoots for a while, then it sets up flower buds and blooms on top of the roof. Instead, you need to cut a stem down to an inch or so from the ground. There it breaks bud and grows up with several new stems to 3 feet tall—where it blooms *on*, not over, the trellis.

RENOVATION FOR OLD VINES

Gardeners commonly renovate old, abandoned vines of all kinds by cutting them down to the ground, or more accurately, to a foot above. Or you may cut a vine way back to a manageable framework and then retrain the rampant new growth in coming years. The vines rarely, if ever, die. Instead, they grow back amazingly fast and look better than ever. Okay, *occasionally* making a big cut on a really old clematis stem/trunk will kill it. So if it has three big, old stems (by big, I mean ¾- to 1-inch diameter), only cut one or two this year. Save one for backup. If you have only one really big, old stem, grit your teeth and do it. Or you could decide you like the way your vine blooms on top of the basketball hoop.

MY BEST ADVICE

Having witnessed many people's successes and failures with vines, I proffer the following advice: New gardeners get to plant one and *only one* vine per arbor, trellis, or wall. Give your vine a lot of room. Really, *a lot more room* than you are planning. And use an arbor or arch that is much bigger than the ones you commonly see in garden centers. By the time a vine gets going and blooming on one of those, you won't be able to walk through it. The arbor needs to be 2 to 5 feet taller and wider than you so that the vine can gracefully spill off. A clinging vine needs a lot of room too, like one entire side of your house. It won't work to put it on the mailbox post. That's not enough space. And, given that many vines have an ugly phase, put that arbor or trellis *away from the front porch*,

Some Common Vines

TWINERS

Akebia (*Akebia quinata*). Semievergreen, small purplish blooms. Because of small blooms, vine is best located outside the back door or a window. Its ugly phase is fall/winter (black spots on leaves). Can produce unwanted seedlings and can rip off siding.

Clematis (*Clematis*). Beautiful flowers, interesting seed heads. *C. montana* and *C. armandii* are most vigorous. Many others are more well behaved. Ugly phase is winter (tangled mess) for all, including the evergreen *C. armandii* (yucky leaves). Difficult to get out of shrubs and trees.

Grape (*Vitis*). Ornamental and fruiting. Nice leaves, plus grapes. Most kinds could cover up a tree, easy. Annual pruning and tying needed. Grapes bleed (run sap) if pruned too late in the winter; scary, but doesn't hurt the plant. A really nice new purple-leaf ornamental grape is now available, *V. vinifera* 'Purpurea'.

Honeysuckle (*Lonicera*). Sweet-smelling flowers. Ugly phase is summer (chronically aphid-ridden) and winter (tangled mess, the "honeysuckle mattress").

Kiwi (*Actinidia*). Makes kiwi fruit, has nifty fuzzy stems. The fruiting kiwi vine needs to be tied to a stout and sturdy trellis. It wants 30 feet, which is the length of a house. Male and female plants are needed for fruit (most kinds) and, remember, one mature vine can produce fully one ton, that's 2,000 pounds, of fruit. There is a wonderful variegated ornamental species (*A. kolomikta*). Its leaves are green, pink, white, and rose on the same plant; many leaves are green splashed with white. It can burn in direct sun. It needs only 15 feet.

Passion flower/Passion vine (*Passiflora*). Exotic-looking flowers. Ugly phase is winter (tangled mess, dead stuff on bottom).

Wisteria (*Wisteria*). Beautiful blooms and, when pruned regularly, can have an interesting winter structure. Reckless, fast growing, and strong. It gets under shingles, rips up fences, tears apart balconies, sneaks with runners on the ground over to distant plants, and jumps onto nearby trees. Prune off 90 percent of new growth every year. These are the runners/whips, soft, and about as thick as an electrical cord. Leave unpruned the stiff parts: the trunk, scaffolds, and flowering spur systems spaced roughly 1 foot apart.

CLINGERS

Boston ivy (*Parthenocissus tricuspidata*)/Virginia creeper (*P. inserta*). Great red fall color. These deciduous vines have nice winter pattern, especially on concrete walls with seams. Difficult to get off wood siding for painting, gets under shingles. Both need a lot of wall space, like 30 by 30 feet.

Climbing hydrangea (*Hydrangea anomala petiolaris*). A lovely, well-behaved vine. Pretty white flowers. Looks good in the winter. The only clinging vine recommended for growing up an established tree's trunk. Good for low walls.

Ivy (*Hedera*). *H. helix* (English) and *H. canariensis* (Algerian) are considered too vigorous. But others are better behaved. One, *H. helix* 'Congesta', a cathedral ivy, is a truly small vine with interesting overlapping spires when grown on a wall. Needs only 2 by 2 feet. Good for foundation walls, fences, the water meter (with a cutout for the dial face), lamp posts, and so on.

Trumpet vine (*Campsis*). Cool, orange, trumpet-shaped flowers. Needs a lot of wall space, like 20 by 20 feet. Not well behaved. Spreads by suckering roots. When dug, tiny bits left in soil grow into plants.

HOOKING VINES

Climbing rose (*Rosa*). Beautiful, sweet-smelling flowers. Needs tying. Bend young canes horizontally to promote flowering. Ugly phase is summer/fall (black spots on leaves). Like others of its kind, stems of these plants can cause pain (thorns).

maybe down below in the garden. With some distance, the vine still looks elegant even when the leaves are mildewed, black spotted, aphid-ridden, or gone for the winter.

Summary

Many vines are pruned heavily, either once in a while or annually. This is done to keep them blooming and/or fruiting nearby, or to prevent them from overcoming the house, the tree, or the garden. Hard pruning can minimize the ugly stage in the life of many vines.

CLEMATIS *(Clematis)*
by James "Ciscoe" Morris

One of the plants that sometimes give pruners a problem is clematis. This is because there are three different kinds of clematis, and each kind needs a different style of pruning.

The key to pruning clematis is bloom time. One type of clematis blooms in summer or fall. Another blooms only in spring. A third type blooms in spring, followed by another bloom in summer or fall. Often it's difficult to tell which type you are dealing with. If you don't know, it's probably wiser to wait a year to find out and then prune accordingly.

Summer Bloomers

The easiest clematis to prune are those that bloom in summer or fall (bloom after the end of May). The classic summer bloomers are the *lawsoniana* hybrids. The huge blossoms flower on wood produced in the spring. These late bloomers are best pruned to within about 2 feet of the ground every

Figure 13.1 Summer-blooming clematis **A.** Summer bloomer pruned in spring **B.** Summer bloomer in mid-spring **C.** Summer blooming!

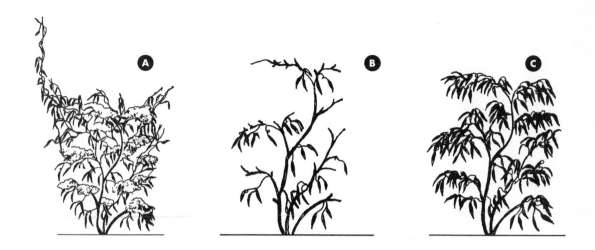

Figure 13.2 Spring-blooming clematis **A.** Spring bloomer blooming **B.** Spring bloomer pruned in late spring **C.** Summer regrowth

year. The summer and fall bloomers can be pruned in fall, once the vine takes on that dead look, or in early spring before growth begins (see Figure 13.1). I prefer pruning them in fall so I don't have to see that ugly, dead-looking foliage all winter long. When planting summer-blooming clematis, I usually prune it to within 6 to 12 inches of the ground for the first two to three years. That promotes low branching for a fuller plant with more flowers.

There is at least one exception to this rule. That is the relatively rare *C. maximo wicziana.* This plant blooms with small, fragrant, white flowers late in summer and is generally evergreen here in the Pacific Northwest. To preserve its evergreen nature, it should be pruned before growth begins in spring in the style described for *C. armandii* below.

Spring Bloomers

The spring-blooming clematis include the fragrant *C. montana* and *C. armandii.* These bloom only on the previous year's growth. Prune them a month after the bloom fades in spring (see Figure 13.2). These plants quickly resemble rat's nests if they are not kept under control. I prefer to keep them thinned out in a style that I refer to as the tracery effect. To achieve this, prune out all but two or three basal stems. Allow only as many lateral stems as the trellis can support without looking crowded. Prune all other growth back to the main branches. To prevent *C. armandii* from becoming bare at the base, pinch low-growing branches and train laterals to cover the base.

Repeat Bloomers

Clematis that bloom in the spring *and* again in the summer (or fall) are the most

Figure 13.3 Repeat bloomer **A.** Spring repeat bloomer **B.** Pruned in spring after bloom **C.** Fall bloom

confusing. The China native *C. lanuginosa* with its attractive 6-inch flowers is a good example. These bloom on old wood in spring and new wood in summer or fall. To preserve the old wood that will produce the spring bloom, prune lightly in fall or late winter. Remove only deadwood and weak, spindly growth. In spring, immediately after the bloom, cut back branches that flowered to the main framework branches (see Figure 13.3). This will promote the new growth that will bloom in fall, and again in spring. The only problem with the spring and fall bloomers is that the need to preserve the old wood for the spring bloom makes it necessary to leave the ugly dead-looking foliage on the trellis all winter long. I guess a little ugly foliage during the winter is a small price to pay for two displays of spectacular clematis flowers each season.

The Young Clematis Vine: A Note from Cass

I caution gardeners not to heavily prune a clematis before it gets established, which can take up to five years. Sometimes hard-pruning a young clematis can kill it. (Although many books recommend cutting new clematis vines to three buds, i.e., 2 inches, I assume, to create multiple stems.) In fact, it seems to me that new clematis vines are prone to dying at the drop of a hat in any case. Don't bump it, or step on it, or let your dog near it for a few years. Maybe protect it with a little chicken-wire fence. But if you do that, don't let the vine grow *through* the fence; later, the clematis will be tough as nails.

WISTERIA *(Wisteria)*

"Wisteria is Latin for work." I wish I knew who said that. How true it is! Under those beautiful color photos of arbors splendidly vine-laced and hung with glorious lavender blooms, there ought to be a warning label: "This Vine Can Be Dangerous." It wants to cover . . . everything!

Ciscoe Morris, renowned Northwest media horticulturist and author of the preceding section on clematis pruning, tells a story about the time he was house hunting. He saw a home advertised for sale in the paper—three bedroom, two bath, in a desirable neighborhood. The price was unbelievably low. Upon arriving at the site he realized why. Two ancient wisteria vines had overcome the home, actually lifting it off its foundation. Their stems were as big as tree trunks. I doubt it was an exaggeration. I have seen wisteria tear off balcony banisters and smother entire trees, and everyone knows what they'll do to your roof and gutters.

I guess I didn't know when I planted mine against the railing of the covered porch eleven years ago. But I'm not sorry, either. Despite the work, there is nothing quite as wonderful as a wisteria. I love the high excitement of watching the spring buds plump up and then expand. It's so . . . erotic. Later, when it's in full bloom, I watch people point and sigh as they pass my house. It makes my entryway look so horticultural. And wisteria smells sweet. In the winter the long fuzzy pods dangle down just above my head, as if asking to be petted. And I must oblige.

Early Training

I read a lot of pruning books. They amuse me. I especially like the one that insists that you make your wisteria vine single trunked. To do that, I think you'd have to guard it twenty-four hours a day with a flashlight. Although I have seen single-trunked wisterias, the more common sight is a main trunk composed of twisted and coiled stems. They look like an unruly rope. Wisterias just grow

like that. I don't know why they don't girdle themselves, but they seem to do just fine.

If you want to force side branching at a particular point, you head-back (lop) the main stem at that point (see Figure 13.4). In my case I planted a vine at the front porch post. I wanted some framework scaffolds to run along the handrail. *Scaffold* is a word meaning one of the main branches of a tree, or in this case a vine, as opposed to the main trunk or the many smaller side (lateral) branches. Then I wanted the main trunk to continue up to the little porch roof and grow along the trellis over the entryway stairs. At the place where the little vine was headed back—the level of the handrail—four or five new shoots developed. Two of the new shoots were tied into position to become the handrail scaffolds. Another one was tied to the post to continue up as the main trunk. Another shoot was shortened (to about 3 inches) in hopes of forcing it to bloom. And the last shoot was cut completely off to prevent overcrowding.

People are often reluctant to head-back a wisteria, wanting it to get as big as fast as it can, and not wanting to hurt the poor little dear. But trust me, heading will in no way slow it down, and a small cut on a young plant does little harm. It simply makes it branch out. Major scaffolds on a wall or lattice should be spaced at least 1½ feet apart to allow room for the blooms to dangle down without running into each other.

All along the major scaffold branches (about every foot or two) you will want to create persistent frameworks of lateral branches reminiscent of the spur systems

Figure 13.4 Training a wisteria vine **A.** Use a heading cut where scaffolds are wanted. **1.** Cut tip. **2.** Cut off low runner. **B.** Train new shoots that came from heading cut. **3.** Tie up. **4.** Tie down. **5.** Shorten. **6.** Remove. **C.** After cuts **D.** It blooms in the spring! **7.** Trunk. **8.** Scaffold. **9.** Bloom.

found on an apple tree. These spur systems hold the fat flower buds that expand into blossoms. Each little spur system will be a woody framework of branches ranging from about the size and shape of a hand to (after many, many years) roughly the size and form of a forearm.

Instead of growing a series of these tidy, well-behaved spur systems, the young wisteria branches will send out a lot of skinny, rapidly-growing, soft, vegetative

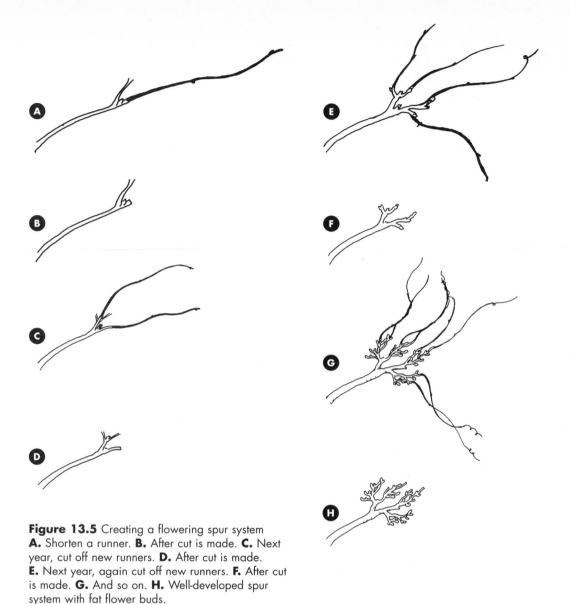

Figure 13.5 Creating a flowering spur system **A.** Shorten a runner. **B.** After cut is made. **C.** Next year, cut off new runners. **D.** After cut is made. **E.** Next year, again cut off new runners. **F.** After cut is made. **G.** And so on. **H.** Well-developed spur system with fat flower buds.

shoots (which make leaves, not flowers) in the spring and summer. These shoots are called *runners*, or sometimes *whips*. You will need to force some of these runners into becoming a spur system by heading them back to 3 to 6 inches from where they join their parent scaffold branch (see Figure 13.5). The majority of the runners should be completely cut off at the scaffold. Most of the shortened runners will fatten up and become spur systems, but some may die and become stubs. And still others seem determined to be vegetative, taking off with a vengeance next year and refusing to produce flowers. Don't ask me why.

Arbor or Trellis

Wisterias are often allowed to run to the top of an arbor or overhead trellis and to spread out, with the blooms dangling down from above. Quite lovely. This too necessitates frequent pruning or the wisteria eventually piles up on top of itself, creating a mess of dead canes below and preventing blooms from hanging down. After it has been trained to a framework of scaffolds and spur systems, you will need to cut off 90 percent of the *new* runners every year and shorten the rest. Whenever necessary, whack back any lateral runners that try to escape off the sides of the trellis or that threaten to climb into neighboring plants or structures.

I think that wisterias look best trained to an overhead trellis. Such an arbor or trellis needs to be very strong and sturdy. Use 4 by 4s, at the very least, as the main posts and the top piece should be made of 2 by 4s. Forget those flimsy lattice things you see for sale in catalogs or at garden stores. Your wisteria will eat it for lunch. The smartest trellis I've seen is a system of metal pipes, sunk in concrete, disguised with some lattice.

If the wisteria trellis is attached to the house, I strongly recommend that you plant the vine on the *farthest* post and let it fill in by growing toward your house. You will be glad that you gave yourself that slight edge in later years as you find yourself tugging and tearing runners out of your gutters and shingles. And trust me, you need only one wisteria.

Standard or Tree

With the help of a very sturdy stake or two, a wisteria can be trained into a sort of small free-standing tree. This is commonly done in the South. When the young vine reaches the top of the stake, whack the wisteria back to force it to bush out. The resulting young shoots later become the main scaffolds or framework of the tree canopy. The idea of the wisteria tree appeals to me since it can be situated in the middle of the yard, far from anything else. There it can be vigilantly watched and pruned on all sides.

Summer Runners

With all wisterias, scores of runners will reach out into empty air every summer, hoping to grab onto a nearby helpless victim. These runners are roughly the thickness of a phone cord. Cut them off before they strangle a sleeping dog or trip the gardener. This can mean pruning every month if the runners are in your way, say on your front porch. In any case, be certain to prune them off before winter, when they harden off (stiffen and become woody, holding tightly to shingles, tree limbs, etc.) and are more difficult to remove.

In the summer I whack back the runners just to get them out of the way (making them about 5 or 6 inches long). I do more detailed thinning and pruning in the winter, when all the leaves have dropped off and I can see what's going on. After the summer pruning, my wisteria vine looks sort of like a feather boa, just to give you an idea. By the way, those runners can be used to make a tasteful simple wreath. Just wind them into a circle. Same with grape vines.

Underpruning

The most common mistake is to not prune a wisteria enough. More than 90 percent of the *new* growth (the zillions of long runners) needs to be cut off annually. A single runner can grow 12 feet in one year. After the framework is established, shorten many of the runners to six buds. Remove the vast majority completely, every year! (See Figure 13.6.)

Overpruning

I didn't think it could be done, but I have witnessed three novice pruners overprune wisteria. Given a mature flowering vine, the pruner is tempted to remove not only the runners but the desirable, woodier, persistent spur systems as well. Very old vines have flowering spur systems that are as long as your arm. If they are pruned off or even shortened too much, the vine will appear sparse and have too few blooms. And the next year, such overpruning will result in a wild (wilder than normal) resurgence of flowerless runners. The general idea, then, is to shorten or remove all the long, wild runners, and leave all the spur systems to flower like crazy.

Radical Renovation

If it gets away from you or you have moved into a home that already has an enormous wisteria tangle, grabbing and strangling everything in sight, show no mercy. Lop, saw, and chainsaw whatever is necessary to get it back down. I suggest you cut several feet below where you want the regrown vine to be, since you will experience an upsurge of new shoots the following spring.

As with all heading cuts, the new growth will occur directly beneath the cut and will head up from there. You will need some room to let the wisteria regrow over the next few years. New growth will be vegetative (not flowering) and rampant for a few years. I wouldn't be surprised if some major stems die back partially or totally, if you make cuts 1 inch in diameter or more. But I doubt that you will kill the plant. As some stems die back, cut off the dead bits. Other stems will supply the replacement shoots to be tamed in upcoming years.

Tools

My relationship to grapes and wisterias changed dramatically when I finally bought a specialized tool called an ARS long-reach pruner. No, it's not a traditional-type pole pruner. It's a lightweight, expanding, aluminum pole, with a trigger and a standard scissors-type pruning head. Some (interchangeable) heads have a sort of "grabber," perfect, I imagine, for pulling tough runners out from under shingles and fascia boards. Such a tool saves hours of ladder work, but can cost about eighty dollars. I got mine from the A. M. Leonard tool catalog (800-543-8955; *www.amleo.com*); ask for the wholesale catalogue.

The long-reach pruner is only good for water sprouts and vines. It lacks cutting power for thicker or woodier branches. The only other tools required for wisteria are loppers and hand pruners. Occasionally you

Figure 13.6 A. To promote blooms, remove most runners and head-back others. Finish pruning in the winter, when you can see. **B.** Next year's blooms **C.** Summer runners: Watch out, here they come! Cut them back every two weeks to get them out of the way. **D.** Finish pruning in winter, removing runners but leaving woodier parts. **E.** Each year there are more and longer blooms, and trunks and scaffolds thicken.

may need a pruning saw. Don't forget the twine and nails or whatever you use to tie up the vine. And retie as needed to prevent girdling.

My Wisteria Won't Bloom

The most common comment I get at classes is "My wisteria won't bloom." It's natural for these vines to take between three and seven years to start blooming. I have read that frequent, proper pruning may help them to begin blooming sooner, or at least more. On the other hand, some people have old vines that have never bloomed. I'm told that these are seed-grown plants or "mules."

I have often heard root pruning recommended to force an older vine to bloom. Basically, this means that you use your shovel to cut the roots in a circle (or dotted circle) a foot or two from the vine. I have also heard people recommend fertilizer formulated to encourage blooms (relatively low in nitrogen). However, I have been faced with such a vine and had no luck with either technique. In that case, as with all nonperformers, removal is the best option, and no one will blame you for it.

How to Kill Your Wisteria (and Other Woody Plants)

If you just cut the offending plant to the ground, it will not die. Instead it will regrow rapidly. If it, or any other woody plant that you want to kill, is impossible to dig out, I recommend using Roundup (glyphosate). Roundup is a liquid herbicide often used to kill dandelions and other weeds. Farmers use it to kill weeds before planting, since it

does not poison the soil. The herbicide binds tightly to soil particles, making it unavailable to kill other things. It is quite deadly to the plants it touches, though, and is translocated throughout the plant system including the roots. Although I would never declare this or any chemical (organic or nonorganic) safe, it seems to pose the least threat to the environment, given what we know.

As an herbaceous weed killer, Roundup is mixed with water and sprayed on weeds. This is best done on a dry, hopefully warm, spring day. In two weeks the weeds will be yellow and dead, and the soil will be ready for replanting and mulch (to prevent weed seeds from germinating).

In the case of woody plants, like the non-blooming wisteria, volunteer holly, blackberry, ivy, cotoneaster, or what have you, you use Roundup as a "cut-stump treatment." Purchase the jug of concentrated Roundup, usually about 18 percent active ingredient (the glyphosate). You'll use only a small quantity of liquid, to which you'll add the same amount of water. The directions should say "Apply a 50 to 100 percent solution of this product to freshly cut surface immediately after cutting." They don't say how. I use a glass rubber-cement bottle that I have gone through great pains (involving emptying glue and then peeling residue out with my finger) to prepare for use as an herbicide container. It has a brush built into the cap, and the bottle fits nicely into my tool-belt pocket. But it is an imperfect system, as the cap corrodes and leaks, and it is illegal to store the herbicide in that container. I regret that there is no appropriate commercial applicator available. Be sure to wear rubber gloves and safety glasses, and take care not to get any in a stream or on yourself.

The cut-and-paint system is best done in late summer, not spring or winter. The only serious problem I have heard of arising from the use of Roundup as a cut-stump treatment is the situation where a desirable plant, usually a tree, is "attached" to the sucker, sapling, or tree being cut and painted. Trees of the same species in close proximity can have roots that graft to each other underground. One man e-mailed me to say that after he poisoned the stump of a bigleaf maple he cut down, the poison "flashed-back" into a nearby bigleaf maple and killed it. Think the situation through, please.

Roundup used as a cut-stump treatment could be a powerful tool in the war against invasive exotics such as ivy, Scotch broom, and wild clematis. Unfortunately, those good people who are most willing to do the work (the volunteers) are often the least willing to use chemicals of any sort. I can tell you,

though, that Roundup is the last chemical that even organically minded professional gardeners give up. And I would be sorry to see it banned.

Summary

Prune wisteria a lot, removing up to *90 percent of the new foliage* every summer. Cut off all those skinny runners and/or shorten some to about 4 to 6 inches from the scaffold branches or trunk. This will encourage them to turn into persistent, blooming branch systems (spur systems). Leave all the older, previously shortened branch/spur systems that are attached to the main trunk(s) and scaffold framework. You can tell the branch/spur systems from the runners because they are thicker and stiffer (woodier), and have relatively fat flower buds on them. Summer pruning is done just to keep the wisteria from taking over the world. More precise pruning is done in the winter, when all the leaves are off and you can see all the trunk, scaffolds, spur systems, and runners.

CHAPTER FOURTEEN

Trees

205

Thank God for Dr. Alex Shigo. I feel lucky to be living at the same time as Dr. Shigo, and to have been privileged to hear him speak in person on numerous occasions. Dr. Shigo is a Ph.D.–type doctor, as opposed to a medical doctor (M.D.). He has been described as the "Sir Isaac Newton of Arboriculture" (the study of trees). As the chief scientist for the USDA Forest Service, he did pioneering research on how and why trees decay (rot). And he has finally described exactly how a tree limb is attached to a tree. Before Shigo's work, engineers could not explain how a limb could withstand wind stresses and snow loads. These are only two of his contributions to the field of arboriculture.

Not only has Shigo done an incredible amount of primary research, he is a powerful public educator. He travels extensively throughout the world speaking (and listening) to the arborists who actually work on people's trees. And he tells them that many of his "discoveries" are actually not really new, but that his main job has been to make them known. He says, "I carry the club." Presumably, he means the club used to wake people up by hitting them over the head.

TREE BIOLOGY AND PRUNING

Shigo's research has now been generally accepted as the "New Tree Biology" (which is the title of one of his books), and it is revolutionizing the practice of tree care. I include this information here because a lot of new research (in the past ten or twenty years, both by Shigo and by others) counters what many people hold to be true. The following is a partial list of conclusions based on these new scientific findings:

• Wound paints and pruning seals do not prevent decay in trees.

• "Flush cuts" cause rot.

• Fertilizing a sick tree does harm.

• A tree limb is not really attached to the trunk, except for a small portion at the base of the limb.

• Adding amendments (like peat moss) to a planting hole increases neither the growth rate nor survival rate among newly planted trees.

• After a tree is transplanted, pruning-back branches to compensate for root loss reduces, rather than encourages, reestablishment.

• Weaker trunks develop on those trees that are tightly staked at the time of planting.

I could go on, but you get the idea.

For those wishing to find out more, or for those who still have serious doubts about any of the above, I recommend getting a copy of the third edition of *Arboriculture Integrated Management of Landscape Trees, Shrubs and Vines* by Richard W. Harris, James R. Clark, and Nelda P. Matheny (published by Prentice Hall, Upper Saddle River, New Jersey, 1999). Arborists just call it "Harris." It's a very large and expensive textbook, but it comes as close as anything I've found to being the Compendium-of-All-Horticultural-Knowledge. It references and summarizes the major scientific findings in the field. Unfortunately, like most textbooks, it makes for some very dry reading. Those wanting to go right to the source will want to locate either *A New Tree Biology* (1986) or *Modern Arboriculture: A Systems Approach to Trees and Their Associates* (1991), both by A. L. Shigo (published by Shigo and Trees, Associates, Durham, New Hampshire). These are also large textbooks, and like Harris they may be hard to find in the local library. If you don't care about the subject that deeply, you may just continue through the tree section of this book, which you already know is lightweight, cheap, and easy to read.

Compartmentalization

The world can be roughly divided into inanimate objects, plants, and animals. Animals often avoid injury and death by moving away from the wound source. Pain, caused by fire, for example, is the signal to move away. Trees cannot move away from the source of an injury. (An old saying is "Trees will stand for anything, because they can't run.") When an animal is injured, it must stop the bleeding and mend the damaged part (the broken bone). When a tree is injured, it must stop the *decay* (same as rot) that wants to eat it up, and grow a new replacement part, say a new limb. If you back the car into a tree, thus breaching the protective bark, the rotting organisms can then charge in and start to eat (decay, rot) wood. The decay begins with the injury. A good analogy in humans is gangrene that follows a war wound. Unfortunately, there are no antibiotics for trees. And pruning paint or wound seal does *not*, as we all once believed, keep decay from entering the tree. The tree does the defense work internally.

Trees are the largest, longest-lived organisms on the planet. The reason is an incredible defense mechanism called *compartmentalization*. When it is injured, a tree *walls off* or *compartmentalizes* the injured area internally by chemically altering the wood in predictable patterns. Trees don't heal; they set up barriers to rot and then try to outgrow it. Sometimes a tree compartmentalizes well, and only a small pocket of rot remains sealed off inside the trunk as the tree grows larger. Or perhaps decay spreads up and down in a long column. It varies. The only wood that is guaranteed not to decay after an injury is the new wood—the rings of wood laid down after the tree was damaged. If you see a hollow tree, you will know that the size of the hollow is exactly the size the tree was when it was topped or injured.

Compartmentalization is why that pocket in your tree where a limb rotted out doesn't get bigger; it just makes a cute home for a squirrel. It's easiest for a tree to wall off a dead or dying limb (see Figure 14.1). It's somewhat harder for the tree to wall off a gash on the trunk (see Figure 14.3). It's hardest for it to wall off the rot that comes charging down the trunk when a tree has been topped (see Figure 14.2). It's sort of the difference between bruising your knee, cutting off your hand, and cutting off your head.

This new understanding of tree biology means that arborists no longer bother to dig out a rotten "cavity" in a tree and fill it like a dentist. And we especially don't dig back into "sound wood" or drill a hole to drain water out of a cavity, since both these activities make a brand-new wound, allowing decay to enter previously protected areas of the tree. The tree must then set up new barriers, taking up valuable space and energy.

Figure 14.2 Look inside: pattern of decay after a topping cut

Figure 14.1 Look inside: pattern of decay from a stub cut limb

Whether your particular tree dies back totally or partially when wounded depends a lot on how well it walls off wounds generally. This varies according to a tree's species or genetic makeup—even among members of the same species there is genetic variation. There are several species of trees that don't compartmentalize well. In the trade they're called "rotters." They include bigleaf maple (*Acer macrophyllum*), alder (*Alnus* spp.), willow (*Salix* spp.), and poplar (*Populus* spp.).

You want to help these plants by prompt removal of injured limbs and by avoiding wounding or cutting (pruning) healthy green wood. Cut out the deadwood and little else. Leaving deadwood rotting on a tree acts, as Shigo says, like "a big stick of sugar" drawing in the rotting organisms. Besides, it looks bad.

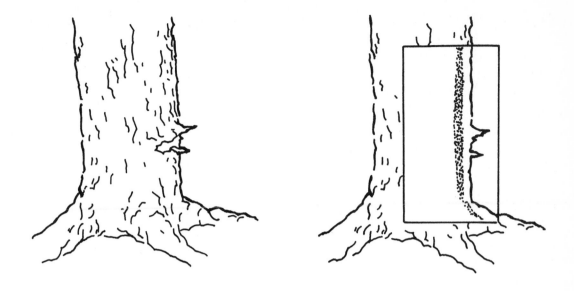

Figure 14.3 Look inside: pattern of decay after a trunk injury

The Branch Collar

Shigo tells us that branch wood is different from trunk wood. This is a hard one to get your mind around, but it explains how limbs are held onto, and into, trees. In the spring, a tree will wake up and add a layer of wood (the new ring) to a branch. Then the trunk wakes up and puts on its own new layer of wood. Where the trunk wood meets the base of the limb, it laminates over the limb, creating sort of a bulge called the trunk/branch collar. For short, this area is now referred to as just the *branch collar.* The branch is, for the most part, separate tissue from the trunk and is just held in place, buried inside the trunk by each year's new ring of wood. When a knothole drops out of a piece of lumber, you are seeing the branch wood drop out of the trunk wood.

This lamination process is repeated every year. When you prune off a limb for whatever reason, you should be careful to cut off only the branch wood and avoid cutting or wounding the trunk wood. This means you cut *to* the collar but *not into* it, since that would open up the trunk to decay.

If you cut *too far out*, though, the branch will die back to the collar, leaving a stub (see Figures 14.4 and 14.5). The dead stub changes color and, in response to the cut, the collar plumps up. Next year the collar starts to creep out the stub, trying to enclose it (this process is called *wound closure*).

In general, the right place to cut is almost like a dotted line where the branch starts to get fatter near the trunk. People always want me to tell them the right "angle" to make the cut, but that angle varies, as do the collars themselves. Some species have

Figure 14.4 Where to cut **A.** Stub cut (too far) **B.** Collar cut (just right) **C.** Flush cut (too close)

big and fat collars, some species have their collars inside the trunk (another hard one to visualize). But by studying illustrations and looking at the collars on real trees, you'll soon get the idea. Looking at recently dead branches, with the plumper collar and different colored wood, can help you determine the characteristic angle of your tree's collar (see Figures 14.6, 14.7, and 14.8).

Figure 14.5 Look inside: patterns of decay from **A.** stub, **B.** collar, and **C.** flush cuts

Flush Cuts

Older arboricultural literature recommends cutting a limb off "flush" with the trunk. Shigo recognized and explained how damaging flush cuts are to trees. The practice of flush cutting began as a misinterpretation of a true observed phenomenon. When a limb is removed, the tree responds by covering over the wound in the process called wound closure. With a flush cut, closure can happen faster than when a proper collar cut is made. Wound closure is important because it seals off the *entryway* for decay and allows the tree to continue adding rings of healthy new wood. Even if the entryway is closed, some decays can continue internally, but the real problem with flush cuts is that, unlike collar cuts, they open a second door through which decay reaches trunk wood (remember that trunk wood is different from branch wood). Any possible benefit of rapid closure is far outweighed by the unnecessary damage a flush cut does by opening up the trunk to decay. Arborists of the past mistakenly equated closure with the tree being "healed."

Also note that while it is true that rapid closure can be the sign of a healthy tree, artificially inducing closure with flush cuts is still bad. It is sort of like making a hospital patient get out of bed and run. While it is true that a person seen running is probably a healthy person, causing a sick person to run will not make him well.

How Trees Die

People mistakenly assume that since a tree didn't die right after having nails or a car driven into it, it's all right. Wrong! Trees usually die from a series of blows over a long time, and when one dies it's usually because of the proverbial straw that broke the camel's back. You may have a giant column of dead rotten wood walled off inside your tree from some old wound and when the drought hits, well, whammo! You have a dead tree. Your trees can wall off a lot of abuse, but that doesn't mean you should abuse them.

How to Prune a Tree Limb

When pruning heavier branches and ones that have narrow crotches (branch attachments), it is wise to use a multicut system of removal (see Figure 14.11, page 215). Remove the weight of the branch first by cutting it off farther out from the trunk. Start by making an undercut, then saw from the top down. The undercut will prevent your saw from getting stuck. Once the weight is gone, more accurate pruning to the collar is easy. Then, at the bottom of the collar, also make a correctly angled undercut. This will prevent tearing the bark when you make the final cut from the top down (see Figure 14.9). If it is a very narrowly angled branch crotch, you may be forced to saw completely from the bottom upward; otherwise, you will inadvertently cut into the collar (see Figure 14.10). This is awkward, but necessary, since the nicest thing you can do for your tree is to make *a good collar cut*. In fact, most pruners spend a fair amount of time correctly positioning

Figure 14.6 Branches die back naturally to the collar. **A.** The collar is usually obvious as a bulge.

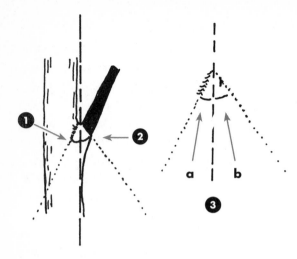

Figure 14.7 If no collar is visible, locate the branch bark ridge and use geometry. **1.** Branch bark ridge **2.** Collar **3.** Angle *a* = Angle *b*

themselves, checking from different sides, before they begin to saw.

Summary

The nicest thing you can do for your tree is to figure out where the branch collar is and cut the limb off to, but not into, it. The branch collar usually looks like a bulge at the base of the limb. If it is a big limb, take the weight off it first by cutting the limb off farther out. For the final cut, make an undercut first, before sawing down. This will prevent ripping the bark. If the crotch angle is narrow, you may have to make the entire cut by sawing from the bottom upward. Don't bother with pruning paint or seals. They don't work.

PRUNING YOUNG TREES

A young tree is one that is less than fifteen years old. Shigo says it's a tree that is still

all dynamic mass. Such a tree is difficult to damage with pruning. But, whereas the young tree *can* take a lot of pruning, it generally doesn't *require* much, since most of the limbs of a young sapling are temporary and will be removed as the tree grows up. But by knowing what to cut and why, the pruner can solve many problems before they become serious and much harder to correct later in the tree's life.

The main goals of young tree pruning are (1) removing suckers, (2) removing temporary limbs, and (3) minimizing included bark.

True Suckers

Suckers are the straight, thin, rapidly growing shoots that arise from the trunk, the *base of the trunk* (which is called the *trunk collar* or *butt flare*), the roots, or below a graft union. Trunk suckers are often caused by wounding, such as flush-cutting limbs or mower/string-trimmer damage. Suckers can also occur when a graft union no longer suppresses the growth below. Remember, suckers are *not* the same as water sprouts, which occur on tree *limb*s when they have suffered injury or mal-pruning.

Graft Union Suckers

The *graft union* is the place where two parts of a plant are spliced together, usually a desirable top portion (the *scion*) attached to the more vigorous, original trunk or roots. The graft union on a weeping cherry tree will be high up on the trunk and will look like a bulge just beneath the weeping branches. The trunk below belongs to a standard

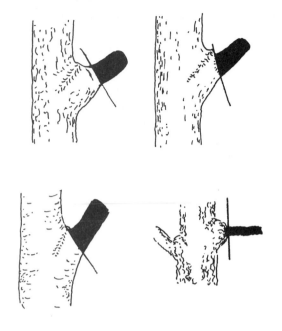

Figure 14.8 All are correct collar cuts: There is no set angle for a cut.

cherry, the weeping limbs just above are the desirable branches. On other trees, graft unions on the trunk, either near the crown or near ground level, can be spotted as a sudden change in bark color or trunk diameter.

Graft unions sometimes fail, especially if the tree has suffered from drought, malpruning, late freeze, or other cultural stress. When this happens, dormant buds below the union begin to grow out into suckers. These suckers must be removed on a young tree (even if they have gotten rather large) or they will overtake the tree (see Figure 14.12).

Getting Rid of Suckers

You have the greatest chance of success by correcting sucker growth on young trees. Cut the suckers off just as they meet the trunk. If a sucker is a few years old, it may even have developed a collar. Cut to it, but not into it. Cutting suckers too far out (leaving stubs) or too close (flush cuts) stimulates even more suckers to grow. But note that even if suckers are pruned "just right" they may keep returning to plague the tree owner for a lifetime.

Moderately better luck can be had by pruning in the summer, though even this is not a magic bullet. The best "cure" for suckers remains prevention, and that is done by keeping the tree healthy.

Ground-Level Suckers

Suckers sometimes arise from below ground level, from a young tree's roots located near the trunk. This is often the result of the tree being planted too deep. This is a common problem both in the landscape industry and in volunteer and homeowner tree-planting projects. A survey conducted by the Bartlett Tree Research Laboratories found that 93 percent of the test group (363 trees) were planted too deep by professionals (see "National Epidemic Reported: Improper Planting Is Killing Trees," by E. Thomas Smiley, pages 36–39 in the December 1991 *Arbor Age Magazine*). This is indeed an astounding percentage. Not only do these trees send up troublesome suckers, they fail to thrive and many can die before reaching maturity. (Shigo once said that if he was granted one

Figure 14.9 A common mistake in limb removal: No undercut causes bark to tear.

wish, it would be that trees not be planted too deep.)

If you find such a tree, and it is young, dig it up and replant at the correct level. If it is too large to dig, just pulling the soil away several inches from the trunk collar (hopefully with positive drainage) can help immensely. You will know where the correct level is by carefully digging down the trunk with a trowel until the trunk flares out, turning into the major roots of the tree. This is the *trunk collar* or *butt flare*, and in a correctly planted tree it would be above ground, with roots disappearing just under the soil. If the tree has been planted too deep for a few years, know that some new roots may have developed in the higher soil level. They are an emergency system, like their above-ground counterparts, water sprouts. Such roots are thin and pale and they don't enlarge where they meet the trunk. Ignore them and continue to dig down looking for the characteristic flare of trunk collar, which will be the tree's original and correct soil level.

Temporary Limbs

As the urban tree grows up, it is usually necessary to remove the lower limbs to create clearances for people, cars, houses, and such. Almost all the limbs the new owner sees on a young tree are these *temporary limbs.*

A limb on a trunk "feeds" the portion closest to it, making that part of the trunk stronger, and giving it good taper. A poor nursery practice is to tightly stake a sapling tree and quickly limb it up. This creates a taller tree, faster. But they are weak trees

Figure 14.10 Another common mistake in limb removal: Cutting from the top down, the narrow angle forces a flush cut.

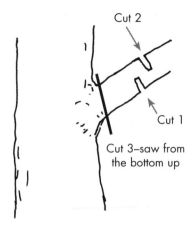

Cut 2

Cut 1

Cut 3—saw from
the bottom up

Figure 14.11 The three-cut system. On narrow, angled branch crotches, you may have to saw entirely from the bottom upward.

that may even flop over when untied. When limbing up a young tree, you need to do it neither too soon or too late. Delaying pruning until the limbs have become large is equally bad for the tree. Older trees are less able to deal with the larger pruning wounds. Also, if cuts are made one directly above the other, pockets of rot may coalesce between them. It is therefore best to vary cuts at different heights and sides of the tree over the course of years.

A good rule of thumb is that at any given time two-thirds of the length of the tree trunk should be covered in a leafy crown. Another good rule is to *prune off temporary limbs before they become half the diameter of the trunk.*

If the young sapling tree is planted on a narrow median strip, the only limbs in existence may interfere with people walking down the sidewalk. In this rare situation, it is recommended that the temporary limbs be headed-back, out of traffic's way, but allowed to continue feeding the lower portion of the trunk (see Figure 14.13). This is one of the few exceptions to the rule, "Don't head-back tree branches." When enough of the crown is above head height, begin to slowly remove the temporary limbs, perhaps two a year from opposite sides and different heights on the trunk.

And, of course, all cuts should be made to the branch collar.

Included Bark and Double Leaders

The other target of early pruning is included bark and the correction of double leaders. When a tree has two equal leaders (a *leader* is the uppermost or leading part of the trunk), separated at a narrow angle, bark can get trapped between them (called *included bark*). There is no connecting wood holding the two leaders together. As the two leaders expand they may push each other apart, and the tree can break. Another common included-bark situation arises between the

Figure 14.12
Remove suckers from the base of trees.

Figure 14.13 To accommodate foot or vehicular traffic, **A.** head-back temporary branches (remove them in 2–3 years). **B.** Now pedestrians can walk by.

trunk and a large side branch when the crotch angle is narrow. As the tree grows larger, the area of disconnect increases, as does the weight of the limb. These limbs are the ones prone to breakage, damaging the tree and ruining its good looks. Worse yet, if the tree is on a right-of-way or near a structure, people or property could get hurt. A little enlightened intervention early in the life of a tree can prevent a major disaster twenty years later.

Not all narrow crotches have included bark. If the attachment is a good one, you will see a little rumple of bark at the point of juncture. If there is included bark, the bark will disappear in a fold. V-shaped crotches often have included bark. U-shaped crotches are okay (see Figure 14.14).

If you find an included-bark branch on a young tree (a young tree that is going to grow up to be a big tree), go ahead and prune it off to the collar. In the case of a double leader (in which the two main leaders are the same size, with a narrow crotch), one of the leaders should be removed. The result can look quite severe, and the tree may even become lopsided. But fear not. The tree will grow new scaffold limbs higher up on the trunk and right itself naturally. Because there is no collar on a double-leadered tree, the cut will seem too steep or flush; but it is a proper cut nonetheless (see Figure 14.15).

Figure 14.14 Spotting included bark on a narrow-angled crotch **A.** In a V-shaped crotch the bark disappears into the trunk. This is a weak attachment. **B.** In a U-shaped crotch the bark is pushed up. This is a strong attachment.

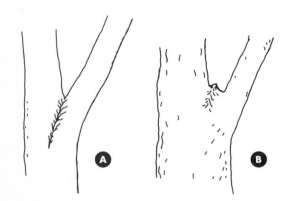

The Causes of Included Bark

A fair amount of branch crowding, including double leaders and included bark, is again the result of poor nursery industry practices. A three-year-old sapling looks like a buggy whip (it has no side branches). Nursery people discovered that homeowners would more readily buy a tree if it looked like a miniature tree with a crown. Such a tree is created by heading back the sapling, forcing branches to grow out in a cluster at the top. Unfortunately, the person who bought the tree must then spend the next several years training it back to a central leader and then slowly removing the lower, temporary branches as it gains height. And so it goes.

Other trees just seem prone to growing with included bark and double leaders, especially trees with an opposite branching pattern. Responsible nurseries maintain a strong central leader on shade trees and do follow-up pruning to alleviate overcrowded branches.

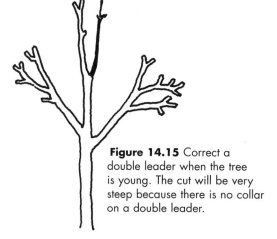

Figure 14.15 Correct a double leader when the tree is young. The cut will be very steep because there is no collar on a double leader.

Exceptions to the Rules

Small maturing ornamental trees (as opposed to large, shade trees like oaks and elms) may already have their major limbs chosen, and they should not be trained back to a central leader. And they may be crowded at the point where the major limbs meet up. Certain cherry trees are an example. To "correct" it would mean ruining the tree.

Learn the natural habit and the estimated mature size of your tree. A nursery person can readily supply this information. Take, for example, the Florida or Eastern dogwood (*Cornus florida*). It often grows with an open, U-shaped, or even V-shaped double trunk. These forms have even more aesthetic interest than the single-leadered ones. And since dogwoods are sensitive to pruning cuts, don't try to make one into a single-leadered tree. The crown of a purple-leaf plum tree (*Prunus cerasifera* 'Atropurpurea') is likely to have mostly included-bark scaffolds. To try to eliminate them would be to eliminate the entire crown, creating a nightmare of water-sprout regrowth and perhaps even killing the tree. And, since this tree rarely gets large enough to do major damage when the limbs fail, the situation is best ignored. Another small tree, the Japanese maple (*Acer palmatum*), often has a crown consisting of included-bark scaffolds. Many of the new *fastigiate* (narrow growth form) trees developed to fit street right-of-ways consist mainly of included-bark limbs. But since these limbs are of relatively small size, and their angle to the trunk remains acute to the end, they are not considered dangerous.

On a medium- or large-growing young tree, you will sometimes come across a side branch or double leader that is too large to remove (i.e., a cut more than 2 or 3 inches). In this instance, attempt to suppress *one* of the leaders or the competing branch by selectively heading it back to a large lateral.

Summary

Young trees can take a lot of pruning, but they don't usually need much. Remove any suckers growing from the base of the tree. As the tree grows up, you may remove the lower limbs, a few at a time, from opposite sides of the tree, to allow for foot traffic. A few thoughtful cuts minimizing included bark (which causes weakly attached limbs) can prevent serious damage from occurring many years later. The old headmaster's adage goes "As the twig is bent, so grows the tree." It's true for the student, and it's true for the tree.

BIG TREES

There is a famous quote from William Blake that goes: "The tree which moves some to tears of joy is in the eyes of others only a green thing which stands in the way." Perhaps your tree is in the way of a water view, or of foot traffic, or maybe you just feel that it has gotten to be too much. And maybe you have some safety concerns. But since, unlike the people Blake writes about, you actually like your tree, you may just want to prune it.

If that is so, you will need to hire a qualified, well-insured arborist to do it. Only a fraction of the people in the "tree service" business are really qualified. I am reminded of an old cartoon kicking around the Plant-Amnesty office. It shows a tree worker and a hapless customer looking at a tree that has been "pruned" to look like a very short, sharpened pencil. In the caption the tree worker is saying, "I told you I was honest and hard working, I never said I knew what I was doing." Buyer beware! Later in this section you will find information on how to hire an arborist.

Terminology

Writing about big trees, and pruning big trees, is complicated by the fact that there are so many terms floating around, most of them poorly defined. And the terms and definitions keep changing. Many are rough equivalents but not exact synonyms. I've listed some of these below. The exact meaning of each term will be contained in the

The Key Terms

Big tree; shade tree (big and deciduous); large forest tree (deciduous or coniferous and native)

Small tree; patio tree; ornamental tree; flowering tree

Crown thinning; thinning; lacing; safety pruning; crown cleaning

View pruning; vista pruning

Crown reduction; dropcrotch pruning; de-horning; selective heading

Utility pruning; line-clearance pruning; directional pruning; V-pruning; rabbit-ear pruning

Interlimbing; layering; windowing

Topping; round-over (smaller topping into a ball shape); heading

Risk assessment; hazard tree evaluation

Spurs; gaffs; spikes

third edition of the epic trade book *Cass Turnbull's Guide to Pruning*.

Dangerous Trees

Many people want to prune their trees because they are concerned about safety. Every time a big storm hits, the news programs on television feature homes crushed by fallen trees and tree limbs. This brings on what we call the "second wave of damage": Fearful tree owners pay to have their trees topped in the misguided belief that this is the right thing to do (see Figure 14.16). It is not, and neither is dropcrotch pruning (both of which are dealt with in Chapter 1, Basic Cuts).

If you have concerns about safety, the rational thing to do is hire a qualified arborist to do a "risk assessment," or what we all used to call a Hazard Tree Evaluation.

Trees don't fall over or break apart because they are too big. They "fail," as it is called, because there is a flaw. Some common causes of failure are included-bark (see pages 215–217) trunk or butt rot, root rot, poor soil structure, insufficient trunk taper, severed roots from construction damage, saturated soils, and a host of other things—including previous bad pruning!

An analogy to having a risk assessment for your tree is having a building inspector assess the potential damage to your home in the event of an earthquake. We all initially think about skyscrapers as being more at risk during an earthquake than smaller buildings. But we learn that whether or not the building "fails" is really more a matter of factors other than size. A well-constructed skyscraper will

Figure 14.16 Topped tree five years later **A.** Water sprouts become weak new crown. **B.** Column of decay continues down the trunk (inside).

stand when a smaller, old, brick building, situated on a mud flat, will "fail."

A similar situation is true for trees. Unfortunately, it is difficult for arborists to see inside trees or tell what is going on under the ground. But they do know how to read a lot of signs that escape the average tree owner. After a hundred-year storm hit Seattle, with massive destruction to trees and property, I asked several arborists how many of the tree failures they could have predicted. I was surprised at the answers, which averaged 90 percent. I would have thought a lot less. Perhaps it was the gift of hindsight.

Risk Assessment

There is a sort of formula that arborists use to rate the relative risks posed by trees. They assign a number to each of three factors and then add all the numbers together. First the arborist determines the most likely point of failure—a limb, a trunk breakage, or the entire tree falling over. Then he or she assigns numbers to the following: (1) the likelihood of failure, (2) the weight of the part that will fail, and (3) the presence of a target. The third factor, the target, is the most variable. A building, especially a home, directly beneath the tree would have a high rating. A parking lot might get a medium rating because during the night nobody's parked there. Or the target factor could get a low rating—for example, in the case of a tree in the woods that is not near any path or trail. I was surprised to learn that paths and roads have a relatively low rating because at any given moment a person or a car is not likely to be directly under the tree, especially at night. Whenever someone comes up to me with concerns about their tree, I ask, "What would it hit if it fell down?" If it is out of the way, somewhere in the back yard, I am not particularly worried. If it is a giant old cottonwood that has recently developed a lean, situated directly above the baby's room, with mushrooms growing out of the trunk, I say, "Get an arborist out there tomorrow, or better yet, today!"

I do not do risk assessments myself. Like the young medical student, I see symptoms everywhere, but I am not qualified to make the diagnosis. It takes years of experience picking up after trees that have "failed" and a lot of training to do a proper job.

Only a fraction of the arborists who know how to prune will have the additional experience to do a risk assessment. If you do not

live within range of a qualified arborist, you should order the "Hazard Tree Packet" from PlantAmnesty and do the best you can.

WHAT CAN BE DONE

No tree can be declared "safe"; a strong enough wind will blow down anything. Also, like a doctor doing a physical exam, the arborist might miss something. The problem is compounded by the fact that we can't talk to our patients and say, "How have you been feeling?" There is also no modern medicine for trees: no antibiotics, no bypass surgery, and no kidney transplants. So if a tree is very sick or dangerous, the answer is usually to take it out. The key to plant health care is prevention (as it was for humans two hundred years ago). A saying from John Davey (the father of modern arboriculture) is "Good health defies disease." That's as true today as it was in 1910. Most of the tree owner's job is to protect the tree from drought stress, construction damage to the roots, and malpruning. Please note that the vast majority of the average tree's roots are in the top 3 feet of soil, and they extend far beyond the drip line of the tree (the imaginary circle on the ground directly beneath the outermost branch tips). (See Figure 14.17.) In general, the kind of root system that is depicted on a thousand product labels and logos does not exist in nature. That picture, the one that shows the crown of the tree mirrored by the root system, is responsible for thousands of tree deaths every year.

People want their trees declared totally safe or totally dangerous, but most trees fall somewhere between these extremes.

Figure 14.17 The roots on the left are what we *think* it looks like underground, but in reality the roots are shallow and widespread, as on the right.

Occasionally we will find an obviously high-risk tree. Such trees must come out, and fast. But if the tree in question just has some flaws, there are mitigation measures that can be taken. These measures (cabling, bracing, thinning) are, in my opinion, overused and over-relied-upon. They *do not* guarantee safety; they simply lower the risk.

The most obvious, and least used, solution is to move the target: Shift the picnic table, move the swing set, relocate the bike path. If a much beloved, historic tree has become iffy, you should fence it off, to keep people from harm's way. And you should know that *the vast majority of damage done to people and property by trees comes from limb breakage*, not from the fallen tree sensationalized on the TV evening news.

The other things that can be done to lower the risk of damage are cabling (a cable is strung between two parts of the tree), bracing (a rod or bolt is put through two parts of the tree), and thinning. Thinning can be done to remove broken limbs, to reduce wind resistance, or to lessen the weight of

an at-risk branch. All three techniques have the potential to do more damage than good. So, here again, find an arborist with good judgment, good credentials, and years and years of experience. Then ask for his or her opinion. And the main thing is to listen and then—here's the hard part—*follow their advice.* They will not want to be pinned down as to whether or not a tree is dangerous, for obvious reasons. But you still want a summary of the best of their knowledge and judgment. A good question to ask is, "What would you do if it was your tree?" They hate that question. A good arborist will not encourage you to retain a dangerous tree, no matter how much you love it. Nor will he or she encourage you to remove a perfectly sound-looking tree simply because you suffer from a bad case of arborphobia. The good arborist likes trees but is objective and experienced enough to know when they need to come out.

PRUNING BIG TREES

There are other reasons to prune large trees: to develop a view, to create clearance, to make a big tree seem less imposing to the owner, or to enhance its natural beauty and health. First, here are a few general things to know about big tree pruning.

As Dr. Shigo reminds us, all pruning cuts are "wounds." On trees, 90 percent of all cuts will be true thinning cuts. Selective heading is reserved for a very few limbs, under special circumstances—to repair a previously headed branch, or to shorten the limb that is hanging over the chimney (but which is too big to be thinned off entirely), or to shorten a limb that is "overextended" (for example, one that grew from a water sprout).

The amount of live wood taken off, and the size of cuts, is a lot less than I first surmised when I started hanging around with arborists. (See Figure 14.18.) It is the forsythia that can take a lot of heavy pruning, not the oak tree. And know that a mature tree will not need as much pruning after the initial "cleanup." You can have your arborist back every three to five years for a touch-up if you like, and if you live close to a large tree, I would have it inspected every five to ten years. The average healthy, full-bodied, middle-aged shade tree can have about one-eighth of the foliage removed without doing harm. Most of the work is deadwooding, though. The older, more experienced arborists who speak at conferences can often be heard to say, "The longer I am in the business, the smaller and fewer my cuts become." The very outside limit for tree pruning is about one-quarter of the foliage, and that is under special circumstances. The various kinds of pruning that I describe in my view tirade below (see "Trees and Views," next page) are the same as ones used for other reasons.

The older the tree is, the less live-wood pruning it can withstand, both in the total amount of foliage removed and in the size of the cuts. I think of the *average* tree's life

---

Figure 14.18 Mature tree pruning: **A.** Remove smaller side branches for clearance; **B.** the older the tree, the smaller—and fewer—the cuts.

span as roughly equivalent to ours, not the hundreds or thousands of years popularized in stories. Also, a tree in ill health should not be heavily pruned. With old and sick trees, almost all the pruning done will be dead-wooding. Minor adjustments can be made. Like elderly people, old trees just can't adapt well to big changes. Keep them comfortable and be gentle. But unlike people, many trees reach their maximum state of beauty when they are well aged.

TREES AND VIEWS

The word "view"—like the word "top"—causes my stomach to clench. Both of these words will jump out at me, whether spoken in a room or printed on a sign. That's because I associate them with so much tree damage. Every month someone calls PlantAmnesty to report that their neighbor has topped, cut down, or poisoned their tree to get a view. The desire for water views, or distant vistas (say, of the valley or the mountains), has become a driving force in real estate. The "sweeping view" is the ultimate status symbol of the '90s and '00s. Some communities even have "covenants" to force people to top or remove their trees whenever someone uphill complains, no matter how far away their house is or how newly arrived to the neighborhood they are.

People—even good, ecologically responsible people—can easily succumb to view fever. It is a lot like gold fever. There is free money for you, if your neighbor would just get rid of that unimportant tree. Personally, I can't wait for the day when status symbols are such things as the amount we sacrifice for the public good and the degree to which we use recycled materials.

Don't be fooled. Nobody owes their neighbor a view. If you want to cut down your own tree, well, that's a different matter. The trouble is in the language. People say "my view" as if they owned it. They do not. They *own* a window that may or may not have a view. And that view can change over time. Just as the crime rate in your community, the economic health of your region, and the state of your schools affect the value of your home, so too does the presence or absence of a water view. It is perfectly okay to go to your neighbor and try to bribe them to remove a tree. But you shouldn't demand they do so. You wouldn't expect your neighbor to remove the top story of their house to improve your view, would you? Their tree has real value to them. Not only does it add a dollar value to their property, it creates privacy. And unlike a view, it works as a green utility to the benefit of the entire city. It creates oxygen, cools the city, slows runoff, cleans particulate pollution, and stays the creation of smog—something that ruins everybody's view! And you expect your neighbor to remove it. Sheesh!

Can you tell I have strong feelings on this subject? I do. I even got to use the term "view monger" on the front page of the *Wall Street Journal* once. Someone has to speak up for the trees, or they will disappear, quietly and one at a time, from every hillside facing water. In fact, this is already happening, since every tree on a hill is in the way of several people's "uninterrupted views."

But there are some things that an arborist can do to improve a view. Most of them will make the tree a more acceptable *part* of the view. If you examine calendar photos and landscape paintings you will discover that a foreground, such as a tree, is an essential part of the picture. If it were true that the best view is of "uninterrupted" water, then people on ocean liners would find the vast empty Pacific breathtaking. They would sit in their deck chairs a thousand miles from land, ooh-ing and aah-ing at the vast expanse of "uninterrupted" water. Instead, it is boring, boring, boring! A water view is most spectacular when it is contrasted with something else in the foreground—like islands or, you know, trees.

VIEW PRUNING

Arborists cannot prune to make a tree invisible, as many people seem to think. Thinning can make a tree seem more airy and delicate (see Figure 14.19, below right). Crown raising,

by taking off some lower limbs, can help you see the water below. Occasionally, if the tree is quite close to the viewer, it may be successfully windowed. This is done by pruning out a few larger and smaller limbs to create a layered look. It often helps to remove a few limbs on the other side (but not exactly opposite) to create a visual balance. Not all trees can be windowed successfully, but some lend themselves to it by virtue of their natural habit—pines, some cypress, and some cedars. PlantAmnesty publishes a great little booklet titled "Saving Trees and Views," should you need more illustrations and information on how to prune your tree or to create a saner view covenant.

We also sell a "View Packet" that is helpful if you are having to battle view mongers in your own neighborhood. My best advice to you is (if you are not bound by law to comply) to firmly refuse to do anything to your tree. If you can, force yourself to be rude. Accommodating view seekers does

Figure 14.19 Pruning for view (left to right): **A.** Windowing **B.** Skirting **C.** Thinning

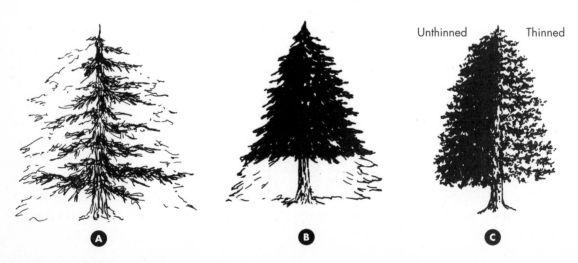

Unthinned   Thinned

Ⓐ   Ⓑ   Ⓒ

not appease them. It has the opposite effect. They feel validated and will be back soon with more demands. So now you know my real feelings on the matter.

HOW TO HIRE AN ARBORIST

It can seem so difficult to find a qualified arborist that many tree owners try to skip it altogether. They just want to get enough information so that they can tell a "tree service" what to do. This is a bad idea. There is simply too much to know and too much skill involved.

And under no circumstances should you be doing the pruning yourself! The tree business is among the most dangerous professions in the nation. It ranks right up there with blasting, logging, and underwater welding. I personally know of three arborists who suffered major accidents, causing a coma, amnesia, and the breakage of almost every bone in the body. The workers' compensation rate for arborists reflects this. Currently it is $2 per person hour in Washington State, which partially accounts for the seemingly high hourly rate that real arborists charge. They also must invest in expensive equipment—chippers, stump-grinders, enormous dump trucks that are forever breaking down. And then there is the liability insurance that they should carry. When I make a mistake, someone's peony dies. When an arborist makes a mistake, a person is injured, a car is crushed, or a home is damaged.

Also, tree care is a highly competitive profession. A great deal of an arborist's time is spent on bids and estimates. And since they will see you only once every five years or so (if they get the job at all), there are a lot of unbillable hours, which have to be recouped in the final rate they charge each customer. The take-home message is this: Arborists need to charge a high hourly wage, and they deserve it. They are, after all, risking their lives. What other professional whom we hire does that?

So take the time to find, and be willing to pay for, a qualified arborist. Start by looking in the yellow pages of your telephone directory. Open it to the section headed "Tree Service." Depending on where you live, between 10 percent and 100 percent of the advertisements will list "Tree Topping" as a service. Cross them off the list. Then look for a professional affiliation. Most good services are members of the ISA (the International Society of Arboriculture) or the TCIA (Tree Care Industry Association, the organization previously known as the NAA or the National Arborist Association). What is it with everybody changing their names, anyway?

Look for the words "ISA certified." Anybody can call themselves an arborist. It's just a word, like "landscaper." It means "tree person." An ISA-certified arborist, on the other hand, has passed a rigorous test on tree knowledge. They will carry a white card in their wallet that they are just dying for someone to ask them to show. You can get a list of certified arborists by contacting the ISA (800-335-4391). An ad that says "Licensed, Bonded and Insured" doesn't really tell you much. Besides, a lot of the bad tree boys lie. Ask for the phone number of their insurance carrier. Then call to make sure that they are carrying at least $1 million in liability.

Another way to find a good arborist is to check with someone who would know. That is *not* the guy at work who just had Acme Whackme Tree Experts in to top all his trees. Your friend may be able to identify good plasterboarding when he sees it, but not good tree work. If your city has a City Forester or City Arborist, ask them for some recommendations. Or try the head person at the Parks Department.

Once you start interviewing arborists, have them write everything down. If you are collecting bids, and even if you aren't, have them use the American National Standards Institute's (ANSI) A-300 Pruning Standards. You don't have to know what they are. But your arborist should. If you came home to a topped tree, you would be able to sue for damages because you specified the work by these standards. To get a copy of the standards, write the TCIA at 3 Perimeter Rd, Unit 1, Manchester, NH 03103, or call 800-733-2622. You can purchase a pruning standards packet that contains the A-300s, plus several other pruning standards and articles, plus an article that compares the standards, by contacting PlantAmnesty at *www.plantamnesty.org*, or write to us at P.O. Box 15377, Seattle, WA 98115-0377.

What's to Know About Arborists

A tree service business that has a large advertisement, or a lot of employees, or that has been in business for many years, is not necessarily better than the smaller, two-man operations that are springing up everywhere.

Good arborists do not need a bucket truck to get into trees. They climb them, getting in with ropes and ladders. At all times they are tied into the tree, suspended by a rope that is attached to the top of the tree. They prune their way down and out, at times walking far out on very thin limbs. The other end of the rope is tied to a body harness called a saddle. Thus, if they fall, they swing to the trunk. It is fascinating work to watch—they climb and rappel in trees like trapeze artists or rock climbers. When pruning, they more often use pole pruners and large handsaws than chainsaws. Nor do they climb trees using spikes that are attached to their boots. Those spikes (a.k.a. gaffs or spurs) cause damage to trees, sort of like puncture wounds on people. Spikes are used when trees are being removed—that is, killed.

Arborists have very large territories. If you live very far away from a qualified arborist, consider going in on tree work with some of your neighbors. Line up a couple of days' worth of work, ask your prospective arborist to schedule you in the slow season, and—if you know they are good—you might offer to hire them sight unseen. Have your local bed and breakfast put them up in exchange for some tree advice.

If you live way, way out in the country with no hope of getting a qualified arborist, you will just have to do the best you can. If you are an amateur tree lover with a thirst for more tree knowledge, PlantAmnesty and the National Arbor Day Foundation are two good sources for more information about trees. Contact the NAF at 100 Arbor Avenue,

Nebraska City, NE 68410, or call 402-474-5655.

If you are a budding professional arborist, both the ISA and the TCIA have a great deal of information for you, including training tapes, trade magazines, and conferences with lots of helpful field demonstrations.

Summary

• If you need work done on a large tree, hire an ISA-certified arborist and have him or her bid to A-300 pruning standards.

• Big trees can be thinned, limbed up, or windowed. But the amount of foliage removed should not exceed roughly one-eighth of the total live canopy. Deadwood is okay to take out and doesn't count against the pruning budget. The older or the unhealthier a tree is, the less can be done to it without causing harm.

• If you have safety concerns, hire a qualified arborist to do a risk assessment.

• Do not do large tree work yourself. It's very dangerous.

PRUNING TREES FOR POWERLINES

There is no good way to make (or feasibly keep) a big tree small. It just can't be done. They just grow faster and look uglier. And we can't let trees grow through the powerlines or the lights would go out every other day (and a lot of people would get electrocuted). This is unfortunate, since trees are pretty and wires are ugly. The best solution is to remove the big trees (that's the hard part) and replace them with smaller-growing ones. Or we could site the large-growing trees farther inside front yards so that they can crown out *over* the wires.

Undergrounding the utilities of major arterial streets, over the course of many years, is feasible and to my mind worth the cost and traffic aggravation. But reflect that it would *also* require the removal of long rows of large, existing trees. And the initiative for undergrounding would need to come from the public (not the utility companies). The combination of negatives—traffic trouble, increased utility rates, and removal of trees—could prove very unpopular.

Without permission to remove trees, the very best that line clearance crews can do is to prune trees to grow around the wires (usually in a V shape). This still looks funny, and it isn't good for trees. But it is better than topping, and there just are no other options (see Figure 14.20).

POLLARDING

Pollarding is a form of pruning "art." A special ornamental effect is achieved in keeping a big tree small: The thick trunk is in strong contrast to a relatively small, compact crown. Some trees are pollarded to accentuate secondary features, such as increasing leaf size (*Catalpa, Paulownia*) or stimulating bright-barked water sprouts (*Salix*). Correct pollarding is achieved through species selection, early training, and extensive, dedicated annual maintenance. Like other examples of pruning art, pollarded trees are rarely planted as individuals, but are best suited to mass plantings and/or as part of an overall formal design.

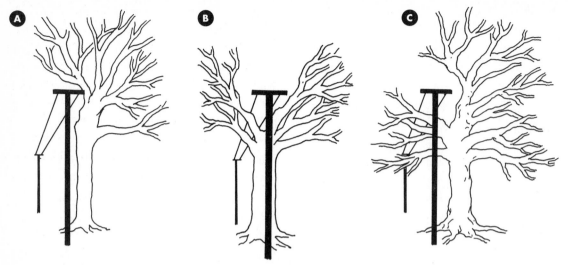

Figure 14.20 Three examples of proper line-clearance pruning: not a good thing, but doing a bad thing well. **A.** After under trimming **B.** After through trimming **C.** After side trimming

Pollarding vs. Topping

Pollarding bears a superficial resemblance to tree topping. But then again, to a man from Mars a surgery looks a lot like a mugging. In both cases somebody puts a knife in the subject's stomach and relieves him of all his money. The big difference is that one of the procedures maintains the long-range health of the subject. Pollarding, like topping, eliminates the natural beauty of a tree's branch structure. It is extremely high maintenance, just like tree topping. Unlike topping, it maintains the long-term health of the tree. In Europe, pollarded trees have survived for five hundred years, actually living longer than their natural counterparts.

How Did Pollarding Start?

Pollarding began in Europe as a practical way to harvest a tree without killing it. A young deciduous tree would be headed back at a point above the reach of foraging deer and livestock, and then regrown. The resulting water sprouts (also called suckers by some) would be cut off every year or two to be used as animal fodder, made into baskets or brooms, or bundled together for firewood. Soon the tree would form a callused knob from which the water sprouts would regrow. The water sprouts regrow annually from dormant buds on the pollard head and are cut off again and again at their points of origin.

How Is Pollarding Done?

The right species must be used. Species that are traditionally pollarded include plane trees, sycamores, *Paulownia, Catalpa*, linden (Tilia), tree-of-heaven (Ailanthus), and horsechestnuts (Aesculus).

Pruning Art

Pruning art breaks the general rules of pruning to achieve certain special effects. Successful pruning art always meets three criteria:

• The species chosen lends itself to the technique by virtue of its natural shape and degree of toughness.

• Manipulation of the plant is intensive. Pruning begins when the shrub or tree is young, and pruning annually, for the life of the plant, is guaranteed.

• The art form reflects a specific formal style and therefore matches the overall intent of the garden.

Here is a short glossary of pruning-art terms.

Topiary: Sculpting of plants. Tightly sheared geometric shapes, or likenesses of animals or even people. Topiary is often seen in estate gardens and formal rose or flower gardens. Plants chosen generally have fine leaves, can break bud anywhere, and are tough enough to take repeat shearing. Boxwood, English yew, and Japanese holly are commonly used. Sometimes ivy or other vines are trained on a framework.

Espalier: Plants are trained in two dimensions, usually flat against a wall. The technique was originally developed for fruit trees for ease of production, but its pleasing effect was soon adapted to other plants. Some plants commonly espaliered are apples, pears, quince, and pyracantha.

Pollarding: Major limbs of young trees are headed, and subsequent new-shoot growth is annually cut off to swellings called pollard heads. The result is a large-leaved "lollipop" tree, often used as an accent in formal gardens. The stark, gnarled winter silhouette adds interest in an appropriate setting. The term "pollarding" is often misapplied to common tree topping. Trees commonly pollarded include catalpa, mulberry, and plane.

Cloud pruning: One of several highly stylized Japanese pruning art forms. Cloud pruning is often mistakenly referred to as bonsai (*bonsai* means "in a pot"). Pines are thinned out dramatically, and the buds that elongate into shoots called candles are pinched each spring to cause a "puff of clouds" look to the ends.

Pleaching: The branches of adjacent trees are interwoven when the trees are young to create living gazebos, arbors, or covered promenades. Commonly used plants: willow, hornbeam, and apple.

Coppicing/Stooling: Plants are cut to the ground annually to accentuate their bright stem color or to create especially large leaves. Examples of plant materials used are red twig and yellow twig dogwood, white-stemmed brambles, catalpa, and smoke bush.

The Essential First Cut

The tree trunk or branches are headed back to the point where the pollard heads are to be located. The first training cuts on the tree should be less than 1 inch in diameter and should be made when the tree is young (Shigo defines a young tree as one that is under fifteen years old). Starting with large cuts on an older tree is unacceptable. The pollard head protects the trunk from rot. If the pollard head is removed, the trunk rots out and the pollard is ruined.

Pollard Styles

Usually trees are trained to a single head or to a series of pollarded branches originating from one point. As a simple guideline, one-third of the total height of the tree should comprise the crown and two-thirds the trunk. If the pollard heads are located too far out on the branches, the branches may break. Other styles exist, including vertical and "free form."

Sprout Removal

Sprouts that regrow from the pollard head are removed every year. Annual upkeep is essential not only for aesthetic appearance but also for tree health. Removing the sprouts every year from the time the tree is young ensures that the tree never becomes dependent on more canopy than it can grow in one year. Furthermore, if sprouts are left to become older, they develop heartwood and become less able to react to the cutting, once again allowing rot to enter the tree.

To determine whether a certain tree is a true pollard or simple mal-pruned, ask the following questions.

1. Is a suitable species used?

2. Are all cuts made during the life of the tree under 1 inch in diameter?

3. Does it have a pollard head (or heads)?

4. Are sprouts removed every year?

5. Was it chosen and planted in this spot to be used as a formal pollard? (i.e., is it part of a larger overall formal design, such as castle grounds, a rose garden, or a boulevard?)

6. Is it likely that the tree will have the sprouts removed every year through several "owners" for perhaps a hundred years? (i.e., are people being charged admission to the garden where the trees are located, or are they city trees on the public dole?)

Summary

Pollarding looks like tree topping, but it isn't. Unlike tree topping, pollarding protects the long-term health of the tree. To be real pollarding, the process starts early in the life of the tree. No cut should ever be greater than 2 inches in diameter. Pollarding can and does keep a large tree small, but maintenance is costly and can never be deferred. Numerous shoots must be removed annually for the life of the tree. Pollarding is a very formal style and should match formal surroundings.

DOGWOOD *(Cornus)*

I like the entire genus of dogwoods. There is a reason the old favorites are old favorites—they're nice. The dogwood trees (as opposed to the dogwood shrubs such as *Cornus stolonifera* and the ever-so-cute but hard-to-grow dogwood ground cover, *C. canadensis*) have nice flowers and fall color. Many have attractive fruits, and some have an elegant winter branch pattern.

Water Sprouts

With regard to pruning, the most important thing to know is that dogwood trees throw water sprouts at the drop of a hat (see Chapter 3, Suckers and Water Sprouts). Prune too much (and it doesn't take much), and the next growing season will bring a bushel basket of water sprouts growing from the site of each cut.

With most trees, professionals advise that you can remove up to one-fifth of the foliage once every five years or so. But when pruning a dogwood tree, I say you should prune even less, maybe something like one-eighth of the foliage, or perhaps even one-sixteenth. If your dogwood doesn't grow a bunch of water sprouts from the pruning cuts in a year's time, then you have not overpruned, and you may try some more. Or not, if you don't want to tempt fate.

Bleeding and Timing

I am told that dogwoods bleed if pruned too early in the year. I have never seen this myself. When a tree "bleeds," it oozes sap from a pruning wound at a scary rate. I have read that bleeding does not hurt the plant, but it does bother the tree owner. The bleeding will stop once the tree's leaves emerge. For these reasons, and others, you usually prune in the early dormant season or in summer.

Sunscald

A dogwood's bark, especially that of the eastern dogwood (*C. florida*), is thin and prone to sunscald—another reason not to overthin. I have heard a garden columnist advise people to shade the trunk by planting shrubs to cover it. But I think this just makes everything look crowded and messy. I would rather people just retain enough lower limbs on the tree trunk itself, or if not, try to see that the tree is protected by high shade of other trees nearby. Dr. Shigo has stated that there is no such thing as sunscald caused solely by exposure to sun, not even on a dogwood. His work indicates that the splitting bark (sunscald) is a result of two cuts being made—one directly above the other—or that it comes from improperly placed cuts, specifically flush cuts (which remove the collar). In either case, the take-home message

is avoid limbing-up dogwoods whenever possible.

Common Sense Pruning

That doesn't mean that you shouldn't prune. If a limb is growing out into the pathway, prune it off to the branch collar. And certainly take off any deadwood, which is easy to spot in the summer because the dead branch has no live leaves on it. Old, previously mal-pruned or anthracnose-ridden trees will have plenty of deadwood. The greatest pruning secret is to remove deadwood. Good pruners do it first, and do it always. We also look for any obviously broken or damaged branches.

Size Reduction

Do not attempt height control or reduction! It won't work. Even using proper selective heading cuts, a dogwood tree will explode into a wild regrowth of ugly water sprouts. Prune those off and three times as many grow back!

Only on rare occasions is the selective heading cut used on a tree, especially a dogwood tree. I can remember such a cut I made on a previously mal-pruned eastern dogwood (*C. florida*). The branch in question had been headed before, and the end of it sported a nasty snarl of water sprouts. It was not an option to take the limb off entirely because it was too large and, in addition, the cut would have left an unbalanced-looking tree. So I followed the branch back from the tip to a place where there was a large, well-placed lateral branch and cut back to there. The remaining cuts on the tree were all true thinning cuts, removing lateral branches at their point of origin.

Thinning

Many of the remaining branches to be removed will be located near the crotches. Pruning out small branchlets from the space nearest where the branches attach to the trunk seems to make the tree look better defined and cleaner. On many dogwoods, especially the eastern dogwood, you can also accentuate the elegant branch structure by taking out some (never all) of the duplicating or parallel branches. In this species a branch of tends to have a smaller branch attached to it that exactly parallels its parent. Pruning off the "baby" branch may make your plant look better (see Figure 14.21). This sort of general thinning is the artistic part of pruning and is quite enjoyable. But be careful not to overprune. This is hard once you start seeing how much better your tree looks thinned out. The overriding law is to stay within the pruning budget—and remember, the budget is extremely small for dogwoods.

In general, you should work from the bottom up and the inside out, going in a generally upward spiral fashion. When confronted

Figure 14.21 Remove the parallel "baby" branch.

with a difficult pruning decision, I have found it best to skip it and move on. Just remove those branches that you are quite certain need to be removed and that will not leave a large "hole." Whenever I find myself paralyzed with indecision, I just move over to another part of the tree. I know I can come back later, after the rest is done or when I have viewed the tree from many angles.

Rehabilitative Pruning

Because dogwoods have such a lovely branch structure and because they water-sprout back so horribly, gardeners consider the mal-pruning of them as particularly bad. The three common forms of mal-pruning are topping, shearing into a ball or other shape, and overthinning. The good news is that, given enough time, dogwoods can be pruned back into good shape. But it's hard, and it takes nerves of steel. The overwhelming impulse is to remove all the horrid-looking water sprouts, but that won't work—more just grow in their place.

The four steps to rehabilitative pruning are (1) wait, (2) thin, (3) wait, and (4) thin. The water sprouts will shoot way, way up, but they will eventually arch over and turn into youthful, pretty decent looking branches. The problem is that they will look different from all the original old branches, which are more curved and generally better looking. It is the contrast between the two types of branches that drives people crazy. As a professional I have developed specialty pruning that is done to mitigate the intolerable contrast. This keeps the tree owner calm long enough for the tree to outgrow the mal-pruning. It also does help the tree regain its natural shape sooner. Such pruning is counterintuitive, and it is very hard not to overprune while working on the tree. It will take five years or so before the tree is fully restored.

This is what you do: Take out all of the deadwood and stubs. Then wait a year. Go back in and take out just *a few* of the water sprouts from some of the clusters along the branches. Take out more of those that are closest to the branch crotches. Wait another year. Now, begin to make the two branch types (the old curved and the new straighter) look more uniform. Do this by removing some of the pretty curved branches, leaving straighter old growth (that's the part that doesn't make sense). Then cut off some of the most impossibly ugly, long, or wrong-way shoots of the new growth, leaving the shorter, more curvaceous new shoots. Now the top and the bottom (or the interior and the exterior) more closely resemble each other. Only do *some* of the pruning now. Come back next year or the year after and do more. One year you will come back and everything will look pretty good. Ah, success.

If you are having difficulty identifying a tree as a dogwood, refer to the old horticulture joke: How can you tell a dogwood? Answer: By its bark.

Cornelian Cherry

Cornus mas is a plant lover's tree because it blooms very early (February) with small, cheerful yellow flowers, and, like forsythia, it blooms before the leaves come on. In the fall, the cornelian cherries have big black fruits reminiscent of cherries (hence the name). Plant lovers tend to be blind to the faults of this tree: It lacks, shall we say, structural grace. Its branches tend to be skinny and straight, crossed like Ts, and parallel all over the place in a most unfortunate way. Only in great age do they develop more arching grace. Go easy on these trees. Pruning more won't make the branches any prettier, and water-sprout regrowth could make it a lot worse.

Eastern Dogwood

The eastern dogwood (*C. florida*) is a favorite small garden tree. It comes with either pink flowers or white, and there are even some with tricolor leaves. They bloom in May. They have the classic "turban's cap" buds—good for winter identification. They have good fall color. And they have the elegant branch structure I love to look at in the winter. They are more densely branched and shorter than the western dogwood (*C. nuttallii*). Many eastern dogwoods grow with a spreading double leader—which, by the way, should *not* be corrected into a single-trunked tree by people who have read more about pruning than they have actual pruning experience.

Dogwoods are also extremely prone to a nasty disease called anthracnose, in which all the leaves turn crispy brown in the summer and then fall off. Not all the eastern dogwoods have the disease. The healthy ones I see tend to be living in tall, open shade or mild sun as opposed to being tightly jammed in a courtyard. Good circulation is important. However, don't try to create good circulation by overthinning. You will just cause a billion water sprouts to regrow, and they really make the tree thick and prone to disease. On the other hand, cutting down the Douglas fir next to your dogwood can help. If you are not averse to a chemical program, there are products that can be sprayed on the tree that will effectively control the disease. Or you can just learn to live with the sight of crispy leaves in the summer.

By the way, all the dogwood trees look a little more drought stricken than they actually are. In the summer, the leaves directly exposed to sun start to fold, looking roughly like taco shells. This is normal and is even an identifying characteristic of the tree. This is not to say it's okay not to water. It's just something to know.

Kousa Dogwood

The kousa dogwood (*C. kousa*) seems to be somewhat disease resistant (meaning it doesn't get anthracnose as badly) and it is quickly becoming a new favorite small, street tree (especially for under powerlines). It can be a multitrunked, twiggy tree that in older age develops a nicer fan-shaped branching habit. Sometimes it blooms so heavily it pulls the limbs over. Very impressive. It is one of the trees that, when I was first becoming interested in gardening, I actually stopped the car and tracked down, going through several yards to find out what it was. (The others were ginkgo and paulownia.) The reason I was interested was that it bloomed solid white in the summer (when most everything else was through blooming) and then *faded to pink*! Ooooo! All the girls

will want one. The same pruning rules apply as with other dogwoods.

Western Dogwood

My favorite dogwood tree is our native one, *C. nuttallii*, but I never recommend planting it because it is extremely susceptible to, and defenseless against, anthracnose. I have seen many trees die from this disease and it makes me so sad. Western dogwood is a much taller and more openly branched tree than the eastern dogwood. Its flower bracts are a creamy yellow-white, tinged slightly green. The flowers load up the trees in early spring, and one can see why it is British Columbia's provincial tree if you drive the country during the bloom time. They're everywhere and they're beautiful. And sometimes there is a second bloom in the fall. They have, in my opinion, the nicest branches, like delicate ripples of water, and nifty seed heads.

My opinion is not shared by all. When I was first learning gardening, I found two city gardeners in a Parks Department truck and picked their brains. I asked, "What's the difference between the eastern and western dogwoods?" They agreed that one was much denser that the other and they both said one was better than the other, though it turned out to be a different tree for each.

In an effort to simulate the feeling of a western dogwood in my yard (but without the anthracnose problem), I purchased an 'Eddie's White Wonder', a cross between the eastern and the western dogwood. I like it, though the flower bracts are not quite the same. It does have lovely fall color and only gets a little anthracnose at the bottom (where there is less air circulation). For several years I would go outside to find the top foot of the tree broken. I never figured out why, though I suspect a crow or squirrel had something to do with it. Following each break it would send up several new shoots, and I always felt I should be a good pruner and go up on a ladder and train it back to a single leader. But I found that if I just put it off long enough, the tree would choose its own new leader and the other competitors would subside into side branches. Now when people ask me if they should train a new leader on a broken top, I'm not sure what to say. Sometimes you should work on it (to prevent a double leader from developing), and sometimes you can ignore it and it will go away on its own. I have found this to be true of many problems in life. The hard part of problem solving is knowing which kind is which.

Summary

Because dogwood trees water-sprout easily, prune them lightly. No size reduction is allowed! Use thinning cuts, preferably small ones, and always cut to the collar. Remove no more than one-eighth, and more like one-sixteenth, of the live crown. Taking out deadwood is always okay and doesn't count against the pruning budget.

FRUIT TREES

Ask five knowledgeable gardeners how to prune fruit trees and you may well get five very different answers. This is because fruit trees have been grown for centuries as food sources rather than as ornamental trees.

Therefore, everybody and his brother have developed a system to maximize fruit production and to make it simple to pick all the fruit, fast, and to make it easy to spray and to do more intensive pruning to produce more and more fruit.

If you want to maximize your fruit production, most county extension services have inexpensive bulletins. They will explain early training of young trees, pruning for production, and what to do with that old apple tree to bring it back into good shape. You will learn the single-leader method, the open-center method, and the modified central leader method. You will learn about Type IV tip bearers with "blind wood." You will learn how to spread open young limbs (some people use clothespins) or to shore up old limbs with 2 by 4s to keep them from breaking. All the information in these bulletins will help you produce lots of fruit, but if it seems like too much work and you don't want to learn that much, try the Turnbull method of pruning fruit trees. It is less work, and you don't have to concentrate as hard. It makes your tree look good and will produce enough fruit to feed all your friends and family before the fruit rots.

Pruning Errors

First, let's go over what not to do. The two most common errors in pruning fruit trees are: (1) topping and (2) creating umbrella trees whose crowns are laden with water sprouts. Topping is unequivocally bad for any tree, including fruit trees. The water sprouts that shoot back up from a topped fruit tree will not only be ugly, they are too busy trying to get enough leaves back in order to feed the tree to make much fruit.

However, many orchardists will reduce the height of apple and pear trees using the dropcrotch method of lowering trees. Dropcrotching means you selectively head back to a side branch of a decent size, say one-half the diameter of the parent stem. This is hard on the health of old trees and opens them up to rot. Younger trees (fifteen years old or younger) withstand this height reduction better. Dropcrotching reduces the amount of water-sprout regrowth, compared to topping, but does not eliminate it. On an old apple or pear, do not make a dropcrotch or thinning cut that exceeds 2 or 3 inches in diameter at most. Do not use it as a way to keep your ornamental tree small. Don't prune too much (no more than one-fourth of the total leaf surface) in any one year. And don't try to fix it all in one year. If you have a tree that needs a lot of work, do it over several years.

The second error is the creation of "umbrella trees." This is the result when the pruner cuts to an outside branch year after year (called *bench-cutting*)—something you might be tempted to do if you already know something about pruning.

Apical Dominance

We now need to understand apical dominance. This is the only hard, technical part. Here is some basic tree and plant biology, which, when you get it, will make everything else clear to you, and you can also impress your friends with some fancy words. First, we will talk about the last bud on the end of a branch (the terminal bud). This bud

releases a chemical that, moving via gravity, keeps the buds on down the line rather subdued. Think of it as the boss bud. When you cut off the end boss bud, or even bend it over, the chemical flow is disturbed and the other buds begin to grow.

Umbrella trees have terminal (boss) buds that are too low. Gravity prevents the chemical from reaching buds down the line, so a crown of water sprouts develops at the top. To help keep your old apple tree from producing excessive crown water sprouts, thin back low branches (they look like hooks) to a branch facing more up and out (see Figure 14.27c on page 241).

Pick out a major (scaffold) branch and follow it with your eyes. Does it dip down quite far, crossing other, lower scaffold branches and cluttering things up? Then you may selectively head back (prune) to one of its side branches that faces more upward and outward (a 40-degree to 60-degree angle is ideal). The scaffold branch now ends in a boss bud with greater *apical dominance*. This will reduce the number of returning crown water sprouts farther back as well as improve the looks of your tree. Keep in mind apical dominance if you attempt to reduce the height of your apple or pear tree. It is a good idea to cut back a tall vertical branch to a shorter branch that also faces upward (see Figure 14.22). Basically you are not trying to eliminate all vertical branches; you are simply replacing them with shorter, younger, and fewer vertical branches. This retains some apical dominance and allows the tree to grow a little every year. It's like a volleyball game—you rotate out a few of the tallest

Figure 14.22 An upright 1-inch branch (width of two fingers) can be cut back to a half-inch side branch (width of one finger).

old water sprouts every year. You may have a forest of water sprouts that are the result of previous bad pruning. If you remove all of them, they all come back. Leave some to apically dominate the rest, shorten some to create a second story up, and thin out the rest. Note that the natural state of many old fruit trees is an umbrella, which is all right if the umbrella is low down on the tree where you can get the fruit, and if you don't care how it looks. But often the umbrella occurs high up on the tree, shading out the fruit below, and spoiling the overall good looks of the tree.

Pruning Fruit Trees

So, how do you prune an apple or a pear tree? The easiest way is just to prune it like other trees: for health and good looks. First,

and always, take out the deadwood. Be thorough. Then take out some of the worst crossing or rubbing branches and the worst branches going the wrong way. These are the ones that start on one side of the tree, head the wrong way through the center, and come out on the other side. Also, thin or selectively head back some of the branches, especially toward the top (even a few big branches, up to 1½ inches in diameter) to increase light penetration and to lower your tree. This helps ripen the fruit lower down. It increases air circulation, too, which is important in order to discourage the numerous bacterial and fungal diseases that spoil the fruit. Look for narrow, weak big-branch crotches. Heavy, fruit-laden branches need to be strong. Narrow crotches are the ones that break. Now, you could stop here and you would have a pretty good-looking apple or pear tree without too much trouble. It will have fruit. But if you want to do more, read on.

Pruning for Fruit Production

Certain kinds of branches make more fruit buds or spurs than others. These are the ones that are situated in a not-too-horizontal position. You can pull or push new branches into such a position, or you can just start cutting out the ones that aren't in the right place and leave the ones that are. Nature makes fruit by sending up a young, straight-up soft branch. It flowers on the tip, and the flower turns into a fruit. The weight of the fruit pulls this supple branch over. As a branch gets older, it stiffens in a more horizontal position (see Figure 14.23). As the branch tips over, the apical

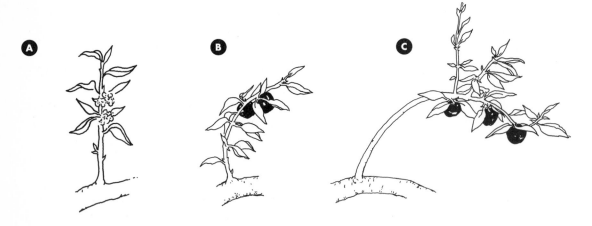

Figure 14.23 A. Vertical shoot flowers. **B.** Flowers become fruit, weighing branch down to a 45-degree angle. **C.** A more horizontal branch develops laterals and sends up new vertical shoot.

dominance of the terminal bud weakens, and buds farther down the branch are released to form nice little side branches (laterals) and on them, teeny, tiny ¼-inch branches called spurs. These tiny spurs have fat flower buds (fruiting buds) rather than skinny leaf buds. We want the laterals and spurs.

Figure 14.24 Head laterals to force fruit spurs.

In the winter, it is the fat-budded spurs that you see on trees that make you think what you're looking at might be a fruit tree. You can encourage some, but not all, of your side branches (laterals) to make spurs by heading (also called tipping back) to two or three buds. This works on pears and apples, but it doesn't work on cherries. And plums, apricots, and peaches are totally different. Now, if your main branch gets pulled too far over—past 90 degrees—apical dominance is diminished, too many buds are released, and those miserable water sprouts start charging back up.

In some senses, pruning fruit trees breaks all the rules for ornamental tree pruning. You try to keep your tree small, something that should never be done to other trees. Pruners often reduce fruit trees dramatically, which would be extremely bad pruning on a maple or oak. We also head a lot. We head side branches (laterals) to force them to make spurs (see Figure 14.24). We shorten major scaffold branches with heading, especially young ones, so that they won't swing in the wind and lose fruit (see Figure 14.25). Heading causes these branches to get fatter or stouter. We need stout branches to hold up heavy fruit. On apples and pears, especially, we do a lot of heading.

Other Fruit Trees

Peaches, nectarines, and Japanese prunes are pruned quite heavily, with scary-looking large heading cuts. Instead of setting up persistent spur systems, as apples and pears do, these trees make fruit on new wood. The heavy pruning is done to force renewal shoots to grow, and also to keep the branches short enough that they don't break under the fruit load.

And then there are the cherries and European plums, which you shouldn't prune much at all. Deadwood removal is always okay.

Let's recap what we've gone over thus far. Prune your fruit tree like any other tree:

1. First, and always, take out all of the deadwood.

2. Take out the worst crossing, rubbing branches.

3. Take out the worst wrong-way branches.

4. Take out some, not all, of the water sprouts.

5. Remove weak crotches if they are or will become part of the main framework (scaffold) branches (see Figure 14.26).

6. Thin (don't strip) all those branches rather than heading them, and do more thinning on the top to encourage light penetration and air circulation.

When dealing with water sprouts on your apple or pear tree, remember to cut some out altogether; leave some alone (don't cut off

Figure 14.25 Training a young fruit tree

Before

Growth After

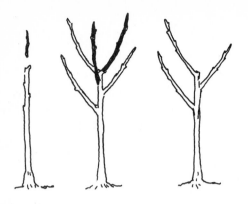

Figure 14.26 Heading a "whip" is done to create a low crown. In year 3, remove crowded branches and those with included bark (weak crotches).

the tips), since they will flower and fruit and be pulled over and produce more spurs later; head back some water sprouts to thicken them up into second-story branches. Try to head-back to another upright side branch and not to a horizontal branch that would water-sprout back madly (see Figure 14.27).

If you want to encourage more fruiting on your apples and pears, you can prune for more horizontal branches. You can bend back laterals to force more spurs to form. See, you're an expert already!

More About Fruit Trees

• Pruning of young trees (under six years) is done to develop strong, low framework branches and not much else. In fact, it may take a while longer for your tree to fruit. Go easy in the early years. There are some newer varieties that fruit earlier.

• Old trees can be invigorated by heavy pruning to produce new wood and spur systems, although you may experience a temporary

drop in production when you cut off older and lower limbs or "hooks."

• Summer pruning of fruit trees is all right if the tree is vigorous and healthy and well watered. Spotting deadwood is easy in the summer. Summer pruning can be useful in reducing the spread of fungus-bacterial diseases that like damp weather, and it will help reduce water-sprout regrowth. It generally slows the growth rate and will help restrict the size of your tree. It is harder on the plant, however, so go easy, and never prune during a drought.

• Many fruit trees need a cross-pollinator tree in the neighborhood. The cooperative extension service in your area has lists of what type of tree pollinates what for you and which fruit trees do well. Cross-pollinators are something to consider when you are planning your orchard.

• New dwarf varieties called "spur type" apples don't need to be pruned to make them set up spurs. They do it themselves. In fact, be careful that you don't prune the spurs off.

• Bee activity is needed for pollination. If it has been a very wet spring, you may not get enough bee activity. Bees, like some Parks Department workers I know, won't work in the rain. On the other hand, if you don't see any bees and it has been sunny, it may be that someone in your neighborhood has inadvertently killed them with pesticides. Misapplication of some commonly used pesticides can wipe out entire hives. If your neighbor doesn't read the label and applies something like Sevin on plants in bloom during the middle of the day, a bee might bumble into a flower and

Figure 14.27 Renovating an old apple tree: **A.** Remove some water sprouts up to 2 inches in diameter.

B. Shorten some water sprouts to a side branch or bud.

C. Remove lowest "hooks" to reduce the recurrence of water sprouts and make the tree look better.

D. Finished apple tree.

then carry the poison back to the hive and kill the entire hive. This is a tragedy for the orchardist as well as the bees.

• Fruit trees need sun in order to flower and fruit. If your tree never sets fruit, stand next to it and look up. If you see big trees or condominiums, this may be your problem. You're in too much shade. Try removing your fruit tree and planting a vine maple, Japanese maple, or some other understory tree that will look nice and do well in these conditions.

• Fruit trees, especially Gravenstein apples, sometimes get into the habit of bearing fruit every other year. This routine can be somewhat modified by pruning. If you wish, you can ignore it. Your tree may be too young. You'll have to wait, be patient! Or your tree may be too old. You'll have to prune it or remove it and replace it with something you like better.

• You can improve the size and quality of your fruit by thinning branches so that more light gets to the interior of the tree. Also, you can thin spurs and baby fruit so that more energy gets put into the remaining branches or buds for bigger, tastier fruit. (Mother Nature will do some fruit thinning for you. In the "June drop" the tree will shed away any small apples that have not developed seeds.)

• There is a difference in the severity of pruning of European and Japanese plums. Japanese plums should be pruned heavily, like peaches; the strong upper wood should be cut back to weaker branches. European plums should be pruned very lightly. Japanese plums and European plums will not cross-pollinate each other.

• These days you don't have to suffer with big fruit trees; nurseries now have new dwarfing rootstocks. So if you want fruit and less work, chop down that old tree and plant a new dwarf one. Dwarfing rootstocks come in small, smaller, and very small. Check them out with your extension service. A really smart-sized fruit tree is about 4 feet tall. Unless, of course, you love that old tree—then keep it.

• Do not try to make your cherry tree small again by topping it. It won't work. They have yet to develop a really good dwarfing rootstock for cherry trees, although there are a few available. That's why that big bucket truck with the 70-foot extension is called a "cherry picker."

• People often want to lower cherry trees because they cannot stand the waste of the fruit on the top where they cannot reach. Removing the top will not actually increase cherry production down low. Other people welcome the day when the tree gets tall enough that the birds leave the lower cherries alone.

If much of the information in this section seems very confusing and self-contradictory —well, it is. Even people who specialize in fruit tree pruning are often unsure and easily swayed to other methods and ways. Take heart—teachers send students out to practice on apples and pears because these trees are so forgiving. In Eastern Washington, machines mow them to force fruit production. Stay away from topping—especially your cherry tree—and you'll do okay.

Summary

• Traditionally, fruit trees, like roses, are for people who like to prune and spray a lot. Try buying very, very disease-resistant, and very dwarf trees to reduce these maintenance chores.

• You can, if you like, prune fruit trees as you would ornamentals, for health and good looks, and leave it at that.

• Horizontal branches bear more fruit than vertical branches.

• All fruit trees are not created equal.

Group A: Head a lot. Prune hardest.

Peach, apricot, nectarine, Japanese plum

Group B: Keep young trees short. Head laterals to encourage fruit spurs. Prune less than Group A.

Apples, pears

Group C: Hard to keep trees short with pruning. No topping. No heading laterals. Train early by bending branches. Prune least.

Cherries, European plums

JAPANESE LACELEAF MAPLE

(Acer palmatum 'Dissectum'*)*

The laceleaf maple is king. Who would deny it? The magnificence of its winter branch pattern is such that even most hedge-shear maniacs will halt before its awesome delicacy and grace (see Figure 14.28). If you're looking for the perfect focal point for a small and frequently viewed area, you'd be hard-pressed to do better.

But just how to properly prune a Japanese laceleaf maple is a source of great concern for the average homeowner, and a source of great joy (and income) for the knowledgeable professional.

Figure 14.28 The Japanese laceleaf maple has beautiful winter branching.

What Doesn't Work

Don't try to keep a laceleaf maple small. I have seen gardens where people have diligently tried to contain them, using selective thinning cuts to keep the top down and selective heading to restrain the width. But the heavily thinned branches seem to rapidly age, peel, and crack—a sign that dieback is next. Overthinning and overpruning can also stimulate a resurgence of shoots, which are always a warning bell that something is wrong.

The most common cause of mal-pruning is mis-siting. Usually the dainty baby maple is perched at the front stairway's edge, ensuring inevitable obstruction of foot traffic. The best solution to the severely mis-sited tree is to transplant it. Go ahead. We (that's the royal "we," meaning John Turnbull) recently salvaged a forty-year-old laceleaf maple (8 feet by 8 feet by 5 feet tall) and transplanted it to the Turnbull Home for Orphan Plants. When moving a Japanese maple, take special care not to break the branches—they are quite brittle. Immediate water is the key to success, as is diligent watering the first full year.

I have only seen one full-grown Japanese laceleaf maple that has been successfully reduced in size. It was in a Japanese garden within a larger botanic garden in Missouri. Farther on in the same landscape was its twin. But that one looked sadly nipped and nibbled on, no doubt from a similar attempt to "control" it.

The Miracle of Deadwooding

Gardeners love to get their hands on an old, neglected laceleaf because they are assured of transforming a scraggly brown mop into a piece of artwork. I remember one impressed client who said, "I thought I just didn't have the right kind." And it's so easy! Eighty percent of the work is simply the removal of collected dead leaves and accumulated deadwood. Just gently run your fingers through the branches, combing out the leaves. I always feel like the hairdresser of the Goddess Flora. Then the gardener "thumb prunes" out the tiny dead twigs that have occurred since last year. They are easy to spot, since they are light gray in color, not matching the rest of the living branch. Using thumb and forefinger, the pruner gently squeezes, until the dead twig snaps out (see Figure 14.29).

Larger dead and dying branches should also be removed. They are usually located at the bottom and inside of the tree, where they have been shaded out. Which brings me to correct positioning. Work from the bottom up and the inside out. Like an auto mechanic, the pruner is often found lying under the tree, legs sticking out, working on

Figure 14.29 Thumb pruning

his or her back. It's a fine place to spend a warmish summer day

Prune not only the dead branches but also the limbs that have been so severely shortened that they are of no further use (and would probably die sooner or later anyway).

Figure 14.30 Summer pruning: Assume the position.

Timing

I like summer pruning because you can gauge when the tree has been sufficiently opened up to see inside to "the bones." Laceleafs tend to get a bit heavy and thick looking in full sun, and they can be successfully thinned out to give them a lacy feel. Take care not to thin or overthin in very hot weather, since the bark is easily sunburned (despite how it sounds, sunburning the bark on any tree is a serious problem). Or you can prune laceleafs in the early winter. For novices it is easier to follow the branch patterns when the leaves are off, but it can be harder to spot dead wood. To make sure a limb is dead, use your hand pruners to peel back a tiny bit of bark. If the thin sheath of cambium just beneath the bark is green, the branch is still viable. If it is brownish or worse, cut away!

Not long after the winter solstice, the sap begins to rise in maples, and if you prune before the leaves are out, you are likely to see the cuts "bleed." I am told that this doesn't permanently damage the tree, but it looks scary, and most good gardeners wait to do major work until the leaves are out. Once in late January I cut a large limb on a sunny day. It wept heavily, and I worried that as the temperature dropped to below 30 degrees that night the wet area might freeze and crack.

Tools

More so than on any other plant, it is important to use high-quality, sharp pruning tools when pruning laceleaf maples. The cuts must be exact, neither leaving the hint of a stub, nor cutting too close (see Figure 14.31). In

Figure 14.31 Where to cut **A.** Don't cut too far out; it leaves a stub. **B.** Don't flush-cut; it's bad for the plant. **C.** Cut just right.

the first instance the stub dies back and ruins the good looks of your elegant plant; in the other case, the flush cut can open the branch to disease and decay. I vividly recall my Japanese pruning instructor showing us "shell pruning." He ran his hands along the branch and extolled the virtues of "smoothness" and "agedness" in our pruning endeavors. The

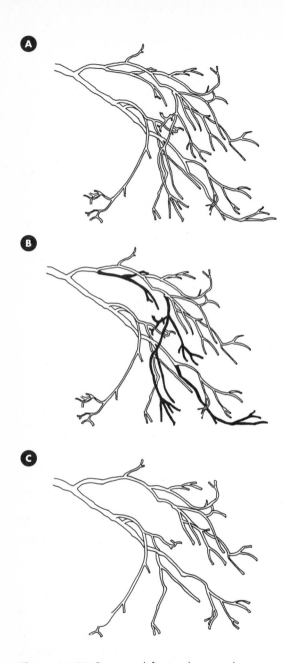

Figure 14.32 Creating definition between layers **A.** Original side branches. **B.** Remove lower branches with selective heading and thinning; always cut to upper, out-facing branches. **C.** Layers are separated on the finished branch.

branches on laceleafs are so brittle, and the bark so thin, that it's easy to make pruning cut mistakes, tears, or stubs. Invest in a professional pair of bypass pruners and an ARS-type folding pruning saw. ARS, Felco, and Corona are the three brands recommended most. Julie Hale, a PlantAmnesty gardener, has located a special tool called a Japanese keyhole saw, which works especially well to make the fine and exacting cuts required on Japanese maples.

Some little maples are so engineered that their skirts drag in the mud. That is to say, the lower limbs flow down to the ground and beyond. Remedy this situation by taking off some of the lower limbs entirely to the trunk (even some fairly big ones) and selectively heading some of the others. Always cut back to a side branch that is big enough to take over as the branch end. Usually the side branch is at least one-half the diameter of the parent stem, and faces out.

The rest of your pruning is done either to solve a problem (e.g., removing the one most interfering limb that sticks out into the sidewalk) or to lend definition to the plant (see Figure 14.32). Thinning out branches uniformly throughout the plant will give it that airy look. Be careful not to "strip" them all out to the ends. Better to take some large and some small branches, frequently standing back and walking around to judge your progress. It helps me to think that I am separating various layers of limbs rather than thinning each branch separately. When selective pruning, always take off the lower portion of a branch, cutting it back to a side branch that "leaps" upward and outward. It reminds me of opening an umbrella.

Remember, it's easy to take it off, hard to put it back. New pruners tend to overthin. It is true that you take out crossing/rubbing branches, but remember you are not trying to eliminate them all, especially if they represent a fair portion of the plant. To remove all the crossers/rubbers would mean total destruction of a laceleaf, whose branches tend to wander and double back in curious ways. It is more important to spot the branches that wander too far from one side of the tree to the other, that are too straight (not as pretty as curving ones), and that have little taper to the stem (see Figure 14.33).

Finish by thinning the top of the plant, which I find the most difficult part of the job. I often do this portion from outside. In the end the plant should have a uniform "beaded curtain" or "lace" effect.

The entire process of pruning a large, neglected laceleaf maple can take between one and three hours, so remember to be patient and move slowly. In the end you will be amply rewarded. The laceleaf does all the work, but you'll get all the credit. Long live the king!

Summary

The art of fine pruning is seen at its best on the Japanese laceleaf maple. Working from underneath the plant, flat on your back, deadwood and remove dead leaves first. Then use a combination of selective thinning and selective heading cuts to lace-out the plant. Favor branches that curve pleasingly and those that face upward or outward.

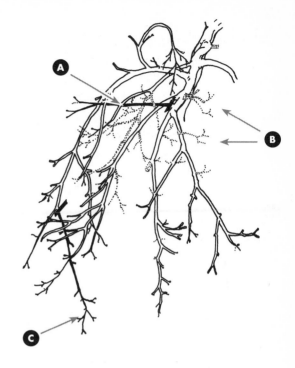

Figure 14.33 Remove deadwood (dotted lines), some branches that rub, and ones with little taper or curve. **A.** Too far, too straight, no taper **B.** Deadwood **C.** Touches the ground.

Create layers. Save the topmost part for the end, with final touch-up pruning being done from outside. Do not try to keep this plant from getting larger.

JAPANESE MAPLE *(Acer palmatum)*
Pruning Japanese maples is easy, and it reveals the inner beauty of the tree so that it can be seen even in the summer when it is cloaked in leaves.

When I landscaped my yard almost twenty years ago, I put a Japanese maple (the kind that makes a small tree, not the weeping Japanese laceleaf maple, which was previously discussed) in front of the living-room window. Through the years I have watched it grow. I love how the raindrops hang on the limbs like a string of pearls. I love how a winter snowfall traces a white line atop each of its dark and delicate limbs. Because it's a deciduous tree, it was a good choice for the south side. My south side isn't blazing hot and totally exposed, as it's a bit set back from the street and it's in temperate Seattle. I suspect that in a more severe climate a southern exposure might scorch the leaves. The Japanese maple is an understory tree, preferring a slightly shaded and sheltered spot. The shade, in turn, results in the classic open canopy that shows off the Japanese maple's fine trunk and branch structure.

Thank heavens my maple lets the precious winter sunlight in, but keeps the hot summer sunlight out. But because it's in a sunny spot, it grew up thick and full. After only a few years, my window was totally obscured. I signed up for a Japanese pruning class to learn how to prune it so that I could continue to see through it. Now I sit on the sofa with my morning coffee and newspaper and peek through the branches. I can observe my little corner of the world without totally exposing myself to it. I make note of neighbors walking to the bus stop and the kids going to school. And I can take appropriate action when I see stray dogs enter the forbidden territory of my yard or a squirrel start to dumpster-dive for bulbs.

My tree has grown quite large, standing 20 or more feet, crowning out over my front porch roof. Ever since we adopted a full-sized Japanese laceleaf maple for the back yard (Little Red), we refer to the one in front as Big Red. Sometimes in the afternoon the sun casts a shadow of delicate leaves inside the house. It looks like someone painted a Japanese mural, except that the gray shadow leaves will occasionally shift and sway on the wall. And looking directly out at the tree is impressive too. The window frames the trunks, which curve and recurve artfully.

To add to my viewing pleasure, a flock of the tiniest little round birds comes to visit my tree every fall. Out of nowhere they start appearing, zipping in one by one, and soon the tree is chock full of tiny, chirping budgies. They busily groom the branches, defying gravity as they do, sometimes hanging upside-down or walking up vertical limbs to eat unseen insect tidbits. And then, after a while, the birds leave. It ends as it began, with just one or two birds flying off at a time. And then suddenly they're all gone. The tree is empty and quiet again.

My Mistake

The Japanese maple I brought home was a perfectly globe-shaped, multiple-trunked tree. I thought myself pretty smart to situate it far enough, about 4 feet, from the window. As it turned out, it was still poorly placed, growing easily thrice as big as I had imagined (and still going). Years ago rain-laden limbs were hanging down, intruding onto the pathway, onto the porch, onto the roof, and into the wires (the telephone line). Not so smart after all. Had I chosen a fan-shaped tree I would have had a much easier job training it to stay out of harm's way. I feel guilty every time I have to prune another limb.

Japanese maples—like snowdrop trees, dogwoods, and many other small trees—are mis-sited by landscape designers all the time. They place them as a garden's focal point, too close to the walkway or road, as if "small tree" meant "doesn't grow." Small trees or shrubs will still shock the owner with their increase in size over the years. Yet these plants are correctly labeled because when they grow up, they will still be relatively much smaller than the vast majority of trees (which are 40 to 80 feet or higher). As you may have surmised, I know most of the common garden mistakes because I've made them myself.

Heading-Back Temporary Branches

At the suggestion of a friend I tried containing my tree's size by selectively heading-back its limbs, all over, every year. Selective heading means making a branch shorter by pruning it back to a smaller side branch. (Selective heading is the right way to make a branch shorter.) Each cut I made was less than ¼ inch in diameter. I kept pruning Big Red in this way for several years. I did the tree no harm, but I still failed to stop it from increasing in size. The tree just seemed to redouble its efforts to grow to its predetermined size.

I watch landscapes over years, and I've seen many people try to keep Japanese maples and most other trees small, both the right and the wrong way; I've never seen it work. Actually I saw it once. A two-story Japanese maple had been arduously pruned for a water view from the upstairs windows. The owner wanted to know if her arborist had "butchered it." I said no, it looked amazingly good for an attempt at the near impossible. The result of years of dropcrotching was that the branches splayed out like a giant candelabrum. I told her that it would be better for her to choose: tree or view. (Later I heard that I had told her to "take the tree out!")

Over the long haul, I suspect that the best you can achieve with dedicated, annual pruning for size control is about a 10 to 15 percent reduction in size as compared to an unpruned tree. The constant time, money, and effort it causes rarely justify the difference. I now think of tree pruning as a way to channel or direct growth, not as a way to stop or even to slow down growth. One good adage I've heard is "You exert your control over trees when you choose which one to plant."

Selective heading works only as a temporary holding measure to keep lower branches out of the way until such time as they can be completely removed. You might well ask the question "Why not remove them as soon as they are spotted as being in the way?"

It is recommended that the lower limbs of all young trees be kept for a few years. The reason is that the photosynthate made by those limbs (or, more accurately, by the leaves of those limbs) is used to strengthen and fatten the lower portion of the trunk where they are attached. And we want strong, well-tapered tree trunks because they are less likely to break in windstorms. For street trees, owners are admonished to shorten and keep the lower limbs until two-thirds of the tree is above head height. Then the limbs should be removed slowly, one or two a year on different sides of the tree trunk and at different heights. Avoid pruning two branches located one directly above the other during the same season.

On the other hand, you shouldn't wait too long to remove the lower limbs on a Japanese maple or any other tree. In nature, the young, lower limbs are naturally shaded out as the forest grows up. In the city and in the open, the limbs are surrounded by sun and will stay on indefinitely. Your job is to prune them so that they don't interfere with foot or vehicular traffic, before they get too big. How big is too big is, of course, a relative situation. For example, a 2-inch-diameter branch on a massive 100-foot tree is nothing, but on a 15-foot Japanese maple, it's a major limb. Taking off large limbs does harm to trees, even when done properly, so minimize the damage by timing your pruning cuts just right. Not too soon, or too late in its life—but just right.

Branch-Collar Cuts

Hopefully, all readers know how to make a proper collar cut by now. If not, be sure to read the section "Tree Biology and Pruning" at the beginning of this chapter. Remember, the very nicest thing you can do for your tree is to learn where to make the cut. (Skip the pruning paint—it doesn't work. Skip the fertilizer spikes. Skip the trunk wrap.) New pruners are apt to cut off the bottom part of the collar. A few years ago I instructed my apprentice on collar cuts and assigned her to cut off a lower limb of my maple—just to help her get her courage up. I came out later to find an oval face, instead of a round face, on the trunk. (*Face* is a term referring to the light-colored area that shows where the cut was made.) It hurt like a poke in my eye; a flush cut on my tree! As soon as she left, I rubbed a bit of dirt on the face, hoping to hide it from my arborist friends.

Thinning

Generally speaking, pruning a Japanese maple consists of thinning out the tree using a combination of larger and smaller thinning cuts spread evenly throughout the crown (meaning you don't just strip out all the internal branches). You start from the bottom and work up and out. First, remove all of the deadwood: dead twigs, dead stubs, and dead limbs. They are easy to spot in the summer because they have no leaves. But even in the winter deadwood is a different color from live wood. On Japanese maples it's gray and snaps out easily when pressure is applied.

Also look to remove interfering branches, say the one that sticks out at eye level into foot traffic. Before you do, though, consider how your tree will look without that particular branch. And what, then, will your next move be? Plan a few steps ahead. Sometimes it helps to have a friend standing outside the tree. You jiggle the branch you want to remove and they tell you if it will look right. Then switch places. Perhaps you should head it back for now. Perhaps not. If the in-the-way branch is a major portion of the tree, it is often a better solution (though certainly more difficult for people to accept) to move the pathway to accommodate the tree.

Other candidates for removal are branches that rub other branches—if they're not too large, that is. More than once I've seen people destroy their tree by blindly following the pruning rules.

After this, the rest of your pruning is to create definition between the layers of branches. As you work up the tree, follow the individual scaffold branches with your eyes. Look to remove branches that head too far up or dip too far down (see Figure 14.34). In my mind, I think of the floating lady in the magic trick. The magician appears to pass a hoop over her body to prove that she is not suspended from wires. My branch is the lady, and as I move the imaginary hoop over her I run into the wrong branches (too far up or too far down). I cut them off, leaving a relatively level plane. The Japanese pruning term for this sort of thinning is *fan pruning*.

Keep moving as you prune, lest you over-thin the tree. When considering any particular area of branches, I prune only the easiest choices. When I find myself at a loss as to which branch to cut, debating in my mind the pros and cons of removing this or that branch, worrying if I will create too big a hole, I take it as a signal to move on. You needn't, and probably shouldn't, finish cutting off all the "wrong" branches. Remember, you can come back to it later—later in the day, or even next year or the year after.

The Pruning Budget

The overriding factor in pruning is the pruning budget. This is rarely referred to in pruning literature, but it is critical. In fact, if you prune out *all* the "wrong" branches in a Japanese maple or any other plant, you have overpruned it. Each plant has a set point, and if you prune more than it likes, you stimulate water-sprout regrowth and/or dieback of branches. The set point varies by species, but in general the pruning budget for trees is much less than for shrubs. The commonly quoted "one-third" rule is for forsythias, not maples. Try to limit yourself to removing no more than one-eighth or less of the leaf

Figure 14.34 A. Thinning a branch includes the removal of a dead lateral (dotted line) and laterals that reach too far up or down. **B.** Finished branch.

canopy in a year. (Deadwood doesn't count in the budget—it's dead.) You can come back next year for more, assuming that you don't do too much now.

Go especially easy on young trees (less than five years old) in your landscape. In an effort to get that open, fan-tree look, people are apt to prune too much too soon. How will you know? Next year the tree grows out with fast, skinny, floppy new shoots. They look a lot like suckers or water sprouts except that they originate from perfectly good, uncut tips of branches. My friend Tina calls them "maple squirts."

The pruning budget also varies among different members of the same species. There is a variegated (two-tone) Japanese maple that has become quite popular recently that is naturally much more stiff and twiggy. I've been asked to prune it to make it look more like its airy and graceful cousins, but I resist. It is much better to let it grow for a few years and then begin the thinning process, slowly, and wait to see how it responds next year. If the tree responds with a lot of weak and spindly shoots, it has been pruned too much. Do less, not more, in the future.

Correcting Mistakes

One common mistake in pruning a Japanese maple is overthinning. Another mistake is to top or tip it. Although I think of the Japanese maple as sort of a delicate tree (perhaps because of the thin bark or because it gets sunburned and windburned), it recovers pretty well from the various forms of mal-pruning. New branches will form out of the regrowth of water sprouts.

I remember gardening for a charming Scandinavian lady in Bellevue. She loved her garden. The hepaticas in it reminded her of home. She fed me cookies and very strong coffee at lunch. Among my chores was seeing what could be done with the three full-grown Japanese maples that had been topped a few years earlier. They were a mess. The mal-pruning had simply been a mistake on her part. People see topping done and they assume it must be okay. Well, two of the three trees looked quite a bit better after some rehabilitative pruning. The worst one, however (cuts 2 inches in diameter!), never made it back and finally had to be cut down.

The first step to rehab pruning is *wait*, and it's the hardest. It's impossible to believe that all those horridly floppy water sprouts will ever turn into anything substantial, but they do. Over time (a year or two) they actually stiffen and lift back up. It's true. I swear. I've seen it with my own eyes. Then you can begin to take off the lesser of the new branches: The ones that still flop, head the wrong way back into the center of the tree, or are too crowded with the others in a cluster. Deadwood and especially dead stubs from mal-pruning are always fair game, and the biggest aesthetic improvement will be in removing them. Do your rehab pruning (except the deadwood) over a few years. If you take off too much, too soon, guess what happens? A bunch more water sprouts are stimulated into growing out.

Summary

Japanese maples are good candidates for thinning. They take an average amount of pruning, for a tree. Remove no more than one-eighth of the live crown, plus all the deadwood. You may want to prune to create layers, called fan pruning. No heading, no size control. If removing a lower limb or two solves a problem (like interference with foot traffic), then do so if the limbs aren't too large (no thicker than half the diameter of the parent trunk).

MAGNOLIA *(Magnolia)*

Every year I regret more and more every cut I've ever made on a magnolia tree. That's because no matter how few or how small the cuts, they always seem to turn into a mess of water sprouts, ugly as sin and impossible to get rid of.

That's a real shame, given that the branch patterns of the deciduous magnolias are some of the best Mother Nature has to offer. I have to stop myself from bringing pruned branches home from work. (My house would be full up in a week with the interesting flora I come across.) Not only do the magnolia's branches divide often, but the tips are fattened like fruit-tree spurs, and they end in eminently touchable fuzzy buds, an identifying characteristic of the species.

The three most common magnolias in the Pacific Northwest are the saucer magnolia, the evergreen or southern magnolia, and the star magnolia. Take care not to ask too much of a magnolia tree, or she will punish you for a lifetime. But given just the right spot and the freedom to grow unaltered, a magnolia will reward you with much of the best that trees have to offer: bloom, scent, and a lovely winter silhouette.

Pruning Magnolias

My best advice about pruning magnolias is— don't. Having said that, I confess that sometimes I do. If the lowest limb stretches into the driveway or runs through an unmovable shrub, I may prune it off to the trunk or to a likely upper lateral. If an upper scaffold dips down too far, crowding another major limb, I may lighten it up with many small thinning cuts or I may remove a large lateral or two. Then it springs up and out of the lower network of limbs. That looks better. And I have been known to thin an old crowded branch. This is good fun, and the results are a crisper, cleaner-looking branch pattern.

But earlier this year I noticed an unflattering, straight water sprout on a star magnolia that I had headed back the previous year, ever so lightly and selectively, to get it out of the concrete pathway. Now when I prune, I do so with even greater guilt and apprehension. I suggest you do too. And avoid it altogether if you can.

Rehabilitative Pruning

The good news is that magnolias are good compartmentalizers. This means that if some misinformed, well-meaning neophyte tops the heck out of a magnolia tree, the tree won't die. The tree will instead wall off the incoming rot organisms, explode into a bazillion water sprouts, and grow back to its original size in a year or two. Of course, it looks horrid, as does any magnolia that has been mal-pruned—topped, tipped, or overthinned. Overthinning is, by definition, pruning to the extent that water sprouts are formed in response to the cuts. (Overthinning is harder to determine in many conifers, since as a general rule they can form few waterspouts in response to cuts.) In the case of magnolias, whether or not any particular thinning cut responds with water sprouts will depend on several factors: the size of the cut, how well it is made, the total amount of foliage being removed, and whether or not the remaining branch is exposed to sun. You may get away with making a few small, internal, well-made collar cuts. Otherwise, expect to see water sprouts next growing season (see Figures 14.35 and 14.36).

If you leave the water sprouts growing long enough (and they do get long!), they will turn back into branches. It's true! With a little judicious reduction in the numbers of sprouts (cutting out a very few of the smallest, wrong-way, or crowded sprouts in each cluster), you can eventually, over the span of four or five years, get a crown of sorts back on the tree. I have personally trained a group of water sprouts from a skinned-up saucer magnolia back into a blooming branch system. Not as lovely as the original, but passable, and I no longer have to remove water sprouts that make the tree look such a fright for half of the year.

When rehabilitating the crown of a previously mal-pruned tree, I am more tempted with magnolias than other plants to head-back some of the skyrocketing water sprouts in hopes of building a crown with some lower internal branching. I'm not thoroughly convinced this works, but a knowledgeable arborist of my acquaintance assures me that it does.

Figure 14.35 A. Removing a lateral that is too large will **B.** cause water sprouts to grow.

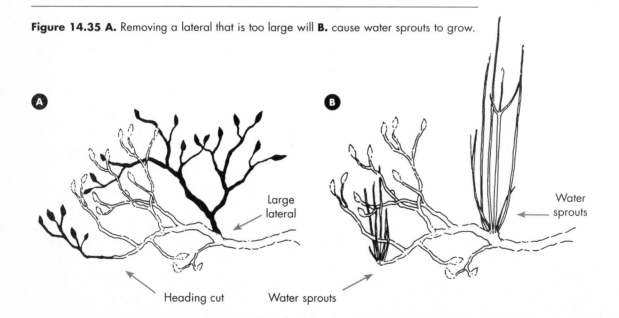

A

Large lateral

Heading cut   Water sprouts

B

Water sprouts

Figure 14.36 A. A few small, internal, well-made pruning cuts will **B.** not result in regrowth and water sprouts.

Saucer Magnolia

The saucer magnolia (*M. x soulangeana*) is a really nice tree. It gets listed as a small tree in garden books because it tops out at about 20 to 30 feet. That's small in the world of trees. It's like saying an orca is small. That's small for a whale, but still really big for an animal. Thirty feet is a lot bigger than most people think when they plant something called a "small tree." Furthermore, folks don't really pay much attention to the part of the tree description that says the tree will get to be as wide as or wider than it is tall. The low, broad-spreading habit of the saucer magnolia makes it desirable, but it also means that it'll eat up half the average front yard. When people begin to realize this, about ten years after planting the tree, they usually respond by limbing up the tree. I don't like this solution because it defeats the nice spreading shape that the tree is meant to have. I also find that it results in water-sprout regrowth, and frequently the next-highest limbs will dip back down to the ground. (With most other trees, especially large-growing ones, limbing up works well.)

With a saucer magnolia, I just recommend that people keep removing grass so they don't have to mow under the low-hanging limbs. And I advise planting a nice ground cover and spring bulbs in the bed. By the way, it is important to note that magnolias rarely transplant successfully—another reason to consider their site carefully.

Although it takes up a lot of room, I nonetheless consider the saucer magnolia a gardenworthy tree. Not only does it have an exquisite winter branch structure, it blooms with enormous pale purple flowers of heady fragrance. They are impressive without being gaudy. Even before they bloom, the elongating buds—like white candles standing on the branches—add to the intense excitement of oncoming spring. I love to watch them. And, to my knowledge, neither the saucer nor the star magnolia is plagued by any serious diseases, unlike many other flowering trees.

Later in summer, the magnolias set up some very interesting seed pods; the husk splits open to reveal a spiral of shiny orange pearls. I wonder if the formation has something to do with the fact that magnolias are one of the most ancient orders of plants. You might miss the pods if you are not looking. But the discovery and admiration of odd pods is an example of the rewards awaiting those who do their own maintenance. You get these little treats, if you are paying attention.

The saucer magnolia has large leaves, which add some contrast to the summer landscape. But better yet, those big leaves decompose through the winter, leaving a finely netted, leaf skeleton—lovely as lace. I don't get to bring those home either.

Evergreen or Southern Magnolia

Some people like the evergreen magnolia (*M. grandiflora*), preferring evergreen plants to deciduous ones in general. The enormous green leaves of the evergreen magnolia have a contrasting feltlike brown backing that looks good in floral arrangements and wreaths. Broadleaf evergreen trees are relatively rare in our area. This accounts for the fact that an early explorer misnamed Magnolia Bluff in Seattle. The trees he saw lining the bluffs weren't magnolias, they were madronas (*Arbutus menziesii*), our very own native broadleaf evergreen tree.

Like those of the saucer magnolia, the flowers of the evergreen magnolia are also big and fragrant, but they tend to bloom off and on, rather than putting on one big show. These trees get much taller than the saucer magnolia and therefore can be limbed up more successfully, if access is needed. However, it is preferable whenever possible to leave the lower limbs on this and all magnolias. Besides, if you limb them up all the flowers are overhead. This makes

planting an evergreen magnolia down the hill, or below the second-story balcony (off to one side), a good idea.

I must confess I bear a grudge against evergreen magnolias. It's their leaves. They don't decompose—and they're slicker than ice. I worry about little old ladies slipping on them, and not-so-little or not-so-old maintenance gardener ladies too. This feature makes them a bad choice for sidewalk plantings and patios. Raking them up is like raking up shingles. And the limbs are weak, breaking under snow loads (except the 'St. Mary' and 'Victoria' varieties, perhaps). I have also seen a few trees get a virus disease that causes the leaves to die. It's not a big deal, but it's another strike against them.

On the other hand, I know many other gardeners who especially like the evergreen magnolias. It really is just a matter of personal preference. As you advance in the world of gardening, you become disenchanted with the most common species and more enamored of the rarer and often less showy varieties. My personal feeling is that the reason many, if not all, of the most popular plants are most popular is that they really are the best. I think if you lined up a bunch of those smarmy horticulturists who (for some inexplicable reason) had never seen a magnolia tree before, they would pick out these three as the best.

Star Magnolia

Now the star magnolia (*M. stellata*) is truly a small tree (when it grows up). The mature ones I know are about 10 by 15 feet. For the first decade or two the star magnolia will serve as a nice shrub. Its flowers resemble stars, with straplike white petals. It has the characteristic fuzzy buds, articulate branch structure, and the magnolia's penchant for throwing water sprouts when pruned. Like all the magnolias, it should be planted where it can reach maturity in height and width without restriction.

You can get into trouble limbing up star magnolias, because then you'll have to remove the water sprouts two or three times a year for eternity. (Boy, does that get old fast.) But I have seen star magnolias sold on standards as trees. A standard is a long straight trunk upon which the crown is grafted. These trees, as well as the shrub form of star magnolias, are available with either pink or white blooms.

Other Magnolias

Despite my preferences, you might care to know that horticulturists in our area will be more impressed by finding a cucumber magnolia with yellow flowers (*M. acuminata subcordata*), a bigleaf magnolia (*M. macrophylla*) with fabulous 1- to 2½-foot leaves, or a Campbell's magnolia (*M. campbellii*) with flowers like water lilies on bare branches in March. There are many others. But rest assured, magnolias, no matter what variety, are never considered banal.

Summary

Magnolias are very touchy, and it doesn't take much pruning, even selective pruning, to set off the water-sprout response. Therefore, deadwood only. If you do prune, do so minimally, using small, internal thinning cuts whenever possible.

ORNAMENTAL CHERRY, CRABAPPLE, AND PURPLE-LEAF PLUM TREES (*Prunus* and *Malus*)

This spring I got a call from a lady who said, "I pruned my flowering plum tree according to the instructions in my pruning book. I took out all the crossing branches, the ones headed into the middle, and the water sprouts. There's nothing left, I think I may have killed it!" Although she may have, the more likely scenario is that it will explode into water-sprout regrowth over the course of the next year.

Plums (*Prunus* x *blireiana*, *P. cerasifera* 'Atropurpea', and other cultivars), crabapples (*Malus* spp.), and flowering cherries (*Prunus* spp.) suffer from a great deal of mal-pruning because they have fairly confusing, and to some, upsetting branch systems. They are also usually at a height that most pruners can get to (although height doesn't seem to stop people when they get a hankering to top their birches—the single most abused tree in the Seattle area). The branch patterns on plums, crabs, and cherries naturally cross back and forth. Andrea, my mentor, described it as "dancing branches." I think they look more like someone took the lid off a box of bunnies.

Don't

Watch out! The main reason these trees are difficult to prune is that they are extremely prone to water-sprout regrowth. Water sprouts are the straight, skinny, rapidly growing shoots that are the result of mal-pruning and other forms of stress. These trees just seem to have itchy buds. Walk past them with a pair of Felco pruners and they're likely to throw enough sprouts to turn your hair white. ("Oh, is that what happened?" I can hear someone saying.)

The other problem with plums and cherries (not crabs) is that they are horrible compartmentalizers. (Can I get a "Prunus with an absence of malus" joke in here somehow?) That is to say, they die back readily if branches are shortened (headed). When the jerk who owns the apartment building down by the Jack in the Box in my neighborhood topped five full-sized purple-leaf plums, two died stone-cold dead within the first two years. The rest grew back to exactly the same size (except now their winter branch pattern is ruined and they all have suckers growing from the graft union). I have even seen young cherry and plum trees die from numerous small heading cuts (less than 2 inches). The fact that these species are so sensitive makes me resist even the slightest bit of size reduction.

I remember buying my 'Mount Fuji' cherry many years ago. At first I longed for the branches to be lower and more horizontal. To my delight, I found that over time the limbs folded down and out. A few years later, I realized that they don't stop growing. The lower limbs kept lowering. Eventually one branch headed into the parking space. The one on the other side lowered into foot traffic. I headed one branch back selectively, cutting back to a largish side limb. The other one I cut off completely. This year the tree

is near dead, mostly because of a virus (no inside leaves) and the brown rot (killing branches from the tip back). But I'm certain that the pruning hurt it as well.

It is not uncommon for homeowners with very old, broad-limbed cherry trees to ask to have them pruned back "just a little" to stop them from getting too wide. I never oblige. It's just too hard on a cherry tree, in my opinion, which is old at age forty (see Figure 14.37).

I was most unnerved when some grossly topped cherries (3-foot-diameter trunks, 1-foot topping cuts) that I pass on my way to the Center for Urban Horticulture survived, resprouted, and seemed to be doing fine. Two years later they were gone. I wish that plants responded more predictably to bad pruning, and did so within the first month. Would that trees had vocal cords too. Unfortunately, the

Figure 14.37 Resist size reduction in pruning: **A.** Water-sprout regrowth from "proper" crown reduction **B.** Dieback from heading-back "a little"

death and dieback from topping, heading, and repeat-stripping is bad for trees in a statistical sort of way. Smoking cigarettes only kills some people (not all), and then only after a long period of time. The ill effects of bad pruning often take years to show up. By then no one connects the cause with the effect. The trees are dead and gone.

The Other Common Pruning Mistake

It is important to avoid stripping out the center of a plum, crab, or cherry. New gardeners frequently overprune in this way. If a little is good, a lot is better. But as in cutting hair, it is important to know when to quit. Overthinning is a little harder to forgive when done by experienced professionals, but it is extremely common. In particular, we had one such well-loved arborist here in Seattle. He was the darling, in fact, of some of the wealthier garden clubs. He routinely stripped out these trees to "accentuate" the branch pattern. We sarcastically called him Art the tree shaper. Of course the trees bloomed pathetically, and the tree owners were locked into the expensive re-removal of water sprouts every year, forever. He died a few years ago, but I still run across many examples of his work, living monuments to his ego and his misguided love of trees.

An entire subset of well-educated arborists in the San Francisco area have subscribed to this sort of overthinning; readers down there will have a hard time discerning those arborists who prune well from those who prune too well when talking to them or to their devoted customers. However, I can offer the following advice: With few exceptions, a properly pruned tree will not regrow into a forest of water sprouts the following spring. (The exceptions include elms, which tend to water-sprout no matter how lightly you prune them, and espaliered fruit trees.)

Deadwood

Ninety percent of your cuts should be dead branch, dead stub, and dead twig removal. Summer pruning will make it easier to spot the billions of tiny dead twigs in your cherry tree. I hope you have strong knees and a good aluminum three-point orchard ladder, because such a chore can take up to three hours on a large, old, neglected flowering cherry. But it is well worth the effort.

When I teach grounds crews how to prune we eventually get to the field demonstration, and afterwards a novice is apt to say, "I didn't realize what a big difference taking out the deadwood would make." And next year the job will take only a fraction of the time. For you new pruners, remember to do the deadwood first and to spend almost as much time placing and setting your ladder as pruning.

Live Wood: Remember the Pruning Budget

Now let's move on to pruning live wood. It helps to think of plants as having a pruning budget, which you can spend any way you like. On crabs, cherries, and ornamental plums, the live-wood budget is small (because of problems of compartmentalization and water-sprout regrowth). For example, you can have three big cuts and ten small cuts, or twenty small cuts, or five large cuts, or any combination thereof; but remember you will *not* be allowed to remove *all* the crossing/rubbing, wrong-way branches. So consider carefully before you cut. Choose to remove those branches that will give you the greatest aesthetic improvement (see Figure 14.38). Look for the worst first.

Look for branches that actually touch each other (crossing/rubbing) but that have not grafted to each other (as sometimes happens). If they are not too big (more than 1 inch in diameter), maybe you can cut one out and leave the other, better-placed one. Usually you choose to leave the branch that heads out from the center, but not always. Especially on these trees, the branches' natural habit is to backtrack. I like the description of thinning out trees that says "Every space is filled, but with fewer branches." Try to restrict your cuts to true thinning cuts, taking a small lateral off a parent stem rather than making selective heading cuts that reduce a limb by cutting back to a lateral.

You get more aesthetic bang per buck by removing branches that crowd near the branch crotches. But be careful, it looks so good to take out some of the laterals that you might feel compelled to continue out the branch, leading to overthinning. It is also a common desire among new pruners to cut off all the small twiglets commonly found on cherry tree trunks and branches, to give them that clean look. But remember, these twiglets bloom in the spring and are quite pleasing. Leave as many as you can bear.

Pruning students are admonished not to stay too long in any one place, lest they over-prune. Keep moving, keep moving. When I consider an area of crowded branches, I first try out several possible cuts in my mind's eye. If I am at all in doubt, I don't prune; instead I leave it and move on to something I am confident should be pruned. This is another way to keep yourself from overthinning a tree.

Especially resist the temptation to remove branches at the upper crowns of crabapples in order to smooth out the tree's profile. It invariably causes an upsurge of water sprouts, which *really* ruins the outline. You'll never get rid of them by repruning, and the tree will, in fact, become more labor intensive and unmanageable every year.

The best looking purple-leaf plum trees I've seen are ones that are very old and have never been pruned. Go in, take out "the dead," and leave the rest. Young plums have a lot of water-sprout/sucker-like growth inside the crown. This is normal, and if you

Figure 14.38 Correct pruning: Choose to remove branches that will give you the greatest aesthetic improvement. **A.** Dead stub **B.** Wrong-way branches **C.** Suckers insist on removing it you will get to do more of it every year till you die. The other alternative is to leave those long skinny shoots and let them age, curve gently, and become graceful branches after ten years. Nonintervention is the best strategy.

Do, however, remove any and all true suckers—those that originate on the trunk, graft union (looks like a bulge), or roots. This is a common problem found on crabapples. These suckers will ruin the looks of your tree if allowed to remain. If the suckers originate below the graft union, they will grow up into large trees, overtaking the originally selected plant. Due to mower abuse, my local pizzeria now has three large, green-leafed, white-blossomed plum trees and only one of the original small, purple-leaf, pink-flowering plums that were planted on the parking strip.

Rehabilitative Pruning

I watch trees and landscapes over years, and I am constantly amazed at how well most of them recover, given half a chance. About four years ago, at a condominium I frequently drive by, the landscapers stripped out four purple-leaf plum trees as part of their grounds maintenance program. That spring, the trees shot back up with a ton of water sprouts thick as the hair on a dog's back. Over the next two years the sprouts turned back into branches about the diameter of my wrist. Once they reached the height of the previous tree, they began to arch out and put on side branches (see Figure 14.39). I couldn't believe my eyes. Most of the lesser water sprouts remained puny or died off.

This example goes to show that after a tree has been tipped, topped, or stripped, the next course of action is to *wait*. Getting "on top of it" early will simply put your tree back into a spasm of regrowth. In fact, it's probably best to wait three or four years to do any crown restoration. The exception is the removal of deadwood (stubs, twigs, and branches) as it occurs. After the tree has reached its original height, you may slowly, gently, and over the course of a few years thin out the crowded areas where several branches originate from the same point. Back at the condo complex, the trees reestablished without any help just in time for the next crew to sweep through and tip them all back (arghhhh!).

For a tree that has been clipped into a perfect globe, thin out the lower portions, trying to make the tree more uniformly branched. Grounds crews or condo owners who have inherited globed or umbrellaed trees may simply have to scowl and bear it as trees are resheared until they die (the tree or the person). Few people can endure the middle phase (waiting) in crown restoration. It reminds me of growing out a "perm" or a bad dye job.

Summary

Don't top these trees. Don't tip them or shape them into balls, boxes, or hamburgers. Don't clip your crabapple into a cute umbrella every year. Don't try to turn a fastigiate (skinny) cherry tree into a horizontal tree or cut it back into a diaper shape. Avoid shortening (heading-back) major limbs and overthinning. As a general rule of thumb,

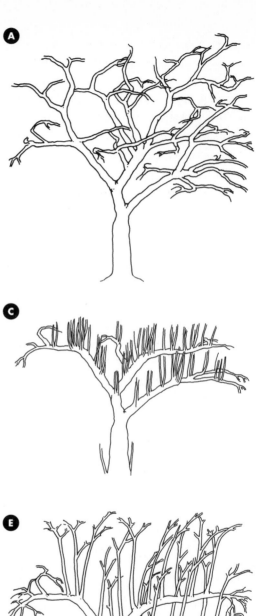

Figure 14.39 A. Original cherry tree B. Overthinned tree: Laterals are stripped. C. The cherry begins to water-sprout. D. Wait! Another year. E. About four years later: The new crown forms.

restrict yourself to pruning less than one-eighth of the living canopy in a year. If water sprouts return at the places you cut, you either overpruned or sliced into the branch collar. Don't restrip trees that have been mal-pruned in the past. I don't care what your old pruning book says.

Do thin lightly, and avoid pruning altogether if you can. Removing deadwood and dead stubs is always in order and doesn't count against the pruning budget. Take out a few of the worst crossing/rubbing and wrong-way branches. Clean out the branch crotches a bit. Take no more than an eighth of the live crown and put up with a lot that is "wrong."

WEEPING CHERRY
(Prunus subhirtella 'Pendula'*)*

"It was a weeping cherry, now it's a crying shame!" So said my co-worker upon seeing a brutally headed weeping cherry tree. It was a double shame, since weeping plants clean up so nicely with a good pruning job. I am always pleased to see a weeping tree of any kind at the site of a pruning demonstration. They're great for giving people a clear idea of what can be done with thinning and without having to get out the ladder.

The Most Common Mistakes

The worst mistake is topping or any other general whacking done to a cherry tree. Genetically speaking, cherries are bad compartmentalizers. That means that they are more likely to rot out and/or die back from such rude pruning. Worse still, they are loaded with dormant buds that are just itching for an excuse to turn into a forest of the straight, wild-looking shoots called water sprouts.

Another common mistake is evenly shearing the branch ends off, like a hair trim. This isn't so hard on the tree's health, but it looks a lot like a "Moe" haircut, and it creates bunching at the ends. The preferred way to prune is to carefully cut each strand back to an out-facing bud or lateral branch. And stagger the cuts at differing lengths around the tree.

Yet another common error is tidying up the topmost portion of the crown by removing that errant branch that sticks up unpleasantly (see Figure 14.40). Next growing season the result will be the growth of two or three more errant branches (water sprouts) beginning exactly at the site of the pruning cut and growing very straight up from there. Remove those and . . . you get even more! So resist the temptation to make your tree a perfect umbrella. Those weeping cherry trees that are perfect are genetically programmed to be so—for example, *P. sargentii* 'Snow Fountain'.

The errant branches of the more commonly planted weeping cherries will eventually droop down as the tree ages, evening itself out naturally. If you look at mature trees in your neighborhood, you will see that they are always a bit asymmetrical in their growth habit. It's how they increase in size.

It's likewise ill advised to try to stop a weeping beech from increasing in size. They don't water-sprout as vigorously as cherries, but like almost all trees, they too resist being kept down.

Suckers

Suckers from graft unions must be removed. Sometimes I drive by a big cherry or plum tree that has mostly white blossoms with a smattering of pinks lower down. The white belongs to the vigorous rootstock that broke free and has outgrown the chosen variety. It's a lot like the "Exorcist" story. Most plants have the weeping part sort of spliced onto the trunk, and you will see that graft union as a bulge at the top. Sometimes there is another bulge (graft union) between the trunk and the rootstock. Keeping your tree healthy, well watered, and properly pruned will help keep Mr. Hyde out of the picture. Should you spot a straight shoot from below that lower graft, saw it off promptly even if it requires a rather big cut.

Deadwood

Deadwood is the next thing you should search out. It's pretty easy to find on cherries. They are commonly and horribly afflicted on the west side of the Pacific Coast mountain ranges with two terrible diseases, blossom blight/brown rot (a fungus) and bacterial canker. Brown rot fills the trees with tiny dead twigs and causes the branches to grow even more kitty wampus than they do ordinarily. In the spring, the disease enters through the blossoms (which later hang on and look water-soaked) and the branch dies from the tip back. At the point where the

Figure 14.40 Young weeping cherry with errant branch **A.** Don't remove errant branch. **B.** Do remove lowest branches and ones hanging closest to the trunk. **C.** Errant branch folds down in time.

Figure 14.41 Dieback and lesions on a cherry tree

disease is finally stopped by the tree, the next nearest bud or twig will grow out (usually at an unsightly 45-degree angle). Nearby and on many branches both large and small, you'll find sunken spots called cankers or lesions, which are another sign of disease (see Figure 14.41).

Bacterial canker (a bacterial disease) causes even larger cankers or lesions on the branches and trunk. It favors injured trees, like those that suffer from mal-pruning. If you follow "the rules" and cut out all diseased branches with lesions on your average cherry tree, you will destroy it! Pesticides, even when dutifully applied, are often ineffective. So it's best to just cut out all the little dead twigs (which can be very time consuming indeed, and is easiest when done in the summer), and rake up all the leaves in the fall on which the disease overwinters. But what a difference deadwooding makes! The

ragged ugly mop turns into a lady's dainty parasol.

In the case of very small weeping cherries (easy to get to), the meticulous removal of dead twigs plus the increased air circulation can significantly reduce both diseases (I've eliminated brown rot on one client's patio tree). Larger, harder to get to cherries will still be chronically afflicted with diseases in wetter, warmer (warm to the fungi) climates. Pruning simply gives the tree a fighting chance and makes it look better. I think of cherry trees as the sick kids of the plant world. There are so many cherry tree diseases (for all the cherry trees), in fact, that the Washington State Cooperative Extension publishes a little booklet titled "Why Cherry Trees Die" (publication number EB0668). It's good for both sides of the mountains and has great descriptions and photos. Contact your local county cooperative extension office if you want to order a copy (look for them in the blue pages, under "County").

Thinning

Thinning in general is the other pruning to be done. You see much improvement by thinning where all the branches meet up together at the top. There you will usually find several big dead stubs where the last pruner failed to cut them off completely. Carefully saw these out. Don't scar the bark of nearby limbs or the trunk, or you will stimulate bothersome water sprouts.

Then remove a few of the lesser crossing or crowded branches. People always want to cut the top back, which, as mentioned above, may get you into deep trouble.

Instead, go inside and remove the branches that are being shaded out underneath. Especially *target the branches that hang closest to the trunk* (see Figure 14.42). Follow them up to their larger parent stems and thin them off where they join it. Trust me, this process will make a huge difference.

Additional definition can be achieved by selectively heading some of the weeping branches that hang down, crossing into branches below. Follow the offender back to a good-sized lateral (at least half the diameter of the branch to be removed). Choose a lateral branch that is located on the upper side of the parent stem that is to be shortened. Look for one that heads out from the center of the plant, and make your cut there. This process can be used to raise

Figure 14.43 Weeping birch

the skirt, should it be trailing too low or on the ground.

Other Weeping (and Curly) Plants

These same general procedures apply to the other great weeping plants (you will find *pendulata* in their botanical names): weeping willows, beeches, spruces, pines, and birches (see Figure 14.43). Thinning will also help turn a wall of weeping blue Atlas cedar into a lovely beaded curtain. But don't attempt to thin out a weeping giant sequoia (it looks like a giant muppet); that one is best kept full bodied.

A good general thinning and deadwooding also does miracles for curly plants (they often have *contorta* in their names), such as Harry Lauder's walking stick (*Corylus avellana* "Contorta') and corkscrew willows. There are several plants that both curl and weep, such as Camperdown elm and some mulberry trees. They too will benefit from similar thinning.

Figure 14.42 Working underneath and inside, remove branches closest to the trunk; cut to scaffold or out-facing branches.

Summary

Take out the deadwood first. Then prune off some of the worst crossing/rubbing branches, but not all of them. Most pruning is done from under and inside the plant. Remove limbs that hang down closest to the trunk. Selectively head lower branches to upper, out-facing laterals. To lift the skirt, prune to out-facing buds or lateral branches of sufficient size. Go easy on the cherry trees because they water-sprout easily, removing no more than one-eighth of the live canopy, and ideally less.

JAPANESE PRUNING OF PINES

by Don Brooks,
Kubota Garden, Seattle, Washington
(This article was originally published in the PlantAmnesty newsletter.)

Pine trees, pruned to reflect those in the exposed mountains and on sea cliffs, have been part of Japanese gardens for centuries. You need not have a Japanese garden to bring these techniques into your garden, as the styles are pleasing and timeless. Hours spent communing with your tree as you shorten candles in the spring, strip needles in the fall, and prune as necessary become a special time—you and your tree together.

The pines in Japanese gardens are pruned to create a desired image, a hint of places you might wish to be. Random elements are removed and harmonious ones are created or retained. You begin by assessing the type of landscape you have or want to have and then create a design to fit that situation. Elements to consider include the species of tree, the establishment of trunk lines and

Figure 14.44 Trunk lines in the trees are prominent features, so it is helpful to divide them into three basic styles.

The formal upright: These trees are peaceful, growing quietly and not exposed to very harsh conditions.

The informal upright: Occasional stress, such as wind, affects the top.

Slanting: Continual stress is evident here. The trunk line can strongly lead your eye to another area of the garden.

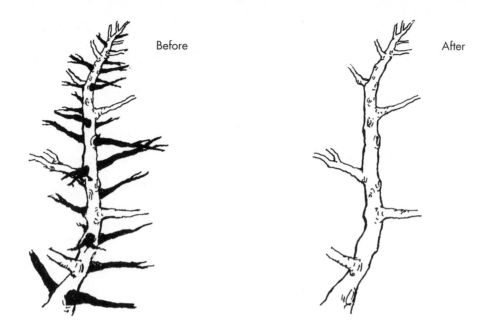

Before   After

Figure 14.45 Establish scaffolds that radiate in a roughly spiral fashion up the trunk, with closer spacing toward the top.

branch structure, the position, and a whole host of others.

Virtually any tree, including pines, can be pruned in what is thought of as the Japanese style. Traditional landscapes in Japan have often been regarded as having masculine or feminine characteristics. The "masculine" landscapes are exposed, rugged areas where the trees feature angular movement, rough bark, and sparse foliage. "Feminine" landscapes are more sheltered and have smoother bark, gentler movement, and more lush foliage. Most landscapes and trees have a combination of these characteristics. "Masculine" species include shore pine, *P. contorta*; Austrian pine, *P. nigra*; Japanese black pine, *P. thunbergiana*; and Scotch pine, *P. sylvestris*. "Feminine" trees include

Japanese red pine, *P. densiflora*; Japanese white pine, *P. parviflora*; and eastern white pine, *P. strobus*.

Trunk Lines

Trunk lines in the trees are prominent features, so it is helpful to divide them into basic styles (see Figure 14.44). After the trunk design has been chosen, either by you or by the tree, you are almost ready to begin pruning. It's important that you always work safely. Trees over 18 feet and trees leaning over water require special ladders or ropes, so it's worth the effort to try to establish your tree at a height and a location that will allow future access, with your fingers, to all parts of the tree.

Figure 14.46 Branch pruning, top view **1.** Remove dead wood. **2.** Remove straight center lines. **3.** Remove old needles. **4.** Pine pushed to the limits of photosynthetic endurance.

Figure 14.47 Branch pruning, side view **1.** Before: Remove branches that hang too far down or project too far up into next layer of scaffolds. **2.** After. **3.** Before: Remove straight lines. **4.** After.

How to Begin

Stand back now and look at the entire tree from all angles. Most styles are based on triangles, as you can observe in the illustrations. The heavier, longer, thicker, and more widely spaced branches occur nearer ground level (see Figure 14.45). Near the top, short, thin, and more closely spaced branches are seen. The branches are usually on the outside of curves to accentuate movement. Throughout the entire tree, straight lines are discouraged (see Figures 14.46 and 14.47). In beginning to prune a pine, consider that once something has been removed, it cannot be put back. Visualization or perhaps a sketch of what you want is helpful. I recommend that novices take it easy and begin with the obvious dead, diseased, and crossing-branch removal, then follow with needling, candling, and finally pruning. This is somewhat the opposite order of the more experienced gardener but is a safe approach until you feel comfortable with the job.

Needling

Each year a new set of needles emerges from the new shoots (candles). In the fall of the year, every two-year-old or older needle is removed by grasping them between your thumb and fingers and pulling, pinching, or twisting them off. The result is an extremely light and airy appearance that offers full views of the trunk and branches as well as admitting light, air, and water. This look lasts until early the next summer, when the new needles join the old.

Figure 14.48 Expanding candle on pine

Candling

The new growth tips are called candles (see Figure 14.48). The central candle will become the continuation of the trunk or branch, with the side candles becoming the side branches. Straight lines are rarely encouraged in these trees, so usually the central candle is completely removed. Timing is important here, and it varies greatly, depending on climate, species, and location. Each tree will have to be timed individually.

Figure 14.49 Candling: Usually take the center entirely; shorten the others.

I like to get the candles when they can still be snapped off with the finest pruning tool of all, your fingers.

Pine branches produce a highly variable numbers of candles, from one to as many as twenty. It is most common to select two or three side candles that will grow into a zigzag pattern, as illustrated (see Figure 14.49). Those few that are left are shortened by pinching off the tip at the appropriate length. A reasonable question to ask is, "What is the right length?" With this artistic form of pruning, there is no correct answer, so simply rely on your sense of proportion. One or two inches is normal. Pinching the tip, if carried out early enough (late spring at the latest), stops its growth at that point and allows it to set buds for next year. Too late in the season, and you run the risk of killing the candle. A good rule of thumb is to perform the operation while the candle is flexible enough to use your fingers. If you wait until pruners are required, you will be cutting the soon-to-expand needles in half and will be risking future bud production. It helps to think of candling as pruning on a small scale. The goal is the same as that of all good pruning—to direct growth in an aesthetic and healthy manner.

Timing

The timing of pruning is problematic. Traditional pruning time in Japan is in the fall, but they have wet and warm summers and cold and dry winters. Few areas in North America have the same conditions. I've noticed Seattle pines killed by excessive fall pruning if a hard winter follows. Hard spring pruning

followed by an especially hot and dry summer can also kill them, so I have adopted a strategy of moderation. A little here and a little there. I always try to prune by removing less than one third of the total needles per year. My ideal is to take four or five years to get a tree in shape. My tools are hand pruners, both Western spring-loaded types and Japanese scissor types, and a small folding saw. My goal is the same as with candling: the creation of curves and zigzags and the avoidance of straight lines.

Branch Styles

I like to divide branch treatment methods into three broad categories. We'll call them the Kyoto (or Imperial) style, the Tokyo style, and the Oriental style. Each requires different amounts of time and labor, and each has a dramatically different look.

The Imperial style can be called the highest form of maintenance in the Japanese garden. Indeed, in classical times a seven-year apprenticeship was undertaken before a gardener was allowed to work alone on a pine. This method requires attention at least twice a year, including candling in the spring, needling in the fall, and pruning as needed. The goal is to create a branch structure so open that a small bird can fly through anywhere. I've experienced this many times, and it's always a magical moment.

The Tokyo style was developed several hundred years ago in response to a shortage of resources. Some things never change! This style essentially omits the needling phase. This leaves much more visible branch pads but less visible branch structure. Candling

Figure 14.50 "The Dieter's Guide to Cloud Pruning"

operations are still carried out by hand and give individual branches an undulating and soft appearance. Needles eventually become shaded out, thus giving the underside a brown, dead look that should be periodically groomed.

The final style, the catchall Oriental style, can include candling with hedge trimmers and poodle pruning. Problems with these techniques include masses of exposed dead needles and the usual aesthetic concerns that typically accompany any action carried out in the least amount of time possible.

In my fifteen years of serious gardening, I've discovered two things that calm my thoughts during periods of stress. One is hand-weeding moss beds and the other is pruning pines. Years of careful observation, both in the wild and in cultivated gardens, as well as years of touching pines, will leave you with the same feeling of peace and satisfaction.

CHAPTER FIFTEEN

Ground Covers

273

At first it might seem obvious that ground covers are those plants that, well, cover the ground. Duh! For many gardeners the term implies masses of low-growing (but not always, according to some garden books) plants that carpet the ground. But then it gets a little more complicated. Ground-cover plants can be shrubs (junipers, heathers, and such), self-seeding annuals or perennials (like sweet woodruff or violets), and clumping perennials (like epimedium or ornamental grasses). Or they can be—what I think of as the truest ground covers—plants that spread by above-ground or below-ground runners. They will differ in their pruning and cultural needs according to which type they are. I intend to focus on the ones that spread by runners or roots. Examples are ivy, hypericum, ajuga, pachysandra, and vinca.

THE MYTH

I often hear the statement that "ground covers will choke out the weeds." Balderdash!

On the contrary, the crisscrossing mats of stems, whether above or below ground, can protect dandelion or grass roots from the would-be weeder's pokey-tool. It's one of the reasons I often find myself hating vinca. And the presence of ground covers can also preclude the use of pre-emergent herbicides, making a problem like "horsetail coming through the kinnickinnick" impossible to solve. Because of these difficulties, I am beginning to think that these sorts of ground covers are a bad idea for so-called commercial sites, the ones with small maintenance budgets (aren't they all?).

The Truth Behind the Myth

Like most things people repeat, there is *some* truth to the statement that ground covers suppress weeds. But there are qualifications. If the newly planted ground cover and the weed grow up together, they will remain friends for life. But if the weed seed introduces itself years later, when the ground cover has become a solid carpet, the weed will find no home. The seed either lands on a leaf or, if it manages to somehow to make its way down to the soil level, is shaded and cannot germinate.

So the take-home message for ground covers is to be religious in keeping the weeds out for the first three years, or until the ground cover has become a thick, uninterrupted carpet. It's a lot of work. It takes vigilance. But after that you will reap the benefits. In the future, the time you spend on weeding will indeed be a lot less than if you had left the ground barren.

And if, at some point in later years, you do spot a bit of grass poking out of your creeping thyme (or any other ground cover or plant), do not (as we are all prone to do) pass by, ignoring it, pretending not to see it, hoping subconsciously that it will be choked out. You must rather descend upon it like a vengeful god and dig it out! Forget what effort it takes, even if it means digging up and tossing out some part of your ground cover. You must destroy the offender! Actually, I find it a little refreshing to have a part of one's life where pigheaded intolerance is a good thing. Rest assured that the ground cover will return, but weed-free. Whereas, if you ignore the weed, it will increase and become more vigorous each year, eventually ruining the entire area.

The Trouble with Ground Covers

The trouble with spreading ground covers is the same as with many of the herbaceous perennials—they tend to be either too vigorous or too puny. Whether or not they are "just right" will vary widely, depending entirely on the situation.

The shade-loving ones sometimes creep out into the sun, where they look yellow and scraggly (pachysandra, ajuga). Or you apply mulch to the beds to slow down the weeds (which it does), only to find that a nearby ground cover takes off and colonizes an entire area you wanted for some other reason (strawberries that send out stringy

runners come readily to mind). Not only that, several of the spreaders are notoriously hard to eliminate once they have claimed a third of your garden as their own (and that is the truest determining characteristic of a weed), examples being hypericum (St. Johnswort) and bamboo.

General Pruning and Care

Many spreading-type ground covers (ivy, pachysandra, ajuga, hypericum) simply adore mulch. If you want them to increase and do well, just add two to four inches of a lightweight (which is to say sawdust-based) compost (like Steerco, my personal favorite) over the ground and watch them take off. You can even spread it a half-inch thick right over an established patch, doing so right after you have weeded it. I sometimes fling shovelfuls of mulch into the beds. This is called "broadcasting." Just make sure a goodly amount of the ground cover's green leaves poke up through the mulch when you are done.

With the other sorts of ground covers, like self-seeders and woody shrubs, mulching is a different matter. Because mulch reduces seed germination, you wouldn't want to spread it over, say, your sweet woodruff patch. It would smother it. On the other hand, if your ground cover is made up of woody shrubs like juniper or heather, mulch won't hurt them, but you must remember to not bury the main stems or to cover over the plants themselves.

A lot of ground covers, and especially the "stringy" ones (such as ivy, vinca, and lamium), like to accumulate at the base of shrubs, crisscrossing over low branches and slowly clogging up the base of the plant. It looks bad. And here your main chore (aside from zealous weeding, as just described) is to get it out of the crowns of shrubs like azaleas and rhododendrons.

This is not a delicate matter. Use your hand pruner and your gloved hands to cut and rip the strings out of the bases of plants. I promise you will discover a marked improvement in the way your landscape looks. Creating definition between the layers of plants is one of the main purposes of pruning, and one of the best ways to create a sense of order in a yard that seems overgrown or out of control. While you're there, you might want to remove a few of the shrubs' lowest limbs. These are the ones most likely to be used as a ladder by the overachieving ground covers (and morning glory, and root weevils!). You'll spot them easily, as they are the ones currently being pinned down by the strands of vinca or ivy. Usually (but not always) prune them off completely, cutting back to the main stem.

Sometimes your ground cover—say, ivy, lithodora, or vinca—has gone too far to the edge of the bed, where it bunches up unattractively like water behind a dam. Or perhaps it has totally obscured the rockery or spilled out into the pathway, menacing pedestrians. Earlier, when it first casually spilled over the rockery or softened the hard edge of the bed or path, it may have looked attractive, but now, a few years later, it has become too much. Most people's first reaction is to shear the plants back even with the bed edge, path edge, or top of the rockery. And as long as that look appeals to you, there's no problem. But if you so desire, you can achieve a more natural look with selective pruning.

First, hold up the upper portions of the "rug" and cut off the underneath parts. It's sort of the opposite of sweeping things under the rug. Then snip what's left in an uneven, sort of shag-haircut manner, so that the planting mimics its earlier stage of development. The ground cover then cascades casually over the rockery, dipping up and down in a random fashion. Or it recedes back from the bed edge as if it hadn't yet grown that far out.

Some ground covers send out running stems above ground (ivy, ajuga, vinca, lamium, strawberry) that take root wherever they touch the soil. It's their way of getting around. You should stand back from the planting and determine whether all the ground cover you see is wanted. Look at the big picture. I often rip out the portions that have reached the bottom of the rockery or have gone into other plantings—or when I feel there is just plain too much. Don't be afraid. It will all come back if you don't like the results of your decision, and (here's the bad news) even if you do.

ENGLISH IVY *(Hedera helix)*

Most professional gardeners hate ivy. I even hate writing about it (probably because it is so ubiquitous). But I don't hate ivy as much as many ecologists I know. Here's their story.

English ivy has been listed as a weed by the Washington State weed control board because of characteristics that make it potentially dangerous to our native areas, not just to your back yard. Unlike many ground covers, it does well both in deep shade as well as the sunny sites that most ground covers prefer. It spreads and roots in a large variety of adverse soils and situations. All of this makes it a good ground cover for freeway plantings and steep hillsides with no irrigation, but it also spells trouble for our native areas. It spreads itself around by seeds (pooped by birds) into native areas, where it takes off, submerging and killing our native understory plants. It creates what has been called "a green desert." Not good at all.

Ivy also climbs up the trunks of big trees, reaching quite high, and then creeps out the limbs. I have never seen ivy totally overtake the photosynthesizing green canopy. (On the other hand, the escaped wild clematis—*Clematis vitalba*—in the Seattle area does easily climb 125 feet into a Douglas fir tree, spill out over the canopy, and entirely block the needles' access to sunlight. I think that wild clematis poses a greater threat to our local forests than does ivy.) Those of us in the field of horticulture disagree about just how dangerous ivy is to big trees. But everybody agrees that it is not a good thing. It covers the trunk, hiding signs of decay from arborists who might otherwise see that a tree is dangerous. It adds weight to a tree, and big ivy stems on younger trees have the potential to girdle. Furthermore, it looks bad, especially as it gathers in the upper canopy like a giant green snot gob. The latter, as you might have guessed, is my opinion on the matter.

Gardeners have always hated ivy because it requires high maintenance and there is just so damn much of it. First I'll tell you how to maintain it in sites where it is wanted. Then I'll tell you how to eradicate it, if that is your plan.

Maintaining Ivy

In the back of my mind, I've been working on something like the "Ten Essential Gardening Tips" for the new professional gardener. So far, I have six: (1) Take the time to remove a stone from your shoe. (2) Go back to the truck for the right tool. (3) Don't nest one 5-gallon white spackle bucket inside another. (4) Go back to the truck and put your rain gear on when the *first* raindrops hit. (5) Don't try to untie knots with gloves on. (6) When working on a bank of ivy, never put your hedge shears down. You'll spend the next hour looking for them!

Shear, Rip, Pry

Most maintenance of ivy on banks and fences consists of shearing it back so that it doesn't keep piling on top of itself. Use hedge shears to do this chore. Don't worry about cutting strands that may parent a portion you are trying to keep—that part has probably rooted-in and is no longer dependent on the umbilical cord. You want your ivy to tightly hug the fence, especially the bottom where it meets the ground. It often looks better to remove large portions of ivy that have overtaken ornamental rocks or the rocks of your rockery. It's a lot like peeling giant oranges. The contrast between the rocks and the ivy is a good one.

On very old clumps of ivy, you will find "mature leaves" that look entirely different than the juvenile leaves we associate with ivy. Some people think it is a different plant altogether. But these mature leaves are usually associated with the seed heads (white flowers on a stalk, which later develop into black berries) that are the enemy forces headed out to ruin our woods. So, if you see these, you are honor-bound to cut them off (see Figure 15.1).

You need to peel ivy off buildings and tree trunks. But if you do this in the spring, it is back up the wall or the tree by July. So if you have only one time to prune during the year, do it in the late summer or fall and it will stay done all winter. If you wait too long, though, the aerial roots will "harden off" and be much more difficult to dislodge. If you get to the stems while they are still in their first year, they give up more easily. I use the blade of my hand pruner to pry the aerial roots off. Cut, pry, cut, and pry. See why we hate ivy?

If you need a ground cover for shade, I recommend pachysandra. It is a very tidy, evergreen, and well-behaved ground cover. And, nobody hates it.

Radical Renovation

You can't really go too far in shearing and cutting ivy. In fact, when a bank of ivy has been let go for way, way too long, it can and should be renovated by shearing and lopping off (with your loppers) every last stitch of green. Take it way down to the woody nubbins. It comes back in about a year. Go ahead, cut and pry out some big thick stems too.

Okay, there is a slight possibility that it might not *all* make it back. So, maybe avoid doing this really drastic thing on the ivy in a

Figure 15.1 Ivy seedhead and mature leaf

narrow parking strip, in the blazing heat of August, or next to a highly reflective surface like Seattle's Holman Road. But, in general, it's okay to shear the top layer of leaves anytime, as long as it looks good to you. Radical renovation is okay when done in the spring or winter. After renovating, do a thorough job of hand-weeding, followed by mulching.

To Eliminate Ivy

Unlike many of my colleagues, I am not inclined to condemn an entire family on the basis of the sinful behavior of one member. Because of English ivy, several other *Hedera* species are suspect: Baltic (*H. helix* 'Baltica'), Algerian (*H. canariensis*), and Hahn's self-branching form of *H. helix* are the most worrisome. The others I am not particularly concerned about. I am personally more agitated whenever I see something from the polygonum (knotweed) family show up in a client's yard. I don't trust any of them! In my opinion, they (and this group now goes under several new species names, making them harder to identify) are far more likely to ruin your yard. Unlike ivy, they aren't likely to seed into the woods. But one, Japanese knotweed (*Polygonum cuspidatum*), has escaped and is considered a nuisance, if not a threat, to the environment.

To eliminate a field of ivy takes a fair bit of determined work, but it can be done. And, more and more, it *is* being done, since it is now considered the socially responsible thing to do. For the most part, hand-grubbing is what's entailed. My husband uses what he calls "the amazing rug-roll technique," which he learned at a PlantAmnesty renovation workshop (see Figure 15.2). He uses a short-handled spade (the kind with a flat, square blade) to loosen, dig, and pry the layer up, and then rolls it back sort of like a rug. It works well to have one person on his or her knees undercutting as another person rolls it back. The advancing roll provides a specific leverage effect that pulls out the roots as it rolls. When I work alone, I use a hand tool that I call the "baby mattock" for the same operation. It chops and loosens the soil, releasing the roots as I roll the ivy toward me. One must have a hand pruner in a holster readily available, too. Having the proper tools is the key to success. Some people get an allergic reaction to ivy, so you may want to wear gloves.

After hand-grubbing the majority of the ivy out of your shrub bed, or peeling it off your walls or out of your rockery, you will need to deal with what I call "the mother root" or, as others term it, "the root of all evil." You'll know it when you see it. It's big and impossible to dig out. I have seen some old ivy stems that are as big as two inches in diameter. If you do not destroy the underground heart of this root, it will grow back into a new vine in a year or two. There may be an acceptable cultural way to do this. Stab it out with a pry bar? Cover it up with a dark, plastic sheet of some sort? But I do not personally know of any that work. I use Roundup (glyphosate), a liquid, systemic, contact herbicide. This means it kills what it touches by being absorbed and moved throughout the plant. I use the cut-stump treatment described in "How to Kill Your Wisteria (and Other Woody Plants)" in Chapter 13, Vines. I just hope my organic friends forgive me for this sin. I also hope that, in this case, the ends justify the means.

In my opinion, Roundup poses a lot less serious threat to the environment than the ivy. According to the scientific data available, glyphosate does not build up in the food chain, or cause birth defects, or hurt your liver. It doesn't stay active in the environment. It is unlikely to move through the soil to get other plants or reach the water table. This is because it binds tightly to soil particles and is no longer available to poison other things.

This is why farmers use it. It kills the plants it touches but does not poison the soil. They can just plow the weeds under and plant corn, or whatever. Because there is no active residue with Roundup, seeds (including weed seeds) will readily germinate the next day. There are good philosophical reasons not to use any herbicides, and I respect people who have sworn them off completely. But my personal decision is to use the big guns, sometimes, when I feel the other options are limited and the need is great.

So I cut the main stem just above the mother root with a pruner or lopper or saw, and then *immediately* (within one minute) brush on a concentrated dose of Roundup. The dose is 50 percent water mixed with 50 percent of the concentrate (the concentration on the jug is listed as being around 28 percent active ingredient). It is my unsubstantiated opinion that full-strength may work less well. Leave about an inch of woody stem—not more, not less. If you leave more, the plant might wall off the area before the poison gets into the root. If you cut lower, two bad things could happen: One, you cut so low that you get dirt on the cut, which inactivates the Roundup. Or two, if you cut too low, and it doesn't work for some other reason (like rain or who knows what), the stem will break bud and grow back. But because you cut so low, you won't be able to get another big, cut surface to paint the second time around. So leave yourself a margin of error, which is to say about 1 inch of stem. When it becomes obvious that the poison failed, wait for a while, then recut and repaint. The best time of year to do this is summer. Wear safety glasses and gloves.

The third step in ivy elimination is follow-up. As with all weeding systems, you only get about 80 percent the first time around. The next year, you need to pick up the strays. Do it by hand. There are no magic substitutes for hand-weeding. Not black plastic, not weed-barrier fabric, "not nothin'." Trust me. If there were, I'd know about it. The third year and thereafter, only tiny amounts of

Figure 15.2 "Hey, did we bring extra epoxy to glue this ground cover down?"

care will need to be taken. I would never expect total victory, though, with this or any other weed situation. Battles are won, but the war is never over.

HYPERICUM *(St. Johnswort)*

The second most hated ground cover is St. Johnswort (*Hypericum calycinum*). I know a gardener who hates it so much he won't use the herbal remedy made from it that is used to treat depression. Like ivy, it is extremely aggressive and difficult to get rid of once established. And it is quite common. As the saying goes, "Familiarity breeds contempt." But I remember the first time I saw the flower—I thought it must have come from heaven, all yellow and silky and delicate. If you have fallen in love with it and long to possess some, I recommend you get any of the *shrub* forms of hypericum, which have the same pretty flowers as well as interesting multicolored berries. Unlike the spreading ground cover, the shrubs are considered "choice."

The Trouble with Hypericum

In the Puget Sound area, both the ground cover and the shrub tend to get leggy, and they develop dark orange to brown spots on their leaves. I refer to this as "leaf crud." A leaf crud is any one of a number of diseases that make the leaves *look* bad but do not actually endanger the plant. You can get rid of it and tidy up the hypericum planting by radically cutting the plant back to an inch or two off the ground (yes, it is really scary looking!). Do it in the spring. By the end of the season, your shrub or ground cover will be back—tidy, full-bodied, with fresh clear leaves and flowers.

In the Seattle Parks Department, where I worked for several years, we would lower the wheels on our mowers and mow the ground cover to an even swath of 2-inch, really ugly barren stems. We could then get to the weeds, which we dug up or poisoned, and then we might or might not have added a light mulch. Everything grew back incredibly tidy and uniform, and looked great for several years. Additional irrigation may ward off the recurrence of "leaf crud," which I tend to associate more with stress, specifically drought stress, than with the presence of moisture (which encourages the fungal leaf cruds). If more water makes it worse, then reduce the flow and try making things drier.

SALAL *(Gaultheria shallon)*

Salal is one of our handsome native ground covers. It is of the sort that creeps by underground stems. It can be both too fussy (because it is difficult to get established) and too vigorous (since some time after it gets going, it spreads and can't be stopped). So take care where you plant it. In some gardens it is the perfect accompaniment to the trees and shrubs. In others it becomes an overbearing houseguest.

Old patches of salal can get too tall, woody, and leggy. Old salal gets a leaf crud of its own, with the leaves developing black spots. Like ivy and hypericum, it not only withstands, but may actually benefit from, a radical renovation done every ten years or so. In the spring, cut every stem back to about an inch from the ground, two inches at most. People try to be nice by cutting higher. Don't. It actually looks worse right after you do it, and the results are not as good when it grows back. In a year it will all come back, perhaps spreading more evenly, and the leaves will be fresh, green, and unspotted. Thoroughly weed the area while you can see the ground. Add mulch while you're in there. Add extra irrigation if there is a terrible drought. But otherwise, don't worry—be happy.

Summary

• Creeping ground covers such as ivy, vinca, lamium, ajuga, St. Johnswort, and strawberry bunch up in the bases of shrubs and should be cut and pulled out.

• Creeping ground covers can be reduced to a more manageable size by ripping out unwanted portions, by undercutting the bottom portion of plants, and by snipping back the leading edges into an uneven, natural form.

• Ivy is considered a threat to native areas, and a lot of trouble by maintenance gardeners. Prune annually by hedge shearing. Rip and pry it off walls and tree trunks. Eradication is encouraged and can be achieved using "the amazing rug-roll technique." The judicious use of the herbicide glyphosate (Roundup) as a cut-stump treatment can stop the vine from returning.

• Ivy, hypericum (St. Johnswort), and salal can all withstand radical renovation done in the spring. This will modify the height of the planting and can eliminate, at least for a while, leaf-marring diseases.

• For more information about invasive plants and weeds, contact your regional noxious weed control board or the Department of Natural Resources for more information about invasive species in your area. Here in the Northwest, go to *www.dnr.metrokc.gov/ wlr/lands/weeds/weed_control_board.htm.*

CHAPTER SIXTEEN

Even More Plants to Prune

AUCUBA, FATSIA, AND SKIMMIA

Aucuba, fatsia, and skimmia might fit nicely into a group of plants some gardeners might call "loser shrubs." But one of the conclusions I have drawn from twenty years of gardening is that any plant, when used to its highest and best advantage, is valuable and admirable. There are no bad plants, just plants in the wrong place. That place could be the North American continent. And I realize there are people out there who need to know how to prune them, dull as they may be. So here goes:

AUCUBA (*Aucuba japonica*)

The right and best place for an aucuba is in the low-water-use, part-shade-to-almost-full-shade part of the yard. I have seen aucuba used most effectively as understory in the woods. You know the place. It's where the rhododendrons are too leggy, suffering from lack of water, and blighted by powdery mildew.

Aucuba is a broadleaf evergreen shrub that grows about 5 to 6 feet tall and just as wide. The ones most frequently used have variegated leaves, usually gold and green. I'll never forget finding them in the nicest garden for which I have ever been the caretaker. That estate belonged to a wealthy lady of impeccable taste who was also a keen gardener. Her variegated aucubas brightened up the area under the conifers, and they hid the compost pile and made a good backdrop for a perennial border. A leafy branch of aucuba, placed together with daffodils and a few other green and gold elements from her

garden, looked fabulous in a vase. Aucuba leaves also proved useful for creating holiday decor.

I have found that most people develop a dislike for a particular plant because the specimens they've seen were in the wrong place, planted too close together, and/or chronically mal-pruned or diseased. Aucuba, for example, looks spectacularly horrid when planted in the sun and sheared by the grounds crew, as it so often is.

The Trouble with Aucuba

I put aucuba in the mounding-habit pruning category rather than in the tree-like shrub category because of its soft (more herbaceous) branches. The tree-likes have stiffer, more intricate branching systems that make them good candidates for thinning. I have seen only one aucuba successfully skirted and thinned. Most often such attempts succeed only in revealing numerous skinny, wiggly, black, and basically yucky branches hidden beneath the leafy canopy. Therefore most pruning done to aucuba will be limited

Figure 16.1 Aucuba pruning

to tidying up the perimeter (only if necessary) with the grab-and-snip method, and making a few selective heading cuts, hidden down inside the plant (see Figure 16.1).

Radical Renovation

Aucuba also responds well to cutting back to near ground level. If you attempt this type of pruning, for whatever reason, do it in a kind season (not too hot, not too cold, and not too dry) and do it to healthy plants only. Don't prune it higher up, trying to be nice. Half measures avail us nothing. Cut low down—1 inch to 1 foot above ground level. Radical renovation is like surgery; it's really hard on the health of the patients. Sometimes they die. And it is not a regular maintenance procedure. It should be done only, say, once in ten or fifteen years to rehabilitate a previously mal-pruned plant.

Note that radical renovation, like most other kinds of pruning, usually fails at keeping a plant smaller than its genetically programmed mature size. For an aucuba, that size is about 5 feet by 6 feet. If your aucuba doesn't have that much room to grow, consider transplanting (although my husband, the Transplant King, says aucubas are not good subjects for transplanting) or total removal.

FATSIA *(Fatsia japonica)*

Personally, I like fatsia. It's tough. It likes the shade. It can be pruned to fit a tall, narrow spot. And it's unusual, having a sort of tropical-looking leaf. Some people are embarrassed by them.

One unfortunate habit of fatsia is that it holds on to its older leaves after they turn yellow, then brown, and eventually black. So you may need to groom your fatsias regularly, cutting or brushing off the offending leaves as necessary. Some years are worse for spent leaves than others. I'm not sure why.

Pruning

Fatsia is definitely in the cane-grower category. You can remove entire canes (even those 2 or more inches in diameter) by cutting them to the ground. This can thin the shrub out, or it can fix a specific problem, such as a branch that's interfering with foot traffic, or crowding another shrub, or rubbing the house. If you don't remove too many canes, it may stay thinned out. If you remove a few more you may, on the other hand, stimulate new canes to arise from the base, eventually making the shrub thicker and bushier.

These two seemingly opposite effects of removing canes (thinner and bushier) are a puzzler for people. It reminds me of the question I asked my mom when I was a little girl. Watching her as she was cooking, I asked, "Does stirring something make it hotter or cooler?" Her answer was "It depends." Quite an impossible and frustrating answer for a little girl, but true nonetheless.

You can readily make any desired selective heading or selective thinning cut. You won't ruin the plant's looks or stimulate ugly water sprouts. And you can even make a large, horrible-looking, nonselective heading cut anywhere along the entire length of a cane, with every expectation that it will break bud and grow out some nice-looking side branches in a year's time. And it is quite acceptable to radically renovate a fatsia by cutting *all* the canes to an inch or two or three above the ground.

SKIMMIA *(Skimmia japonica)*

This is another shade-lover. Every once in a great while I see a nice-looking group of skimmia. I say "group" because skimmia is *dioecious*, meaning that you need both a male and a female plant to get a nice set of red berries. These berries often appear simultaneously with the white flowers, which, shown against the deep green leaves, make a pleasant sort of Christmas-like motif. Skimmia is also in the "rare and much needed in the Northwest" category of shrubs under 4 feet.

The Trouble with Skimmia

But I have seen only two or maybe three instances of good-looking skimmia. More often, and familiar to all professional gardeners, is the mite-ridden, bleached-out, sucked-to-pale-lime-colored leaves of the average skimmia planting. There is a list of Northwest plants so plagued by diseases that gardeners avoid recommending any of them. As one looks down the list, a vivid picture bubble of the disease-ridden plant pops up in the mind's eye. Cherry = blossom blight/brown rot. Blue spruce = spruce adelgids. Crabapples and plums = scab. Dogwood = anthracnose. Rose = black spot and powdery mildew. Skimmia = mites.

In general, I'd say you have a better chance of avoiding the mite problem if you plant your skimmia in the shade. I've always assumed that giving it plenty of supplemental summer water would help too. But experience confounds me. One of the instances of a good-looking skimmia is the one I cut to the ground and transplanted to a spot under a blue Atlas cedar, where it receives no water, ever, that I can determine. It's one of the few things I put there that survived, and it looks great. Go figure.

And, if the homeowner doesn't know any better, I suppose the pale lime-green foliage of his or her skimmia could be considered a nice contrast to the other, darker green leaves of most landscape plants. Yeah, that's it; it's a 'Golden' variety.

Pruning

Radical renovation is okay for a skimmia if it is needed for some reason. Generally this plant is pruned like others in the mounding-habit category—which is to say gentle size reduction and tidying of the shrub, using the grab-and-snip technique. Sometimes you can even head back branches nonselectively, cutting to a point inside of the shrub. There it will break bud and grow out with nice-looking new branches quite readily. And sometimes you can even thin out a skimmia, as you would a tree-like shrub, revealing a nice branch structure. It will bush out rather quickly, though, and maintaining it as a thinned-out shrub can be labor intensive.

CEANOTHUS *(Ceanothus* spp.*)*
by Bill Wanless

For many gardeners in the Northwest, the amazing blue color of the ceanothus flower is the big draw. Some stop there; others are delighted to learn that there are also pink- and white-flowering species. The small- to medium-sized leaves have their own glossy green charm, and the many forms that ceanothus takes, from prostrate shrubs to 20-foot ones, both evergreen and deciduous, provide many possibilities to explore (see Figure 16.2). Over fifty species can be found from Canada to Mexico and from the East Coast to the West Coast.

Sounds great, let's go to the nursery and load up! Well, first we need to get a full and balanced picture here. The big "cons": some are not cold hardy; they are often short lived; they seem confusing to prune; and, of course, they have their own pest and disease list. Depending on where you live, there may be only a handful of choices. Nevertheless, you decide to forge ahead, and now you have at least one plant to put in your garden. Before going further, here is the plant culture part of the show. Make sure the soil drains well (or slopes), don't pile mulch up against the trunk, and do not give it summer water! Also, don't forget that in the Northwest, it will get at least one and a half times bigger than the size shown on the tag.

Pruning

OK, so what do you need to know about pruning? First, decide what you're trying to achieve. Will you be pruning it as a hedge? Training it against a wall? Making it tree-like? Or are you just concerned about health and general beauty? These answers will help determine what to do and when.

One of the best ways to approach pruning is to divide the world of ceanothus into evergreen and deciduous. In general, evergreens

need a light touch, while deciduous ones can be pruned quite hard. The next question is "When do they bloom—in spring or late summer?" Like most maintenance pruning, ceanothus pruning is best done shortly after the plant blooms (easy to remember), when it is beginning the process of developing next year's flowers. If you prune a summer-flowering plant in the spring, you will miss the show that summer!

As with most plants, the process of encouraging a pleasing shape must be started when the plant is young. Attempts to correct the form later on are often a dismal failure.

Figure 16.2 Ceanothus

Evergreen Ceanothus

For evergreen ceanothus, prune as little as possible. You really don't have to do much, if any, pruning, and the plant will be fine. If you want to promote a denser look, tip-prune only the new growth. The temptation to do more drastic shaping can lead to bad judgment. I have cut back evergreen ceanothus branches to reduce the plant's size, taking care to cut where there are clearly new side shoots. But cutting back farther into older, thicker branches beyond that green zone will likely leave you with ugly dead stumps. A too-large evergreen ceanothus is one of those plants that leaves you with only one option—removal.

Deciduous Ceanothus

This type of ceanothus does better with routine pruning. In the first couple of years, try to develop a permanent framework: Cut back main stems by about half to outward-facing buds, and cut side shoots back to about 6 inches or so. From then on, don't be quite so heavy-handed, just prune back to the framework you created. Unlike the evergreens, deciduous ceanothus can be radically renovated (cut back close to the ground)—you get to start over!

As with all woody shrubs, an important part of your pruning routine should be the removal of any dead or damaged branches. A little bit of thinning can't hurt—just look for the worst of the small branches starting to grow into or across the center of the plant. These two steps improve a plant's health by limiting opportunities for pests and diseases and make your plant more beautiful. If you have chosen one of the larger species, one option you have is to arborize the shrub—to make it more tree-like by heavier thinning. Ideally, this should be done as the plant grows, but can be done later if you do it over two or three years. One last note—in my experience, a mature ceanothus most likely will not transplant well, so choose a good spot the first time.

All this fuss and bother may persuade some people that ceanothus is not worth it. However, I think Michael Dirr summed it up best in his book *Manual of Woody Landscape Plants*: "A final thought takes the author and the reader to Edinburgh Botanic Garden almost 16 years past where the first rich blue Ceanothus stopped me in my tracks. The camera nearly imploded. This form is listed as 'Edinburgh' and is almost justification for traveling to Scotland." Then again, my Scottish heritage doth cloud my vision at times.

DAPHNE *(Daphne* spp.*)*

I was pleased to be in the audience when somebody asked garden writer Marianne Binetti why their daphne, a longtime garden resident, had suddenly died. Marianne responded that daphnes just up and commit suicide every once in a while. That remains my favorite Mariannism. Yes, it's true. The daphnes are a finicky lot. But they are well worth the trouble. My own garden, which started out twenty years ago with a semblance of grace and theme, has degenerated into a hodgepodge of salvaged plants and a collection of two genera—*Hydrangea* and *Daphne*. I can't help it.

Winter Daphne *(Daphne odora)*

You can't beat daphne. My front yard has many sweet spring smellers—*Daphne odora*, osmanthus, hyacinths, pieris. I needn't have bothered with any but daphne. *D. odora* easily wins the best-fragrance awards—first, second, and third place. During bloom time, I spot passers-by hunting her down with their noses, so heavenly sweet is she. And she lifts my spirits every day for over a month—the rather bleak month of February—and on into March. Now that's a hardworking, gardenworthy plant. I've never had an employee who didn't develop a crush on daphne. I'm still in love with daphne twenty years later. She is my second "Daphne O." The first one died when I tried to move her. Even though I had been warned "Daphnes don't transplant," I thought it would be different for me.

My "Daphne O." looks pretty bad much of the year, especially during the winter and on cold spring days—her leaves are cupped and bleached. And in the summer too, as there's a bit too much sun where she's planted. The entire shrub is rather floppy. In a really cold winter she totally defoliates (but she refoliates by summer). Nevertheless, she enjoys "most favored plant" status.

In some people's yards—yards suffering from neglect and maltreatment including shearing—daphne does great. Other times, in perfect conditions, she dies. To paraphrase Freud, "What does daphne want?' We're not really sure. We are told to plant daphne in well-drained soil, give her 3 hours of shade in the summer, and reduce summer water to a minimum. These plants are drought tolerant, and, in fact, they are prone to "water mold." Daphne prefers a pH of about 7, so in the slightly acidic soils of the Pacific Northwest, a little lime may be in order.

I recommend that everyone try a daphne, and see if she likes you. If she doesn't make it, don't take it personally.

Pruning

I have resisted commenting on the pruning of daphnes, including *D. odora*, since my knowledge is incomplete. I'll clue you in to my current knowledge base, under the assumption that some knowledge is better than none. Given the touchy nature of the beast, most people are afraid to experiment on their daphnes, as am I. In researching the topic, I pass on my favorite quote from the 1972 edition of George E. Brown's *The Pruning of Trees, Shrubs & Conifers*: "Normally these shrubs do not require pruning and their response if carried out is so varied that the advice is, do not try it."

That said, I do, from time to time, prune *D. odora* using the grab-and-snip technique. Usually I do that in spring to get some flowers to bring inside. Also, this shrub gets pretty floppy, and it's perfectly okay to cut off, or cut back to a side branch, any branch that's lying on the ground and extending onto neighboring plants (see Figure 16.3). And one can try to perk it up by removing some of the longest branches lying on top of others. And, although I always resist pruning for size constraint, I have done it under certain conditions. The plant is generally 4 feet tall by 5 feet wide at maturity, and you should count on that when you site your shrub. But it will get up to 8 feet tall and as wide, and I have a client who complains that his *D. odora* is swallowing up the yard (most people would be gleefully beside themselves to have such a robust and healthy plant). But as it was actually engulfing a pathway and a little bridge, I did indeed prune hard, rather ruthlessly cutting back branches to side

Figure 16.3 How to prune *Daphne odora*: Remove branches shown in black.

are very poisonous, as are all parts of all the daphnes. If this plant survives, it gets to be about 4 feet tall. It is a deciduous shrub that the *Sunset Western Garden Book* describes as having "rather gawky, stiffly twigged, erect growth" (see Figure 16.4). For pruning instructions, see the George E. Brown quote on page 289.

branches deep inside the plant, and even making some rather nonselective heading cuts. I was pleased to find that all of them broke bud like crazy and greened back up nicely. Hmmmm. It makes me wonder if such a shrub could be radically renovated.

February Daphne *(D. mezereum)*

More than one *D. mezereum* has died in my yard. I was relieved to hear from the nurseryperson that they no longer carry this plant because it gets a deadly virus. So maybe it wasn't my fault, after all. On the other hand, I saw a lot of these in Alaska, and rather large ones at that. So is it a tough plant or a delicate one? Well, it's a daphne. I still really want one. But *D. mezereum* is definitely a plant lover's plant. That's because it's basically just a stick that covers itself in a purple sweater of sweet-smelling flowers really, really early in the year. The rest of the time it is pretty unremarkable. Oh, I guess I should say it has some nice red berries later on. Those berries, by the way,

Figure 16.4 *Daphne mezzereum*

Garland Daphne *(D. cneorum)*

Daphne cneorum (pronounced knee-OR-um) is a low, ground-hugging mat that almost always dies—which is why, I guess, the books refer to it as a "choice rock garden plant." I never plant it any more. If you are tempted to try it, I've found some interesting advice on its maintenance. I quote again from *Sunset*: "A noted rock garden authority recommends throwing rocks at your *D. cneorum*: the rock bruises the stem and holds it against the soil in a layering process."

Daphne burkwoodii

D. burkwoodii, including the nice varie-gated form 'Carol Mackie', is one of the lesser daphnes that are becoming more and more common (see Figure 16.5). And we are all glad to see it. It has small leaves, grows 3 to 4 feet tall and just as wide, and here in the Northwest it loses its leaves in winter (although the books call it semi-evergreen). It has pretty little nosegays of sweet-smelling, white-fading-to-pink flowers in late spring and again in late summer. It turned out to be the perfect plant for the spot at the base of my wisteria. I had been looking for something that didn't get too big to act as an anchor and a counterpoint to the mega-show that my wisteria puts on, and that would bloom at the same time. (Other good companion plants for wisteria are ceanothus and 'London Pride' saxifrage.) It's nice to have some shrubs that are smaller than rhodies, camellias, pieris, and, well, just about everything. And with smaller leaves too, for more contrast in our yards. A *D. burkwoodii* in one of my customers' yards is doing well under the canopy of some cherry trees, where other plants failed to thrive; it's holding its own against the life-sucking mass of cherry tree roots.

For pruning instructions, see Brown's advice on page 289. In a personal confession, I will admit to a pruning experiment perpe-trated on my own plant last year. Because the shrub was getting a bit too big and a bit too leggy for its spot, I, well, I sheared it mid-season. Yes, I did. I just wanted to see what would happen. It's part of my job descrip-tion to test for pruning information. My *D. burkwoodii* branched out at each cut end and was bushier and shorter and tidier. So far, so good. Then the leaves fell off for the winter and all the "hydras" at each cut end (which had collected a mess of those dead leaves) were visible. It looked like heck. I guess I knew that one of the criteria for a good "shear plant" (hedge plant) is that it is evergreen so that the ugly heading cuts are never seen. Duh! Can one radically renovate this shrub with any luck? I don't know.

HOLLYWOOD JUNIPER *(Juniperus chinensis* 'Torulosa'*)*

I'm fond of Hollywood junipers. Talk about a plant with character! Every time I see one I sing the first bars of "Hollywood" ("Hollywood—dah, dah, dah, dah, dah, dah, dah—Hollywood"). These shrubs have got "good action," twisting upward like giant green flames (see Figure 16.6). Some people do find these plants a bit strange, so they should be sited carefully, not placed next to some other oddball plant such as a weeping birch or a corkscrew willow. I think they're great when used either as a mass planting or as a single accent.

Figure 16.5 *Daphne burkwoodii*

Figure 16.6 Hollywood juniper

Hollywoods are relatively small for a conifer, starting out as a handsome shrub and eventually becoming a 15-foot tree. I've seen them used effectively planted in a row separating two parking lots. Another great use I admired was as a contrasting footing to a really big, multi-angular apartment complex. Hollywoods were the perfect choice for the long, narrow space on top of a rockery next to the building, and above the street and sidewalk. Yet some idiot grounds-keeper still felt compelled to level out the tops. And that chore couldn't have been easy. What is it with people that they have to straighten and smooth out nature? It drives me nuts. But you already knew that.

Hollywood junipers are also versatile among conifers in that they can be pruned in a number of ways. There isn't much you can do in the way of pruning with, say, a spruce tree. But Hollywoods can be practically espaliered, or extensively thinned, or skirted up and made to look more tree-like.

The Don'ts

Don't shear your Hollywood juniper, and don't head the branches back to make it into a roughly rounded shape (see Figure 16.7). That wouldn't hurt it, as junipers are great compartmentalizers, and they can't water sprout, so that's not the problem. But such pruning is an aesthetic travesty of the highest order!

And you should also be aware that junipers, like most conifers and needled evergreens, can't break bud and put on new green needles and twigs if you have cut back into the barren branches (the dead zone). If you hack off every speck of green on your forsythia or laurel, it might not look good, but it will create a whole set of new replacement branches (starting out as water sprouts). Not so for junipers, so take care! Before you remove a limb of any juniper, plan a couple of moves ahead. This can save you heartache later.

Figure 16.7 Hollywood juniper looks great unpruned.

The Do's

Do inter-limb, thin, and/or skirt-up as needed. (All three of these techniques are described here.) And always give due consideration to the possibility of leaving the plant alone—the best and cheapest form of plant management.

Inter-limbing

Inter-limbing, also called layering or windowing, is the procedure of removing some of the main limbs, taking them off where they meet up with the trunk. Stagger the removals: To achieve a natural and pleasing effect, take one limb off this side, then one off the other side at a different height. Generally speaking, one would use this technique to solve a problem. For example, you could remove some lower limbs to accommodate pedestrian passage on a path, and then inter-limb above to ensure that the plant didn't look top-heavy or lopsided. Or, if the juniper is in front of a window and you want a partial view or a whole one, inter-limbing might be the answer.

In another situation, I had a client who had topped back her Hollywood in an ill-fated attempt to keep it under the eave. In response, the topmost side branch took over as the new leader and shot up, clearing the gutter admirably. My strategy was to let it continue up, while allowing some space between it and the eave. To make it look acceptable to the homeowner, I had to do quite a bit of thinning and inter-limbing below so that the top and bottom matched each other in density. I also cleaned up the stubs and meticulously removed any exposed tiny dead twigs. (Such deadwooding is always a "must" in conifer pruning!)

Thinning

Thinning, also known as lacing, involves removing many smaller side branches from the scaffold (main) branches (see Figure 16.8). (Here again, if you don't have to thin, leaving the shrub alone is a choice.)

Figure 16.8 Hollywood juniper thinned out.

I can think of an instance where I spent an hour or two thinning. The Hollywood was planted in that awkward space between the house and the walkway. By thinning off all the twigs and branches headed into the walkway, and with meticulous deadwooding, I made the plant into a rather successful espalier. As with inter-limbing, an artistic eye is needed. Thinning a branch means that you "take some and leave some" along the length of the branch. Don't confuse thinning with stripping or poodle-balling, in which everything along each branch is removed, leaving only tufts of green at the ends. Thinning and

Figure 16.9 Okay: Arborized.

deadwooding can be a good way to fix your mistakes if you've unwittingly cut back your Hollywood juniper leaving stubs and exposing dead twigs.

Skirting

Skirting is also known as arborizing, limbing-up, or crown raising. By taking off several lower limbs, you can turn a large shrub into a small tree. I have admired a double-trunked Hollywood at a commercial site in the north end of Seattle that somebody skirted to good effect. The rest of the work on that property was pretty awful. So I think our landscaper just lucked out. To decide whether or not your Hollywood is suitable for skirting-up, take a peek inside and ask yourself, "If I take all the lower limbs off, will it look like a nice tree with a trunk that leans and twists and has good taper? Or will it look like an ostrich, with a skinny silly leg and a big round top?" (See Figure 16.9.) Remember, we want trees, not lollipops!

Is Cloud Pruning an Option?

Finally, I should report that at a lecture I attended on Japanese-style pruning, the teacher mentioned that the Japanese were beginning to use Hollywoods to replace cloud-pruned pines in formal gardens. (See the table "Pruning Art" in Chapter 14, Trees, page 229.) As there would be no candle-pruning required, and presumably a lot less "needling" involved, it would be a lot less work. I must say it made me squirm to consider the results, which might look a lot like poodle-balling (or not), given the eye of the pruner (see Figure 16.10).

Figure 16.10 Not good: Poodle-balled.

SARCOCOCCA AND DROOPING LEUCOTHOË

Here are two nice lower-story shrubs that will definitely be on the word list for the Horticultural Spelling Bee, along with *fuchsia*, *mycorrhizae*, and *phytophthora*.

SARCOCOCCA (*Sarcococca* spp.)

This plant comes in two types. Tall sarcococca (*S. ruscifolia*) gets about 4 to 6 feet tall and 3 to 7 feet wide. Low sarcococca (*S. hookeriana* var. *humilis*) spreads by underground runners and grows about a foot tall. Both are tough plants that like the shade, including deep shade. They are tidy, are prone to few diseases or pests, and have glossy, dark green, narrow, pointed leaves along rather cane-like branches (see Figure 16.11). The *Sunset Western Garden Book* says that these plants are "of great value in landscaping shaded areas—under overhangs, in entryways, beneath low-branching, evergreen trees. They maintain slow, orderly growth and polished appearance in deepest shade." I include them on the extremely short list of plants recommended for that difficult, narrow space between your walkway and the side of the house. Gardeners also like them because they have tiny fragrant flowers in late winter and early spring. Sarcococca won't impress anybody on a garden tour, the way a tree peony or a black daylily would.

Figure 16.11 Sarcococca before pruning.

But clever designers will work it into almost every shade-garden plan. They know that the homeowners will be pleasantly surprised by its olfactory treat. Consciously or not, they'll also appreciate its easy maintenance.

Figure 16.12 Sarcococca after pruning outer canes to ground level; note walkway.

Pruning

In general, this plant doesn't need or want much pruning. It occasionally crowds a wall or a window or a pathway, at which time you can cut out the outermost canes, removing them at ground level (see Figure 16.12). Sometimes one or two of the newer canes will shoot up awkwardly, overstretching the accepted perimeter of the shrub. Cut it back to that side branch or, if there isn't one, cut it completely to the ground. Although I don't think of sarcococca as being a problem plant, I do sometimes find that it suffers from mysterious defoliation of some canes. Those are also candidates for removal.

I guess all this means that sarcococca is generally pruned like a cane-grower but sometimes like a mounding-habit plant. And I feel compelled to tell you that it is sometimes listed as a good plant for a low, formal hedge. Yes, it is. In fact, I've seen it used that way in a garden. It was sheared into a 10-inch-high hedge that edged a square planting bed . . . and it looked just fine!

DROOPING LEUCOTHOË (*Leucothoë fontanesiana*)

How's that for a plant name? Leucothoë is pronounced "lew-COE-thew-way," at least by me. I especially like the little marks above the ë. And then there's the assonance, "droop-ing" and "lew-coe-thew-way." Does it mean there might be something called a "slovenly dove tree"? An "embarrassed pieris"? Or a "parsimonious escallonia"?

Anyway, leucothoë. It's another lower, slow-growing shrub with gracefully arching branches (see Figure 16.13). It grows 2 to 6 feet tall, spreads by underground runners, and takes shade or gentle sun. Its leaves are larger than sarcococca's, and they are leathery green, turning bronzy in the fall. It has clusters of creamy white flowers in spring, resembling those of lily-of-the-valley and, well, drooping. There's a really nice

---

Figure 16.13 Drooping leucothoë

multitoned variety called 'Rainbow' that has leaves that are yellow, green, and pink!

Drooping leucothoë is pruned pretty much the same as sarcococca. Except I wouldn't shear it. It reacts very badly to nonselective heading cuts—the headed branches die back. It also suffers mysterious dieback of lower, internal branches that haven't been pruned. This is not a big problem, though. Just prune them out. And, in fact, to make this plant look generally better, I recommend pruning out some of the lower inside growth even if it's alive and healthy. If necessary, canes can be cut to the ground, and a little selective heading using the grab-and-snip technique is okay too.

STRAWBERRY BUSH (*Arbutus unedo*)

Many years ago when I worked for the Parks Department, I got a call in October from someone who had visited one of my parks and was dying to know what that shrub was that had yellow, orange, and red balls and little white flowers on it. It took me a moment to locate it mentally. "Oh, that's a strawberry bush. *Arbutus unedo*," I said. Now *there's* a practically flawless plant. It has a beautiful branch structure featuring twisting, peeling red branches in old age. It has glossy broadleaf evergreen leaves, and it's almost pest and disease free. I guess specimens occasionally freeze to death in a very cold winter around here. But in general, it tolerates a wide variety of sites and conditions, including windswept beaches and clay soils.

And then there are the balls and flowers, ornamental but understated. The fruits (the "strawberries") are edible but rather bland

and mealy. The clusters of urn-shaped flowers are characteristic of the family Ericaceae. *Arbutus unedo* is little brother to our endangered madrona trees (*A. menziesii*), and I may be wrong, but I think of it as big brother to the manzanitas, also beautiful but hard to keep alive.

Your average strawberry bush gets to be 8 to 35 feet. That's pretty dang big. (And it's probably why many garden books and many people call it "strawberry tree.") Mostly what is sold is *A. unedo* 'Compacta', which is more in the 6- to 10-foot range. There is a true dwarf, *A. unedo* 'Elfin King', that stays about 5 feet tall—good for your planter box or entryway pot, flowering and fruiting all year long.

Thin Out or Limb Up

Generally speaking, you can choose to do nothing to your strawberry bush for many years. When it gets old and looks too imposing, you can thin it out to reveal the nice internal branch structure. And thinning it out makes it airy and delicate looking. If you take off many of the lowest side branches too (called skirting or limbing-up), then a large, mature strawberry bush turns into a nice, small strawberry tree. Such a process is called *arborizing*. Strawberry bushes do not water-sprout easily, so they can be pruned a fair amount. My guess would be that up to a third of the foliage can be removed without stimulating sprout response. Follow the instructions in Chapter 12, Tree-Like Shrubs. Start with the deadwood. Thin off many small side branches, spreading those cuts evenly throughout the plant. Take some,

and leave some. Don't confuse thinning with "stripping," in which all the laterals are skinned off, leaving only a little foliage at the ends of the branches. Or, on the other hand, you can just leave your strawberry bush fully foliated and dressed to the ground, especially if you want it to be a screen.

Grab-and-Snip

I suppose someone might need to tidy up a strawberry bush at some point, or slightly reduce its size. If it is being allowed enough room to grow to its adult size. I don't suppose a great deal of harm will be done by making a few judicious selective heading cuts.

Locate the branch that sticks up over your window; follow it down to where it meets up with a shorter side branch, and cut it off there. Repeat with the next-worst branch that interferes with foot traffic or touches the house or whatever.

You are forbidden to shear this plant, because it is so nice. But I suspect that it puts up with such treatment pretty well. At least the one down at Dick's Drive-In seems to be doing okay. I probably shouldn't say so in print.

Radical Renovation

Arbutus unedo does stump-sprout, however. And that's some good news if it has been over-thinned or has frozen to the ground. Or if, for some unfathomable reason, you need to cut it to the ground and regrow it. I saw a large, lovely old arborized *A. unedo* freeze three or four years ago. It has regrown from sprouts that arose from the trunk, 1 to 6 inches above ground level. Those sprouts eventually turned into a new bush about 4 to 5 feet tall, but at this point, their stems are straight and thin. It will take another eight years for them to twist and curve, and become the well-tapered trunks of the original.

VIBURNUM DAVIDII

The eye longs to see something new. When arborists from around the world gathered in Seattle for an international arborists' conference, guess what tree they admired? Madrona? Bigleaf maple? One of our towering conifers? No, it was none other than the naturalized mountain ash, *Sorbus aucuparia*. Yes, it's true. I'm not making it up.

I overheard a similar conversation while accompanying a tour group from a national botanic garden conference here in Seattle a few years ago. As we passed through the various areas of Freeway Park, I heard murmurs of appreciation and a request for identification of the shrub *Viburnum davidii* (see Figure 16.14). This is such a common plant here that it's often regarded with disdain and referred to simply as "davidii." But for the folks on the tour, who were seeing it with fresh eyes, it was a focus of admiration.

And, I must admit, I too like "davidii," for a variety of reasons. It's in the group of much needed 5-foot-and-under plants so useful for design purposes here in the great Pacific Northwest. It has an interesting broad, quilted leaf (also good for contrast), and it's evergreen. I guess I'm just fated to stick up for underappreciated plants like "davidii"—the way I do for topped trees and maligned junipers.

Figure 16.14 *Viburnum davidii*

Viburnum davidii is pretty tough. It takes sun or shade. In the sun it grows about 2 feet tall. In the shade I've seen it get, oh, 3 or 4 feet tall. The only place I've seen it fail to thrive is in heavy clay soil. It also tolerates a wide variety of pruning methods. It can be reduced in size using the time-honored grab-and-snip method. It can be thinned out. And it can be radically renovated. So which pruning category does this put it in? Cane-grower, tree-like, or mounding-habit? The answer is Yes.

Grab-and-Snip It Like a Mounding-Habit Shrub

If the plant has gotten a bit tall in places, you locate the branch that sticks out the farthest, follow it down to the interior of the shrub, and cut it off to a side branch. Then look for the next-longest branch and repeat. Do this all over, always selecting the worst first, until your shrub is shorter and tidier, but natural. When you do this pruning, concentrate on the places where dissimilar elements meet up. For example, create a bit of space where the plant meets the house or where it crowds into a different shrub.

Remove Canes to the Ground

Another way to prune *V. davidii* is to remove some stems completely by cutting them to the ground. If you cut out the tallest ones, this will reduce the overall height of your plant. But mostly I find that the canes I'm cutting are those closest to the walkway, because the shrub is disrupting foot traffic.

Thin It Out Like a Tree-Like Shrub

Maybe your "davidii" isn't too tall or unkempt. Maybe you like the size, but it just looks a little shabby. Maybe you, or someone who shares your living quarters, just whacked at it using many nonselective heading cuts, turning your shrub into a stub-fest. A little thinning and a lot of deadwooding will fix it right up. This plant has a nice branch structure, so why not reveal it? And you don't really have to worry about over-thinning it because it isn't prone to the water-sprout rebound effect. Prune at will. Aesthetics will be your only consideration.

Radical Renovation

From time to time I radically renovate *Viburnum davidii*, cutting it to a low framework. What's left is a patch of 2- to 4-inch-tall, utterly leafless branches. This is scary to look at and not a nice thing to do to a plant. But this viburnum is quite tolerant, especially if it is not already stressed out and you do the cutting in the spring, a gentle season.

Radical renovation shouldn't be used as a regular maintenance procedure, which raises the question "Why would you do it?" Often the reason isn't a good one. For example, a client of mine (well, it was her husband, actually) was bothered by the fact that a really nice stand of *V. davidii* spilled over their two-lane driveway.

Why do people object to plants hanging over their hardscapes when they don't interfere with traffic? I don't know. After all, the point of these plants is to soften the straight lines and sharp angles of our hardscapes. In this case the "davidii" was doing its job. To my eyes it was the perfect transition plant, stepping down from several tall rhodies and a camellia and gently spilling onto the concrete.

What is the matter with people that they are compelled to cut a plant straight off back to the edge of the driveway? It drives me crazy. Theses are the same folks who cut tree limbs off to the gutter line, and shear junipers back to *reveal* the ugly curb rather than hide it. All I know is that these aesthetically challenged people are in the grip of some shared and deeply subconscious drive to control Nature, whether it serves a purpose or subverts one. It's a form of territorialism, perhaps.

Anyway, my client's hubby whacked back the "davidii" straight to the edge of the driveway. It looked bad, you can well imagine. So I waited till spring and cut the entire patch (about 7 feet across and 2 to 3 feet high) down to about 2 inches high, weeded it, mulched it, and watched it grow back to a nice 1-foot mound in one year.

Another client of mine had a well-sited stand of *V. davidii* on the side of her house, between a walkway and a window. But after 20 years it had gotten a little too big for its spot, menacing people walking the narrow side yard. Thinning and cane cutting worked for a while. Eventually it got up over the window and began to look leggy, so I did a "rad-reno." A short, dense patch of *V. davidii* grew back and worked there for about five more years, and then the same problems started recurring.

Much of gardening, and certainly much of pruning, is really a temporary measure that's simply buying time for the existing design. One of my favorite maxims is "Pruning, like marriage, is the art of compromise." Sigh. I have resolved myself to this truth.

THE WHACKABLES: LAVATERA (TREE MALLOW), *SENECIO GREYI*, PEROVSKIA, FUCHSIA, AND CAPE FUCHSIA

There's nothing like teaching to bring clarity to one's subject. I was cooking up a new pruning slide show last year, "The Whackables, the Shearables, and the Untouchables," when several truths—ones that I actually already knew—were brought into much stronger relief.

These truths especially pertain to the Whackables.

Some, and perhaps all of the plants so listed, belong to a group that horticulturists refer to as *subshrubs*. And last year for the first time, I actually *got* what subshrubs means. It means that they are somewhere between being woody shrubs (such as snowball bush or rhody) and being true perennials—herbaceous flowering plants that die back to the ground every winter (such as peony or iris). And what difference does that make? It means that you prune the subshrubs differently than either shrubs or perennials. You can—and in many cases should—cut them way, way back every year, and it also means that you should do this pruning in spring, not in early or late winter, or early spring.

Here are the truths that became more apparent: Timing of pruning is important only if plants are being nonselectively headed (as opposed to selectively pruned); large non-selective heading cuts are more prone to dieback than small cuts; and the Shearables (lavender, rockrose, broom, and heather) are not the same as the Whackables.

(Many other plants—true shrubs, which are annually or occasionally cut to the ground or to a low framework—are dealt with elsewhere in this book. They include hybrid roses, red twig dogwood, and butterfly bush. Untouchable trees and tree-likes include cherry, crabapple, plum, witch hazel, double-file, wintersweet, magnolia, and dogwood. And they are not actually untouchables—they are more accurately "touch lightlys.")

LAVATERA (*Lavatera thuringiaca* or *L. assurgentiflora*)

I like to plant lavatera, whose common name is tree mallow, in new landscapes because it is such a great immediate-gratification plant. It grows really fast and blooms like crazy all season. Its flowers are usually some shade of pink and are reminiscent of hollyhock flowers (see Figure 16.15), although they're not quite as good; on the other hand, the foliage isn't prone to rust the way hollyhock foliage is. Used as a cut flower, lavatera is almost immortal in a vase. But it can be a

Figure 16.15 Lavatera bloom

rather short-lived plant in the ground. These characteristics make it excellent filler in a new landscape, to be interplanted among other shrubs, giving the homeowner something big and gratifying to look at until the choicer, slower-growing "real" shrubs can get up and going.

I had a client who didn't like the particular shade of pink that flowered on her lavatera. I thought it was spectacular, especially blooming against the purple smoke bush behind it. So it came home to live in the "orphans' corner" at the side of my house. Like so many plants that get heeled-in, it stayed there for quite a while. It grew quite tall—8 to 10 feet—and blocked the unwanted view from my dining room into my neighbor's vestibule. I was delighted to see its abundant pink flowers outside my window, month after month, for several summers. Then one winter, the tall main stem cracked under a snow load or perhaps from its own weight. I've seen that happen elsewhere too. I assume that this is one reason that gardeners often cut it to a very low framework every year. Such pruning also keeps it shorter and less leggy than it would be otherwise. (See Figure 16.16.)

I cut back the broken branch of my heeled-in lavatera. It was about 2 inches in diameter, and I cut it cleanly at about 5 feet high, making a large nonselective heading cut. I had every expectation that it would break bud in the spring, grow out rapidly, and bloom like crazy that summer. It didn't. Instead it died. Unfortunately there was little branching below to assume the job. Oops!

Similarly, I got poor performance from several lavateras, a perovskia, and a *Senecio greyi* that I cut back to low frameworks in a client's yard (at her request). The difference between this and other similar cut-backs to the same plants was the timing and the weather. My conclusion is that cool and cold weather can set back lavetera, and many of these above-listed plants, especially if the cuts are large. So it's better to wait until danger of frost is past, when dormant buds start swelling, which is to say mid- to late spring. Not fall, not winter, and not early spring. *Timing is important when plants are nonselectively headed.* And the problem isn't even that the plants actually freeze back, but that they can just get sort of poopy for

Figure 16.16 Hard cut-back of lavatera.

the whole next year. So don't cut back when they are going to sleep in the fall, or when they're sound asleep in the winter or early spring. But cut them back in mid-spring (like April or May). Think of it as a rude alarm clock: "Buzz, buzz, buzz . . . Time to wake up and get going!"

I also noticed this year that when I told a student to cut back an "out-of-control" lavatera at a renovation site, he assumed that he should "clean it up" too. So he headed a main stem back to about 3 or 4 inches off the ground (okay so far) and then thinned off all the smaller side branches (oops!). It's quite likely that the large headed-back branch (the cut was about 3 inches in diameter) would die back; but all the little headed-back side branches, had they remained, would have lived, grown out, and become the new shrub. As they were removed, though, the whole plant kicked the bucket. *Big headed-back branches are more likely to die than little headed-back branches.*

'Twas no great loss, however, as lavatera is, as I have often said, a fast-growing, readily replaced, filler subshrub. And, furthermore, even when it is pruned correctly, (headed back when the plant is neither too old nor too young, neither too high nor too low, neither too soon nor too late), it still ups and dies sometimes.

Be aware that there are several species of lavateras (*Lavatera*) and mallows (*Malva*) that are true annuals: They grow, bloom, set seed, and die in one year. Some are nice self-seeding annuals; others are considered self-seeding nuisances. Ask your friendly

Figure 16.17 Senecio foliage

neighborhood nurseryperson which kind the one you want to buy is.

SENECIO GREYI

Some folks call *Senecio greyi* "dusty miller," like several other plants of this color. (Its botanical name has been changed to *Brachyglottis greyi*, to my unending annoyance.) It's what we call a foliage plant. It has gray leaves that are about the size and shape of dimes and nickels growing all along the branches of a mounding, 2-foot subshrub (see Figure 16.17). Its summer flowers are little yellow daisies that may or may not be of use to you and your design intents (just cut them off if you don't like them). Its main feature is the foliage because of the valuable color contrast it provides to other plants in the garden, and it is an under 5-foot lower-story plant of the sort that is much needed in the average Pacific Northwest garden. Even so, it can get "too big" and a bit leggy, and it can be cut back hard in the spring to keep it smaller and somewhat more compact (assuming it gets enough light).

What do I mean by "cut back hard"? Well, I mean you can cut it back by about half its size if it's not too old (try not to make cuts over ¼ inch in diameter) or too young (give it a year or two to get established before you start whacking). In either case, wait until mid-spring for best results.

PEROVSKIA *(Perovskia atriplicifolia)*

Perovskia, commonly known as Russian sage, is another gray plant. Instead of a mound, though, this one is made up of spires of gray leaves. In summer, its blue flower spikes look great in your mixed border. I like to say its name with a Russian accent, rolling that *r*.

It can get to be about 3 feet tall. Once established, it can also be whacked back. On this one you can go really low, to a few inches or to the ground. Again, do it in the spring, not the fall or winter while you're cutting back all your "real" perennials. It gets pretty crummy looking in the winter when the gray leaves freeze and hang limply along the stems. You can brush them off with your gloved hand, leaving the interesting gray, spiraling stems for winter interest. They remind me of the outline that your sparkler makes as you whirl it around on a warm, Fourth of July night. I think I'll declare this plant a subshrub too.

HARDY FUCHSIA *(Fuchsia magellanica)*

For a long time I've daydreamed about designing a yard that *blooms* in the fall (not one that simply turns color or has berries, but truly blooms like a spring garden). I'd have river lilies, abelias, asters, sasanqua camellias, a lot of those yellow daisies that start with *heli*, hardy cyclamen, colchicums, real fall crocus, and hardy fuchsias. I'm sure you'll think of some others for me.

Hardy fuchsias will also be on the Horticultural Spelling Bee list, along with schizostylis, phytophthora, and *Clematis maximowicziana*. Hardy fuchsias are like the non-hardy fuchsias that you get in hanging baskets for summer, except that their flowers are generally less big and blowsy (see Figure 16.18), they don't bloom as long, and they winter over in your yard as deciduous shrubs. Around the Pacific Northwest they occasionally freeze to the ground in winter, becoming a jumble of ugly sticks covered in ugly dead leaves. But, magically, in spring they will send up a host of new shoots that will become an entire new, blooming shrub that same year! When this happens, you want to get in and cut out all those skinny dead stems to the ground, or nearly to the ground, *before* all the new soft, easily broken new shoots arise. I think that's February or maybe March. And I think this makes the hardy fuchsia more accurately a "semi-hardy" shrub.

Figure 16.18 Fuchsia bloom

Because hardy fuchsias readily renew themselves like this, some people cut them to the ground whenever they think they've gotten too big. I tend not to prune for this reason alone, just because it's too much work and the size difference isn't really that much: In two years it'll be the same size as it was before. But you won't do any harm.

And I suppose I should mention that fuchsia is sometimes listed as a plant that can be used as an informal hedge, with dedicated annual pruning higher up.

There are many hybrids. Some hardy fuchsias become really quite large shrubs. I'm thinking of that one with tiny, dainty, pale-pink flowers, dangling down like earrings or little fairy ballerinas. Cute, cute, cute. And so understated. But the bush gets really big, like 5 or 6 feet tall and as wide. That can be a surprise. You can, if you need to, head back all of those branches in the spring to 4 or 5 feet in an effort to restrain the size of your shrub. It won't hurt it, and it will bloom just fine. Then after a few years you'll get tired, and move it or enlarge the bed.

CAPE FUCHSIA *(Phygelius capensis)*

Cape fuchsias are the new kids on the block. I noticed they started becoming more common a few years ago, and I think of them as a perennial, or maybe something I might call a woody perennial, or maybe a semi-hardy, deciduous subshrub thing-a-ma-jig. There's a lot of new stuff that was supposed to die in the winter that keeps hanging on, winter after winter. You know, like dracaena and New Zealand flax *(phormium)* and the cannas. They were hardy for a while. And then they weren't.

Cape fuchsia is a good-looking plant. It grows about 3 to 4 feet tall, with tubular off-pink or red flowers that dangle in clusters, attracting hummingbirds. It looks pretty delicate, but actually it's really tough. It takes hard pruning (cut it back every spring by about half, or it seems to get out of hand). And, as many gardeners are finding out, it spreads by underground roots, making it a bit of a nuisance at times and in places. These new plants are easily transplanted, making them a good (or perhaps a bad) gift for your friends or for the plant sale.

In summary, I must warn that *the Whackables are different from the Shearables* (heather, lavender, rockrose, and broom). Both groups are best pruned in the spring, because in both cases we are using the nonselective heading cut. But unlike the Whackables, the Shearables will not reliably return if cut back into barren wood. So remember: Shear them, don't whack them.

CHAPTER SEVENTEEN

Three Fruit-Bearers

FIGS

At a PlantAmnesty "Meeting of Like Minds," plant expert Hildegard Hendrickson gave us a presentation on how to grow figs in the Northwest. Here are the take-home messages, written down for you before they slip out of the grasp of my recall.

Figure 17.1 The classic fig leaf

Why Grow Figs?

Figs don't travel or store well when they are fresh, and they won't ripen after you pick them. These two facts make fresh figs an extra-special treat that you pretty much have to grow yourself, or know someone who does, to enjoy. And what a sweet treat they are.

Why Doesn't My Fig Fruit?

The most common question about figs is "Why doesn't my fig bear fruit?" The answer is probably that *you have the wrong kind.* Many kinds of figs from around the world need a specific pollinating wasp that we simply don't have here. Many other varieties require more heat units than are available in the Pacific Northwest. But even if you have

the right kind, you may not get figs *if you don't give your tree enough hot sun.* Even the varieties that do well here need at least eight hours of full sun, ideally against a wall on the south or west side of your house or some other structure—with no overstory of Doug firs! Figs don't need much water either—in fact, if you give them less water you'll get sweeter fruit. And please note that figs do not need a cross-pollinator.

Nomenclature

Why does one never see a Latin botanical name attached to an edible fig? Figs have been in cultivation for millennia. Much crossbreeding has occurred over the centuries, and misnaming is rife. Literally hundreds of varieties exist, with very confusing nomenclature. Synonyms abound—some varieties have six or more different names; and to make things even more complicated, the same name is sometimes used for more than one variety.

Even experts have difficulty distinguishing among some varieties. I believe this is why Hildegard spent time showing the leaves of different varieties and describing the various color combinations of skin and flesh. When someone tells her that their fig isn't producing, she tries to figure out the kind of fig in question by asking color and leaf-shape questions (see Figure 17.1). The take-home message is that if your fig doesn't produce, dig it out and plant new one—or, if you are adventurous, you can graft a scion from a good one onto the rootstock of your loser.

Hildegard recommends the following varieties for the Pacific Northwest: 'Gillette',

'Desert King', 'Lattarula', 'Brown Turkey', 'Petite Negri', and 'Brunswick' (also called 'Vashon Violet' here in the Northwest).

Pruning

Figs produce their little baby fruits on the wood of last year's growth. This means that, if you or your hubby whacks your entire plant to the ground or hat-rack it in spring, you won't get fruit that year. If you let it grow back, it will produce fruit the following year. Sometimes a hard freeze will kill the plant down to the roots. Fear not, it will grow back and produce fruit next year.

This is not to say figs shouldn't be pruned. *Au contraire!* Figs are extremely tough— they don't rot from heading cuts, and they renew themselves with suckers. Hildegard says you can prune a fig either like a fruiting tree (see Figure 17.2), with a single trunk, or

Figure 17.2 Fig pruned like a fruit tree.

as a shrub, with many canes originating from the base, but still getting pretty dang big.

Hildegard does her major pruning in early spring while the fig is still dormant. If we get a late arctic blast after it has leafed out, the tender tips can be injured. This is also a good time to start new fig trees from cuttings.

Pruning as a Small Fruiting Tree

Until recently, Hildegard liked to prune her fig like a little fruiting tree so she could tie bird netting around the crown and gather it in at the trunk, thus foiling a host of backyard wildlife that wants to eat all her precious figs. (She stresses that sharing with wildlife just doesn't work because crows will peck one bite out of each and every fruit.) But she has recently changed her mind about pruning techniques: She now plans to grow her future figs as bushes, especially since her 'Desert King' fig has decided to reach for the sky. The 'Lattarula' and the 'Neverella' can be more easily controlled.

Hildegard didn't really detail how she prunes her figs as trees—I suspect she uses a combination of crown reduction (dropcrotch) pruning to keep the trees shorter and periodic removal of water sprouts from the scaffolds. She says she doesn't have a rigorous regimen for pruning. Because so many water sprouts grow from each place a cut is made, she prunes when she thinks pruning is needed and her pruners are in her pocket. She does recommend removing all the suckers that keep springing up near the base. I've noticed that after a warm, wet spring or after dropcrotch pruning, fig branches may suddenly splay down in a most unfortunate manner. Just so you know.

Pruning as a Cane-Growing Shrub

If you prune your fig like a cane-growing shrub, you will be using the "shotgun method" sometimes applied to hydrangeas. Every year, cut some canes to the ground, or an inch or six above. Even cuts as big as two inches in diameter and nonselective cuts are perfectly okay—after all, it's a fig. Then head (top) some of the canes to about two feet above the ground (more or less) to force them to branch. These nonselective heading cuts are often scary looking, but if you don't make such cuts, be aware that one cane (especially on the 'Desert King' variety) can grow straight up for way too long before it sets fruit. Leave the existing shorter canes unpruned so that they will bear fruit that year. Hildegard says it's as important to net bush-pruned figs as to net tree-pruned figs.

When I asked her what would happen if a fig tree was allowed to grow, she pointed out that the tree would get really, really big and the fruits would get smaller, less tasty, harder to pick because they are out of reach, and impossible to net.

Letting Her Rip

I suggest that if a fig is being used as a small ornamental tree, just let her rip—almost no pruning needed. Avoid all but the lightest of thinning, since figs water-sprout quite easily, and we don't want that! I think a fig would look its best, and would require the least maintenance, that way.

Fig Crops

In warm climates, figs produce continuously. In our area, most figs produce two crops a year. We normally get to eat only the spring, or "breba," crop. The fall crop rarely ripens here, because the weather is cold and dark. (Hildegard says, though, that her 'Appalachian Brown Turkey' sets only one crop—in the fall, and it ripens, though the figs are small.) If you do happen to get a second crop, you can ignore it—you don't need to remove the unripe figs.

Pests and Diseases

We have no serious pests or diseases on figs here. Isn't that nice?

Harvesting Fruit

Generally speaking, unripe figs won't ripen after they're picked. Wait until the perfect moment, when they are very, very ripe. This perfect moment is when the fig hangs or droops straight down, with a little drop of honey at its base (see Figure 17.3). Hildegard

Figure 17.3 Fig as it ripens

strongly emphasizes that *figs should not be picked before they are completely ripe.*

Storing Fruit

Hildegard recommends cutting figs into quarters and letting them dry out halfway— that is, only until the pieces are still slightly soft and very sticky—in the open or in a fruit dryer. Then store them, layered on sheets of aluminum foil that are then placed in pint-size airtight plastic containers, in the freezer so they won't mold.

Root-Pruning

Figs are excellent candidates for root-pruning and transplanting. In fact, the roots can be quite aggressive, invading other areas of the garden and sometime spawning more fig bushes—bushes that you don't need or want. Root-prune mercilessly by jumping straight down on your shovel all around the fig's drip line every five years, in the winter or as needed. (To avoid this problem, you could grow your fig in a large pot, in the sunniest place in your yard or on a sunny balcony.)

GRAPES

The editor of a garden magazine once told me the tale of a property owned long ago by a pioneer grape grower. The old vintner fell upon hard times, and his property lay fallow for many years, the vines becoming an immense woody tangle that produced only a few small clusters of grapes. Eventually, he sold to a fellow who raised and trained mules for mule teams, a common mode of freight hauling at the time. One year the mules escaped from the paddock and ate their way through the entire hillside of vines. The next year the vines produced like crazy and remained easy to access and harvest. The moral of the story is "Any ass can prune a grape."

Grapes That Fruit on One-Year-Old Shoots

For novice pruners, the hardest part of pruning grapes is the incredible amount of material that must be pruned off every year. You know those huge fields of wine grapes that you see in the winter, where hundreds of vines are trained to trellises and each one looks pretty much like the letter T? Well, to get the vines to look like that, 99 percent of the new growth is cut off every winter. In the spring shoots come flying off those Ts, and each one can grow 6 feet or more. But there are way too many, and the shoots grow way too long, so in the spring and summer most are removed. Those that remain get shortened to a couple of leaves past two or three sets of flowers to allow for two or three bunches of grapes on each stem.

Figure 17.4 Grapes

Grapes That Fruit on Two-Year-Old Canes

To complicate things, there are other grapes (dessert or table grapes) that fruit on second-year shoots, called canes. Dang! Harder to visualize and figure out what is going on. Basically, you always leave a permanent framework consisting of a trunk and maybe scaffolds (thick, gray, shaggy, woody) and cycle out old canes. Keep some of this year's shoots (soft, green, skinny); they'll get a bit woodier, thicker, and browner and become next year's canes, which will sprout their own spring-summer shoots that will bear fruit. Don't worry too much, though, just whack away, leaving a few youngish shoots and canes. Cut some canes back to three or so buds so that they look like a spur or a thumb (or a stub). These will produce new shoots that turn into canes (that have shoots and grapes) for the near future. For these vines, you are cutting off only 90 percent of the new growth every year, cycling out older canes and training up a new crop. Trunk, Cane, Shoot. Trunk, Cane, Shoot.

When to Prune

Just prune back your grapes every winter to look like the grapes in the accompanying illustration (see Figure 17.5). They tell the real story—thank God for the illustrators! Your job is to make your vine look like the illustration, *every winter*. You can do repetitions of the illustration if you want to cover more territory on your trellis or arbor.

When I say "prune in the winter," I mean in deep, dark winter. One of the most characteristic features of grapes is their tendency

Figure 17.5 Winter pruned grape

to bleed profusely if pruned either too early in the winter or too late. PlantAmnesty gets a couple of panic calls every spring about grapes *bleeding* at a terrifying rate. We assure the callers that they will be okay and the vine will stop bleeding sap once the leaves are out. So do your winter pruning in the middle of winter, when the weather is very cold and your vine is hard asleep—say, late December to early February. In late spring or summer, when the leaves are out and fruit or flowers have set up, you can go back in and prune away excess canes and shoots. Simplifying the mess will allow more sunlight to hit fewer grape clusters, thus making them fatter, juicier, and sweeter. Heading is okay on most vines, including grapes, so don't worry.

Note that when you're tying new canes into place for next year, they are apt to snap off if pulled too hard and too early in the spring. So wait until summer or fall, when they are slightly hardened off.

A Final Note

Arthur Lee Jacobson, author of many fine books including *Trees of Seattle*, says raccoons and possums are a terrible problem for local grape owners. Although he has no advice regarding possum deterrents, he does say that baby powder will put off raccoons. So I look forward to seeing y'all at work inside your grape vines next summer with hand pruners and baby powder bottles in hand!

RASPBERRIES

Not much has given me more pleasure than the tiny raspberry patch I planted 23 years ago in my back yard. Every summer I pad out there, sometimes in my socks, to raid the bush. I inspect the canes, choosing the darkest berries, perhaps with a bit of white showing at the top where they are already trying to slip off—an indicator of maximum ripeness. Yum, yum. Others I gently tug. The ones that release easily are the sweetest. The raspberry bush I ravage today will miraculously provide an entire new crop of ripe berries tomorrow. And I encourage my neighbors to pick them too. The more you pick, the bigger the ones that remain become. You can't over-harvest, shorting yourself the next day. You just get more. And it's free! You can't beat free.

Figure 17.6 Raspberries

And the people from PETP (People for the Ethical Treatment of Plants) want me to let you know that fruits (and maybe nuts) are the only plant parts that actually *want* you to eat them. Think about it.

For me, the annual grazing of raspberries captures the essence of summer—that and the smell of sun-warmed conifer needles underfoot as I walk to the mailbox.

Pruning

Sometimes what seems obvious to me isn't obvious to others. I was reminded of this during a recent garden consultation. The new homeowner asked me how to prune his raspberries. I told him to remove the old, dead canes (by cutting them off at ground level). Which ones were the dead ones seemed obvious to me—they were all dry, gray, and brittle. He said he thought maybe he was supposed to keep those because they were "the good ones" that had had berries that summer. Hmm.

Pruning "Regular Old" Raspberries

Every year the raspberry bush grows new bright-green canes in the spring. They just have leaves, no flowers or fruit. But the next spring they get flowers that turn into raspberries that ripen in July. Then they die at the end of the year, turning into the aforementioned dry, brittle, gray canes. After they are through fruiting, or during the fall-winter cleanup, you cut them to the ground. What's left in the raspberry patch is the greener one-year-old canes, which will bear fruit next summer.

Figure 17.7 Regular raspberries **A.** Year 1 **B.** Year 2 **C.** Year 3 (dead)

Pruning Everbearing Raspberries

That all sounds pretty straightforward.

Then the hybridizers got to work and invented the "everbearing" or "fall-bearing" raspberries. I call them the "confusion-bearing" raspberries.

I was on a radio garden show when somebody called to ask how to prune them. I hemmed and hawed. The host, certain that it couldn't be all that hard, Googled the term. As he read aloud from the screen, I could see the cloudy look come over his eyes.

So here goes the spiel on everbearings:

The first year a cane grows up, flowers, and bears raspberries on the *top* half, *in the fall*. The cane overwinters and then bears fruit on the *bottom* half the following *summer* (in June or early July). Then it dies. If you *want* to (you do not *have* to), you can cut the top half off after it fruits in the fall. Then, after the bottom half has fruited the next summer, you cut out the rest of the cane

out down to the ground 'cause it's pretty much dead now.

Since this type of raspberry patch will be made up of both one- and two-year-old canes, you should be harvesting raspberries in both summer (last year's bottoms) and fall (this year's tops). Hence the term "everbearing."

So I assume some of you now understand how to prune everbearings. It all makes perfect sense to you.

Then there are the rest of you: those who have had the read the previous paragraph a couple of times and thought they understood, but by the end of the day couldn't explain it to their neighbor, or on a radio program. My advice to you is to just do what's "obvious" by looking at the patch. Cut out the "finished" tops (the ones that have borne fruit), and cut the completely finished, dead-looking canes to the ground. Or forget the cutting-in-half part and just cut the completely dead ones completely out. Leave the live-looking ones. That oughta work.

Don't worry too much. It's not like your raspberries will stop bearing fruit if you don't prune them. The patch will just get clogged with a bunch of old dead canes. Which reminds me. Although I am a far, far cry from being an expert on raspberries, I've made the following observation. Raspberries want to colonize. They keep creeping out from the center of the plant, and all the really good canes seem to be at the edges. That makes them a bit hard to manage.

And, for those of you who are still stymied by the pruning of everbearing raspberries, I proffer the following third option. In a local newspaper, garden columnist Mary Robson answered the question "How would you prune everbearings?" thus: "You did ask how I would prune them, so I'll tell you. I would cut all the canes to the soil line. This is not only super easy but it also allows the plants to put all their energy into making new canes and the biggest fall crop possible. (For summer fruit I'd add a couple of June-bearing cultivars like Willamette, Chilliwack, or Centennial to my planting.)"

"What a happy life it would be only to cultivate raspberries."

—Alice B. Toklas

Figure 17.8 Everbearing raspberries **A.** Year 1 **B.** Year 2 **C.** Year 3 (dead)

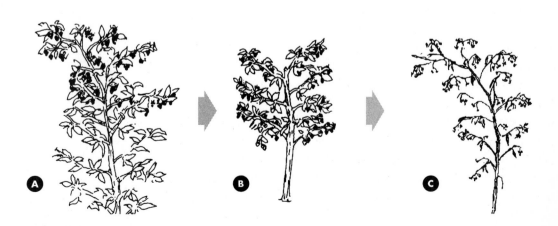

CHAPTER EIGHTEEN

Taming the Native-Plant Garden

315

"Nature abhors a garden." I wish I could remember who said that. It's so true. Unless we tiptoed into the woods and built a cabin without touching the ground, what most of us have is a disturbed site. Upon it, we impose an artist's conception of Nature, which is not really a natural area at all. Rather, it's planted with an assortment of species that may or may not have occurred naturally on that site, or even occurred naturally with each other. The site will become a battleground, not a self-sustaining woods, and we will eventually need to intervene.

As soon as the plants are put into the ground, the forces of entropy are unleashed. Exotic invasives (laurel, holly, Himalayan blackberry) and not-so-exotic invasives (grass, dandelions, shotweed) move in to take up residence. And then we discover that even some of our chosen plants are way more prolific than others—even outright aggressive. Three, four, and five plants will begin to occupy the same space. Everything is everywhere! Furthermore, no matter who planted the garden—the avid amateur, the native-plant biologist, or the professional designer—in five or ten years it reveals itself to have been overplanted. We are all driven to make it look reasonably right at the beginning, only to find that we have yet again underestimated the mature size of shrubs, or how many trees to put together. We foolishly thought the day would never come to tell on us. *But now the day is here.*

I am frequently asked to renovate overgrown gardens—and, increasingly, overgrown native-plant gardens. To bring order out of chaos—and to do so in a way that the garden will still appear natural, or perhaps even a bit wild—is big fun and a real challenge. For years I have enjoyed making people's woods prettier. But before I tackle the area outside the front door, the owner must first face *The Unpleasant Truth*: Pruning, renovating, and all other gardening activities are unnatural acts! The very principles of making a garden look better are antithetical to what might be considered the golden rule of Nature—to maximize diversity. In other words, Nature, especially in a disturbed area, loves a mess! Birds and bugs and critters love a half-uprooted, topped, rotten tree, leaning on a shrub that is full of deadwood, with broken brown fern fronds, surrounded by prickly bushes impaling gobs of dead bigleaf maple leaves. On the other hand, your

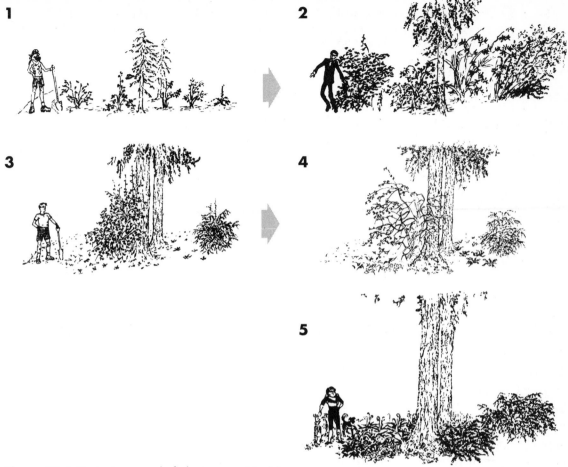

Figure 18.1 Strategic removal of plants every 5 to 15 years.

newts, lizards, and snakes wish you would leave a pile of rubble and dried weeds in the back yard.

You may even have supplied the local fauna with some of these messy areas on your large property. But most folks want something a little more pleasant at the front door. Here, I try to mimic a more established ecology. Maybe not the lovely monoculture of the climax forest, with a single sylvan grove and a carpet of oxalis—but something more along the line of a shady forest floor at the Mount Adams campground.

Renovating an overgrown native-plant garden means separating layers, taking out some of the dead brown stuff, reducing the number of plants occupying the same place, and deleting other plants completely just to make a nicer-looking garden (see Figure 18.1). This is tough on some folks, who will react according to deeply held subconscious beliefs, such as:

Plants are either all good or all bad.

Natives are the good plants and therefore all should live.

"Natural" means not interfering—I like the overgrown look.

A good pruner could just prune it back to the right sizes and nothing would have to die.

But . . . actually . . . something will. Have to die, that is.

REMOVE PLANTS

Let's start by killing the exotic woody invasives, shall we? Things like laurel, cotoneaster, and holly. Most people can agree on that. But this is not as easy as one would hope. If you cut them to the ground, they just grow back (with the possible exception of old, woody Scotch brooms). A holly, for example, could easily outlive you, even if you cut it to the ground every other month for 30 years! Long after you've turned to dust, it will have sprung up to 20 feet and made a merry Christmas scene. Digging a plant up can be way, way more work than seems worthwhile. It will probably destroy nearby desirables, and it can turn up a host of weed seeds to boot. But then, aren't nettles just more native plants?

A Sawsall and an 8-foot pry bar (which my husband calls "the tool of ignorance: $8 rent, $30 buy") with fulcrum might work if it can be maneuvered into place. If you can spare $200, you can get yourself a Weed Wrench. They're cool. Ecological restoration workers use a $500 Roundup (glyphosate) injection gun (JK Injections) system to apply concentrate to the freshly cut stems or to inject invasives such as Japanese knotweed. I use a 99-cent touch-up plastic paint canister with brush in lid and 9 percent glyphosate as a cut-stump treatment for any and all unwanted woody brush. (Apologies to my 100 percent organic friends). For more information on my method, see the section "To Eliminate Ivy" in Chapter 15, Ground Covers, page 278.

So let it be a lesson to you new people to patrol your garden every fall and pull these nuisances early on, when they are 1 to 2 inches tall and can be easily dispatched with a pair of pliers.

Next up, and a little harder for the native-plant novice, is removing the native invasives. Our native plants like it here. Some *really* like it here, and several are perfectly adapted to outcompete anything else you have on your property. Some are underground spreaders that are harder to stop than the ones that just have babies all over the place. In either case, you are wise to remove some of these overly aggressive native plants. I've seen salmonberry (*Rubus spectabilis*) invade and conquer the mossy woods and open fields with amazing success! And remember: Horsetail, fireweed, and crows are native; foxglove, cattails, and red-winged blackbirds aren't. It's okay to hate a native plant on your property. You can ban it from your garden; but don't worry, it's living happily someplace else nearby! In regular gardening parlance, the term *vigorous* is sometimes code for *invasive*. In restoration ecology, the phrase *very successful* can mean *invasive*. So listen closely to plant descriptions and choose wisely.

On the other hand, sometimes you *want* some thicket-producing natives. A mixed

Figure 18.2 Prune to keep walkways open.

hedge of deciduous and evergreen shrubs (like Oregon grape, ocean spray, redtwig dogwood, hazelnut, red-flowering currant, and elderberry) will protect your forest edge from the invading non-natives. Or you may want a shorter, spreading thicket along your pasture fence (with plants such as snowberry and wild roses), which you keep from spreading by haying the field every year.

But these same plants can overwhelm your front-doorstep garden. You may want to remove just some or all of those, depending on the design and whether or not they are making themselves a nuisance. Sometimes the native garden has already become completely overwhelmed, and the only course left is to just surrender and pull out the losers—deleting, say, the huckleberry and sword ferns that have been totally submerged and overcome by the salal and ocean spray. Pretend you designed it that way.

In general, no more than two plants should occupy the same spot. Pick two that look good together, or that offer high-low contrast, and edit out the others. A special case exists along the walkway, where the best choice is to have only low materials at the edge, with nothing too threatening or crowding at eye level (see Figure 18.2). Now that we have removed unwanted woody plants by any means necessary, let's proceed to the next job.

DE-VINE AND GET THE BROWN OUT

Stringy groundcovers can muck up the good looks of a mixed planting. I often delete native vines, strawberry, and ankle-busting native wild blackberry or restrict them to a dedicated area of their own.

And, even more un-Naturally, I am apt to hand-rake (or just push down onto the ground) the worst of the brown leaves and other brown stuff (dog-paddle out dead fern fronds and bigleaf maple leaves caught up in the shrubs, and make sure the curled brown leaves under the rhododendrons are raked out of sight). Tamp down or remove dead twigs and downed branchlets that fall from your conifers in every storm. Clean the path. The finer deciduous leaves get to stay, and areas farther from view can stay completely

Figure 18.3 Thin plants to reduce crowding

leafed and naturally mulched. To make up for the removal of debris, I sometimes have to reapply a mulch. Arborist's conifer chips most closely mimic the forest floor and work to suppress weeds. If you have your own chipper, you can feel good about the small recycling cycle you use to clean up material and then mulch with it, now nicely shredded.

When working my way through the landscape, I leave sword ferns if they're in the right places and gleefully relocate the rest, as I consider them to be a near-perfect plant for understory in both native and non-native shade gardens. They're great to use to complete designs that have been disrupted by the removal of large, unwanted woody plants.

I love almost all the ferns, but the maidenhair and deer ferns are especially choice and fabulous to find in a garden. But, as anybody who has worked with me can tell you, I make war on lady ferns (*Athyrium filix-femina*). In my view, they have too many babies that show up inside desirable shrubs, then die back and leave the shrubs stuffed with ugly dead, broken fronds in the winter. I hate them. I use a baby mattock to murder each and every one I can find, with a zeal that scares even me.

PRUNING

There's just no guilt-free living anymore. When I was a kid, I let the water run in the sink as I brushed my teeth. We burned piles of autumn leaves, and we turned over rocks on the beach to molest the marine life. And until recently, I used to say that deadwooding was always good and you couldn't go wrong—that is, until a lady told me she left the dead twigs on her lilac that were the perfect size for some particular bird to build its nest. Drat! It's true! Deadwood of all sorts is good for Nature. Unfortunately, our trees and tree-like shrubs look better with the deadwood pruned out. Actually, everything looks really good pruned that way. So carry on with the deadwooding, with the knowledge that there may be some places you will choose to leave it. Then properly dispose of your gardener's guilt by composting it on the

Figure 18.4 Take off lower limbs crowding ground cover.

site with all the other aforementioned dead twigs, leaves, and plants.

At the beginning of this book I've written about how to prune plants according to one of three basic habits (cane-grower, tree-like, and mounding habit). The native-plant list at the end of this chapter shows the pruning habit of each tree and shrub, as well as botanical name, height, and degree of vigor. I have also included the notations DNP (do not plant, i.e. banned by Cass) and CPF (Cass's personal favorite). Keep in mind that pruning plants for size control is largely unsuccessful for all but the briefest time. In landscape renovation, refereeing between plants or making individual plants look more attractive are the real goals of pruning.

I can think of three common scenarios that are particularly applicable to renovating the native-plant garden. One is when two plants of equal size are crowding each other. Prune some of the branches of each that are headed into the other, as well as doing a general thinning throughout (see Figure 18.3). Now the shrubs mingle like two slow dancers, not two barroom brawlers.

A second situation arises when two plants of different sizes are too crowded. In this instance, prune off the lowest limbs of the taller plant to accommodate the understory plant (see Figure 18.4). For example, remove the lowest limbs of the vine maple that grows through the low mahonia under it.

Thirdly, pruning can do wonders for trees or tree-like shrubs, especially those near a building, such as a vine maple next to the house. First take out the deadwood. Then prune off the branches that touch the building (see Figure 18.5), if to do so does not exceed the pruning budget. The *pruning budget*, you may recall, is the combination of the branch diameter and amount of foliage that can be removed without causing water sprouts or rot or dieback in any given plant. For trees the limit is about one-eighth to one-sixteenth of the total foliage in a given pruning cycle (every five to ten years). The size of the thinning cut for an understory tree should not exceed about 1 inch, most often much less. Use other pruning guidelines just to make it all look better: Thin out crossing/rubbing, broken, diseased, wrong-way branches (though never exceeding the pruning budget).

Figure 18.5 Prune branches that touch buildings.

A TOUCH OF CHARM

By now you should be feeling pretty good about your native garden. I'm always amazed at just how much material can be removed from a garden without anyone's being able to tell that it's been touched. The garden still looks natural and even lush, but now it's nicer to view, with greater depth and detail. However, before you leave well enough alone, I'd like to put in a plug for the very lowest level of greenery. Now that several of the giant shrubs are gone, you have room to put in low ground covers, self-seeding annuals, and choice perennials that can give the native-plant garden that "*Ooh, aah!*" quality. So, when you can, leave some empty spaces on the forest floor, especially near the door and the walkways. You can then add a carpet of "successful" (wink, wink) ground covers like oxalis, *or* vancouveria and bleeding heart, *or* bead ruby (false lily-of-the-valley). You could salt the edge of the wood with robust, self-seeding annuals like fringecups, lupine, or columbine. For a more delicate area of well-matched, not-too-vigorous small guys, use deer ferns, foam flower, and vanilla leaf. And for the ultimate in woodland perfection, include a few trilliums, fawn lilies, and, God willing, a living patch of bunchberry!

Intervention complete! You can rest and be proud of your reasonable facsimile of the beautiful and wonderful wild woods. And those of you who can't stand this sort of strong-handed intervention in your beloved native-plant garden: You're in luck. It's your garden and you can do whatever you want with it, or nothing at all, because in the end, you're the only one it needs to please.

Valuable List of Native Plants

BEHAVIOR KEY

VS = Very successful

S = Successful—sometimes OK, sometimes trouble

Spreads = Spreads by underground roots, may be difficult to control

V = Vigorous

WB = Well-behaved

SD = Sometimes dies, but nice

DNP = Do not plant (banned by Cass)

CPF = Cass's personal favorite

See the PlantAmnesty Pruning Guide on their website for pruning according to the following Plant Habits:

PLANT HABITS KEY

T = Tree

TL = Tree-like

CG = Cane-grower

M = Mounding habit

TREES

COMMON NAME	BOTANICAL NAME	HEIGHT	HABIT	BEHAVIOR
Vine maple	*Acer circinatum*	25'	T	WB
Pacific dogwood	*Cornus nuttallii*	60'	T	WB, but water-sprouts easily. Thin lightly. Gets a chronic disease. CPF
Beaked hazelnut	*Corylus cornuta*	20'	TL	VS (seedlings), water-sprouts, thin lightly
Pacific crabapple	*Malus fusca*	40'	T	
Garry oak	*Quercus garryana*	75'	T	WB
Silktassel	*Garrya elliptica*	25'	T	WB

LARGE SHRUBS (OVER 10 FEET)

COMMON NAME	BOTANICAL NAME	HEIGHT	HABIT	BEHAVIOR
Serviceberry	*Amelanchier alnifolia*	20'	TL	
Redtwig dogwood	*Cornus stolonifera*	15'	CG	VS
Ocean spray	*Holodiscus discolor*	15'	CG	S
Indian plum	*Oemleria cerasiformis*	15'	CG & TL	
Ninebark	*Physocarpus capitatus*	13'	CG	
Red elderberry	*Sambucus racemosa*	13'	CG & TL	S

MEDIUM SHRUBS (10 FEET AND UNDER)

COMMON NAME	BOTANICAL NAME	HEIGHT	HABIT	BEHAVIOR
Douglas spiraea	*Spiraea douglasii*	4'	M	
Tall Oregon grape	*Mahonia aquifolium*	4–8'	CG	V, can be renovated
Salal	*Gaultheria shallon*	1–5'	G	VS, spreads, can be renovated
Twinberry	*Lonicera involucrata*	9'	CG	
Mock orange	*Philadelphus lewisii*	9'	CG & TL	
Red-flowering currant	*Ribes sanguineum*	6'	CG	V
Nootka rose	*Rosa nutkana*	10'	CG	VS, spreads, can be renovated
Common snowberry	*Symphoricarpos albus*	5'	M	VS, spreads, can be renovated
Evergreen huckleberry	*Vaccinium ovatum*	6'–10'	TL & M	WB, CPF
Red huckleberry	*Vaccinium parvifolium*	10'	TL	WB, CPF
Salmonberry	*Rubus spectabilis*	10'	CG	Spreads, DNP
Thimbleberry	*Rubus parviflorus*	4'	CG	Spreads

PERENNIALS/FLOWERS

COMMON NAME	BOTANICAL NAME	HEIGHT	BEHAVIOR
Thrift/Sea pink	*Armeria maritima*	1'	
Goat's beard	*Aruncus dioicus*	5'	WB
Western bleeding heart	*Dicentra formosa*	1.5'	V, spreads, CPF
Western tiger lily	*Lilium columbianum*	5'	
False Solomon's seal	*Smilacina racemosa* (syn. *Maianthemum racemosum*)	2'–3'	
Starry false lily-of-the-valley	*Maianthemum stellatum* (syn. *Smilacina stellata*)	3'	VS, spreads
Foam flower	*Tiarella trifoliata*	1'	WB, choice
Western trillium	*Trillium ovatum*	1.5'	WB, CPF
Evergreen violet	*Viola sempervirens*	.5'	Spreads
Fawn lily	*Erythronium oregonum*		WB, CPF

GROUND COVERS

COMMON NAME	BOTANICAL NAME	HEIGHT	BEHAVIOR
Vanilla leaf	*Achlys triphylla*	1'	SD, but nice
Kinnikinnick/Bearberry	*Arctostaphylos uva-ursi*	1'	Gets leaf crud sometimes, don't water it
Wild ginger	*Asarum caudatum*	.5'	WB
Low Oregon grape	*Mahonia nervosa* (syn. *Berberis nervosa*)	3'	Spreads, but can be useful
Bunchberry	*Cornus unalaschkensis* (syn. *Cornus canadensis*)	1'	Dies, but very cute, CPF
Beach strawberry	*Fragaria chiloensis*	1'	Stringy
Twinflower	*Linnaea borealis*	.5'	SD
Bead ruby, aka false lily-of-the-valley	*Maianthemum dilatatum*	1'	VS, spreads, CPF
Wood sorrel	*Oxalis acetosella*	1.5'	VS, spreads
Inside-out flower	*Vancouveria hexandra*	1'	S, spreads, CPF

ANNUALS/BIENNIALS

COMMON NAME	BOTANICAL NAME	HEIGHT	BEHAVIOR
Fringecups	*Tellima grandiflora*	2'	V, self-seeder, easy to pull
Western columbine	*Aquilegia formosa*	2'	Self-seeder, choice
Lupine	*Lupinus polyphyllus*	.5'–3'	Self-seeder

FERNS

COMMON NAME	BOTANICAL NAME	HEIGHT	BEHAVIOR
Maidenhair fern	*Adiantum aleuticum* (formerly *A. pedatum*)	2'	WB, CPF
Deer fern	*Blechnum spicant*	2'	WB, CPF
Sword fern	*Polystichum munitum*	3'	WB, workhorse, CPF
Lady fern	*Athyrium filix-femina*	2'	DNP

Regional Pruning by Plant Habit

The laws of nature are the same the world over, and that includes the rules that govern pruning. Just the names of the species change. When I give a slideshow on pruning to people in another part of the world, I have a local gardener adapt the list of their most common plants to the three-habit system described in this book. I use it to make a local brochure to hand out at the class. These lists are found below, organized roughly from west to east. Because many plants can be rightly pruned in several different ways, you will find some species listed in more than one category. Pruning either way will be correct. Which way you choose will be determined by what you want from your shrub.

HAWAII

Mounds (grab and snip)
  Bougainvillea
  Bush thunbergia
  El Dorado
  Firecracker plant/Coral plant
  Gardenia (including Tahitian gardenia)
  Hibiscus
  Ixora
  Natal plum
  Naupaka
  Oleander
  Snow bush
  Yedo hawthorn (*Raphiolepis*)

Cane-growers (cut canes to the ground)
  Beefsteak plant
  Bird of paradise
  Candle bush
  Chenille plant
  Crepe gardenia
  Croton
  Cup and saucer
  Dwarf umbrella tree
  El Dorado
  Heavenly bamboo (*Nandina*)
  Heliconia
  Lantana
  Mussaenda Queen Sirikit
  Pagoda flower
  Panax
  Snow bush
  Ti

Tree-likes (thin out, making many small cuts)
  Angel's trumpet
  Bush thunbergia
  Camellia
  Crepe myrtle
  Gardenia (including Crepe and
    Tahitian gardenia)

Jatropha
Mussaenda Queen Sirikit
Pagoda flower
Powder plant, Haole Lehua (*Calliandra*)

SOUTH-CENTRAL AND INTERIOR ALASKA

USDA Zones 1–4

Mounds (grab and snip)
Cotoneaster
Potentillas (cane-like, too)
Spiraeas

Cane-growers (cut canes to the ground)
Forsythia
Honeysuckle (*Lonicera* spp.)
Red twig dogwood (*Cornus stolonifera*)
Roses
Shrub willow
Siberian pea shrub
Ural false spiraea

Tree-likes (thin out, making many small cuts)
Amur chokecherry (*P. maackii*)
Amur maple (*Acer tataricum*)
Common chokecherry (*P. virginiana*)
Crabapples
Currant
Lilac
Mayday tree (*P. padus*)
Mountain ash (*Sorbus*)
Mugho pine (*Pinus mugo mugo*)
Prunus
Rose tree of China
Serviceberry (*Amelanchier*)

Viburnums
American cranberry bush
(*Viburnum trilobum*)
Highbush cranberry (*V. edule*)

Water-sprout easily, so prune lightly
Cotoneaster
Crabapples
Prunus spp.

Can be pruned as a hedge
Cotoneaster
Siberian pea shrub

INLAND NORTHWEST

USDA Zones 2–5

Mounds (grab and snip)
Barberries (some canes)
Box honeysuckle (*Lonicera nitida*)
Boxwood (*Buxus*)
Burning bush
Holly (*Ilex* spp.)
Potentilla
Snowberry (*Symphoricarpos*)
Spiraea

Cane-growers (cut canes to the ground)
Butterfly bush (*Buddleia*)
Forsythia
Hydrangea
Kerria
Oregon grape, wild Oregon grape
(*Mahonia* spp.)
Red twig dogwood (*Cornus stolonifera*)
Roses
Weigelas

Tree-likes (thin-out, making many small cuts)

Deciduous azaleas
Elderberry (*Sambucus*)
Enkianthus
Huckleberries (*Vaccinium* spp.)
Kalmia
Lilac
Manzanita (*Arctostaphylos*)
Pieris (*Andromeda*)
Rhododendrons
Spindle tree
Winter snowball

Viburnums
  Doublefile viburnum
    (*V. plicatum tomentosum*)
  Highbush cranberry (*V. edule*)
  Leatherleaf viburnum
    (*V. rhytidophylloides*)

Water-sprout easily, so thin lightly

Cherry
Cotoneaster
Crabapple
Dogwood
Fig
Filbert (hazelnut)
Magnolia
Parrotia (*Parrotia persicaria*)
Plum
Witch hazel (*Hamamelis*)

Will take heavy thinning or arborizing

Laurel (*Laurus*)
Pieris
Pine
Rhododendrons (mature)
Strawberry tree (*Arbutus unedo*)

Tough tree-likes (can be headed into hedges or let go natural)

Laurel (*Laurus*)
Privet (*Ligustrum*)
Pyracantha
Yew (*Taxus*)

SAN FRANCISCO BAY AREA

Sunset-Western Climate
Zones 15, 16, 17
USDA Zone 10–A

Mounds (grab and snip)

Abelia
Aucuba
Barberries
Escallonia
Evergreen azaleas
Evergreen viburnums
Gardenia jasminoides
Grevillea 'Noellii'
Hebes
Hollies
Japanese holly (*Ilex crenata*)
Mexican orange (*Choisya*)
Myrtle
Oleander (sometimes trained into tree)
Pittosporum tobira 'Wheeler's Dwarf'
Rhaphiolepis indica
Rockrose (*Cistus*)
Rosemary

Cane-growers (cut canes to the ground)

Bamboo
Hydrangea
Lilac
Nandina/Heavenly bamboo

Oregon grape
Roses

*Tree-likes (thin-out, making many
small cuts)*
 Bottlebrush
 Camellia
 Cherry
 Cotoneaster
 Fig
 Hopbush (*Dodonaea viscosa*)
 Lilac
 Magnolia
 Manzanita (*Arctostaphylos*)
 Myoporum laetum
 Pacific wax myrtle (*Myrica californica*)
 Pieris japonica (*Pieris andromeda*)
 Pine (*Pinus* spp.)
 Pineapple guava
 Pittosporum eugenioides
 Rhododendrons
 Strawberry tree (*Arbutus unedo*)
 Tea tree (*Leptospermum*)
 Tibouchina (*Tibouchina urvilleana*)
 Toyon (*Heteromeles arbutifolia*)

*Tough tree-likes (can be headed
into hedges or let go natural)*
 Laurel (*Laurus*)
 Photinia
 Privet
 Pyracantha

SOUTHERN CALIFORNIA

Mounds (grab and snip)
 Abelia
 Azalea

Boxwood
Cotoneaster
Escallonia
Euonymus
Gardenia
Grevillea 'Noellii'
Hebe
Hibiscus
Manzanita (*Arctostaphylos*)
Mirror plant (*Comprosma repens*)
Natal plum (*Carissa macrocarpa*)
Pittosporum 'Wheelerii'
Plumbago
Rhaphiolepis indica

Cane-growers (cut canes to the ground)
 Apidistra
 Aralia
 Bougainvillea
 Forsythia
 Hibiscus
 Lantana
 Nandina/Heavenly bamboo
 Oleander
 Oregon grape (*Mahonia*)
 Schefflera spp.

*Tree-likes (thin out, making many
small cuts)*
 Acacia
 Aucuba japonica
 Bottlebrush
 Bush cherry (*Eugenia*)
 Camellia
 Carolina cherry
 Fern pine (*Podocarpus gracilior*)
 Ficus benjamina
 Ficus nitidu

Pink powder puff
  (*Calliandra haematocephala*)
Melaleuca
Orange jessamine (*Murraya paniculata*)
Pepper tree (*Schinus*)
Pineapple guava (*Feijoa sellowiana*)
Pittosporum tobira
Privet (*Ligustrum japonica*)
Strawberry tree (*Arbutus unedo*)
Sweet olive (*Osmanthus*)
Victoria box (*Pittosporum undulatum*)
Xylosma congestum
Yesterday-today-and-tomorrow
  (*Brunfelsia pauciflora*)

Tough tree-likes (can be sheared)
  Boxwood
  California privet
    (*Ligustrum ovalifolium*)
  Eugenia
  Photinia
  Photonia x *fraseri*
  Privet (*Ligustrum japonica*)

ARIZONA LOW DESERT

USDA Cold Hardiness Zones 9–A, 9–B
AHS Heat Hardiness Zones 10 & 11

Mounds (grab and snip)
  Bougainvillea
  Brittlebush (*Encelia farinosa*)
  Bush rosemary
  Butterfly bush (*Buddleia*)
  Cape honeysuckle (*Tecoma capensis*)
  Cassia
  Chuparosa/Desert honeysuckle
  Convolvulus/Bush morning glory

Creosote bush (*Larrea*)
Dwarf coyote bush (*Baccharis*)
Euonymus
Fairy duster (*Calliandra eriophylla*)
Indian hawthorn (*Rhaphiolepis indica*)
Indigo bush (*Dalea*)
Japanese boxwood
Jojoba (*Simmondsia chinensis*)
Lantana
Little-leaf cordia
Mexican honeysuckle
Myrtle
Natal plum (*Carissa macrocarpa*)
Pittosporum
Plumbago
Ruellia
Saltbush (*Atriplex*)
Texas Ranger/Texas sage (*Leucophyllum*)
Yellow bells (*Tecoma stans*)

Cane-growers (cut canes to the ground)
  Bougainvillea (if rejuvenating or
    frost damaged)
  Cape honeysuckle (*Tecoma capensis*)
  Chuparosa/Desert honeysuckle
  Indigo bush (*Dalea*)
  Lady Banks' rose (*Rosa banksiae*)
  Nandina/Heavenly bamboo
  Red bird of paradise
  Yellow bells (*Tecoma stans*)

Tree-likes (thin out, making many small cuts)
  Arizona rosewood
  Desert or yellow bird of paradise
  Dwarf bottlebrush
  Hopbush (*Dodonaea*)
  Pomegranate

Texas mountain laurel
   (*Sophora secundiflora*)
Yellow oleander (*Thevetia peruviana*)

Tough tree-likes (can be headed into hedges, or let go natural)
Desert lavender (*Hyptis emoryi*)
Hibiscus
Juniper
Oleander (*Nerium oleander*)
Photinia
Privet (*Ligustrum*)
Pyracantha

RENO, NEVADA

USDA Zones 4, 5A & 5B

Mounds (grab and snip)
Barberry (*Berberis*)
Blue Mist (*Caryopteris*)
Creeping mahonia (*Mahonia repens*)
Firethorn (*Pyracantha*)
Flowering Almond (*Prunus gladulosa*)
Gold Flower (*Hypericum moseranum*)
Mugo pine (dwarf) (*Pinus Mugo mugo*)
Potentilla (shrub form)
Quince (*Chaenomeles*)
Spreading Cotoneaster
   (*Cotoneaster horizontalis*)
Tamarisk (*Tamaris*)

Cane-growers (cut canes to the ground)
Butterfly bush (*Buddleia*)
Dwarf ninebark
   (*Physocarpus opulifolius*)
Flowering almond (*Prunus gladulosa*)
Lilac (*Syringa vulgaris*)

Mock orange (*Philadelphus*)
Oregon grape (*Mahonia aquifolium*)
Red twig dogwood
   (*Comus stolonifera; C. sericea*)
Rose of Sharon (*Hibiscus syriacus*)
Sand cherry (*Prunus besseyi*)
Tamarisk (*Tamaris*)

Tree-likes (thin out, making many small cuts)
Amur maple (*Acer ginnala*)
Black chokeberry (*Aronia melanocarpa*)
Firethorn (*Pyracantha*)
Fragrant sumac (*Rhus aromatic*)
Lilac (*Syringa vulgaris*;
   also under cane-grower)
Mock orange (*Philadelphus*)
Nannyberry (*Viburnum lentago*)
Red chokeberry (*Aronia arbutiflolia*)
Rose of Sharon (*Hibiacus syriacus*)
Russian olive (*Elaenagnus angustrifolia*)
Serviceberry (*Amelanchier*)
Smoke bush (*Cotinus coggygria*)
Staghorn sumac (*Rhus typhina*;
   also under mounds)
Wayfaring tree (*Viburnum lantana*)
Western redbud (*Cercis occidentalis*)

WISCONSIN

USDA Zones 4 & 5

Mounds (grab and snip)
Abelia
Barberries (some canes)
Boxwood (*Buxus*)
Burning bush (or as a tree-like)
Holly

Honeysuckle (*Lonicera* spp.)
Japanese holly (*Ilex crenata*)
Quince (also cane-like)
Snowberry (*Symphoricarpos*)
Spiraea (also cane-like)

Cane-growers (cut canes to the ground)
Alpine currant (*Ribes alpinum*)
Butterfly bush (*Buddleia*)
Chokeberry (*Aronia*)
Deutzia
Forsythia
Hydrangeas
Kerria
Mock orange (*Philadelphus*;
   or as a tree-like)
Ninebark (*Physocarpus opulifolius*)
Oregon grape (*Mahonia*)
Red twig dogwood (*Cornus stolonifera*)
Roses
Sand cherry (*Prunus pumila*;
   also tree-like)
Weigela
Winterberry

Tree-likes (thin out, making many small cuts)
Elderberry (*Sambucus*)
Huckleberry (*Vacciniumspp.*)
Kalmia
Lilac
Nannyberry
Smoke tree (*Cotinus*; or as a cane-grower)
Spindle tree (*Euonymus*)
Winter snowball

Viburnums
   Blackhaw (*Viburnum prunifolium*)
   Doublefile viburnum
      (*V. plicatum tomentosum*)
   Leatherleaf viburnum
      (*V. rhytidophylloides*)

Water-sprout easily, so thin lightly
Buffalo berry (*Shepherdia*)
Cherry
Cotoneaster
Crabapple
Dogwood
Filbert (hazelnut)
Magnolia
Plum
Witch hazel (*Hamamelis*)

Will take heavy thinning or arborizing
Amur maple (*Acer tataricum*)
Pine
Russian olive (*Eleagnus angustifolia*)

Tough tree-likes (can be headed into hedges or let go natural)
Boxwood (*Buxus*)
Privet (*Ligustrum*)
Yew (*Taxus*)

CENTRAL FLORIDA

USDA Zones 9–A, 9–B

Mounds (grab and snip)
Bougainvillea
Boxwood (*Buxus*)
Hollies (*Ilex* spp.)
Indian hawthorn (*Rhaphiolepis indica*)

Ixora
Pittosporum
Plumbago
Spiraea (*Spiraea*)

Gardenia
Hibiscus
Juniper
Sea grape (*Coccoloba uvifera*)
Thryallis

Cane-growers (cut canes to the ground)
Bamboo
Bird of paradise
Ginger
Heavenly bamboo (*Nandina*)
Lady palm
Marlberry (*Ardisia*)
Saw palmetto (*Serenoa repens*)
Schefflera

Tough tree-likes
Boxthorn (*Lycium*)
Oleander
Photinia
Podocarpus
Privet (*Ligustrum*)
Viburnum
Wax myrtle

Tree-likes (thin out, making many small cuts)
Azalea
Bottlebrush
Fringe tree (*Chionanthus*)

Three Views on Sterilizing Your Tools

STERILIZING PRUNING TOOLS, PART I

Dr. Linda Chalker-Scott
(This article was adapted from the Plant-Amnesty newsletter.)

Why, When, and How

Anyone who has made an investment in top-quality pruning tools probably cleans and maintains them on a regular basis. But would you clean them every day—maybe several times a day? While most of us would agree that such a cleaning regime would not be cost effective, there is evidence that such measures can help reduce the transmission of certain plant diseases to healthy plants.

In spite of the ongoing debate regarding tool sterilization, surprisingly little information in the scientific literature addresses this issue. Most of the research has focused on agriculturally important crops: citrus, stone fruits, and vegetable crops. We can extrapolate these results to woody ornamentals, however, and draw some rational conclusions. The focus of this article will be on when, why, and how to sterilize pruning tools.

Types of Pathogens

First, the good news. It is probably not necessary to sterilize pruning tools to prevent transmission of soil-borne or airborne pathogens. These diseases, generally bacterial or fungal, are more likely to be transferred by your hands and clothing than by your pruning tools. Obviously, you should avoid being a direct vector in disease transmission, but you will probably have better success in controlling these diseases through preventative landscape management practices, such as pruning diseased parts, disposing of contaminated leaf litter, and using disease-free compost and mulch.

In contrast, diseases that invade the plant's vascular system or that form oozing cankers are much more likely to be transmitted by contaminated pruning tools. As early as 1906, fire blight infections in nurseries were linked to contaminated pruning tools, and several other researchers have confirmed this more recently. A 1990 study noted that transmission did not occur during plant dormancy but only during the growing season. Fire blight bacteria do not overwinter in the vascular system, which may explain why transmission does not occur during this time. In contrast, one pair of researchers found a 66 percent infection rate during cool, wet conditions in trees pruned with shears treated with bacterial spot. The infection rate dropped to only 7 percent when trees were pruned with infected shears under hot, dry conditions. The authors speculate that the cankers are less infectious when dry; under wet conditions they become gummy, and the inoculum sticks more tightly to pruner surfaces.

Seasonal differences in infection rates were also seen with the fungal pathogen called perennial canker or cytospora canker. This disease can be transmitted either directly onto pruning cuts or from contaminated pruning shears. The authors found that pruning in late spring was worse than dormant pruning. Although the wound-healing rate was slower in winter-pruned trees, the availability of inoculum, the percentage of infection, and the expansion of cankers were less than in trees pruned in the late spring.

Viruses and viroids are the final group of plant pathogens that can be transmitted by contaminated pruning tools. Although one early study reported that infected pruning tools did not transmit poplar mosaic virus, the preponderance of the published literature indicates otherwise. Both citrus viroids and peach viroids have been studied, and both were easily transmitted with contaminated tools.

It seems clear that if pruning tools are contaminated with vascular pathogens or active, oozing cankers, then there is an excellent chance that the disease will be spread to other plants if the tools are not disinfected. Several researchers have studied different disinfecting solutions, with sometimes ambiguous results. In general it seems that any disinfectant will remove virus or viroids from tools. This makes sense, as both viruses and viroids are relatively unprotected and can be killed by direct contact with disinfectants.

Successful removal of other pathogens, especially canker bacteria, is less certain.

Plant pathogenic bacteria do not form spores, and therefore they are not as resistant as fungi to harsh environmental conditions. However, bacteria associated with active cankers are embedded in a sticky mass, which is often difficult to remove from pruner surfaces. In fact, one study argued that disinfectant solutions would not remove bacterial slime from the surface of cutting tools because the pruning blades were covered with microscopic pits. Only when the researchers pre-coated their tools with plastic could pruners be successfully sterilized.

Which Treatment Is Best?

Obviously, the solution to spreading pathogens from active cankers is to avoid cutting into the cankers altogether. For other plant pathogens, several disinfectant treatments have been compared. Again, researchers did not always draw unanimous conclusions.

Disinfectants tested and recommended included the following: alcohol dips (ethanol or isopropyl alcohol); alcohol dips plus flaming (standard procedure for tissue culture); chlorine (Clorox, monochloramine); household cleaners (Lysol, Pine-Sol); Listerine; and trisodium phosphate (10 percent solution).

A further consideration in choosing a disinfectant treatment is how damaging it may be to your tools. The most comprehensive study found Lysol to be the least corrosive and Clorox to be the most harmful to pruning tools.

To disinfect your tools or not—what's the bottom line? To make an informed decision, you need to know your pathogen and its life history, and use common sense:

• If it's a virus or viroid, disinfect your tools.

• If it's a vascular fungus or a bacterium, and/or if it forms oozing cankers, disinfect your tools.

• Avoid cutting active, oozing cankers; wait until they dry.

• If you are pruning irreplaceable plants, disinfect your tools.

• Choose a disinfectant treatment that has been shown to be effective through published research; I would probably not use alcohol, but rather one of the common household cleaners at full strength.

(To order the full text of this article, including footnote references, contact Plant-Amnesty at *www.plantamnesty.org*.)

STERILIZING PRUNING TOOLS, PART II

Dr. Warren Copes
(This article, a response to Linda Chalker-Scott's article, was adapted from the Plant-Amnesty newsletter.)

Tell It to Me Straight

The information below is based on the more common behavior exhibited by a few pathogens (the short answer), and not the total range of known possibilities (a voluminous explanation).

Avoiding a pathogen requires first knowing which pathogen is associated with a plant. Limb dieback may not have been caused by a pathogen. There are no easy rules or generalizations that definitely result in your correctly diagnosing the cause of a plant abnormality. Diagnostics is a knowledge-based skill. Start by learning about the diseases that occur most commonly in your area. People with the Cooperative Extension Service, chemical distributors, garden centers, and landscape companies may have the expertise to help.

Patterns of Pathogen Invasion of Woody Landscape Plants

There are four general patterns relative to where a pathogen may be present in relationship to limb dieback. A fifth pattern does not involve limb dieback but can result in spread of disease.

1. *Plants exhibit dieback or blight and the pathogen is localized in a lesion or canker.*

Diseases such as *Phomopsis* blight on juniper, blossom blight on ornamental cherry and plum trees, anthracnose on sycamore, and black knot on cherry are examples of this type of disease. The pathogen can cause a lesion and girdle a stem at one point, which limits the movement of water and nutrients and causes the limb above that point to die. The pathogen will not have spread far, possibly 2 inches or less, out of the lesion. In this case, a cut can be made in healthy wood that is 4 inches or more away from the edge of discolored wood.

Many of the diseases in this category are more likely spread in water that washes fungal spores or bacterial cells down a limb than on pruning shears. The dieback resulting from *Phomopsis* blight of juniper or blossom blight of ornamental cherry and plum should be removed as it appears. Cankers from anthracnose of sycamore and black knot of cherry can be pruned during the dormant season.

2. *Plants exhibit dieback or blight and the pathogen is present in the discolored wood and in healthy-looking wood well beyond but still associated with the discolored wood.*

Twig blight on lilac, maple, and cherry; fire blight on cotoneaster, crabapples, hawthorne, pear, and pyracantha; and *Botryosphaeria* dieback on Leyland cypress are examples of this type of disease. The pathogen, whether bacterial or fungal, will advance in healthy-looking wood and will be present 3 to 10 inches or more from the dieback. The pathogens often move down the water-conducting tissue (xylem) because there are fewer cell walls and larger openings in the end-to-end cell walls. Amazingly, the wood does not always become discolored immediately as a result of the pathogen entering and growing between plant cells. The discoloration develops due to chemical responses by the plant to limit the pathogen's invasion and due to the activity of the pathogen either before or after it has reached a specific point.

Pruning cuts should be made just above a bud or branch in healthy-looking wood that is at least 12 inches away from the edge of discolored wood. Generally, this is far enough away to be in pathogen-free wood. The main purpose of pruning far enough away from dieback is to completely remove the pathogen so that it won't continue to kill that limb and be spread to healthy limbs. Sometimes a blighted twig or spur may be less than 12 inches away from a larger limb, and such removal would disfigure the tree. In such cases, there is no easy answer. Removing the scaffold limb may be necessary. If you decide otherwise, definitely use a disinfectant, and monitor the tree in case the pathogen was not fully excised and continues to develop. There are times when the pathogen may have moved farther than 12 inches down in healthy-appearing wood. The chances of this happening are a lot lower if the cut is made shortly after blight appears.

Some bacteria can survive on the surface of bark and be swiped from the bark surface across the cut end of the wood. Disinfecting the pruning tool prior to pruning would not have prevented this type of spread. This type of spread has not been recognized as common in the Pacific Northwest. Check with local experts to determine whether it is evident in your region.

3. *Plants exhibit dieback or blight and the pathogen is distributed considerable distances from the dieback and possibly throughout the vascular system of the plant.*

This category includes a range of bacterial and fungal diseases such as leaf scorch of elm, maple, oak, and sycamore, verticillium wilt of maple and many other hosts, and

Dutch elm disease. A few phytoplasma diseases would also be grouped in this category. Diseases in this category usually cause trees to decline and die. These diseases move through the vascular system, but may also move into other types of tissue such as cortical tissue.

Leaf scorch is caused by a bacterium that is transmitted by leafhopper and sharpshooter insects. Symptoms do not develop until after the pathogen has become established and potentially spread throughout the plant. However, because it has such a slow rate of cell division, this disease is probably not transmitted on pruning tools. As a general precaution, plants suspected of scorch should be pruned last or, alternatively, not pruned but removed promptly.

Verticillium species infect the roots first; then spores are produced and transported upward in the vascular system. Limb dieback occurs as a result of root dysfunction, plugged portions of the vascular system, and localized colonization of a branch. Because the pathogen is not evenly distributed throughout the tree, it is difficult to identify where the pathogen would be located and also why the fungus is not commonly spread on pruning tools. On the down side, pruning does not remove the pathogen, which is located in the roots. Trees suspected of having verticillium wilt should be pruned last. As a safety precaution, pruning tools should be disinfected before work at a new site is begun.

Dutch elm disease is a fungal disease that is transmitted by elm bark beetles and root grafts between infected and healthy trees.

The disease is not easily spread on pruning tools, although that can happen. However, removing the dieback in established trees is labor intensive and expensive, so dipping pruning tools in disinfectant after every cut would be a prudent practice, justified because of the seriousness of potential spread. Proper disposal of the wood is also critical. Wood needs to be debarked, chipped, burned, buried, or fumigated.

4. *Plants exhibit dieback or blight and the pathogen is present on the roots or collar of the plant.*

Phytophthora spp., *Armillaria* spp., and various root pathogens can kill a portion or all of a root system, limiting water and nutrient uptake and causing limb dieback. The pathogens are not present in the limbs, and it is not necessary to disinfect pruning tools.

In regard to cutting propagation wood, soil pathogens can be splashed up on foliage and limb surfaces. In this situation, disinfecting plant tissue would be more important than disinfecting pruning shears. The preferred courses of action would be to cut from disease-free stock plants and to prune from stems at a height higher than that reached by water splash.

5. *Plants exhibit a wide array of possible growth abnormalities, such as yellow patterns on leaves or stunted growth, and the pathogen is spread throughout the vascular system or through numerous types of plant tissue.*

The types of diseases in this category are primarily caused by viruses. Numerous viruses can infect woody plants, and each can cause a range of symptoms, further complicated by the fact that multiple viruses can infect a single plant. Some viral diseases may not produce obvious symptoms on one host but may cause severe symptoms when spread to a different host. Cherry leafroll virus can infect, and cause different symptoms on, blackberry, dogwood, forsythia, lilac, and privet. This article is not long enough to properly address the topic of viruses.

Tobacco mosaic virus on ash and hibiscus chlorotic ringspot virus on hibiscus can be readily spread on pruning tools. Many viruses, such as the camellia viruses, the complex of mosaic viruses on roses, and tobacco ringspot virus on hydrangea and forsythia, have not been shown to be transmitted on pruning tools. In general, viruses that can be sap-transmitted have the highest potential of being transmitted on pruning tools. The problem is that transmission on pruning tools has not been demonstrated for many sap-transmitted viruses, and the possibility may range from common to unlikely to impossible. If you suspect a virus, a good general rule would be to either prune those plants last or disinfect pruning tools after each plant, and definitely to disinfect tools between sites.

A Few Comments About Pruning

Properly placed pruning cuts made at the proper time of year allow quicker healing (callus formation) of the cut tissue. Some disease organisms cannot penetrate healthy limb bark but can infect through wounded tissue. The faster a pruning cut heals, the less opportunity a pathogen will have to colonize the wound. The healing process often begins in 24 to 72 hours and is sufficient to prevent many but not all infections. Proper pruning cuts are explained in Cooperative Extension bulletins and in various books on the topic. The best time to prune varies with the plant species and region of the country.

Proper Disposal of Pruned Limbs

Many diseases can still be spread from limbs left on the ground or from wood stacked in a pile on the site. Fungi that cause canker and dieback diseases often can continue to grow and produce spores from dead wood. Since the objective is to limit the spread of disease, the job is not done until you've properly disposed of dead limbs and trunk pieces. The wood can be carried to a different distant site where no susceptible hosts grow. Chipping the wood sufficiently changes the environment so that many of these pathogens will no longer produce spores, and allows the wood to be used for other purposes such as mulch. Composting further changes the substrate so it is preferentially colonized by beneficial rather than pathogenic microorganisms, as well as producing heat that can kill many pathogens. Fungi that cause *Botryosphaeria* dieback, Dutch elm disease, and *Nectria* canker grow beneath the bark; peeling away the bark (debarking) will incapacitate the pathogen.

Verticillium-infected wood should not be piled in an area where susceptible plants will be grown. Chipping will not eliminate *Verticillium* spp., which could contaminate the soil, as it is a soil pathogen.

One Last Comment

This article dealt with only one aspect of disease spread. There is a lot to learn. Don't be intimated by the idea "If you knew what to do, it would all make perfect sense." Learn in steps. Learn about one or a few aspects of plant care at any one time. More important, take time each day, if only for a moment, to enjoy the profusion of colors and fragrances and the awesome tenacity exhibited by plants.

(To order the full text of this article, including scientific names and footnote references, contact PlantAmnesty online at *www.plantamnesty.org*.)

STERILIZING PRUNING TOOLS, PART III

Cass Turnbull

Although I am a bit reluctant to put it into print, I personally don't believe it's necessary for the average home gardener to disinfect his or her pruning tools. And I suspect that the vast majority of even the most careful professional gardeners and arborists don't either. There are notable exceptions. In nursery propagation, where scores of individuals of the same species are being pruned one right after the other, sterilizing tools may be necessary. If I had a group of valuable plants, of the same species, with a known canker or virus disease, I would certainly take the trouble to disinfect. And it's certainly wise for professionals to clean and disinfect their tools between jobs so that they don't introduce some new disease to the next client's yard.

But you are just as likely, or even more likely, to spread disease on your digging tools, your shoes, and your sweaters. And diseases are moved (vectored) in many other ways—by insects, by wind, by rain. Furthermore, I've been told that for many diseases, you have to come into contact with the disease during a particular point in its life cycle in order to spread it. And a great many diseases will attack only one species or a group of similar species (such as fire blight on the family Rosaceae). In general, the thing that gets your camellia is not likely to pass to your dogwood tree.

I vividly recall an International Society of Arboriculture conference in Canada. To the best of my recollection, in attendance were Drs. Alex Shigo, Roger Funk, Dan Neely, and Richard Harris. The question of sterilizing pruning tools was put to them. Shigo said that he felt it was not necessary, and that the important thing was to make a proper collar cut. Then the tree would defend itself from disease. I believe it was Harris who said that in a classroom setting he had not been able to get fire blight (considered an extremely contagious disease) to pass between plants by using pruning tools.

But horticulture writers are so fearful of giving the wrong advice that they always opt for the better-safe-than-sorry answer. There is little actual research on the subject, and most of it is done in laboratory settings rather than in the field, so I wonder. I've pruned a virus-ridden camellia and not transmitted the virus to the camellia sitting next to it. Likewise with roses. The only plant disease for which I have noticed a correlation between the spread of disease and pruning is quince. According to the preceding two articles, one should prune them in the summer or winter and cut well below the cankers. And, although Dr. Copes writes of verticillium wilt that "the fungus is not commonly spread on pruning tools," in Japanese maples this disease is so deadly and so common that most of us would agree to sterilize if it is present, and sterilize between trees in any case as a precaution.

Most plant problems are caused by environmental factors—bad soil, or too much or too little sun or shade or water. Most plant diseases are not a serious threat to the life of your plant (they just make it look bad), and few are transmitted by pruning tools.

So, to answer the question honestly, I would say I don't think people need to sterilize their pruning tools as a general habit. For people in the business, sterilizing tools is awkward and time consuming, and after a while you start to wonder—is it really doing any good? You will have to decide for yourself.

To minimize the potential spread of disease, I can offer a few general rules. Work on obviously affected plants last. Summer or winter pruning is favorable in most cases to wet season/growing season pruning. Use thinning cuts as opposed to heading cuts. With tree limbs, always cut to the collar. Virus and canker diseases seem the most likely to be spread by pruning. When possible, prune 12 inches below cankers, and never through them. But use common sense too. Pruning 12 inches below the cankers on the average afflicted cherry tree would do far more damage than the disease itself! Prune a few inches below other deadwood that you suspect is caused by disease (not deadwood caused by freeze or by being shaded out as the plant grows larger). And, if you see the sudden dieback of limbs on your Japanese maple, you may have verticillium. Be careful.

Summary

I don't think many, if any, diseases are commonly spread by pruning tools—in the nursery maybe, but not in the average home garden. I could be wrong.

Index

C. nuttallii, 233–35, 323

C. stolonifera. See red twig dogwood

C. unalaschkensis, 325

Corylopsis. See winter hazel

Corylus avellana. See Harry Lauder's walking stick

Corylus cornuta, 323

Cotinus coggygria. See smoke bush

cotoneaster

  C. horizontalis, 148–49

  C. microphyllus, 148

  C. parneyi, 148

  C. salicifolius, 148

  C. x *watereri* 'Cornubia', 148

  color of, 148

  crossing/rubbing branches, 151

  deadwooding of, 150–51, *151*

  description of, 147–48

  diseases, 150

  mistakes with, 149–50

  pruning of, 149

  rehabilitative pruning of, 151–52

  selective heading of, *150*

  size of

    description of, 148

    reduction of, 150

crabapple tree, 257–63, 323

crotches, 211, 216

crowding, *320*, 321, *321*

crown, 62

crown raising. *See* skirting

crown reduction. *See* dropcrotching

Cupressocyparis leylandii. See Leyland cypress

cuts

  heading

    definition of, 5, 18

    nonselective. *See* nonselective heading

    selective. *See* selective heading

thinning, 7, 14–15

types of, 4

cut-stump treatments, 203–4, 318

Cydonia, 99

D

daphne (*Daphne* spp.)

  Daphne burkwookii, 291, *291*

  dying of, 288, 289, 290

  February daphne (*D. mezeruem*), 290, *290*

  Garland daphne (*D. cneorum*), 290

  Winter daphne (*D. odora*), 288–90, *290*

Davey, John, 220

dead zone, 88

deadheading

  of hydrangeas, 121–22

  of lilacs, 160–61

  of roses, 128–29

deadwood

  cutting back, 31

  pruning of, 30–31

  signs of, 30–31

deadwooding

  of butterfly bush, 134

  of cherry trees, 259

  of cotoneaster, 150–51, *151*

  of deciduous azalea, 153

  description of, 14, 20, 30

  of evergreen azaleas, *79*, 79–80

  of forsythia, 114–15, *115*

  of golden thread cypress, 181

  of Japanese laceleaf maple, 244

  of juniper, 89–90, 293–94

  of mock orange, 136

  of native-plant gardens, 320–21

  of pieris, 181

  of plum trees, 259

  of quince, 102

English ivy. *See* English ivy
Garland daphne, 290
hypericum, 280–81
myths regarding, 274–75
native-plant gardens, 319, 321, *321*, 322, 324, 325
pruning of, 275–76, 319
running stems from, 276
salal, 281, 324
self-seeding, 274
in shrubs, 275–76
summary of, 281–82
weeds in, 274–75

H

half-moon edger, 55
Hamamelis spp. *See* witch hazel
hand pruner, 40–42
hardy fuchsia (*Fuchsia magellanica*)
blooming of, 303, *303*
pruning of, 303–4
Harris, Richard W., 207
Harry Lauder's walking stick, 142
Hawaii, 327–28
hazard tree evaluation, 219
hazelnut, 323
heading, 6
heading cuts
definition of, 5, 18
nonselective. *See* nonselective heading
selective. *See* selective heading
summary of, 15
heading-back
description of, 6
Japanese maple, 249–50
heathers, 83, *84*
heaths, 83, *84*

heavenly bamboo
description of, 107–8
pruning of, 110
"shotgun" method of pruning, 110, *111*
Hedera spp.
H. canariensis, 193, 278
H. helix. See English ivy
H. helix 'Baltica', 278
hedge(s)
criteria for, 49–51
deciduous, 51
escallonia, 97–98
false front, 50, *50*
formal, 48, *48*
haircut method for cutting of, 49
hardy fuchsia, 304
informal, 48, *48*
laurel, 50
leggy, 48–49
mistakes with, 49
native-plant gardens, 318–19
photinia, 50
power trimming of, 51–52
sarcococca, 295–96
shearing of, 50
shrubs as, 52
size of, 50–51
stranvaesia, 187
styles of, 48, *48*
summary of, 52
trimming of, 51–52
width of, 49–50
Helleborus orientalis. See Lenten rose
Hemlock, 50
herbicides, 203–4, 318
Hollywood juniper (*Juniperus chinensis* 'Torulosa')
cloud pruning, 294, *294*
description of, 291–92, *292*

M

magnolia (*Magnolia*)
  Campbell's, 257
  compartmentalization by, 253
  description of, 253
  evergreen, 256
  M. acuminata subcordata, 257
  M. campbellii, 257
  M. grandiflora, 256
  M. macrophylla, 257
  M. stellata, 256–57
  M. x soulangeana, 255
  miscellaneous types of, 257
  overthinning of, 253
  pruning of, 253–54
  rehabilitative pruning of, 253–54
  saucer, 62, 255–56
  southern, 256
  star, 256–57
Mahonia aquifolium. See Oregon grape
Mahonia nervosa, 325
Maianthemum dilatatum, 325
Maianthemum racemosum, 324
Maianthemum stellatum, 324
maidenhair fern, 325
mal-pruning, xi–xii, 20, 25, 80, 97, 137–38,
    232
Malus spp., 257, 323
Matheny, Nelda P., 207
Mexican orange
  description of, 98–99
  flowers of, 98
  pruning of, 94–95
  radical renovation of, 94–95
  shear-and-shag technique for, 99
  snow loading effects on, 94
  winter damage to, 94

mildew
  on deciduous azaleas, 154
  on rhododendrons, 170
mis-siting of tree-like shrubs, 61
mock orange
  deadwooding of, 136
  description of, 135
  learning, 137
  malpruning of, 137–38
  native-plant gardens, 324
  pruning of, 135–38, *137*
  radical renovation of, 138
  size control for, 135–36
  thinning of, 137
Moon shots, 70
Morris, James "Ciscoe," 130, 194–96
mounding-habit shrubs
  abelias. *See* abelias
  in Alaska, 328
  in Arizona low desert, 331
  artemisia, 84
  aucuba, 284–85
  boxwood. *See* boxwood
  broom, 86
  burning bush. *See* burning bush
  in central Florida, 333–34
  definition of, 68
  escallonia. *See* escallonia
  in Hawaii, 327
  heathers, 83, *84*
  heaths, 83, *84*
  in Inland Northwest, 328
  juniper. *See* juniper
  lavender, 84–85
  Mexican orange. *See* Mexican orange
  native-plant gardens, 324
  pruning of, 68
  quince. *See* quince
  in Reno, Nevada, 332

root, 339

soil-borne, 335, 339

in wood, 338

Paulownia, 228

pearl bush, 180

peegee hydrangea, 123

perennials for native-plant gardens, 324

permanent wilt, 36

Perovskia (*Perovskia atriplicifolia*), 303

Pfitzers, *63*, 88–89

Philadelphus coronarius. See mock orange

Philadelphus lewisii, 324

Phomopsis, 337–38

photinia, 55, 155–59

Photinia x *fraseri*, 155–59

Phygelius capensis, 304

Physocarpus capitatus, 323

Phytophthora spp., 339

pieris (*Pieris japonica*)

deadwooding of, 181

size reduction of, 183

thinning of, 181–83, *182*

"pinching," 94

plant(s)

bloom time for, 34–35

branching patterns of, 5, *5*

habits, 18–19

landscape design using, 54–55

mature size of, 19

overplanting of, 60–61

radical renovation of, 20–21

root mass of, 19

size of, 19

terminology of, 4–5

transplanting of, 57

PlantAmnesty, xii–xiv, 6, 57, 72, 83, 90, 96, 223, 279

pleaching, 229

plum trees

deadwooding of, 259

Japanese, 242

native-plant gardens, 323

pruning of, 259–61

Prunus cerasifera, 257

Prunus x *blireiana*, 257

purple-leaf, 217, 257–63

rehabilitative pruning of, 261

suckers, 260–61

summary of care for, 261, 263

water sprouts, 257–58

pole pruners, 226

pollarding

definition of, 229

description of, 227

history of, 228

reasons for, 228

technique for, 228–30

topping vs., 228

pollination, 240

Polygonum cuspidatum, 279

Polystichum munitum, 325

poodle-balling, 183, 293, 294, *294*

poplar, 208

Populus spp., 208

powdery mildew. *See* mildew

power trimming of hedges, 51–52

powerline pruning of trees, 227, *228*

pruner

anvil, 41–42, *42*

hand, 40–42

holster for, 42–43

long-reach, 201, 203

pruning

of abelias, 69–71, *71*

American National Standards Institute standards for, 226

of bamboo, 109